Sociological Slices

**INTRODUCTORY
READINGS
FROM THE
INTERACTIONIST
PERSPECTIVE**

Sociological Slices

INTRODUCTORY READINGS FROM THE INTERACTIONIST PERSPECTIVE

Editors: GARY ALAN FINE
University of Georgia

JOHN JOHNSON
Arizona State University

HARVEY A. FARBERMAN
State University of New York, Stony Brook

 JAI PRESS INC.

Greenwich, Connecticut   *London, England*

CONTENTS

v

POLITICS AND POWER

SOCIAL MOVEMENTS AND COLLECTIVE BEHAVIOR

SEX ROLES

MARRIAGE AND THE FAMILY

CRIME AND DEVIANCE

PREFACE

The science fiction writer, Theodore Sturgeon, reportedly once wrote, when asked about the allegedly dismal condition of that body of writing, that 90 percent of all science fiction was crap, but, then again, 90 percent of everything is crap. Many sociologists—students as well as teachers—might well sympathize with Sturgeon's assessment. Yet, the remark should not be seen as gloomy pessimism. Think of the brilliant 10 percent. Some science fiction, some sociology, and some student term papers do *not* deserve our scorn.

Editors of any book of readings have the obligation of finding that 10%. This edited collection approaches the field of sociology from the perspective that is known as symbolic interaction. Before they had taken an introduction to sociology course, it would certainly be fair to assume that a very small proportion of students had ever heard of symbolic interaction. In its absence of a strong public image, the perspective is significantly different from Marxism or Freudian psychoanalysis. Actually, the label *symbolic interaction* is over fifty years old. It was coined by the sociologist (and former professional football player) Herbert Blumer in 1937 in a chapter of a social science textbook. In this chapter Blumer distinguished three approaches to social psychology: one grounded in the importance of biological instincts and Darwinian evolution, and a second based on the importance of reflexes and learned responses, as found in writings of behaviorists. The third approach was a new synthesis, based on the work of American pragmatic philosophers, such as George Herbert Mead, William James, and John Dewey. While the term was new in 1937, the ideas on which it had been based had been around for centuries, and portions of the symbolic interactionist perspective can be found in traditions of European philosophy—from the Romantic movement to British empiricism.

Like any perspective that has some measure of longevity, popularity, and intel-lectual vigor, there are different traditions of interactionism—differences that are discussed in more advanced courses. For our purpose we should briefly mention the core elements of the approach. Most interactionists when asked for a central statement of interactionism would first point to Herbert Blumer's 1969 volume, *Symbolic Interactionism*, and in particular to his premises of symbolic interaction:

> The first premise is that human beings act toward things on the basis of the meanings that the things have for them. . . . The second premise is that the meaning of such things is derived from, or arises out of, the social interaction that one has with one's fellows. The third premise is that these meanings are handled in, and

modified through, an interpretive process used by the person in dealing with the things he encounters. (p. 2)

There are differences in interpreting this passage. Some emphasize that all meaning is ultimately negotiated, whereas others accept the existence of real, structural, and physical constraints. Whichever explanation you choose, the passage emphasizes the power of the individual actor in understanding and even *creating* the world. We are not merely acted upon, we act. Meaning is not simply out there or in our own minds, but it emerges though our interactions with each other. This model has had impact throughout the field of sociology. Sociology would look very different without symbolic interactionism and a recognition of the possibilities for human interpretation, particularly in our understanding of the self and identity, small groups, deviance and criminal behavior, mental illness, culture and art, and collective behavior.

In some sense, symbolic interactionists are particularly lucky in that one of the key elements of this approach to understanding human behavior, interaction, groups, and communities, is the belief that one of the most powerful ways of learning is through the rich and detailed example—methodologies that attempt to do justice to detailed understandings of real social situations and actual communities. In bringing these essays together, we particularly looked for those which provide you with a passage into some social world. You will learn about Orthodox Jewish Women, Football Victory Celebrations, Slavery, Student Social Workers, Actors, Alzheimer's Disease, Bailbondsmen, Daycare, Hitler's Speeches, and Japanese Motorcycle Gangs. We hope to have you learn about important sociological concepts through detailed descriptions in these articles.

All of the readings that are included in this volume were culled from a single journal, *Symbolic Interaction*, the journal of the Society for the Study of Symbolic Interaction. The three editors of this volume were editors of that journal from Volume 4 (1981) to volume 12 (1989). We believe that these selections represent the best new thinking on sociology from the symbolic interactionist perspective.

Selecting articles from a single journal has advantages and disadvantages. Among the advantages is the fact that these articles, though they are diverse in many ways, also reflect a consistent perspective. They connect to each other better than would randomly selected articles. Second, given that we three were editors of this journal, we know these articles well and helped to shape them in ways that we felt would make them clearer and more accessible to students. Several of these articles were published with notes that they would be particularly appropriate as assignments for undergraduate students. It is important that articles be written so as to be read by a large audience, not only by a narrow group of specialists.

Obviously, selecting all of the articles from one journal means that many outstanding articles were excluded. Our hope was that this book will be a starting point for your reading, not the limits of it. If some of the articles in this book inspire you to choose a career as a sociologist or to see the world from a sociological perspective then the volume will have been worthwhile. We are not so naive as to believe that each selection will be equally interesting for all students, but we believe that taken together they provide a fascinating introduction to a fascinating field. This is our 10% solution.

The book is organized into eight sections. In each section, we present two or three essays that speak to the general topic of the section. The sections reflect, to the extent possible, basic divisions of the standard Introduction to Sociology class: (1) Self and Society, (2) Roles and Self-Presentation, (3) Occupations and Organizations, (4) Politics and Power, (5) Social Movements and Collective Behavior, (6) Sex Roles, (7) Marriage and the Family, and (8) Crime and Deviance. Since each instructor teaches a class somewhat differently, we recognize that the book will work better for some classes than for others. In selecting these essays we have decided to present them in their entirety, rather than attempting to edit them. Edited selections miss the richness of the presentation of data, which in the case of symbolic interaction seems particularly important. Further, these articles give you a sense of what a sociological article reads like. In this book, we treat you as our future colleagues. Hopefully, this will not be entirely in vain.

It is important to stress that you not take everything that you read in these pages as gospel truth. There is a lot to consider, and a lot with which to disagree. We hope that you will actively consider each statement and disagree with those arguments that do not make sense to you. Don't assume that because some scholar has had his or her work published, it must be better than your own perspective. Raise the points with which you disagree with your instructor and, equally important, with each other. Many of these articles discuss topics that directly speak to your own lives. Symbolic interactionism attempts to understand the world from the perspective of the *actor*— that is, *you*. While you need to give these authors the benefit of the doubt, there should always be doubt.

One hint about reading these articles: at the beginning of each one there is what sociologists call an *abstract*: a brief description of the article. Sociologists examine these to determine what the article is about and whether they wish to read the whole article. You should read these brief descriptions very carefully before starting the article: perhaps several times. This abstract will provide you with a basic guide as to what will come. It is almost a Cliff Notes summary of the text. If you understand the abstract, it is very likely that you will be able to make sense of the rest of the paper.

In closing, we wish to thank those who made this volume possible. Most significant, of course, is the Society for the Study of Symbolic Interaction, under whose umbrella both the journal and this volume are being published. As this organization reaches toward the beginning of its third decade (it was founded in 1974), it has become evident that symbolic interaction as an organized group of scholars and as a intellectual perspective is here to stay. The imagination of the founders of the group, particularly Professor Gregory P. Stone, has provided an inspiration for scholars. We were honored to have been chosen to edit the journal.

Second, we wish to thank our friends at JAI Press, who have been publishing *Symbolic Interaction* for a decade now. Under the firm, supportive leadership of Herbert Johnson, this press has managed to revitalize symbolic interactionist scholarship and scholarship throughout the social sciences. We also thank his colleagues at JAI Press who have labored on the journal: Sue Oppenheim, Marty Smolar, Danielle

Shaban, Nina DuPrey, William Cody, et al. We are proud of our journal, and, while you will certainly find a few errors in these pages—the errors are few.

Third, we extend our gratitude to the many scholars who helped us edit this journal. Over the nine years, ten individuals served as Associate Editors, helping to process and evaluate manuscripts: David Altheide, Robert Broadhead, Gary Alan Fine, Andrea Fontana, Steven Gordon, Jaber Gubrium, Sherryl Kleinman, Frank Kohout, Bernard Meltzer, and William Yoels. They were the backbone of the journal. In addition, we had a series of advisory boards and international editors, who gave the editors advice and contributed to the journal by their presence. There were literally hundreds of scholars who reviewed manuscripts for the journal; the articles that are in this volume are here because these men and women said that they represented excellent scholarship. We wish to note that as editors we are donating all royalties from this volume to the Stone Memorial Fund, which, each year, provides a grant to help subsidize the annual symposium of the Society for the Study of Symbolic Interaction.

Finally, we owe gratitude to the staffs at our home universities while we were editors: the University of Minnesota, State University of New York at Stony Brook, and Arizona State University. At Minnesota, Kent Sandstrom, Dan Martin, and Susan Smith-Cunnien served as editorial assistants, and Gloria DeWolfe and Hilda Daniels provided needed secretarial support. At Stony Brook, Suzanne B. McMillan provided editorial assistance and Kathy Smith and Karen Christenson gave secretarial support. We also thank Kay Korman and Kim Cook of Arizona State for their secretarial support.

Now we turn the volume over to you, our students. The judgement is yours. We hope you learn, laugh, and enjoy, and realize why each of us love sociology and symbolic interaction.

Gary Alan Fine
Harvey A. Farberman
John Johnson

The Bureaucratizing of Impulse:
Self-Conception in the 1980s

Louis A. Zurcher
The University of Texas at Austin

This article selectively reviews and interprets the literature on self-concept and social change. It summarizes the view that in the 1970s the self-conception of Americans, modally considered, manifested a shift from institution to impulse, from social to reflective. The argument is made that in the 1980s the expression of impulse is becoming bureaucratized, newly formated in rationalization and modernization, effectively being institutionalized by assorted societal agents, including sociologists. Speculations are offered about the implications of that change. Several suggestions are made regarding future research on self-concept and the broader notion of "self," particularly by symbolic interactionists and for the purpose of application.

The term "impulse" has had several connotations and denotations in the social science literature. The positive attributions include spontaneity of expression, creativity, autonomy, uniqueness of expression, freedom to oblige one's own inclinations and wishes, capacity to appreciate the present, openness to immediate experience, flexibility rather than rigidity in personality, and ability to self-actualize. Impulse involves those characteristics in choices of conduct and in the expression of feelings or emotions. The negative attributions include exaggerated lability of expression, weak ego or superego, inclination to "act out," incomplete or faulty socialization, distracti-

Reprinted from Symbolic Interaction, 9(2):169–178.

bility, lack of goal orientation, lack of future orientation, weakness of self-control, and proclivity for deviance.

It would appear that self-control and impulse are antithetical, the former socially learned and the latter genetically or physiologically inherent, at least in the old psychodynamic model. From the perspective of symbolic interaction, both self-control *and* impulse significantly are socially learned, negotiated, and differentially manifested according to setting (Mead, 1934; Miller, 1967, 1973, 1982; see also Mischel and Mischel, 1977). In that context, some scholars have reported observations about shifts in the mode of self-expression in the United States from the 1950s to the 1970s. Turner (1976) described a swing in locus of "real" self from "institution" to "impulse." Adler (1972) speculated about the emergence of an "antinomian personality" wherein the expression of impulse and desire took precedence over counsel of discrimination and control. Kavolis (1970) suggested the presence of an "underground self" based upon irrationality, expressiveness, and emotion. Lifton (1968, 1969) identified the Protean Man, Lasch (1979, 1984) the Minimal Self and the culture of narcissism. Veroff, Douvan, and Kulka (1981) described the contemporary "inner American," and Yankelovitch (1981) the "new rules" for self-fulfillment. I speculated about a shift in college student responses to the Twenty Statements Test (Zurcher, 1977, 1983). I coded the student TSTs according to the protocol developed by McPartland, Cumming, and Garretson (1961):

- "A" statements are the most concrete statements and refer to the self as a physical entity. I am five feet ten inches tall. I weigh 150 pounds. I have blue eyes.
- "B" statements identify the self clearly and specifically with institutionalized statuses or roles. I am a professor. I am a U.S. citizen. I am a sophomore.
- "C" statements present characteristic ways of acting, feeling, or responding in social situations. I am a happy person. I worry too much. I am very religious. These statements indicate that the self is not closely identified with an institutional context of norms and roles but is relatively situation free.
- "D" statements imply no particular context, act, or attitude that would indicate identification with social structure or interpersonal networks. They indicate that the self is removed from interactive commitment. The statements are vague and not differentiating. I am a being. I am one with the universe.

I renamed the four categories physical, social, reflective, and oceanic and concluded that student responses, which were primarily social (B mode) in the 1950s, were predominantly reflective (C mode) in the 1970s. This speculation was supported by other TST researchers, notably, Sheinberg (1974), Snow and Phillips (1982), Spitzer and Parker (1976), and Wood and Hughes (1984). I suggested that the increase in reflective responses was provoked by contemporary instability in the roles and social structures upon which the 1950s social responses had been based—that instability is generated by the societal and cultural upheavals of the 1960s. I further suggested that the reflective self-condition did not represent an end point but marked the beginning of a search for new sources of self-definition. If the conditions that generated the reflective self were sustained and sufficiently repetitive and if the person had opportunity to experience all four components of self (physical, social, reflective, and oceanic), then a self-concept consonant with and controlling of change might eventually emerge. I called that the Mutable Self.

> The Mutable Self is a self-concept that affords the individual: first, full recognition of the four components of self and consequently an openness to the widest possible experience of self; second, an awareness of the interaction among the four components of self in varying social settings; third, an awareness of the process experience as well as the content changes within and among the four components; fourth, the flexibility to move among the four components willfully, purposefully, naturally, without rigid fixation on any components; fifth, the ability to integrate the four components and to accept the productive dialectic among them, a dialectic that provokes personal growth; sixth, an understanding, tolerance, acceptance of, and empathy with other human beings who manifest Mutable Selves and for those who do not; seventh, the ability to accommodate, control, and resist rapid sociocultural change and its concomitants without the necessity for affecting defensive stances in or denial of any of the four components of self. (Zurcher, 1977, pp. 35–36).

Flexibility, tolerance, openness, and diversity are themes that characterize the Mutable Self, the sense of self as a continuous becoming, to use Dewey's (1929) expression, a becoming that did not have an end but rather was an end (see also Mischel 1977; Sarbin and Schiebe, 1983). These speculations represented a calculated but certainly precarious leap from a weak empirical finding with TST data to an exploratory interpretation of modal personality—from limited information about self-concept to normative assumptions about self in the context of social change. I have not yet actually studied Mutable Selves, only generated what I thought might be an evocative ideal type. In this article, I follow that same path: I admit confounding the narrower notion of self-concept with the broader notion of self and taking liberties with the intentions of those scholars whose relevant work I cite.

It is now the middle of the 1980s. In which direction is the pendulum swinging? Is it pointing toward real self as institution and real self as impulse or toward the social self and the reflective self? What new formulations of self have emerged to seem to be emerging? Does the Mutable Self obtain?

THE BUREAUCRATIZING OF IMPULSE

The most recent commentaries on the condition of self in the contemporary United States tend to focus on the notion of autonomy. Bellah et al. (1985), for example, have addressed what they perceive to be the increase of atomistic, expressive, and even cancerous individualism among middle Americans. Individual self-serving, the dedicated solo pursuit of one's own impulses, has precluded societal commitment as a good citizen. The voluntary associations that people have chosen to join tend to be defensive enclaves of special-interest groups. Bellah's observations and findings are not unique or new, but they are coherently presented and lend support to the conclusion that an impulse orientation of self remains in force as a "habit of the heart."

I speculate that something more is happening. As Hall (1983) implied in his essay on individualism, the current thrust for autonomy seems to be more complicated than simple self-service. Wood (1977), concluding his analysis of a sample of American diaries written during the past 200 years, suggested that the postmodern self-concept surely manifested an impulse locus. But the expression of impulse had become newly formatted in rationalization and modernization. As I interpret Wood, there was a burgeoning of what might be called *instrumental* impulsiveness, thus the title of this article, "The Bureaucratizing of Impulse."

I am now convinced that it is not a question of self-locus in institution *versus* self-locus in impulse. Much of that productive dialectic seems to have been side-tracked, individually and collectively. Instead, the impulse locus of the sixties and seventies appears in the eighties to have been effectively institutionalized by assorted societal agents. The reflective self is being directed toward reformulation as a rigid social self, with the expression of impulse scripted as conformity to bureaucratic imperatives. The manner in which impulse is expressed, the character of self-control, now occupies a centrality in the agendas of bureaucratic organizations. Perhaps there is nothing surprising about that given the function of bureaucracies, except in what is now the unique dedication and technical sophistication with which the agendas are pursued.

To put it another way, people with impulse selves, with reflective selves, are susceptible to manipulation and apparently are being manipulated toward conformity by agents who control the *marketing* scripts for appropriate expression. In that context, it might be argued that I am more appropriately addressing the "commercializing" rather than the bureaucratizing of impulse. Surely there is a powerful commercial incentive to script impulse for dollar gain, but I believe that notion can be incorporated at least for discussion within the scope of contemporary bureaucratic social organization (cf. Hummel, 1982).

The constructive socialization of human beings, particularly with regard to control of impulse, is of course a prerequisite for the maintenance of society and an obligation of family, school, church, the workplace, and so on. But the outcome should be an individual who is neither all institutional self nor all impulse self—rather, a person in whom these two self-conceptions remain cognitively dialectical, thereby providing a measure of individual freedom for creative autonomy in service of societal good. When impulse is bureaucratized, when it is made wholly institutional, the flexibility and freedom are jeopardized if not lost.

The marketing scripts for the expression of impulse are consistently and power-fully put before the public every day. Those scripts call upon actors to express or channel impulses into the intentional behavior of buying products, believing stories, joining groups, changing attitudes, voting for particular candidates, working harder, choosing a lover, discarding a lover, selecting accounts, defining heroes, villains, and fools, and the like. What is a "Yuppie" if not an individual who has ingeniously or ingenuously merged impulse self with institutional self according to prevalent mar-keting scripts? What are we seeing among undergraduate students on our campuses if not that process? Has professional wrestling become a chic event, have TV soap operas become an obsession, at least in part because those pseudoevents are shapers of and channels for bureaucratized impulse? Is Rambo II a welcomed, structured channel for the staging of emotion? "Charisma," "Joy," and "Ecstasy" are less expressions of spontaneity than they are the names of marketed perfumes. "Love" is a United States postage stamp. "Happy face" figures emblazen bills from electric utility companies. "Self-actualization" is not the ongoing growth process described by Maslow (1954, 1968) but an end product marketed by awareness-training organizations that are subsidiaries of dog food and tobacco companies. Are you only a "three" on our self-actualization scale? Too bad! We can make you a "ten" during one of our weekend seminars in Anaheim, minutes away from Disneyland, for only a few thousand dollars. Allport's (1955) sensitive notion of "becoming" seems to have been distorted into a mindless and spiritless "became."

SOCIOLOGY AND THE BUREAUCRATIZING OF IMPULSE

Surely the bureaucratizing of impulse is a creature of the market but not just created by lawyers, advertisers, media folks, corporate wizards, politicians, and public relations experts. We, too, those of us who have been studying self-concept, labor in that vineyard and sometimes produce sour wine.

Manning (1983), drawing on the earlier work of Burke (1962, 1965), White (1978), and others, has summarized the major styles of discourse (or tropes) employed in field research organizations. He mentions four tropes, which we also know as figures of speech: metaphor, synecdoche, metonymy, and irony. I would add to those the remaining three typically considered figures of speech (simile, personification, and hyperbole) and suggest that taken together the seven tropes classify or at least describe the styles of discourse we have used in the study of the self. For example:

- Simile: The self functions like an executive of the personality.
- Metaphor: His self surged with emotion.
- Metonymy: The C mode replaced the B mode; impulse replaced institution.
- Personification: Her self-esteem precluded the role enactment; her self-esteem demanded consistency.
- Synecdoche: He balanced the self functions of thinking, feeling, sensing, and inuiting in his interaction with others.
- Irony: Self was sacrificed to situation.
- Hyperbole: The self cries out for actualization.

In and among these styles of discourse, we find and report self as subject, object, process, organizer, ego, player, or actor. Self as defense, identity, image, role taker, role maker, role, or person. Self as knower, known, me, I, collective us, collective them. We suggest that the self commands the personality, describes the personality, reacts to the personality, controls the personality, or is the personality. We locate the self-system and define selves as transcendental, creative, altercasting, external, internal, existential, biosocial, premodern, or postmodern. We isolate and categorize selves as untrammeled, archetypal, nuclear, kernel, real, ideal, authentic, inauthentic, alienated, one-dimensional, protean, or mutable.

Ours is a remarkable diversity of scholarly discourses about the self—what it is, how it is, who it is, why it is, what it does, what it should be, what it could be.

I do not suggest that these nomenclatures, nosologies, and typologies are misguided or unimportant. On the contrary, they are extremely important and not at all misguided. I am confident that their accumulation and synthesis one day will lead to an integrated theory of the self. The problem we must avoid along the way is that great evil we all learned about in graduate school but tend to have ignored thereafter—reification of constructs. That is easier said than done, given the manner in which we must market our ideas and the manner in which we must use the rhetoric of social science, as Gusfield (1976) and others trenchantly have observed. When we market our work on the self according to bureaucratic standards, we are pressured, as Peirce reflected, to comply with contemporary fashion and to create reifications "ugly enough to be safe from kidnappers" (Apel, 1981). I wish there were no real examples to make my calculated exaggerations sound. But there are. For example, one of our social science colleagues, not a symbolic interactionist, earnestly reported research about the "fact" that men reveal 65% of their selves and women 85% of their selves when interacting. It is plausible, given vestiges of inappropriate sex role socialization, that men and women in our society still differ in openness of interaction. But do they differ accurately in reified terms of percentage of "self" displayed? Not likely.

THE FUTURE OF RESEARCH ON THE SELF

Given my meanderings in this article and assuming some plausibility in them, where are we to go with our studies of the self? How are we to offset the pressures to bureaucratize and reify our notions of the self, impulse or institution? I have no easy solutions. It is reasonable to conclude that we will continue to develop our marketable constructs. But we can promise that whatever the impositions on our publishable formulations, we will remember and teach that "self" fundamentally is a Sorrel (1914) "myth," a Vaihinger (1924) "as if," an Adler (1939) "creative fiction"—a style of discourse, a trope, a calculated rhetoric. That perspective certainly does not diminish the importance of the construct of self. The human enterprise routinely turns on the "myth," the "as if," and the "creative fiction." Among the styles of discourse before us, it seems most important that we tenaciously grasp the "irony" (Schneider, 1971) of the self-construct—irony here meaning realization of the problematic dialectic between the individual and society, concomitantly with better understanding of the "Yin and Yang" of autonomy and social responsibility. Perhaps we will be able to offset our rejection of a theological "soul" in the contemporary nature of our work and to accept for purposes of theoretical freedom something as broad as Allport's (1955) "Proprium" when considering the self. The Proprium represented the active, organizing, unifying thrusts of the person, drawing upon all the capacities and potentials of mind and body: the healthy, mature, individual steadily exerted propriate striving, becoming more and more unified and balanced in personality. Key characteristics of having reached maturity included acceptance of self, extension of self, humor, insight, and a philosophy of life. Perhaps we will increasingly elect to study the self-concepts of people not only in the structural but in their historical and cultural settings, emphasizing the analysis of human biographies, as argued by Denzin (1985), Bertaux (1981), and Wood (1977) and as encouraged by the inauguration of The Biography and Society section of The International Sociological Association. Perhaps, as Peirce implied, we will not permit the underlying philosophical assumptions of our work to be less than "transcendental pragmaticism" (Morris, 1970; Bernstein, 1965). That purview would demand moving beyond our current preoccupations with micro, meso, and macro aspects of symbolic interaction as discrete elements for analysis. We would see those analytical levels as temporarily useful but soon to be discarded in favor of Peirce's penchant for holistic interpretation—the dialectical, culturally influenced, normatively affected, language based consideration of the individual in his or her place and time—a fuller appreciation of Peirce's observation that self is not only generated by communicated symbols but that it *is* a symbol and should be so considered (Bernstein 1965; Rucker 1969). We might even be able to generate a "transcendental symbolic interactionism," not a new but a better use of the lessons provided us by Peirce, Mead, Dewey, James, Cooley, Miller, and Blumer—a symbolic interactionism no less willing to address the reality of cultural and structural absolutes than it is willing to address the emergence of the situation and the autonomy of the individual—able, as Peirce advised, to encompass science *and* ethics, theory *and* practice, in the keen sociological sense recently advanced by Sjoberg, Vaughan, and Sjoberg (1984) and Littrell (1980). Perhaps we will even be able to come to terms with Peirce's pragmaticist insistence that there are absolutes (moral, aesthetic, ethical) in the human condition (Morris 1970; Winer 1949)—not saying those absolutes are unaffected by situational communication but saying they represent something more in the scope of history than emergent norms or elements of cultural relativity. Fuhrman (1985) has attacked arbitrary notions of the commensurability and incommensurability of abstractions of society and the individual in sociological theory. He has called for a more flexible conceptual framework. Symbolic interactionists can provide that framework.

The American Sociological Association, perhaps cynically considered a bureaucratizer of member impulses, has provided an opportunity for us to advance transcendental symbolic interactionism. The theme of the 1986 ASA annual meeting was "Social Structures and Human Lives." The theme was defined in ASA Footnotes as fostering overarching perspectives that will incorporate macro and micro levels of analysis, will bring human beings back into the social structure, will emphasize the dynamic (rather than the static) character of both human lives and social structure, will recognize the importance of sociotemporal variabilities, and will make appropriate use of both qualitative and quantitative methods. Cross-disciplinary, cross-temporal, and cross-cultural emphases were encouraged. If I did not know better, I would suggest that the American Sociological Association, after a realistic assessment of how Sociology seems to be following Psychology into temporary conceptual bankruptcy, has turned to Symbolic Interactionism with a plea for constructive and constructivist attention. Perhaps also the Society for the Study of Social Problems is looking to us.

The theme of their 1986 annual meeting was "Individual Initiative in an Interdependent World: The Social Problem as an Enterprise." The participants were challenged to confront the long-standing objective subjective controversy on the nature of social problems by squarely taking the social constructionist side and calling for specification of its theoretical and practical consequences. If symbolic interactionists can escape our conceptual reifications and if bureaucratic pressures exerted on us can be measured, we can effectively accommodate those challenges—not as theoretical or methodological ideologues but as colleagues who have developed a pertinent alternative framework. Ours is not the only game in town, but it certainly seems now to have earned the attention of a lot of players.

Other groups of our colleagues also seem to be calling upon symbolic interactionists to provide useful ideas—colleagues such as social workers who are professionally involved in the amelioration of social problems and the salutary application of sociological knowledge. Among the salient questions they put before us are the following: How seriously should the self as actor in efforts directed toward social change be considered? What is the self-concept of effective agents for constructive social change? These colleagues do not want macro versus meso versus micro analyses of self and social change. Their routine professional practice defies such bureaucratic academic abstractions. Instead, they ask: Who will be able to make a difference in solving social problems? Why? How? Where? When will such individuals emerge in socialization processes?

There is a fine opportunity for symbolic interactionists to develop an *applied* symbolic interactionism, to take Peirce's pragmaticism or James's pragmatism more seriously—again, not a new but a better use of the lessons provided us by our intellectual forebears.

Permit me to identify a German term with which Apel (1981) summarized a pertinent portion of Peirce's work. The term is *verständigung*, roughly translated as the process of communicative understanding. It embraces three key elements of philosophical social psychology: (1) the human process of grasping or understanding meaning; (2) the human process of notifying or telling others about that meaning as perceived; (3) the human process of negotiating a mutual understanding or agreement with others about that meaning in a cultural and historical context. Apel argued that the Weberian notion of *Verstehen*, to which we here have so long usefully been dedicated, effectively addressed only the first of those elements: the process of grasping and understanding meaning. That was a limited reading of Weber in favor of Peirce. But I suggest that particularly in our studies of the self, if only to focus what we already know, we substitute *Verständigung* for *Verstehen*.

CONCLUSION

I predict that no matter what rhetoric we decide to use to study self-concept, including impulse and self-control, the agents for societal change will surprise us and we will do our best to catch up with the surprise. I still firmly believe that people with or without our learned observations will be stimulated by contemporary events to evolve toward Mutable Selves and that the emerging global social movements such as the antinuclear initiative will accelerate and validate that contention. Several such activists will engage physical, social, reflective, and oceanic self perceptions with prudent balance toward an important societal end. Gergen and Gergen (1984) have implied, as I interpret for the argument, that the critical activism of women in global social movements for sex role equity similarly will generate Mutable Selves, at least among the participants.

The seemingly problematic aspect in the development of Mutable Selves, assuming that to be a desirable outcome, is the scope of the oceanic component—the value orientations philosophies, theologies, and ideologies that have been internalized by actors. Will they be self-serving altruistic constructs? Kleinman (1985) advised that aspiring younger people in our society indeed seem to be accommodating a "high-tech" based definition of social self, but they are doing so based on a definition of oceanic self still delicately ambiguous and perhaps more inclined toward altruism than is now recognized. What seems to be their bureaucratizing of impulse might turn out to be a hiatus, a "time out" for self in accord with their reading of contemporary organizational imperatives, later to flower as impulse linked to an oceanic perspective—a philosophy, theology, or ideology that is not dogmatic and authoritarian but that manifests the best hopes of Lewin (1935), Adler (1939), Fromm (1941, 1947), Allport (1955), Jung (1933), Murphy (1947), Rogers (1961, 1972), and Maslow (1954, 1968)—a perception of self that includes a flexible understanding and appreciation of the responsible obligations of self in society and a sense of autonomy beyond immediate physical and social gratification. Yankelovitch (1981) reported a broad move toward that state in the United States of the 1980s.

As symbolic interactionists in one way or another concerned with self-in society we have for marketing purposes tended to focus on analysis of self-concept as physical or social or reflective or oceanic, occasionally encompassing more than one of those notions in our work. Pressures upon us have made us cautious. For conceptual and applied purposes, we cannot any longer be so limited. We must consider all four components of self and their integration in historical and cultural contexts. Our intellectual forebears were not cautious. It is time to match their courage, to exceed it, to play our own tune, and to accept responsibility for the resonance that others hear when it is played.

ACKNOWLEDGMENTS

Shortened and revised version of the Distinguished Lecture, Society for the Study of Symbolic Interaction Annual Meetings, Washington, DC, August 1985. I thank Gary Alan Fine and the anonymous reviewers for their constructive suggestions.

REFERENCES

Adler, A. 1939. *Social Interest*. New York: Putnam.

Adler, N. 1972. *The Underground Stream: New Lifestyles and the Antinomian Personality*. New York: Harper & Row.

Allport, G.W. 1955. *Becoming: Basic Consideration for Psychology of Personality*. New Haven, CT: Yale University Press.

Apel, K.-O. 1981. *From Pragmatism to Pragmaticism*. Amherst: University of Massachusetts Press.

Bellah, R.N., R. Madsen, W.M. Sullivan, A. Swindler, and S.M. Tipton. 1985. *Habits of the Heart: Individualism and Commitment in American Life*. Berkeley: University of California Press.

Bernstein, R.J. 1965. *Perspectives on Peirce: Critical Essays on Charles Sanders Peirce*. New Haven, CT: Yale University Press.

Bertaux, D. (ed.) 1981. *Biography and Society: The Life History Approach in the Social Sciences. Studies in International Sociology.* vol. 23. Beverly Hills, CA: Sage Publications.

Burke, K. 1962. *A Grammar of Motives and a Rhetoric of Motives*. Cleveland, OH: Meridian.

———. *Permanence and Change*. Indianapolis, IN: Bobbs-Merrill.

Denzin, N.K. 1985. "A Controversy Over the Method Versus Interpretation." *Biography and Society* 4: 5–10.

Dewey, J. 1929. *The Quest for Certainty: A Study of the Relation of Knowledge and Action*. New York: Minton, Balch and Company.

Fromm, E. 1941. *Escape From Freedom*. New York: Reinhart.

———. 1947. *Man For Himself*. New York: Reinhart.

Fuhrman, E.R. 1985. "Nature, Society and the Individual: Commensurable or Incommensurable?" Unpublished manuscript, Department of Sociology, Virginia Polytechnic Institute and State University, Blacksburg.

Gergen, K.J. and M.M. Gergen (eds.) 1984. *Historical Social Psychology*. Hillsdale, NJ: Lawrence Erlbaum Associates.

Gusfield, J. 1976. "The Literacy Rhetoric of Science." *American Sociological Review* 41: 16–34.

Hall, P.M. 1983. "Individualism and Social Problems: A Critique and an Alternative." *The Journal of Applied Behavioral Science* 19: 85–94.

Hummell, R. 1982. *The Bureaucratic Experience*. New York: St. Martin's Press.

Jung, C. 1933. *Modern Man in Search of a Soul*. Harcourt Brace and World.

Kavolis, V. 1970. "Post-Modern Man: Psychocultural Responses to Social Trends." *Social Problems* 17: 435–448.

Kleinman, S. 1985. *Personal Communication*.

Lasch, C. 1979. *The Culture of Narcissism*. New York: Norton.

———. 1984. *The Minimal Self: Psychic Survival in Troubled Times*. New York: Norton.

Lewin, K. 1935. *A Dynamic Theory of Personality*. New York: McGraw-Hill.

Lifton, R.J. 1978. "Protean Man." *Partisan Review* 35: 13—27.

———. 1969. *Boundaries: Psychological Man in Revolution*. New York: Simon and Schuster.

Littrell, W.B. 1980. "Introduction" (Special Issue on Bureaucracy in the Eighties). *The Journal of Applied Behavioral Science* 16: 263–277.

Manning, P.K. 1983. "Metaphors of the Field: Varieties of Organizational Discourse." Pp. 225–245 in J. Van Maanen (ed.) *Qualitative Methodology*. Beverly Hills, CA: Sage Publications.

Maslow, A. 1954. *Motivation and Personality*. New York: Harper & Row.

———. 1968. *Toward a Psychology of Being*. Princeton, NJ: Van Nostrand.

McPartland, T.S., J. Cumming, and W.S. Garretson. 1961. "Self-Conception and Ward Behavior in Two Psychiatric Hospitals." *Sociometry* 24: 111–124.

Mead, G.H. 1934. *Mind, Self and Society.* Chicago: University of Chicago Press.

Miller, D.L. 1967. *Individualism: Personal Achievement and the Open Society.* Austin: The University of Texas Press.

———. 1973. *George Herbert Mead: Self, Language, and the World.* Austin: The University of Texas Press.

Miller, D.L. (ed.) 1982. *The Individual and the Social Self: Unpublished Work of George Herbert Mead.* Chicago: The University of Chicago Press.

Mischel T. (ed.) 1977. *The Self: Psychological and Philosophical Issues.* Totowa, NJ: Rowman and Littlefield.

Mischel, W. and H.N. Mischel. 1977. "Self-control and the Self." Pp. 31–64 in T. Mischel (ed.) *The Self: Psychological and Philosophical Issues.* Totowa, NJ: Rowman and Littlefield.

Morris, C. 1970. *The Pragmatic Movement in American Philosophy.* New York: George Braziller.

Murphy, G. 1947. *Personality: A Biosocial Approach.* New York: Harper & Row.

Rogers, C.R. 1961. *On Becoming a Person.* Boston: Houghton Mifflin.

———. 1972. "A Humanistic Conception of Man. Pp. 19–32 in J.F. Glass (ed.) *Humanistic Society: Today's Challenge to Sociology.* Pacific Palisades, CA: Goodyear.

Rucker, D. 1969. *The Chicago Pragmatists.* Minneapolis: University of Minnesota Press.

Sarbin, T.R. and K.E. Schiebe (eds.) 1983. *Studies in Social Identity.* New York: Praeger.

Schneider, L. 1971. "Dialectic in Sociology." *American Sociological Review* 36: 667–678.

Sheinberg, S. 1974. "Alienated Youth: Fact or Artifact? Anomie, and Self-Referrent Constructs as Pivotal Variables in a Study of Academic Youth." Ph.D. dissertation, University of Houston, Texas.

Sjoberg, G., T.R. Vaughan, and A.F. Sjoberg. 1984. "Morals and Applied Behavioral Research: A Prefatory Essay." *The Journal of Applied Behavioral Science* 20: 311–321.

Show, D.A. and C.L. Phillips. 1982. "The Changing Self-Orientations of College Students: From Institution to Impulse." *Social Science Quarterly* 63: 462–476.

Sorel, G. 1914. *Reflections on Violence.* New York: Huebsch.

Spitzer, S.P. and J. Parker. 1976. "Perceived Validity and Assessment of the Self." *Sociological Quarterly* 17: 236–246.

Turner, R. 1976. "The Real Self: From Institution to Impulse." *American Journal of Sociology* 81: 989–1016.

Vaihinger, H. 1924. *The Philosophy of "As-if."* London: Paul, Trench, Trubner.

Veroff, J. , E. Douvan, and R.A. Kulka. 1981. *The Inner American.* New York: Basic Books.

White, H. 1978. *Topics of Discourse.* Baltimore, MD: Johns Hopkins University Press.

Winer, P.P. 1949. *Evolution and the Founders of Pragmatism.* Cambridge, MA: Harvard University Press.

Wood, M.R. 1977. "The Post Modern Self: An Analysis of Selected 19th and 20th Century American Published Diaries." Ph.D. dissertation, The University of Texas, Austin.

Wood, M. and M. Hughes. 1984. "Social Psychological Change in U.S. Society, 1957 to 1976: Values, Self-Conceptions, and the Post Modern Self." Paper presented at the Annual Meeting of the Society for the Study of Social Problems, San Antonio, Texas.

Yankelovitch, D. 1981. *New Rules: Searching for Self-fulfillment in a World Turned Upside Down.* New York: Random House.

Zurcher, L.A., Jr. 1977. *The Mutable Self: A Self-concept for Social Change.* Beverly Hills, CA: Sage Publications.

———. 1983. *Social Roles: Conformity, Conflict, and Change.* Beverly Hills, CA: Sage Publications.

The Social Preservation of Mind:
The Alzheimer's Disease Experience

Jaber F. Gubrium
Marquette University

Data from the Alzheimer's disease (senile dementia) experience are interpreted to
extend and refine George Mead's theory of mind. While Mead conceived of mind
as an internal conversation, the disease experience shows that the reality-status of
mind is more practical and radically dialogical in organization. Taken as collectively preserved, mind is circumscribed through agents by means of rule-guided
articulations and closures. Suggestions are offered for a more fully dialogical
appreciation of Mead's view.

In his critique of Watson and behaviorism, George Herbert Mead (1934) presented an
alternative view of mind. It was Mead's contention that mind, self, or intelligence—he
often used these interchangeably (see Mead, 1934:50, 134, 186, 191, 192)—was a
discursive process. Thinking was likened to internal conversation (p. 47). Mead took
care to point out that, while individuals came to have selves or minds, the latter were
not emergent products of nascent structures present at birth, but, rather, were outcomes
of the "social side of human experience" (p. 1). Quoting from Mead:

> Mind arises in the social process only when that process as a whole enters into, or
> is present in, the experience of any one of the given individuals involved in the
> process. When this occurs the individual becomes self-conscious and has a mind
> ... (p. 134)

Although Mead's theory of mind has not been without explanatory controversy
(see Blumer, 1973,1977, 1980; Huber, 1973a,b; Lewis, 1976, 1977,1979; McPhail and
Rexroat, 1979, 1980), mind's "logical geography" (cf. Ryle, 1949:chaps. 1–2) remains

Reprinted from Symbolic Interaction, 9(1):37–51.

individualistic both in symbolic interactionism and in the most recent social behaviorism. While it is generally agreed that self or mind is not an inherent individual possession, it is nonetheless thought to be a state of being located in and about the individual person whose physical presence, with experience, comes to embody it. As Mead (1934: 50) argued against Wundt: "The body is not a self, as such; it becomes a self only when it has developed a mind within the context of social experience." Being self-conscious and socially formed, the individual mind is, in turn, transformed through social interaction.

A variety of commonplace experiences suggests a need to refine Mead's view. In his many dogfight illustrations, Mead asserts that we take it for granted that, while dogs may engage in vivid "conversations of gestures," the gestures are not "significant." The gestures are not products of, nor do they concretize, canine selves. As Mead (1934: 43) says: "We do not assume that the dog says to himself, 'If the animal comes from this direction he is going to spring at my throat and I will turn in such a way.'" The conduct of dogs is understood to be mindless, the outcome of their mutual conditioning. Yet what are we to make of the common experiences where the assumption is relaxed or even reversed? At times, people do take it for granted that dogs, let alone any quick or inanimate object, significantly reference themselves, have minds, and behave accordingly (cf. Casteneda, 1968, 1971, 1972; Wieder, 1980). In light of such definitions and experiences, is not an a priori assumption to the contrary unduly restrictive? More inclusive would be a radically social version of Thomas' (1923) notion of "the definition of the situation" (cf. McHugh, 1968).

While some might judge the interpretation of canine conduct and the consideration of what fuels dogfights as marginal to the symbolic depth of human experience, or the ordinary attribution of mindedness to animals as incidental to the ultimate realities and individual location of selves, there is striking evidence of such conduct in the realm of human affairs. As a case in point, the Alzheimer's disease (senile dementia) experiences of patients, caregivers, and concerned others show that it is not routinely assumed that the demented are mindless but, rather, the assumption, in its own right, is a recurring issue of treatment and caregiving. The patient-oriented actions of the concerned cannot be adequately understood in terms of an internal conversational view of self-location, notwithstanding its social sensitivity. Only the treatment of mind as a social preserve, as an "internal" entity assigned and sustained both by, and for, whomever assumes it to exist, can account for what is taken to be the minded conduct of the mindless, the belief and attitude that the demented have minds when it may be less evident than in the conduct of dogs.

This article presents data toward a more fully social appreciation of Mead's seminal understanding of mind. Following a medical description of the disease and the study from which the data are drawn, four features of the social preservation of mind are examined: (1) the idea of the hidden mind and the problem of its realization, (2) the question of who is mind's agent, (3) discernment and articulation rules, and (4) the organization of mental demise. In conclusion, suggestions are offered for a dialogical view.

THE DISEASE

Called "the disease of the century" (Alzheimer's Disease and Related Disorders Association, 1982), Alzheimer's or senile dementia is now considered to be the single most devastating illness of old age (Reisberg, 1983: xvii). Long after its discovery in 1906 (Alzheimer, 1907, 1911), it was believed to affect those aged thirty to fifty and thus also referred to as a presenile dementia. Recent neuropathological research (Terry, 1978a) indicates that the distinction between presenile or Alzheimer's dementia and its senile form is probably arbitrary, implying that the behavioral and organic markers of both forms of debility are actually one disease.

Alzheimer's is a devastating disease. There is a progressive decline in mental functioning in which victims experience confusion, forgetfulness, depression, disorientation, and agitation. The inability to plan and organize actions leaves one unable to complete the simplest tasks of daily living. While in the early stages, a patient can lead a moderately independent life, severe dementia virtually disables its victim such that one, for example no longer recognizes the once-familiar faces of a spouse or child and is rendered incapable of managing routine activities like eating, voiding, and grooming (see Reisberg, 1981).

However severe the cognitive decline, the victim may be remarkably physically fit. It is said that the only physical markers of Alzheimer's disease may be the senile plaques, neurofibrillary tangles, and ancillary bodies found in the victim's brain, observable upon autopsy. While bioptic examination of the living brain is possible, it is not without considerable risk and rarely done. As such, the diagnosis of Alzheimer's disease remains clinical, based on cognitive evaluation by means of mental status inquiries, family histories, and physical examinations to rule out confounding or concurrent illnesses (Katzman, 1981, 1982; Katzman and Karasu, 1975).

At present, there is no prevention or cure for Alzheimer's disease. While a variety of experimental drugs holds some promise for the treatment of milder symptoms, there is still no effective medical means of reducing severe senile dementia. Medical treatment remains managerial, commonly psychopharmacological intervention. Primarily a custodial problem, the Alzheimer's disease patient becomes the virtual ward of those upon whom he/she is dependent—frequently family members.

The cognitive and pathological status of the disease is even more ominous when its connection with the aging process is taken into account. Although there are repeated reminders, both in the medical and popular literature, that Alzheimer's disease is not normal aging (e.g., Alzheimer's Disease and Related Disorders Association, 1982), there is good evidence that the distinction between the disease and the aging process may be quantitative, not a difference in kind (Tomlinson, Blessed, and Roth, 1968, 1970; Terry, 1978b; Johnson, 1985). As a result, it is not clear whether the inexorably progressive symptoms of the disease are endemic to it or are the characteristics of becoming very aged, prematurely or in due course.

The combination of conditions has meant that Alzheimer's disease virtually has "two victims"—the person afflicted and the caregiver. Its so-called living death devolves into a caregiving problem, not a medical one. Founded in 1979, the Alzheimer's Disease and Related Association (ADRDA), a nationwide network of local chapters and support groups, aims to encourage medical research to eventually find a prevention or cure but, more immediately, to aid, educate, and counsel family members, concerned others, and the public-at-large in dealing with and caring for victims. At the same time, the ADRDA serves as a forum for the mutual support and enlightenment of caregivers.

Both in theory and practice, from medical opinion to custodial concern, the Alzheimer's disease experience is considered to be an interpersonal one, as the "two victims" theme suggests, never the sole problem or burden of the victim proper. The experience virtually exists in the nexus of the "disease that dims bright minds," a now-familiar phrase, and the burden of care. In and about the daily disease affairs of those who coexist there is the abiding everyday problem of mind, the enduring concern over what is left of the patient's self and, if anything, how to decipher it.

THE STUDY

Consideration of the social organization of mind emerged in conjunction with general reflections on field data and the analysis of disease literature from a larger study of the descriptive structure of senility (Gubrium, 1986). Participant observation was conducted in a variety of sites. A small day hospital for the care of Alzheimer's disease patients was studied over a four-month period. Informal activities were observed, as were scheduled events such as therapeutic recreation, reality orientation, activities of daily living, field trips, utilization reviews, staff conferences, and a support group for the patients' primary caregivers. Fieldwork also was conducted in the ADRDA chapters of two cities, focusing on their caregiver support groups. Few of the support groups permitted patient participation. Some specialized exclusively in the concerns of adult children; others were limited to victims' spouses. Local chapter meetings also were attended; their function tended to be more administrative and educational than expressly supportive.

In addition, diverse documents and texts were analyzed for related themes. The mind of the Alzheimer's patient, in theory and in practice, is the frequent topic of both prose and poetry in the disease literature. The presentations and transcribed discussions of medical conferences (e.g., Eisdorfer and Friedel, 1977; Katzman, Terry, and Bick, 1978; Katzman, 1983) show evidence for formal concern for issues raised casually by caregivers: "How does the victim lose a mind?" "How can the mental status of the Alzheimer's patient be assessed when the patient is characteristically incommunicable?" An exploding body of professional and semiprofessional literature addresses the questions, too, presenting the results of controlled studies as well as advice for practical application. With the growth of public concern over the disease and the emergence of an Alzheimer's disease movement centered in the ADRDA, a number of how-to books for caregivers has appeared (see Heston and White, 1983; Mace and Rabins, 1981; Powell and Courtice, 1983). In their own fashion, the books offer a range of practical solutions—rules—for the discernment and preservation of mind. Mind also is thematised in the prose and frequently appearing poems of the disease's folk literature, especially the newsletters of the many local chapters of the ADRDA. It is the poetry, more than any form of written text, that, even in its simplicity and sentimentality, brings the reader or listener to the very heart of mind.

A HIDDEN MIND

A persistent question for all concerned is "What significance is assigned to the patient's gestures and expressions?" For most caregivers, it is evident that the patient, to paraphrase a widely used slogan, at one time had a bright mind now dimmed by the disease. The victim was once intelligible, fully in command of wit and wisdom. As another slogan puts it, the disease seems to steal that mind away. Yet, while the victim's outward gestures and expressions may hardly provide a clue to an underlying human-ity, the question remains whether the disease has stolen it all or only the capacity to express it, leaving an unmanifested, hidden mind.

A focal theme of newsletters and support groups, the issue of the hidden mind bridges two native senses of mind, one individualistic but more structured than Mead's, the other structured but more fully social. Newsletters and support group proceedings show that there is a clear sense that it is individual persons who possess minds. While the social origin of mind is rarely discussed, its social sustenance frequently is. Caregivers and concerned others commonly deliberate over, share information, and offer each other practical advice about how to maintain whatever remains of the Alzheimer's victim's mental life.

In one sense, mind is more structured than Mead's conception in that it is taken to be less an internal communicative process than an objective "thing," an entity owned by the person that, once secured, can be expressed. This is evident in varied common references to "the state of mind," whether a patient has fully "lost his/her mind, when he/she will be completely "out of his/her mind," "what his/her mind is really like," "how to get into a victim's mind," among many similar expressions. In the Alzheimer's experience, such statements are more than casual metaphors; they are taken to be concrete references.

In contrast to this usage is a sense of mind more fully social than Mead's. While mind as entity is, in a manner of speaking, what all concerned are up against, it is at the same time a thing that is existentially tied to all. Because it is hidden—if not completely stolen—by the disease, others are charged with its realization. A common sentiment, it is said to be "up to us" to look and listen carefully for what the Alzheimer's victim is really trying to communicate. A familiar claim, only those who truly love the person, who may hate the disease, can make the difference between the continued realization of the victim's person as opposed to his/her loss to the "mere shell" of a former self. The contrast with Mead is a mind that persists in and through social assignment, the external (public) preservation of self.

The following exchange, drawn from the proceedings of one of the support groups observed, illustrates both senses of mind. The group is comprised mainly of the elderly spouses of Alzheimer's patients. Attention is centered on the mental status of a particular patient. The patient's spouse (call her Rita), asks what to think about her husband's very demented condition of late.

I just don't know what to think or feel. It's like he's not even there anymore, and it distresses me something awful. He doesn't know me. He thinks I'm a strange woman in the house. He shouts and tries to slap me away from him. It's not like him at all. Most of the time he makes sounds but they sound more like an animal than a person. Do you think he has a mind left? I wish I could just get in there into his head and see what's going on. Sometimes I get so upset that I just pound on him and yell at him to come out to me. Am I being stupid? I feel that if I don't do something quick to get at him that he'll be taken from me altogether.

Immediately responding to Rita, another participant, Sara, explains:

We all have gone through it. I know the feeling . . . , like, you just know in your heart of hearts that he's in there and that if *you* let go, that's it. So you keep on trying and trying and trying. You've got to keep the faith, that it's him and just work at him, 'cause if you don't . . . well, I'm afraid we've lost them. That's Alzheimer's. It's up to the ones who care because they [the victims] can't do for themselves.

In the exchange, mind is both individual and social. It is an entity possessed by the victim; yet the possession is also a gift allocated faithfully toward its subsequent realization. It is evident that, in practice, Rita, Sara, and their coparticipants, are literally "doing" mind in order to realize it (see Garfinkel, 1961; Mehan and Wood, 1975). Applying Mead's conversational metaphor, we can interpret their activity as a radically social turn on individual mental life. The status of the victim's internal conversation is, simultaneously, an articulation and practical realization of whomever enters into it. As Sara's response implies, it is those concerned who preserve mind, as ably as they can.

Following Sara's response, several participants question the wisdom of maintaining faith in the face of decreasing evidence that the victim still has a mind. With this, participants directly confront the understanding so central to Mead's view: the status of mind's internal conversation. Participants deliberate over the warrants of their faith. One of them, Jack, asks Sara whether she wouldn't feel foolish to realize that all her faith in, and effort to communicate with, her husband were for naught because, as he claims of his own spouse, "she's like the living dead." He adds:

That's why I'm looking for a nursing home for her. I loved her dearly but she's just not Mary anymore. No matter how hard I try, I can't get myself to believe that she's there anymore. I know how that can keep you going, but there comes a point where all the evidence points the other way. Even at those times (which is not very often) when she's momentarily lucid, I just know that's not her speaking to me but some kneejerk reaction. You just can't let that sort of thing get your hopes up because then you won't be able to make the kind of decision that's best for everyone all around. You know what I mean?

Sara interjects:

Well, I know what you've gone through, and I admire your courage, Jack. But you can't be too sure. How do you *really* know that what Mary says at times is not one of those few times she's been able to really reach out to you? You don't *really* know for sure, do you? You don't really know if those little plaques and tangles are in there, do you? I hate to make it hard on you, Jack, but I face the same thing day in and day out with Richard [her husband]. Can I ever finally close him out of my life and say, "Well, it's done. It's over. He's gone"? How do I know that the poor man isn't hidden somewhere, behind all that confusion, trying to reach out and say, "I love you, Sara"? [she weeps].

In this touching scene, we find that even the attempt to empirically confirm or disprove the supposition of mind can't penetrate its existence or the possibility that it has been altered. Mind's existence seems to be experientially tied, in the final analysis, to the faith of those concerned and to the social preservation of the assignment, to minding. The working sense of mind found in the Alzheimer's disease experience is, at once, individual, social, and discursive. It radicalizes Mead's vision of social individuality. Rather than presenting mind as secured individual property, the Alzheimer's disease experience repeatedly raises the question of how to define it as such. Although essentially hidden, when mind is faithfully assigned, it is an entity, a structure, articulated as much by those concerned as by those for whom there is concern. All are equally mind's agents, in common ownership of those who seek it. Unassigned, mind is no longer in hiding and thereby experientially nonexistent, its apparent expressions meaningless.

THE QUESTION OF AGENCY

As a thing located somewhere behind gesture and expression, mind never presents itself directly to those who take it into account. Hidden as it is, mind must be spoken for. As the Alzheimer's disease experience plainly shows, persons may not be able to speak their own minds. It should be noted, though, that the Alzheimer's disease experience is not unique in this regard, only more visible and urgent in the presentation of what is otherwise a universal problematic. Daily life is full of the pursuit of others' insights into individual minds as well as claims to know individual mind's better than those who ostensibly possess them. As the professionalization of mental concern indicates, agency has even been commodified, a purchasable service available to those desiring expert access to their minds.

Speakers for the victim's mind are a motley set. They may be a formal group, as is the health-care team who reviews a patient's conduct to keep it in tow. In the day hospital observed, the team consisted of a physician, psychiatrist, nurses, a recreation therapist, and a social worker. In varied ways and degrees, each team member spoke for the patient as a means of arriving at a shared sense of his/ her mental status for diagnostic, prescriptive, and therapeutic purposes. In the Alzheimer's disease experience, of course, the caregiver is a key spokesman, his/her assertions warranted by intimate daily contact. At times, the patient may also serve as agent for this own mind; at other times, his/her very vocal, insistent, or seemingly intelligible testimony on his/her own behalf may be discounted because of his/ her disease (see Gubrium, 1980).

There is no guarantee, in practice, who will serve or be accepted as mental agent, only that mind emerges by way of agency.

Before mind is spoken for, the issue of who speaks credibly must be resolved. For example, in ascertaining the victim's mental status, the victim may be taken to speak competently for himself, even at the end stages of the disease when he might otherwise be considered vegetative. As the earlier extracts showed, the concept of "lucid moments" raised the possibility that there were occasions when the virtually fully demented were to be taken as temporary agents for minds still functioning behind the disease. As such, the disease is a communicative malfunction, the lucid moment serving to convey aspects of a mind otherwise hidden. The issue of agency may become lodged in deliberations over the lucidity of such moments, over the question of whether what was said and heard was, in fact, lucid (a clear and distinct expression of the victim's mind) or the mere appearance of lucidity (perhaps a so-called parroting). The discernment of lucidity may itself turn on the assessment of discernment credentials, as one or another party to a deliberation claims to know best in such matters because of experience, education, or insight, among a host of interpretive warrants. Indeed, the figure and ground of warrants and discernments continually shift in the flow of mental discourse.

Mind experientially persists to the extent that some agent preserves it, be the agent the one whose mind is at stake or some other. While in theory, mind is referenced as a thing, it is articulated and realized by a type of existential labor. Agents are themselves practicing features of mind, even though mind, in its own right, is taken to be a separate and essentially hidden entity. As a support group participant explained:

> Look, you and I know that if we don't make a real, loving effort to listen, to really hear, what they're [Alzheimer's patients] trying to say to us, that you might as well call it quits. I know that Dad hasn't said a word for years, but when I touch his hand or put my arms around him—God bless him—he knows. He really knows! You can't tell me he's gone. As far as I'm concerned, Dad's as much with us as he always was. The damned disease has just made it impossible for him to communicate with us. It's an effort and someone's got to believe in them. You just can't ever forget that it's a life and you can't give up on it.

Now, of course, not all of those gathered in this or in other support groups feel as this devoted daughter did. Some cease to be the victim's agent because they consider it foolish to do so, not because it is foolish to care but, rather, foolish to continue caring for something they no longer believe exists. Those continuing to maintain what is called the illusion of the patient's lucidity, who try to preserve the semblance of the victim's former self, are said to be "denying," the irrational sustenance of mind. In contrast, for others, the ultimate question of mind's existence experientially overshadows whatever evidence is brought to bear in the matter. For them, denial is mere rhetoric, someone's way of being diagnostic. When all is said and done, the question remains, as Sara put it earlier, "How do I know that . . . behind all that confusion, [he's not] trying to reach out and say: 'I love you, Sara.'?"

Given the liberal tenor of Mead's philosophy, he understandably tended to limit agency to the individual, embodied articulators of mind, as if to say, when self-consciousness occurs, an individual can speak his/her own mind. Diverse, casual evidence and the Alzheimer's disease data suggest the need for a broader interpretation, cast as discursive and practical individualization. Accordingly, mind is anyone's responsibility, everyone being a potential agent, the person conceivably self-conscious despite himself/ herself.

ARTICULATING MIND

Hidden as it is, mind requires articulation. In Mead's view, it is the individual person, in possession of self-consciousness and sensitive to others, who expresses himself/ herself, to others and to himself/ herself. The Alzheimer's disease experience poignantly confronts those concerned with the everyday issue of articulation. While there are any number of agents for the victim's mind, how do they go about their work? Consider here the social organization of preservation; in the next section, we turn to closure or mental demise.

A difficult task confronts the caregivers and concerned others who seek the Alzheimer's victim's mind: to read outward signs of mind bereft of common meaning. The disease is said to destroy the victim's capacity to communicate by gesture or expression. Left with little or no memory, muddled speech, erratic movement, or other unintelligible activity, in diverse combinations, the usual route to mind is virtually nonexistent.

In the face of this, rules of thumb are offered to facilitate articulation, some based on professional practice, others being "tips" for hearing what the patient is trying to say drawn from individual caregiving experiences. Articulation rules are regular features of the disease literature, especially nursing and social work writings, the advice books for caregivers, and the many ADRDA chapter newsletters.

The foremost rule is that those concerned must be *prepared* to articulate what the patient is trying to communicate. Before the actual interpretation process begins, agents must sharpen their perception so that whatever clues there are to the patient's inner intentions can be captured, obscure and fleeting as they may be. Called "active listening" by some (e.g., Philadelphia ADRDA *Newsletter,* January 1983) and a "special kind of listening" by others (e.g., Bonjean, 1979), preparation is said to require *objectivity.* An active listener attempts to hear without being judgmental, which would confound what the patient means. As explained in the Philadelphia ADRDA *Newsletter* (and reprinted in other chapter newsletters:

> This method [active listening] conveys nonjudgmental interest and a sincere willingness to understand the other person. The result is a clarification of the situation for both the person speaking and the "active" listener, and—in many cases—the person with the problem is able to come up with more insight about his/her problem through the conversation. (p. 3)

The rule not only prepares the listener to perceive the patient's intentions but, through the active listener's effort, both the listener's and the patient's insight into the latter's mind is achieved. As such, active or special listening is preparatory to the common realization of intention.

The preparatory rule has a selection provision. While the active listener should be objective, he/she should not listen to everything the patient conveys, for much of what is said and done is meaningless, arbitrary, or unintended. As a result, one listens for what the patient is *truly* saying, not literal expressions. As Bonjean (1979:8) advises: "Sometimes, listening means attempting to hear what is felt rather than what is reported, what is meant rather than what is actually said." And as pointed out in the Philadelphia *Newsletter*: "In active listening, one listens not only to the literal meaning of the words spoken but also to the emotional content underlying the words" (p. 3).

The active listener fine-tunes for affective messages. This resolves the challenge of communicating with the incommunicable. As defined by the rule, in the final analysis the route to mind is by way of feelings. From physicians to caregivers, those concerned repeatedly reminded each other that, while the Alzheimer's victim may be cognitively deficient, it does not mean he/she doesn't have feelings, the very heart of mind. Needless to say, this puts a considerable interpretive burden on listeners.

Other rules link details of the patient's conduct with particular meanings. Some of the most explicit are described in a widely quoted article by Bartol (1979) titled "Nonverbal Communication in Patients with Alzheimer's Disease." Explicit rules are suggested in the following passages.

> Pacing the halls, restless behavior, and inability to sleep tell us clearly that the patient is anxious, [the patient asking us] "What is wrong with me? Can't you see I am getting worse? How much worse will I get?"
> Withdrawn behavior and signs of nervousness tell us that the patient may be afraid [the patient saying to us] "I am frightened of what is happening to me! Help me!"

Not all interpretive rules are as straightforward. Many emerge from deliberations over the particular meaning of unintelligible gestures or expressions. From professional staffings to support group proceedings and casual conversation, the concerned inform each other of how to interpret the patient's conduct, warranting their claims on grounds as varied as training, expertise, and intimacy of contact. Whether formal or casual, the application of interpretive rules is organized in usage. Rules themselves are interpreted, transformed, and applied as the need arises, working guides for making sense of individual expressions, discovered, interpreted, and applied case by case.

Just as words are believed to stem from mind, feelings are taken to have a source. But what thing do feelings express? The answer lies in the affective analog of hidden mind: the referential heart.

Time and again, in speech and text, those concerned distinguish between the feelings and words the patient conveys, as do rules for active listening. Words and feelings are located, respectively, in references to matters of mind and heart. For some, heart is the mind that has all but failed, the spirit of intention, the heart of mind. As frequently noted, "His mind might no longer be active, but he's still got a heart and feelings."

The heart of mind has the same discursive properties as mind itself. It is a thing, hidden, inferentially describable. Where there can be mental anguish, so, too, there is heartache. Where there is sincerity, there also are heartfelt intentions. Even mind's past— remembrances—has its counterpart in heart's memories. Originally appearing in the Kansas City ADRDA *Newsletter* and reprinted in the August 1984 issue of the Des Moines ADRDA *Newsletter,* extracts from a poem titled "Heart's Memories," said to be written by an Alzheimer's disease victim, share the heart of mind's past:

> I remember you with my heart
> > My mind won't say your name
> I can't recall where I knew you
> > Who you were
> Or who I was.
> . . .
> But I do know you
> > I know I knew you
> And I do love you
> > I know how you make me feel
> I remember the feelings we had together
> > My heart remembers
> It cries out in loneliness for you
> > For the feeling you give me now.
> . . .
> Please, please don't forget me
> > and please don't stay away
> Because of the way my mind acts
> > I can still love you
> I can still feel you
> > I can remember you with my heart
> And a heart memory is maybe
> > The most important memory of all.

While the folk poetry of the disease experience would be judged crude by some, its place in the conduct of the concerned cannot be judged on literary grounds. The folk poetry not only reveals how the ultimate structure of mind is envisioned by those concerned, it is also a way of voicing, by means of words, what words cannot convey. Ironic as that may be, it is taken to articulate the heart of mind, a thing indescribable in its own right.

A commonplace dilemma, caregivers and concerned others frequently complain that they "just can't put into words" the feelings they and/or their patients are experiencing or desire to communicate. It is not a problem of "really knowing deep down," but one of articulation. More than any other vehicle, it is the growing poetry of the disease that succinctly serves that purpose. For example, in one support group session, several participants were struggling to describe to each other the inner feelings of their respective patients. For some time, one caregiver in particular tried unsuccessfully to do so. She claimed to know very well what was in her demented husband's heart, what the disease progressively and insidiously had hidden from her, but had difficulty articulating what she knew. Many agreed that it was hard for them, too. At one point, though, as she once again attempted to describe her husband's heart, she fetched a poem from her purse and read it aloud. On the face of it, its words were no different than the words she had earlier used ineffectively to convey the feelings. Yet, when she had read the poem, her message was received with clear understanding, various members of the group acknowledging that "it said it all." What that was, of course, cannot be described. The point of the poetic message was that, despite its words, it was taken to be clear communication: emotive discourse. The poem was what the poem did; thereby, poetry-in-use became a social relationship—common under-standing, community.

THE DEMISE OF MIND

For some participants, the function of support groups is to teach one to realize, as a veteran put it, "that there comes a point where to keep thinking that they're still sensible and lucid underneath it all is ridiculous and blind." The attitude is not necessarily uncaring but realistic, for, just as those who claim to find definitive evidence of mind and heart in the conduct of their patients, others become equally convinced of their absence. As a daughter explained:

> When all is said and done, for all the finagling they do trying to figure out Mother's strange speech and erratic ways, Mother's just not there anymore. You might just as well be talking to a wall. It's a plain fact as clear as day. All that listening and all the clues in the world are not going to tell you that that brain's still working up there. Everyone should realize that sooner or later. If you ask me, it's more in *their* [caregivers'] minds than in the patient's.

The comment brings us face to face with the social nature of mind and minding. It informs us that, as entities, heart and mind are objects-for-us. The sentiment is that minding should in due course cease, for it eventually represents no conscious thing, nothing. Continued, unrestrained minding itself becomes an affliction—pathological denial—further victimizing the "other patient" of the disease, the victim's caregiver.

In a study of the social organization of death in two hospitals, Sudnow (1967) described dying as a social state of affairs. He reported on the physical preservations and closures linked with interpretations of the social worth of the dying. The Alzhe-imer's disease experience shows that closure is not only social but, for some, program-matic, processed by rules as formal as those serving articulation. The interpersonal relations of the patient and the caregiver are sometimes said to have a natural history. In veteran and professional judgment, it is only natural for, say, the wife of a recently diagnosed spouse to eagerly search for a cure or some other means of sustaining his "once bright mind." Indeed, the search and hope might last for years, well into the most debilitating stages of the disease. For some, the search virtually outlives the victim, as the former caregiver retrospectively attempts to regain the semblance of what the patient "really must have [meant or] felt even though he couldn't even remember his own name, where he'd been, or where he was going." Yet, as those who claim to know from experience or from being expert in such matters, there comes a point when it's only natural to begin closing off one's affairs with the hopelessly demented.

The professional rationalization of intervention is crystallized around a developmental-stage view of the closure process. Discussions and advice columns in ADRDA chapter newsletters and the human service literature of the disease show that Kubler-Ross' (1969) well-known formula of the five stages of dying has been adapted to Alzheimer's disease counterparts. A familiar concern is where the caregiver or a support group "is at." *Is at* refers to some point in the natural history of concern. For example, in regard to a particular caregiver, it may be said that he/she is at the stage of denial or in the acceptance phase, respectively, meaning that he/she refuses to close off his affairs with the person behind the disease or comes to accept the need for closure with what is now only the shell of a former self. Support groups also are said to progress naturally through stages of concern. A group comprised of novice caregivers is likely to dwell on articulation, particularly the cure that will again reveal the minds of those who were once so bright. A group of experienced participants is more likely to have confronted, discussed, and perhaps come to terms with mental demise. Indeed, support groups are described as more or less mature depending on whether they are, as a geriatrician put it, "still preoccupied with cure or are getting their own lives in order."

While in theory the natural history view is a linear vision of closure, even veteran caregivers and mature support groups, on occasion, confront that persistent question: "How do I know . . . behind all that . . . , [he's not] trying to reach out . . . ?" Sometimes, the question rushes ahead of its own deliberation, the fact of it having raised it in the first place taken to be callous and uncaring, the assumption made that, "of course," the victim still has feelings, if not the ability to rationally express them. In the circumstance, closure may be transformed into urgent preservation, with former hard evidence of total mental demise, of so-called brain failure, becoming previously unrecognized clues of the living person behind the disease. There are support groups sessions where ongoing shifts in the discourses of articulation and closure serve to construct, deconstruct, and reconstruct the victim's mind. As such, mind experientially dies and is reborn time and again, in and through formal and informal concern, an ongoing achievement.

CONCLUSION

Consider two principles of Mead's theory of mind in light of the Alzheimer's disease experience. One is the principle of minded individuality; the other is the principle of social formation. As set forth in Mead's eponymous book, *Mind, Self and Society,* the first refers to Mead's treatment of mind as individual property, as an owned internal conversation. The second principle discerns mind as a social achievement, formed and transformed in and through experience, in relation to others. Mead could be interpreted as seeing the principles as in continual dialog, neither one in that regard being a first principle but, rather, simultaneously operative, as Blumerians would prefer (see

Blumer 1969). In this sense, the Alzheimer's disease experience suggests that mind is pervasively dialogical, an individual product of its own discourse.

At times, though, Mead's statements reveal a distinct inequity in the application of the principles. Certain usages suggest that, once enlivened, the individual mind takes on more than an empirically independent existence. Mead speaks of the occurrence of self-consciousness and, then, the presence of mind. But the treatment is such that, while social in development, mind is occasionally described *theoretically* as referencing a self-conscious entity, embodied in the individual, foreclosing the further analysis of the dialogical status of that now separate and distinct internal conversation.

This sense of mind's logical geography constrains the data of the Alzheimer's disease experience, where mind is a poignantly problematic category, the common responsibility and property of those concerned. The concerned may settle their affairs with the heart of mind, concluding that there is indeed a self-conscious, feeling entity hidden somewhere behind the disease, or they may not. In either case, it is continually subject to their brand of epistemological scrutiny. They have the work of assigning and reassigning internality to portions of the common dialog of mind, whose participants include all conversant from victims to caregivers and concerned others (cf. Todorov, 1984).

The practical dialog that now constructs, deconstructs, and then reconstructs mind is not an epistemological dilemma for its participants. They work at its components, they are not numbed by its overall challenge. Thus we sometimes find caregivers raising the question "How can we *really* know?" together with the understanding that knowing is essentially tied to the faith of those concerned. Yet, at other times, they set that aside to deal with the object of their concern, as if to temporarily stop the dialogical whirlwind in order to see through to its major point of reference, to mind.

The Alzheimer's disease experience suggests that Mead's principles be detached from their bourgeois individualism and appreciated as concrete dialogical themes. With that mind becomes a more fully social entity, one born with attention to self-consciousness unfettered by a conclusive self-possession. Not far removed from Mead's internal conversation metaphor, minding is open dialog centered on its essentially unarticulated, but phenomenally describable source: mind.

REFERENCES

Alzheimer, A. 1907. "Über eine eigenartige Erkrankung der Hirnrinde," *Allgemeine Zeitschrift für Psychiatrie* 64: 146–148.

————. 1911. "Über eigenartige Krankheitsfälle des Späteren Alters." *Zeitschrift für Gesamte Neurologle und Psychiatrie* 4: 356–385.

Alzheimer's Disease and Related Disorders Association (ADRDA). 1982. *A Disease of the Century: The Case for the Alzheimer's Disease and Related Disorders Association and its Fight Against Alzheimer's and Related Diseases*. Chicago: A DR DA.

Bartol, M.A. 1979. "Nonverbal Communication in Patients with Alzheimer's Disease." *Journal of Gerontological Nursing* 5: 21–31.

Blumer, H. 1969. *Symbolic Interactionism: Perspective and Method*. Englewood Cliffs, N.J.: Prentice Hall.

————. 1973. "A Note on Symbolic Interactionism." *American Sociological Review* 38: 797–798.

————. 1977. "Comment on Lewis's 'The Classic Pragmatists as Forerunners to Symbolic Interactionism'." *Sociological Quarterly* 18: 285–289.

————. 1980. "Social Behaviorism and Symbolic Interactionism." *American Sociological Review* 45:404–419.

Bonjean, M.J. 1979. *Making Visits Count*. Madison/Milwaukee: University of Wisconsin System.

Casteneda, C. 1968. *The Teaching of Don Juan*. Berkeley, Calif.: University of California Press.

————. 1971. *A Separate Reality*. New York: Simon & Schuster.

————. 1972. *A Journey to Ixtlan*. New York: Simon & Schuster.

Eisdorfer, C. and R.O. Friedel (eds.) 1977. *Cognitive and Emotional Disturbance in the Elderly*. Chicago: Year Book Medical Publishers.

Garfinkel, H. 1961. *Studies in Ethnomethodology*. Englewood Cliffs, N.J.: Prentice-Hall.

Gubrium, J.F. 1980. "Patient Exclusion in Geriatric Staffings." *Sociological Quarterly* 21: 335–348.

————. 1986. *Oldtimers and Alzheimer's: The Descriptive Organization of Senility*. Greenwich, CT: JAI Press.

Heston, L.L. and J.A. White. 1983. *Dementia: A Practical Guide to Alzheimer's Disease and Related Illnesses*. New York: W.H. Freeman.

Huber, J. 1973a. "Symbolic Interaction as a Pragmatic Perspective: The Bias of Emergent Theory." *American Sociological Review* 38: 274–284.

————. 1973b. "Reply to Blumer: But Who Will Scrutinize the Scrutinizers?" *American Sociological Review* 39: 798–800.

Johnson, H.A. (ed.). 1985. *Relations Between Normal Aging and Disease*. New York: Raven Press.

Katzman, R. 1981. "Early Detection of Senile Dementia." *Hospital Practice* 16: 61–76.

————. 1982. "The Complex Problem of Diagnosis." *Generations* 7: 8–10.

Katzman, R. (ed.). 1983. *Branbury Report 15: Biological Aspects of Alzheimer's Disease*. Cold Spring Harbor, N.Y.: Cold Spring Harbor Laboratory.

Katzman, R. and T.B. Karasu. 1975 "Differential Diagnosis of Dementia." Pp. 103–134 in W. Fields (ed.) *Neurological and Sensory Disorders in the Elderly*. New York: Grune and Stratton.

Katzman, R., R.D. Terry, and K.L. Bick (eds.). 1978. *Alzheimer's Disease: Senile Dementia and Related Disorders*. New York: Raven Press.

Kübler-Ross, E. 1969. *On Death and Dying*. New York: Macmillan.

Lewis, J.D. 1976 "The Classic American Pragmatists as Forerunners to Symbolic Interactionism." *Sociological Quarterly* 17: 347–359.

————. 1977. "Reply to Blumer." *Sociological Quarterly* 18: 291–292.

————. 1979. "A Social Behaviorist Interpretation of the Median 'I'." *American Journal of Sociology* 85: 261–287.

Mace, N.L. and P.V. Rabins. 1981. *The 36-Hour Day*. Baltimore: Johns Hopkins University Press.

McHugh, P. 1968. *Defining the Situation*. Indianapolis: Bobbs-Merrill.

McPhail, C. and C. Rexroat. 1979. "Mead vs. Blumer: the Divergent Methodological Perspectives of Social Behaviorism and Symbolic Interactionism." *American Sociological Review* 44: 449–467.

————. 1980 "Ex cathedra Blumer or ex libris Mead?" *American Sociological Review* 45: 420–430.

Mead, G.H. 1934. *Mind, Self & Society*. Chicago: University of Chicago Press.

Mehan, H. and H. Wood. 1975. *The Reality of Ethnomethodology.* New York: Wiley Interscience.

Philadelphia ADRDA Newsletter. 1983. "Summary of January Meeting on Active Listening." Philadelphia ADRDA Newsletter (January): 2–3.

Powell, L.S. and K. Courtice. 1983. *Alzheimer's Disease: A Guide For Families*. Reading, Mass.: Addison-Wesley.

Reisberg, B. 1981. *Brain Failure*. New York: Free Press.

————. 1983. "Preface." Pp. xvii-xix in B. Reisberg (ed.), *Alzheimer's Disease: The Standard Reference*. New York: Free Press.

Ryle, G. 1949. *The Concept of Mind*. Chicago: University of Chicago Press.

Sudnow, D. 1967. *Passing On*. Englewood Cliffs, N.J.: Prentice-Hall.

Terry, R.D. 1978a. "Aging, Senile Dementia, and Alzheimer's Disease." Pp. 11–14 in R. Katzman, R. D. Terry, and K.L. Bick (eds.) *Alzheimer's Disease: Senile Dementia and Related Disorders*. New York: Raven Press.

————. 1978b. "Physical Changes in the Aging Brain." Pp. 205–220 in J.A. Behnke, C.E. Finch, and G.B. Moment (eds.) *The Biology of Aging*. New York: Plenum.

Thomas, W.I. 1923. *The Unadjusted Girl*. Boston: Little Brown.

Todorov, T. 1984. *Mikhail Bakhtin: The Dialogical Principle*. Minneapolis: University of Minnesota Press.

Tomlinson, B.E., G. Blessed, and M. Roth. 1968. "Observations on the Brains of Non-Demented Old People." *Journal of Neurological Sciences* 7: 331–356.

————. 1970. "Observations on the Brains of Demented Old People." *Journal of Neurological Sciences* 11: 205–242.

Wieder, D. L. 1980. "Behavioristic Operationalism and the Life World: Chimpanzees and Chimpanzee Researchers in Face-to-Face Interaction." *Sociological Inquiry* 50: 75–103.

Aces and Bombers:
The Post-Exam Impression
Management Strategies of Students

Daniel Albas
Cheryl Albas
University of Manitoba

In this study we attempted to develop a classification of the strategies students employ to manage self-impressions after grades have been awarded and examination papers returned. These encounters between students are of three types: first, when students who have scored a top grade in this exam (Aces) encounter other students who received a low or even failing grade (Bombers); second, when Aces encounter other Aces; and, third, when Bombers encounter other Bombers. The impression management strategies employed in these encounters are constrained by well-known rules of modesty in regard to one's own achievements and considerateness for lesser achieving peers, dictated by the particular encounter type described above. These rules are spelled out and an attempt made to generalize the findings to a wider universe of interactions.

Goffman (1959) in *The Presentation of Self in Everyday Life* graphically describes how, in the drama of everyday life, people constantly send messages to others with whom they interact concerning their wishes, feelings, intentions, and selves. Some of these messages are intended by the sender and are referred to as "impressions given." Other messages sent are those that are not intended—they escape inadvertently and may even embarrass actors if they are aware of them. These are referred to as

Reprinted from Symbolic Interaction, 11(2):289–302.

"impressions given off." Accordingly, people constantly manage their behavior to communicate impressions that are favorable and advantageous to themselves. In other words, through strategies of concealment and revelation,[1] they practice impression management—a form of communication that employs not only verbal language but also face work, gestures, gait, posture, and the whole panoply of body language. In this article we detail the post-exam impression management strategies students employ either to conceal poor grades or reveal good ones.

By far the majority of empirical studies of impression management deal with strategies of concealment; however, in this article we attempt also to document strategies of revelation. Whether, in the course of impression management, people elect to employ concealment or revelation or a mixture of both depends largely on the total situation and its objectives, dangers, or opportunities; for example, whether the aim is salesmanship, undercover work, or courtship. However, also involved most of the time and constituting a condition more to be coped with than capitalized on are the intense emotions that so often engulf us in so many everyday life situations.

Stebbins' (1972) "expressions of self esteem" can be translated in our present context of "impression management" as attempts to convey the image of a highly estimable person. He describes how actors engage in modest, proud, or conceited behavior with reference to their "accomplishments in lines of activity regarded by [them] and certain others present as major forms of positive self-identification" (Stebbins, 1972, p. 463). In essence, the form of behavior presented to other people whose opinions are valued will depend on the particular situation. Thus, a person may "speak proudly of an accomplishment before one group of people and modestly of it before another." Accordingly we have come to recognize that impression management is a universal and constant process of social interaction; that the problem of coping with emotions and the necessity to obey largely implicit but nevertheless binding rules are the parameters of every actor's role in the impression management act.

A particularly revealing arena for the observation of impression management under emotionally stressful circumstances, and one that is subject to well-known but seldom voiced rules, is the frequently played out drama of returning their papers to students after a test has been graded but the grades have not been posted or in any way publicly revealed. The first intimations students have of their grades is when they go to the front of the classroom and receive the graded paper from the instructor. It is usually a situation highly charged with the emotions of excitement, eagerness, apprehension, and anxiety. Those who have studied thoroughly and think they have done well almost burst with anticipation of an excellent grade, whereas those who were largely unprepared cringe at the almost certain prospect of a low or even failing grade. Students somewhere between these two categories dither in doubt as to whether their hopes will be dashed or their fears will be turned to delighted surprise. As a consequence of the grade they actually receive, all of them, the "Aces," the "Middle of the Roaders," as well as the "Bombers,"[2] know that they must manage the impressions they give if others are to see them in a positive light and if they are to see themselves as highly estimable people. Aces know that if they reveal their marks (as they probably ache to do and so acquire kudos) they must still appear modest and help those who did not get good grades to save face. Even Bombers, who probably wish to conceal their grades know that they must appear to be "gracious losers" and assist others like themselves to save face. In effect, the drama of returning graded exam papers to students is one in which their student identity is very much on the line. It is a competitive situation wherein the awareness context is closed or at least one of suspicion (Glazer and Strauss, 1981). That is, students are unaware of their positions relative to their competitors. We might even think of it as a kind of information vacuum that induces pressure both to find out one's situation relative to that of others and at the same time to project messages which may or may not be accurate but which will protect ego (impression management).

Miall and Herman's (1986) computer search of the literature on impression management revealed that the vast majority of such studies are quantitative in nature and were carried out in laboratory (artificial) settings. The fewer qualitative studies, which are carried out in natural settings, focused heavily on deviants (for example, the mentally disturbed, physically handicapped, or sexual deviants) to the relative neglect of normals. This promotes a situation where a major concept is relegated to "the status of respected little islands of knowledge" (Strauss 1970, p. 53). Accordingly, in this article an attempt is made to extend the applicability of the concept of impression management beyond the "abnormal" focuses of the past to "normal" life situations such as examination behavior. Some wider applications to other everyday life situations are also suggested in the conclusion.

METHODS

This article is part of a larger study of student life and exams conducted over the past 14 years (Albas and Albas, 1984) at a large provincial university in Western Canada. The data come from over 300 individuals who comprise four "generations" of university students. The data originate from three principal sources:

1. Examination logs—These are written accounts by students in which they described in detail how exams influenced their daily lives and noted aspects of exam related events which they perceived as problematic. More specifically, students wrote about what caused them particular difficulty, anxiety, or trouble. The accounts were to be arranged in terms of the what, when, where, and how of examinations as events in their daily lives throughout the academic year. This process incorporated an early in the term pre-examination phase, through the immediate pre-examination phase, the examination itself, its immediate aftermath, and the eventual return to students of their grades. If portions of the logs were unclear or seemed incomplete we attempted to contact the students involved (usually by telephone) to supplement their accounts. Since these logs included descriptions of thoughts, sentiments, and behavior students considered significant, they served as a valuable source of information about student's inner lives we were in no position to observe. The logs also provided an additional base line against which data obtained from observations and interviews could be cross-checked.

2. Interviews—These were conducted by us mostly at the examination site where we intermingled with students before and after exams, and in classrooms after test papers were returned. We attempted to get from students their spontaneous explanations of behavior and practices about which we had questions but had not yet verified. For example, in one class after the grades had been returned we noted a student who persistently tapped his pencil on his desk. We surmised it was a ploy on his part to attract attention to his exam paper, which lay face up on his desk with the grade clearly visible. Of course the tapping could have been a response to a nervous tic or the rhythmic response to a musical motivation. When it was possible to question him a little later, after most other students had departed, he verified our earlier hunch that he was attempting to draw attention to his high grade. In sum, the content of such interviews was prompted by particular "hunches" on our part, suggestions made by students in their logs, and by theoretical implications derived from reviews of relevant literature.

3. Comprehensive observations—To complete the triangulation process information derived from logs and interviews was combined with careful observations of strategies guided by categories that seemed theoretically and semantically apt (e.g., concealment, revelation, or selective revelation).

To ensure that we did not fall into the trap wherein our hypothesized results would come to guide our data-gathering process we scrupulously adhered to the following guidelines: (1) No quotation from logs was used to illustrate any point unless it was replicated (in essence) by at least three others. Most of the time dozens of students reported the same thing in more or less similar words, and (2) We attempted to avoid "leading" students in any responses they recorded in their logs or provided for us in interviews. In all cases we attempted to maintain the integrity and originality of the students responses. Also, careful attention was paid to deviant cases. For example, we did not merely assume that norms were responsible for many of the regularities observed, but rather we paid close attention to deviants to see if they were sanctioned or at least if they broke the sense of social rapport. Deviant cases (from the norms and emerging propositions) led to further reformulation of propositions and the development of a more complex categorization of impression management techniques employed by students.

THE DATA

General Encounters

Use of Revelation

As stated earlier, this study includes strategies of revelation as well as concealment. The first strategy of revelation is "repressed bubbling" wherein students who obtain an unexpectedly good grade are so elated that their joy seeps out in spite of themselves:

> When I have done very well and especially if its a surprise, I feel like telling everyone, but I know its not right [proper]. I try to keep it to myself but I think it shows because I feel this smile all over me—not just my mouth but everything else inside of me is smiling too.

> I usually find it hard to conceal my happiness. I sit through class wriggling and trying not to smile but my friends told me that I had a smile from ear to ear—I just cannot help the seepage.

The norm of modesty forbids overt exaltation and so the elation is expressed in such a way that it is obvious that the person is very happy but, at the same time, could not be accused of "crowing" over the success. These situations test the "dramaturgical discipline" of students almost to the limit because even though they are "immersed and given over" to the action of the moment most remain sufficiently in charge of themselves to be able to "cope with dramaturgical contingencies as they arise" (Goffman, 1959, p. 216). However, some students who receive unexpectedly good grades are unable to muster the self-discipline required and respond by "flooding out" or crying. One male student, unable to contain his joy, clenched his fist, raised it above his head and shouted "All right!"

As a strategy of revelation, repressed bubbling deals with impressions given off by students almost in spite of themselves. At the same time, though, they also employ more intentional techniques to "dramatically realize" identities that otherwise might not be apparent to others. The other strategies we describe subsequently require more "dramaturgical circumspection"—more planning and foresight—if the performance is to be successful (Goffman, 1959, p. 218).

A second such strategy of revelation can be referred to as "accidental revelation." In this situation students return to their seats after they have received the graded test and then permit an "accidental display of the grade" by leaving the test paper face upward as they appear to check through it, all the while appearing to be deep in thought and portraying the general image of humility. Other "accidental revelation" strategies include "very briefly placing the test paper [with grade face upward] sideways on the desk facing in the direction where other students are sitting," or "holding the test paper at arms length while reading it [as if one were far-sighted] thereby exposing the grade to as many others as possible . . . without shoving it in their faces." Another student goes almost as far by "pretending to need to stretch and yawn while I hold the [test] paper in my hand thus displaying the grade for the entire length of the stretch."

A third strategy of revelation involves "passive persuasion." Students who are less bold than those described up to this point but who are nonetheless impelled by an equal desire to make known their "good" or perhaps "unexpectedly good" fortune invoke a strategy of passive persuasion. It involves:

> smiling broadly, or giving some positive sign and then saying nothing. Your rather unusual actions raise the curiosity of other students and friends who will ask you

how you did. Once asked it is then O.K. to "crow", but only for a very short time. The real beauty of this method is that you can move from student to student, or friend to friend . . . smile, "crow", and then move on without appearing to be a braggart or a gloater.

A fourth strategy of revelation is "active persuasion." "Active persuaders" solicit a response from the others by looking about themselves, catching others' eyes, raising their eyebrows in a manner that unmistakably signals inquiry, and perhaps even inclining their bodies toward another in order to initiate conversation. The message is usually so clear that others almost always respond. However, interaction is always a gamble and despite the best of planning it may fail to materialize, as the following example shows. Two male students were classmates in two of their university courses. One student consistently outscored the other, usually by about five to 10%. In the incident described here the student who usually scored higher received his test first. When he went to sit down in his seat the other person "sneaked" a peak at the grade and saw that it was 32 points out of a possible 40. When the student who usually scored lower received his test, he was elated to find that he also had scored 32 out of a possible 40 points. Here is his description:

> However, nobody seemed interested in my mark and I was just dying to tell someone, anyone, but especially this one person. I not only sat beside him, I also angled my body toward him and asked him what he got (as a score). He didn't answer. I spoke even louder and said 'I did a lot better than I thought, I got 32 (out of 40)'. He just kept on reading his test and pretended he didn't hear me [I think]. It was very embarrassing.

This student's identities of "friend" and even as "person" were suddenly and unqualifiedly discredited (Gross and Stone, 1981). However, he went on to note that when he looked around no one was looking at him and those who might have been observing the interaction were turning away. In effect, they were practicing "studied nonobservance" or "tactful inattention" (Goffman, 1959, p. 230).

A fifth strategy of revelation is the use of the "Question-Answer chain rule" (Speier, 1973). Earlier we described how students practice "passive persuasion" by evoking responses from others. This technique assumes that they are able to elicit the curiosity of others and that they are well supplied with friends and acquaintances who will volunteer the question "How did you do?" However, most students find that they must make the first verbal move by asking others how they fared (Q) and then wait for their response (A), which in turn sets the stage for the next question "How did *you* do?"

> It is common knowledge that when you ask another student how well he/she did on a test, that person will not only answer but almost always return the question.

In sum, the tactic is to ask others a question, which, when answered, puts the onus on them to ask a similar question that the initiators of the first question are only too pleased to answer. Thus, the initiators cannot be accused of aggressively bragging about their grade; rather, they are merely modestly complying with a request for information!

Since most students seem to be aware of this tactic, there are also many descriptions of how to cope in the event that they do not wish to respond. This counter-strategy is normally employed when students feel that the grade they received is somehow inadequate and not a good reflection on them. It most frequently takes the form of responding to the first question "How did you do?" in very general terms, such as: "I did O.K."; "not as well as I hoped", "let's just say that I passed", and so compelling the initiators of the sequence to reveal their grades in similarly vague, if less self-gratifying terms. Students who do not abide by these rules of etiquette and persist to pry into the 'information preserves' of others are disliked and often rebuffed:

> Most of my flaunting of marks occurred during my first year at university. After a test was returned the first topic was always "How'd you do?" In mixed company [Aces with Bombers] most people would simply respond 'good' or 'not so good'. I didn't understand that specific replies were not wanted. I would insist on getting an exact mark from them so that they in turn would ask me how I had fared, and I was provided the opportunity to say 90% or 'A'.

This student is now in his senior year and his reputation for flaunting his good grades has resulted in a situation "where it is now difficult for me to do so because few of my classmates are willing to interact with me after we get our test papers back in class." In other words, he has become somewhat of an isolate because of his inappropriate behavior.

A sixth strategy of revelation involves "the foot in the door approach." This more subtle strategy provides a variation on the previous Q-A chain. In this instance actors initiate inquiry, not by asking about another student's total grade but about a specific exam question. They may even use a touch of flattery by suggesting that they flubbed the question and wonder how the other person answered it. This inquiry provides the "foot in the door" for further queries about total grades, and, when the question is returned, they are able to reveal in modest fashion, after an appropriate time of humming and hawing their own good grades.

A seventh strategy of revelation is termed "selective revelation." While some students make it a rule never to reveal their grades to classmates, they are only too happy to share news of their good fortune with other selected audiences, usually friends, parents, or spouses.

> I usually hide my feelings of excitement when I am with classmates and competitors. I remain aloof until I can tell friends who are not in the class and especially my family. After all, they are the only ones who are truly interested in how well I do.

One particularly interesting case is of a student who, in order to ensure maximum revelation (and approbation) of her good grades, involves her mother as a part of her performance team. A "team" refers to "any individuals who cooperate in staging a single routine." An essential moral requirement for teammates is "dramaturgical loyalty," that is, not . . . "betraying the secrets of the team" (Goffman, 1959, p. 212).

In this case considerable dramaturgical circumspection is evident in the student's careful thought that goes into staging the routine as well in her choice of her mother as a team member because, of course, parents have every reason to be dramaturgically loyal, in other words not to reveal to others that they are really cooperating in staging a performance. This is how she describes it:

> I call my mom right away because she tells all of the people she works with. Then when I go home on the weekend and everybody asks 'How are you doing at school?' I respond 'O.K.' In turn, they say 'I heard you were doing really well.' In this way I sound modest and I don't brag because I wouldn't want to say 'Oh, great! I got mostly A's and a couple of B+'s. That sounds conceited. '

Along somewhat similar lines, but a case that defies clear categorization involved a student who retired out of sight of his classmates with his unexpectedly good grade, and then made sure that his "private" revelation—"a big cheer and holler of joy" would be sufficiently loud to reach a considerable audience!

Use of Concealment

Goffman shows that discreditable behavior on the part of actors may not discredit them if it is concealed and unknown. Though discreditable behavior is always potentially discrediting, it is only actually discrediting if it is revealed and the actors stigmatized. Given the normal distribution of grades, then, it is no wonder that some students will seek to conceal their grades and escape stigmatization by their peers. In the words of one student "we become schemers who employ a large repertoire of concealment strategies."

The first technique of concealment involves absenteeism or early departure from class. Students who expect the worst (i.e., a low grade) may not attend class on the day the test papers are to be returned:

> If I know I did poorly on a test and I know on what day it is to be returned I plan to 'accidentally' be away from that class. This way I can prevent others from knowing my mark and so save myself a lot of pain and embarrassment. Later I go to the professor's office and pick up my paper when none of my classmates are around.

Clearly this student is much more concerned with the response of other students than he is with the reaction of the professor. However, there are other students who hate to have the professor identify their face with a low grade. Students who do attend class on the day tests are returned only to find that their assigned grade is one that leaves them shame-faced, usually attempt to avoid communication with their classmates. A tactic widely employed is to leave the classroom at the first available opportunity and assume a manner that conveys that they are not open to conversation:

> I quickly gather up my books and depart in a 'rushed' manner. This allows me to escape from anyone who might attempt to find out how I fared because it appears as if I'm late for something and can't stay around for idle chatter.

The second technique of concealment is "lying about one's grade." Students who are questioned about their grades before they have an opportunity to escape can still conceal their unhappy results by lying about them:

> When I received my grade I felt very ashamed of it because it was the lowest in the class. So, when other students asked me what grade I got, I took it upon myself to lie. I added eleven percentage points to my actual score.

One student, who is also a nun, confesses that she no longer asks others what grade they got because, from her own experience, she knows that she is forcing them to lie.

A third technique of concealment may be described as "emphatic concealment." Students sometimes attempt to convey to others that they are totally "closed" to interaction by assuming a rigid posture, angling their shoulders away from the persons they usually sit beside and interact with in the class, and "rivetting" their eyes to their papers to remove any chance that they will be forced into a position where they have to reveal their grades.

Somewhat less dramatic but nevertheless quite effective strategies students employ to conceal their grades "from the prying eyes of others" include: (1) folding the test paper so that the grade is not visible; (2) keeping the paper literally "close to the chest" and, of course, directly in front of them; and (3) returning to their seats and emphatically putting the paper inside a book or binder, thus implying that the grade received is not a topic open for discussion.

> As soon as I get back to my desk I shove my exam paper into my binder. This action signals to others that I do not want my mark to be public knowledge and that I am not willing to engage in a discussion concerning it. The message is usually received and obeyed.

One student attempts to convey this message more emphatically by placing her book bag on top of the binder into which she has shoved her test paper! Even these seemingly clear ploys, nevertheless sometimes have unplanned outcomes. One student, despite her body work aimed at dissuading others from interacting with her, was approached by a friend who asked how she had scored. This shock led to an uncontrollable bout of coughing on her part, so that the questioner was forced to switch the question from "how did you do?" to "how are you?"

A fourth technique of concealment might be termed "subtle concealment." More subtle students casually veil their mark by strategically placing their elbow over it, or by "accidentally" losing their test paper in the shuffle of other papers. Thus, the grade is effectively hidden from the view of others but the actions are not blatant:

> A too obvious 'cover' fails to serve its purpose because others know you're trying to hide something. So, I discretely cover the grade by draping my arm over it or conceal it by having another sheet of paper over top of the test paper so the grade is just barely (but completely) hidden. In this way it appears as though my arm or the paper just happens to be there by accident.

Students such as these not only conceal, but conceal the fact that they are concealing and thus create the impression that they are behaving "naturally" and that they are open to interaction with others.

A fifth technique of concealment is to "adopt an air of nonchalance." Students who adopt this role-distancing stance do not even bother to look at their grades and attempt to appear as if they couldn't care less about the results: "This tactic is usually successful because if you don't know your mark it's virtually impossible for others to force it out of you."

One exceptional case involved a student who expected to receive a low grade but instead received what in his estimation was an excellent one. At first, his impulse was to advertise his good news. Immediately though the thought struck him that the grade must be a mistake and the professor would certainly notice it if he showed undue excitement. Therefore, his strategy was "to lay low" and "with clenched teeth" and a "disappointed expression" on his face, to read through the test questions and assess the grading. It was only when he found that he had actually done very well and that the grade indeed was correct, that he relaxed and visibly enjoyed his good fortune.

Specific Encounters

Ace-Ace Encounters

These encounters are characterized by an atmosphere of considerable openness because "it's much easier to admit a high mark to someone who has done better than you, or at least as well." A certain amount of bragging is even acceptable because there is no danger of anyone's feelings being hurt. Everyone realizes that everyone else in the group has done well and so the norms of modesty can legitimately be stretched. Bragging often centers on how easy the exam was "so then you can allude to your intelligence without having to appear conceited." In this setting exact grades are likely to be revealed and the "revelation" may be accompanied by a certain staging. One student preceded his announcement of the exact grade to his friends with the following: "I was ripped off on one question where I lost 4 marks, and I lost another 5 (marks) on another question." He paused for a moment and then declared "Still, I pulled off a 90%."

These students almost always critically review each question on the exam. Particularly among students who have been friends for some time, there is an open exchange of the various study tactics they used. And, "whoever gets the highest mark is declared the unofficial winner of the my-way-is-better-than-your-way-of-studying contest." This is an interesting example of a "group culture" (Fine and Kleinman, 1979), which is "anchored in their situationally relevant identity" (Kleinman, 1983, p. 203).

Ace-Bomber Encounters

After a test is returned in class, Aces are almost always willing to interact with Bombers. Most frequently Aces attempt to sense just how poorly the Bombers have performed before the interaction begins. If the Bomber approaches the Ace and appears to be relatively composed, the Ace is likely to respond to the question 'How did you do?' in a very matter of fact fashion. If, on the other hand, the Bomber appears downcast, the most usual response by the Ace will be concealment of the actual grade or revelation "in an apologetic tone and rather quietly so that other students do not hear." Aces are also ready to offer face-saving accounts by immediately commenting on the difficulty and unfairness of the test, denying its significance "its only worth 10% of the total grade" or reminding the Bombers of their disclaimers before they wrote the exam: "As you said, you hardly had any time at all before the test to study." In general, Aces tend to display an attitude of sympathy, commiseration, and support for the dissatisfied Bombers. Aces often go so far as to provide accounts for their own 'lucky' outcomes. Incidentally, such an Ace is the same person who in a group composed of only Aces was heard to remark that the exam was 'a piece of cake.'

Bomber-Ace Encounters

In general, Bombers try to avoid encounters with Aces because the result is usually a feeling of status degradation. "When marks are exchanged you (Bomber) emerge looking like the dumb one" or "you (Bomber) feel like you are lazy and unreliable." Bombers become particularly sensitive to signs of success displayed by Aces, for example, "sitting tall" in their desks, displaying "glittering eyes," "broad grins" or a "jaunty walk," and these signs are often used as cues to identify who to avoid! However, when forced into interaction with Aces, Bombers strive to be gracious and congratulatory. One states that he learned from his parents to "lose graciously and win modestly."

Bombers explain their shortcomings through various accounts and disclaimers, many of which are designed to save face. "I say things like 'I guess it doesn't pay not to study' but my real message is 'I'm not dumb and I could have a mark like yours (Ace) if I did study'." Other Bombers openly admit their guilt: "Given my pathetic effort its just what I deserve." These statements leave the Bombers open to the graciousness and face-saving skills of others.

A dramatic example of the sanctions encountered by an Ace from a Bomber when the Ace breached the norms of modesty, consideration, and courtesy comes from a junior high school setting. This student is now at the university but she will never forget the episode!

> I got 100% on a difficult French test. A not too dedicated student approached me
> and asked me what my grade was. I openly (and naively) revealed it to her. She
> displayed her disgust with me and my performance with a swift kick in my shin.
> I stood there, in front of the class, in disbelief. Then I sat down in my desk and
> felt very guilty!

Bomber-Bomber Encounters

Gatherings of Bombers tend to be closed encounters. Sometimes they even stand circle or cluster together so that their backs are turned towards Aces who may be nearby. Bombers are quite willing to talk about their disappointment with others who are equally wounded by their poor grades. In fact, they often engage in orgies of mutual self pity that they themselves termed "pity parties." In this setting, the discussion takes the form of accounts, most frequently "excuses" (Scott and Lyman, 1968) wherein students attempt to negotiate an identity which does not make them responsible for the final outcome (grade). "I look for someone or something to blame so that guilt can be shared and punishment spared." Many accounts focus on the impossibility of meeting the various obligations that come from having multiple identities. This rather extreme example concerns a husband-father who has a full-time job and who is also taking two university classes: "As soon as class is finished, I have to rush off to catch a bus home or go to work. With all of this going on I can hardly take time off to eat, forget finding enough time to study. " Some of the more typical excuses include: "I had four mid-term exams plus a term paper all due the same week." "I studied the wrong stuff . . . I didn't realize the stories [edited, social science book of readings] would be that important." "I wasn't feeling well for that entire week . . . I had a splitting headache." Many of the excuses given are attempts to elicit sympathy from others and the process is sometimes taken so far that students discredit themselves completely. For example, a student who was just below the passing line was commiserating with two of her friends who had "just made it." In one particular interchange she clearly exaggerated her plight: "I'll probably fail my first year and end up being a bum for the rest of my life." Her friend immediately countered with "Don't feel so badly, you know you can do better. You are actually very intelligent." The second friend present nodded his head in agreement. The student reflected on the conversation for a moment and then stated: "I felt so much better after my friends denied the assertions I inflicted upon myself."

There is a larger proportion of Bombers and correspondingly larger interactional circles of them huddled together seeking mutual support when the grade distribution in a class is very low. The talk often turns from that of a pity-party to scapegoating, which takes the form of a "hate-the-prof-fest." In this instance, professors are portrayed as sadists who enjoy inflicting identity damage on students, slave drivers who demand too much work in a particular course, or just plain incompetents. "I thought the test was totally unfair." "There is no way that test reflects what I know . . . If only she had asked questions on what I know, I could have passed." "The bugger asked all the wrong questions . . He enjoys seeing us suffer." "She has too many tests and assignments, she thinks this is the only class we have to study for." "I sure would like to give the prof a piece of my mind." Each of these proclamations is usually followed by a round of "yeh's" from the other students present.

CONCLUSION

As we implied in the introduction there are two major facets of the universal phenomenon of impression management. The first is to project a favorable image of self, a process that involves identity protection as well as identity enhancement. The second is an expectation that successful people display an appropriate level of modesty when they interact with others and especially that they help those less successful than themselves to save face. These two essential elements of impression management are borne out in our data concerning student behavior when they receive their graded tests. For example, within their own group, Aces did indeed revel in their successes, even to the extent of bragging a little to enhance their egos. However, they also showed remarkable consideration for the Bombers. Clearly, the emphasis is on management, that is, managing the impression to fit the context of the interaction. For example, the Ace who called the test 'unfair' to comfort a Bomber who had scored poorly referred to the same test as a 'piece of cake' when he was with other Aces. We also found that although Bombers certainly do seek solace they also comfort others like themselves during "pity parties."

The converse aspect of the apparently "two faced behavior" of the Ace described above, is that of a student who gave the impression of being disappointed with a grade of 64% but privately hugged herself with delight and relief, since she had not expected even to pass. It was as if she had one role for the public "front stage" and another for the private psychological "back stage." However, she confessed to feeling dishonest, which is perfectly understandable since she had no norm to justify the deception, as did the Ace who was attempting to comfort the Bomber. It is clear from the examples given of the tentative stage by stage feeling out of others before disclosure of their own grades, that most students were not only considerate of others but also manifestly modest-seeming (when circumstances warranted it) in regard to their own grades.

The emphasis of this article has been explicitly on the concealment or disclosure of one's own grade and the management of the impressions given about the relevance of the grade to one's own identity. The counter activity of finding out other people's grades—a kind of "identity search" to locate one's own academic status—is also an important activity, heavily laden with impression management. The kind of impression management involved here would come under the rubric of "espionage" (Wilsnack, 1980) where one seeks "to obtain information from people who do not wish you to have it." To do this one needs a "cover," i.e., a carefully managed set of impressions given that will induce disclosure rather than concealment on the part of others. Our present data do not permit a comprehensive or systematic discussion of "espionage" but they will serve as a basis for further investigation of this topic.

The dramaturgy described in the return to students of their graded examination papers has implications for a much wider universe of situations, some of which we have already tentatively explored. For example, we have noticed that faculty members, who receive replies from journal editors concerning acceptance or rejection of submitted papers tend first to hasten to their offices to open the letter. Rejections are rarely revealed, but in the event that they are, professors tend to evaluate them with the same kind of nonchalant "couldn't care less" attitude of some of the students described earlier. Acceptances are usually advertised in ways also reminiscent of student strategies, for example, covering the general departmental office mail counter with galley proofs.

We also noted that waiters and waitresses manage the impressions they give to their colleagues concerning the "tips" they receive by allowing particularly large ones to lie on the table for a longer than usual time before they are collected, arranging bills in "tip jars" so that the largest ones are on the outside of the roll and so clearly visible, and conspiring with bus boys to exclaim with enthusiastic whoops over large tips so as to ensure the widest possible advertisement of them.

Another situation in which impression management occurs is in those industries where salary raises are not subject to union specifications so workers at the same level may receive unequal increments. Interestingly enough, and contrary to the student mentioned earlier who flaunted his good grades, workers who receive large raises seldom state the exact amount they receive but are more likely to complain (bitterly) about now being in a higher income tax bracket. In effect they reveal their good fortune by implication only.

In sum, all of the situations just noted as well as the student behavior described earlier involve people competing with each other in a more or less closed awareness context where the outcome greatly affects their identity. Perhaps the most important aspect of identity is social status. However, whereas in an open awareness context there tend to be reasonably clear indices of status such as wealth, lineage, knowledge, etc., in closed awareness contexts where status is dependent on grades, salary, or success at publishing individuals will manage impressions to achieve the optimal level of status.

On the basis of the findings in this work we formulated the following proposition. Wherever there exists an ongoing tension between competition and ascendancy on one hand, and approbation and rapport with others on the other hand then individuals will be led almost inevitably to practice various forms of impression management. In the case of students, Ace-Ace and Bomber-Bomber encounters involve minimal status differences so there is little tension between competition for status and the pressure for rapport. Consequently, there is little need for and practice of techniques of impression management. Conversely, Ace-Bomber encounters involve considerable status differences between the interactants that must be balanced against the strong pressures from the student culture for mutual congeniality. As predicted, this opposition produces a considerable amount of impression management.

ACKNOWLEDGMENTS

This article is a revised version of a paper presented at the 1987 Qualitative Research Conference, McMaster University. We thank D. Rennie, R. Clifton, Gary Alan Fine, and the anonymous reviewers for *Symbolic Interaction* for their insightful comments and suggestions.

NOTES

1. Wilsnack (1980) identifies four cardinal strategies of information control. They are espionage, secrecy, persuasion, and evaluation. Of these four strategies, the two most germane to the present study are secrecy, i.e., "keeping other people from obtaining information you do not want them to have"; and persuasion, i.e., "making sure that other people obtain and believe information you want them to have." In this article we will refer to secrecy as "concealment"

and persuasion as "revelation." These changes in terminology seem appropriate because secrecy is really more of a state than it is behavior, and what is being described is behavior. Revelation is the opposite of concealment and though it is achieved through persuasion, revelation is the actual process described.

2. These are terms used by students themselves. The terms "Aces," "Middle of the Roaders," and "Bombers" refer, respectively, to top performers, average performers, and low scorers on any particular examination. Accordingly, an "Ace" in one exam may be a "Bomber" in another. However, high scorers tend to be habitually high scorers, and the same goes for the other two categories. The focus of this article is on the clear differences in patterns of revelation or concealment displayed by Aces and Bombers. The category of students referred to as "Middle of the Roaders," though constituting a numerical majority, are not a focus of this particular article because they do not show consistent differences in patterns of behavior; that is, some of them act like Aces while others act more like Bombers.

REFERENCES

Albas, D. and C. Albas. 1984. *Student Life and Exams: Stresses and Coping Strategies.* Dubuque, IA: Kendall/Hunt.

Fine, G.A. and S. Kleinman. 1979. "Rethinking Subculture: An Interactionist Analysis." *American Journal of Sociology* 85: 1–21.

Glaser, B. and A. Strauss. 1981. "Awareness Contexts and Social Interaction." Pp. 53–63 in G. Stone and H. Farberman (eds.) *Social Psychology Through Symbolic Interaction,* 2nd ed. New York: Wiley.

Goffman, E. 1959. *The Presentation of Self in Everyday Life.* Garden City, NY: Doubleday.

Gross, E. and G. Stone. 1981. "Embarrassment and the Analysis of Role Requirements." Pp. 115–129 in G. Stone and H. Farberman (eds.) *Social Psychology Through Symbolic Interaction,* 2nd ed. New York: Wiley.

Kleinman, S. 1983. "Collective Matters as Individual Concerns: Peer Culture Among Graduate Students." *Urban Life* 12: 203–225.

Miall, C. and N. Herman. 1986. "Fostering Identities: The Management of Information in 'Normal' and 'Deviant' Worlds." Paper Presented at the Qualitative Research Conference: Ethnographic Research, Waterloo.

Scott, M. and S. Lyman. 1968. "Accounts." *American Sociological Review* 33: 46–62.

Speier, M. 1973. *How to Observe Face-to-Face Communication: A Sociological Introduction.* Palisades, CA: Goodyear.

Stebbins, R. 1972. "Modesty, Pride, and Conceit: Variations in the Expression of Self-Esteem." *Pacific Sociological Review.* 15(October): 461–481.

Strauss, A. 1970. "Discovering New Theory from Previous Theory." Pg. 46–53 in T. Shibutani (ed.) *Human Nature and Collective Behavior: Papers in Honor of Herbert Blumer.* Englewood Cliffs, NJ: Prentice-Hall.

Wilsnack, R. 1980. "Information Control: A Conceptual Framework for Sociological Analysis." *Urban Life* 8(4): 467–499.

Self-Mockery:
An Alternative Form of Self-Presentation

Sheldon Ungar
Scarborough College, University of Toronto

The first part of the paper delineates grounds for doubting that enhancing performances are as pervasive as the self-presentational literature suggests. Then, the
notion of structural ambivalence is used to demonstrate that there is considerable
"leeway" in role taking, especially in the case of humorous or playful behavior.
Extending this analysis, it is argued that self-mockery constitutes an important
aspect of the presentation of self. The remaining sections of the paper seek to
define, illustrate and explore the functions of various types of self-mockery. Above
all, it is suggested that self-mockery serves to increase the positive emotional
sentiments among participants.

A central concern of Goffman's (e.g., 1959, 1967) dramaturgical approach to social
interaction is the way in which individuals manage their performances to obtain
favorable reactions from others. According to Goffman, a virtual or ready-make self
ordinarily awaits the individual entering a situation. It is incumbent on the individual
to assess correctly the person that the situation allows and obliges him/her to be and
then act accordingly. To act "accordingly," the individual must effectively establish
and sustain impressions that are consistent with a multitude of rules, obligations,
personal qualities and so on, which arise from both the self imputed to him/her and
the "expressive order" associated with the situation. In short, Goffman (1959, 1967)
contends that individuals seek to convey idealized and, in most instances, self-
enhancing impressions to others.

Following Gottman, a number of experimental studies have investigated the
degree to which individuals present themselves to others in a self-enhancing manner.

Reprinted from Symbolic Interaction, 7(1):121–133.

The results of that research indicate that individuals prefer to present themselves in ways which impress others (e.g., Frey, 1978; Schlenker, 1975; Schneider, 1969). Indeed, that research has revealed that self-enhancement motives are sufficiently strong to occasion self-enhancing presentations even when there is some risk that these presentations could be publicly refuted (Ungar, 1980, 1981).

As might be gleaned from the above, self-presentational theorists and researchers have generally equated self-enhancement with self-presentation (cf. Schlenker, 1980). Yet there are good reasons for doubting that enhancing performances are so pervasive. When actors claim a too positive self image, they are likely to perceive the ensuing interaction as problematic and to become self-conscious or "on" (Messinger et al., 1962). If actors routinely claimed images close to the boundaries of their capacities to carry them off successfully, they would tend to create perpetually problematic environments for themselves. To avoid this hazard and the attendant need to be excessively concerned with defensive maneuvers, it follows that actors are more likely to establish socially adequate, rather than impressive selves. Moreover, and consistent with the social adequacy hypothesis, there is a growing body of evidence suggesting that much of ordinary interaction is constituted by mindless behavior (e.g., Langer and Imber, 1980) or taken-for-granted routines (Collins, 1981).

In addition, the existent evidence on self-presentations may be limited in generality since the research is confined to conveying information about the self to strangers. Ongoing, long-term relationships may dictate different self-presentational strategies. Blau, for example, suggests that "whereas an individual usually conceals his shortcomings and less desirable traits on first acquaintance, he often readily admits them soon afterwards in sociable intercourse, long before the association becomes intimate" (1964: 48). By revealing undesirable qualities, one can attenuate the feelings of envy and resentment that often accompany impressive images; such revelations can also decrease social distance among interactants. And while no studies have specifically examined self-presentations in ongoing relationships, Baumesiter and Jones (1978) did find that actors presented themselves modestly when others already possessed positive information about them.

In the first section of the paper, the notion of structural ambivalence is used to show that there is considerable leeway in role-taking, especially in the case of humorous behaviors. This discussion seeks to provide a view of self-presentational practices that more fully articulates and exploits the "dramaturgical metaphor." As opposed to the constricting focus on self-enhancement, it is suggested that there is an array of self-presentational tactics available to actors. Moreover, an attempt is made to show why self-mockery is an important tactic in the self-presentational arsenal of actors.[1] The second section of the paper seeks to define, illustrate and explore the functions of various types of self-mockery.

Self-mockery is offered as an expansion of the dominant view of self-presentation. As in the case of real (i.e., enhancing) impression management, actors may gain something from mocking themselves. But only in the latter case must they also relinquish something, especially of the "sacredness" of their selves. Self-mocking presentations, like self-enhancing ones, have limitations, and some of these will be discussed in the final section of the paper.

STRUCTURAL AMBIVALENCE AND THE PRESENCE OF LEEWAY

An additional problem confronts the self-enhancement hypothesis. Current formulations of structural role theory (see Handel, 1979) have come to regard inter and intra-role conflict as natural and inevitable. Conflicting or ambivalently structured normative expectations mean that contrary courses of action are simultaneously valued; the actor, faced with opposing norms, cannot anticipate precisely which course of action will be more favorably evaluated by others. In other words when the applicable norms in a situation are inconsistently patterned, actors cannot be assured of gaining favorable reactions by performing in accordance with the "normative order."

But for present purposes at least, the problem that structural ambivalence poses for conducting an impressive performance is less important than the "leeway" it affords in role taking. As several writers have observed, ambivalence serves to attenuate commitment and can give rise to role distancing behaviours (Coser, 1966; Handel, 1979; Stebbins, 1969). According to Handel, the conflicts arising from contrary normative expectations are usually resolved through the negotiation of a working consensus. However—and this is critical—actors only adhere to the working consensus with limited commitment. Indeed, because the consensus that is negotiated to resolve the chronic problem of ambivalence is, in most instances, provisional and not fully binding, leeway or elbow room in which to maneuver can be found (or created) in role relationships.[2]

The prevalence of leeway is also suggested by the social adequacy hypothesis. If people often conduct their performances by mindlessly enacting (appropriate) routines with little regard for new, incoming information, it follows that they will be relatively inattentive to many discrepancies between role "obligations" and role performances. Between the confluence of contrary normative prescriptions, the tentative authority of the working consensus, and the limited role of meaningful congnitions in guiding interaction, problematic events which either necessitate remedial accounts or result in negative identity attributions or other sanctions are likely to be exceptional rather than commonplace.[3]

The presence of leeway is probably best exemplified by role distancing behaviours. Such behaviour is likely to occur when aspects of the identity conferred by the working consensus are either incompatible with the actor's preferred self-conception or likely to be viewed disdainfully by relevant others (Goffman, 1961; Stebbins, 1969). The actor, rather than conforming to the identity-threatening role expectations, expressively conveys his or her "disdainful detachment" from those expectations. Through the use of such tactics as humor or the projection of an unserious self, the actor both withdraws somewhat from the expectation and creates "leeway" to introduce role-irrelevant identities during his or her performance .

Since role distance is frequently constituted by humor (Coser, 1966), it is likely to be accorded an even greater margin of freedom than more serious acts which depart from role expectations (see Emerson, 1969). According to Coser, humor is effective because it "at once highlights and denies the existing ambivalence" (1966: 179). But at the same time that humor expresses the perplexing aspect of the (serious) situation, it creates its own paradox. Humor or playfulness are typically introduced as asides from the official flow of activity, and can be understood as transposing or "keying" the activity from a serious to an unserious framework (Bateson, 1955; Goffman, 1974). This transposition signals that the ensuing activity should not officially "count." The actor is, in effect, asking others to suspend judgment: they should neither take the activity as a direct reflection of him or her nor hold him or her fully responsible for it.

Herein lies the paradox. Humorous or playful behaviour can be construed as either real or unreal. As Fry (1968) observes, the audience is likely to view the activity as either real and unreal at the same time, or to oscillate between these alternative interpretations of the activity.

It is precisely this ambiguity in humor that makes it a potent vehicle in self-presentational practices. By switching to a humorous realm, actors can convey risky or invidious information (about the self or others) without incurring as great a threat to their identities as would occur if the communication was made in a serious realm. In fact, switching to the playful realm can be likened to adopting— however briefly— the role of the fool or court jester. The fool is granted license to stand outside ordinary routines and reveal uncomfortable realities because he or she is never taken quite seriously (Welsford, 1961).

While the role of the fool was institutionalized in Medieval society, the right to engage in foolish behaviour was not reserved for the "fool" or "jester." According to Welsford,

> The greatest seasonal festivals in Christian Europe have a twofold aspect: on the one hand they are occasions for solemn worship, on the other hand they are times of wild feasting, lawlessness and buffoonery. Shrovetide is a season when a good Christian confesses his sins, but it is also the Carnival, when sober citizens will put on a mask and adopt the behaviour of the fool; the Christmas season was once an equally wild time (1961: 70).

Institutionalized occasions for buffoonery seem to have declined significantly in modern societies (Cf. Klapp, 1962). But as Goffman suggests, ". . . brief switchings into playfulness are everywhere found in society, so much so that it is hard to become conscious of their widespread occurrence" (1974: 49). In this regard, the preceding discussion has sought to underscore the extent to which leeway can be found or created in role relationships, especially in the case of unserious or playful behaviour. If the widespread occurrence of playful episodes often goes unnoticed, I would contend that this inattentiveness is not so much due to the frequency of such switchings as to the license accorded them and the significant part they play in "lubricating" social relationships.

In the analysis that follows, I will seek to define, illustrate, and explore the functions of various types of self-mockery. Self-mockery refers to actions—including speech, gestures, contortions, antics and expressive overtones—which treat the self with ridicule or derision. This concept can be clarified by contrasting it with "self-derogation." As opposed to self-derogation, which is usually done in a most serious fashion, to engage in self-mockery is to intend that one's actions be viewed within an unserious framework. The greater seriousness of self-derogation implies that, in comparison with self-mockery, it is more likely to focus on the core aspects of the self, to be done consistently and with greater persistence and detail, and to hold greater potential for creating distress in the actor and/or observers. Self-mockery, then, is more likely to be directed at particular situated identities rather than at stable aspects of the self; it also tends to be episodic or fleeting in nature, and have only immediate or short-term consequences.

TYPES OF SELF-MOCKERY

Two general classes of self-mockery can be identified: status altering actions and aligning actions. In the case of status altering actions, performers mock or caricature their selves so that they can claim something else as a performer and/or re-negotiate the statuses of the participants. For example, performers who are expected to conduct themselves in a too formal or too dignified fashion may briefly project an unserious version of the same activity in order to convey a distinction between their "selves" and the role they happen to be playing. This can serve to debunk role-related pretensions and/or reduce social distance among participants.

By aligning actions, I am referring to the same class of behaviours as are discussed by Stokes and Hewitt (1976). They define aligning actions as forms of conduct which, in the face of potentially disruptive events, simultaneously sustain the flow of actions between individuals and sustain a link between conduct and culture. Aligning actions include motive talk, accounts, disclaimers and remedial interchanges. In appropriating this concept, I am only claiming that the various types of aligning actions are frequently accomplished by engaging in self-mockery. While performers may "appeal to accidents" to avoid being labeled "clumsy" (Scott and Lyman, 1968), I am suggesting that they may be as likely, as one student observer noted, to proclaim, "I'm such a clumsy ox; I'm always doing things like this."[4] By calling attention to their own foibles, performers not only disarm others but also affirm standards or rules in a fashion that is likely to augment positive sentiments among the participants. (Admissions of one's inadequacies can be infectious: other participants may be then likely to recount their own related foibles.)

The last point is critical. In a recent paper, Collins (1981) has convincingly argued that emotional dynamics may be the most crucial mechanism in explaining adherence to social routines and the maintenance of ongoing social relationships. Encounters with others produce varying amounts of emotional solidarity. Individuals will continue or reject further encounters with particular others to the extent that these encounters increase or decrease their positive emotional energies. In other words, individuals are motivated to move towards those encounters which optimize their emotional returns.

Here we arrive at the key function of self-mockery. Specifically, in the ensuing discussion I will attempt to show that self-mockery, if conducted appropriately, serves to increase positive sentiments among individuals and to augment emotional solidarity and personal identification with others.

Status Altering Actions

Performers are likely to mock themselves when they are expected to conduct themselves in a too dignified or a too demeaning fashion or when required performances are either well-above or well-below their capabilities. Status alterations can occur in advance of, during or following the problematic actions.

According to Klapp (1962: 165), "many esteemed statuses in America have a sort of clownish underside. " The professor who feigns forgetfulness or the surgeon who cannot carve a roast or tie a knot are cases in point. Additional examples include rock stars who burlesque their own performances and speakers or celebrities who amuse others with anecdotes about gaffes they have made in the past. A good example is provided by B. F. Skinner:

> I once enjoyed a buffet supper with a group of students. I was sitting in a dark corner, when the hostess, who was Chinese, brought me a plate. She pointed to a dark brown paté of some sort and made a comment that I did not understand. I attacked it with a knife and fork. It had a wonderful crispy crust, and I wondered how the Chinese were able to get that effect so beautifully. I cut into it and put some in my mouth, again admiring the culinary skill of my hostess as I chewed. Then I noticed that the young woman sitting beside me was peeling the same object on her plate. This Chinese delicacy was a hard-boiled egg (Cosmopolitan, March 1983).

Even Presidents of the United States have, in autobiographies (e.g. Johnson and Carter) and interviews, mocked themselves. When anti-American hecklers interrupted a Reagan speech in Canada, the American President eased Prime Minister Trudeau's embarrassment by remarking, "They must have been imported to make me feel at home" (U.S. News and World Report, 1981). In addition, to avoid "taking themselves too seriously," even the esteemed can defile themselves sufficiently to partake in childish antics or ordinary horseplay. The successful executive who meets his or her yacht guests decked out in a sailor's cap and outfit essentially styled for children is a case in point. Artists of all kinds are notorious for their buffoonery while being interviewed or photographed.

The existence of a "clownish underside" can be partly attributed to the ambivalence associated with high status. On the one hand, high status accords the right to expect deference from others. On the other hand, however, there are opposing expectations enjoining persons to treat others as equals. Given this ambivalence and the difficulty sustaining the exemplary role performances often expected from the esteemed, it is not surprising that brief ventures in self-mockery are prevalent. In fact, descriptions of the characteristics of the esteemed seem to routinely contain assertions about their "wry, self-depreciating humor." The following description of Liza Minnelli is probably typical:

> Touching base with New York chic has made Liza aware of just how naive she is, but this very ingenuousness is one of her most charming qualities. She loves to tell of playing among the fabled rich and being invited to dine with Baron Guy de

> Rothschild and his wife. The Baron asked Liza what she would like lo drink before dinner? "I'll have some of your home brew," she said, referring to the Rothschild vineyards. Baron Rothschild didn't laugh, but Baron Alexis de Rede, who was also present, thought the remark wonderfully witty and subsequently staged another party in Liza's honor (Cosmopolitan, December 1981).

In contrast, President Nixon's inability to poke fun at himself was probably one of the factors contributing to his downfall.

Several implications can be drawn from these examples. First, brief ventures into the unserious realm allow the performer to reveal aspects of the self that would otherwise be out-of-place. Furthermore, one can reveal weaknesses or faults and, by viewing them in a humorous vein, still retain one's dignity and status. Such self-disclosure can, like gossip, serve to increase the audience's identification with the performer (cf. Rosnow and Fine, 1976).

Second, status altering actions can reduce social distance or promote status equality—if only temporarily—among participants. It is a sociological truism that deference hinders relaxed sociability. By temporarily relinquishing some prerogative, the esteemed can attenuate the typical effects of status inequalities. In this regard, a study conducted by Aronson, Willerman and Floyd (1966) revealed that a superior person who commits a minor blunder is liked more by others than a superior person who did not blunder. However, they also found that an average person who errs is liked less than an average person who does not.

More generally, I am suggesting that self-mockery can function as an "icebreaker" in interaction among strangers or among status equals. Several examples submitted by students concerned incidents where affected or stilted conversation designed to show one's insight or knowledge were rendered affable by someone admitting that he or she was, for example, a TV addict hooked on soap operas or "Laverne and Shirley."

Persons who do not ordinarily occupy an esteemed status will often mock themselves if they find their social standing temporarily elevated. Thus, when persons perform well-beyond their usual capacities, they may not only disavow any credit for the performance but also recount past ineptitudes. For example, amateur athletes who make surprisingly good shots typically engage in such antics as fondling their racquets or asserting that, "I could not do it again in a thousand years. "

Self-mockery in the face of a momentary enhancement of one's standing is probably best exemplified in the reception of compliments. Generally, compliments produce uneasiness. Moreover, they are often used as an occasion to ridicule oneself. For example,

> Tell one of these ladies she has beautiful skin, and she'll say, "You should see it when I eat chocolate. It breaks out in big, ugly pimples!" Say that she has great legs and you'll hear, "You've got to be kidding! In high school they called me thunder thighs. Whenever I fall off my diet they turn into hams" (Cosmopolitan, July 1981).

Self-mockery is commonplace when individuals' performances are open to the scrutiny of others. Before being taken for a ride, a student observer was told, "I am a terrible driver who should not be allowed on the road." The following type of admission is also commonplace: "It is true that I have no ability to deal with mechanical appliances. New cars break down within hours when I drive them; machines that have never given the slightest trouble blow a fuse as soon as I approach them." Inexperienced speakers commonly call attention to their own anxieties and shortcomings (I'm not used to giving speeches, . . .). Prior to formal ceremonies requiring a show of dignity, individuals often clown and jest (or strike a false note by overconforming or exaggerating their performance to an absurd extreme). Ask individuals to pose for a photograph or a "home movie," and they will inevitably parody themselves or engage in other childish antics.

Jesting can also accompany or follow performances that are well below expectations. Persons who fumble performances may utter, for example, "I must be getting senile" or "I'm too old for this sort of thing." The amateur athlete who bungles a simple shot puts on a ludicrous display: checking the racquet for a "hole" or reenacting a caricature of the original shot are cases in point. Similarly, actions that demean one's identity often elicit self-depreciation. For example, I have observed that people attending programs to stop smoking depreciate their former habit: "I'd want one so bad that I'd go through the garbage bag looking for a decent butt that was dry. Once, when I could not find one, I went out to the car in 20 below weather and found one in the ashtray."

A person cast into a demeaning role, whether intentionally or inadvertently, may take refuge in self-mockery. The following example, which is lengthy but informative, is an attempt to deal with the question, "Why wasn't I asked to subscribe?"

> This has happened to me before. A few years ago, a friend of mine phoned and asked, "What are you doing about Robert L. Schwartz's letter on subscribing to the Newsletter of the Tarrytown Group?"
>
> "What letter?" I said.
>
> "You know," he said. "The one that says 'You are cordially invited to join a special, special group of people—the creative Minority . . .'"
>
> "Well," I said. "Of course the way the mails are these days, you can't"
>
> "Oh," he said. "Oh sorry. . . ."
>
> I also don't want to leave the impression that I have never been selected myself. Just two or three years ago, I got a friendly letter from a Nancy L. Halbert informing me that the "family name Trillin has an exclusive and particularly beautiful Coat of Arms." That was a nice surprise. I don't mean that I've been under the impression that our family lacks distinction. For years, I have seized every opportunity to inform the public that my cousin Keith from Salina once reached the finals of the Kansas state spelling bee and my cousin Neil was the drum major of the University of Nebraska marching band (Vanity Fair, March 1983).

Interestingly, the writer shifts from (seriously) depreciating himself to a false or sham mocking of his family. Through this subtle development the target changes; at the end the author is deflating pretensions rather than seeking absolution for his lack of recognition.

Presumably, individuals call attention to their own faults or failings in order to enlist sympathy, seek reassurance or engender forebearance. But self-mockery creates an ironic distance from their admissions. By viewing their shortcomings in a nonserious fashion, they are inviting others to take less account of their deficiencies. In effect, they are simultaneously providing others with privileged Insights and disarming them by requiring them to discount the import of what they have learned.

As noted previously, self-revelations may induce others to reveal their own shortcomings. Indeed, through a process of contagion, admissions of faults and failings can kindle "rounds" of confessions. In such ritualistic banter, individuals are most likely to reveal past faults or errors (e.g., fizzled dates, bungled interviews) that have little relevance for their present situations. People will also recount past episodes that poke fun at themselves in order to assuage the fears or anxieties of others. Thus, individuals conversing with someone about to get married will relate stories about their initial inadequacies as a cook ("We ate either raw or burned chicken everyday for a year—it was all I knew how to cook"), a housekeeper or a lover, and of course, note that they overcame these problems. Following a botched lecture, novice teachers may take solace in their more experienced colleagues' accounts of even more inept performance.

Aligning Actions

I have suggested that the various kinds of aligning actions can be accomplished by self-mockery. A person questioned about a dubious decision (e.g., paying too much for or poorly selecting an item), may vindicate him- or herself by maintaining that he or she is ignorant, gullible or incompetent ("My mother never let me shop as a child; I always brought home soured milk"). Jesting can be employed to effectuate sin licenses or to suspend judgment: at the start of a party, I overheard a person say, "Ignore everything I say—and I'm only drinking coke!"

Self-depreciating banter can also diffuse anticipated responses to stigmatized identities. Short or overweight persons commonly make themselves the butt of their own jokes to preempt others' comments. In the same vein, at a party to raise funds for probationers, I observed that practically every ex-convict made comments about his trustworthiness (e.g., "Where's the bread"; "This place should be easy to knock off"). Members of stigmatized groups, including many ethnic groups (especially when close to the immigrant experience) often tell ritualized jokes or stories that depreciate their own group. Self-depreciating Jewish humor and books like Portnoy's Complaint are obvious examples; but this phenomenon is hardly limited to Jewish people.

Academics provide a rich source of examples. Since they are stereotypically perceived as living in an ivory tower, engaging in enterprises of little relevance and glossing their inadequacies with jargon, they have developed self-depreciating jokes that can, when aspects of the stereotype are or may be made salient, be employed as disclaimers or accounts. One student noted that a professor who admitted not having read a particular book, immediately recounted the following: "A professor is asked by a colleague whether he has read a book by a certain author. 'Read it? Why I haven't even taught it yet!'" A second example deals with the tendency of mathematicians to make unwarranted assumptions:

> A mathematics professor is busy demonstrating a very complex proof to his students, furiously chalking the blackboard with equations.
>
> "As you can see, step G follows from step F."
>
> "But professor," calls out a student, "is it obvious?"
>
> The professor looks over his work for a moment, and suddenly moves over to another blackboard and starts writing new equations with equal vigor. Half an hour later he turns to the class and says, "Yes, it is obvious" (The Globe and Mail, February 1981).

The role of self-mockery in accomplishing aligning actions can be further specified. A person who fails to adequately greet or pay heed to what is said by another, may first offer a serious excuse and then draw on a ritualized form of self-mockery to redeem the oversight: "I've been in a tizzy recently; like yesterday, I was so embarrassed when I tried to buy a shirt and discovered that I had no money because I had forgot to go to the bank. That wasn't the worst of it. . . ." As this hypothetical example suggests, self-mockery does not necessarily replace more serious aligning actions but certainly can be used in conjunction with them. In effect, ridiculing the self can not only help save face for the offended and indeed the offender, but can effectively display the more painful or serious aspects of untoward actions and yet minimize feelings of indignation or irritation.

Aligning actions are similar in form and content to the status altering actions used for failed performances. The essential difference is that aligning actions pertain to "failings" that are sufficiently offensive to warrant questions or challenges by others. In both cases, however, self-mockery serves to acknowledge the incongruous behaviour and to neutralize or correct the situation. In aligning actions, social control is exercised and standards of propriety are affirmed by humbling and/or ridiculing the self. By switching to a humorous realm, individuals are seeking to effect a split between their true selves (the real) and their debased selves (the unreal) and gain absolution for the latter through laughter or ridicule.

A good illustration of these points comes from a personal accident. At a movie theatre, with an audience of no more than 15 people, I happened to spill my coke on the way to my seat. My natural embarrassment was exacerbated by the applause I received from most of the audience. When I took my seat and started to mumble an excuse, my friend (whom I did not see frequently) proceeded to tell me of a similar incident that happened to him. Apparently, while trying to squeeze by several people to get to his seat, he once spilled his drink and popcorn over the head and fur coat of a lady in the row in front of him. After the film, I, my friend, and several other companions, continued telling tales of prior misadventures.

Several things can be noted about this example. First, the account is provided by an observer rather than by the protagonist, a phenomenon which is made possible by self-depreciation. Second, it illustrates the use of humorous episodes from the past in aligning actions. The recounting of prior episodes that poke fun at oneself may very well be the most common form of self-mockery. Such recountings, by focusing on the past, minimize the cost of what the actor must relinquish. Yet at the same time, they function in a variety of ways to augment positive emotional sentiments. Finally, they can readily give rise to "story chaining" and, like ritualized insults, provide a context in which actors can compete to tell the most clever or accomplished stories.

THE LIMITATIONS OF SELF-MOCKERY

Self-mocking presentations can also be inappropriate or ineffective. In the case of aligning actions, self-mockery is clearly inappropriate for serious offenses (e.g., an accident that causes injuries). More generally, ritualized forms of self-depreciation do not, on their own, remedy incidents that require restitution or have caused sufficient harm to require more weighty remediation. Under such circumstances, episodes of self-mockery subsequent to other aligning actions can be effective in restoring positive sentiments among participants.

Self-mocking presentations can be ineffectual if they are employed too frequently or are not limited to brief interludes. If esteemed individuals incessantly mock themselves, their actions are likely to be perceived by others as spurious or affected. Indeed, such actions are likely to have consequences opposite those intended: they can totally impede relaxed sociability. On the other hand, constant self-mockery by ordinary individuals will probably only serve to create the impression that they are fools or clowns. The "class clown" is typically perceived as an unfortunate or worthless person who is merely seeking attention.

This brings us to a critical point. Self-depreciating presentations are likely to be most effective when the audience already possesses positive information about the performer. Indeed, if an audience is only aware of an individual's shortcomings, self-mockery is likely to be wholly ineffective as a status altering tactic. These hypotheses give rise to several other predictions. Extrapolating from the Baumeister and Jones (1978) study which revealed that individuals were modest only when others already knew about their positive attributes, it can be hypothesized that esteemed individuals or those who have displayed positive attributes are more likely than individuals who do not meet these criteria to engage in self-mockery. It also follows that self-mockery is more likely to occur in long-term than in incipient relationships.

CONCLUSION

The preceding discussion has been rather abstract. Clearly, further research on different self-presentational tactics—utilizing both experimental methods and samples of natural interaction among strangers and persons who do know one another—is required.

The concept of self-mockery is intended to provide a counterpoint to the dominant view of the self and of self-presentational practices (e.g., Schlenker, 1980). In contrast with the view which holds that the self is a sacred object that needs to be handled with care, it suggests that the self can be profaned—and that this can occur without creating problematic incidents. To the view that the self is presented in an idealized or impressive fashion, it juxtaposes the presentation of the self as a ridiculous character. Finally, instead of holding with the gravity of self-presentation and the related notion that interaction is sustained by either conformity to role expectations or by the requesting and giving of different kinds of accounts when "nonconformity" creates problematic situations, it suggests that ambivalence, paradox and leeway are constitutive features of most situations. In the effort to locate the boundary conditions of each of these viewpoints, we can learn a great deal about the presentation of the self.

NOTES

1.   To be fair, it should be pointed out that Goffman is not insensitive to the issue of self-mockery. In fact, his concept of role distance was central to the development of this paper. At the same time, however, it should be recognized that the thrust of Goffman's thought stresses self-enhancement and the importance—even sacredness—of one's face.

2.   Thus Goffman (1957) observes that beneath the working consensus there are often currents of covert communication which are discrepant from the official definitions being expressed. "This unofficial communication may be carried on by innuendo, mimicked accents, well-placed jokes, significant pauses, veiled hints, purposeful kidding, expressive overtones, and many other sign practices" (p. 190).

3.   Employing a line of reasoning that is different from but not inconsistent with the one developed here, Collins (1981) suggests that while calls for retrospective accounts and/or sanctioning occur, "they do not occur very often in relation to the sheer number of micro events that actually take place" (p. 997).

4.   Data used to illustrate self-mockery are drawn from three sources. First, there are quotations cited from magazines. Second, there are personal observations which are noted as such. Finally, all unattributed examples and quotations are based on written observations submitted to the author by 70 students in an interpersonal relations course. Following a brief lecture outlining only the notion of self-mockery, students were asked to submit a written description of the first case of self-mockery that they subsequently came across, no matter the source. Participation was voluntary, and 70 of 120 students made submissions when observations were collected three weeks after the lecture. Unattributed quotations are taken directly from these submissions; examples without quotations summarize one or more submissions. The discussion of the characteristics and functions of self-mockery attempts to capture both the totality of and the variation in the examples. However, it should be clear that the data presented here is intended to do little more than illustrate ideas.

REFERENCES

Aronson, E., B. Willerman, and J. Floyd. 1966. "The Effects of a Pratfall on Increasing Interpersonal Attractiveness." *Psychonomic Science* 4: 227–228.

Bateson, G. 1955. "A Theory of Play and Fantasy." *Psychiatric Research Reports* 3: 39–51.

Baumeister, R. and E. E. Jones. 1978. "When Self-Presentations is Constrained by the Target's Knowledge: Consistency and Compensation." *Journal of Personality and Social Psychology* 36: 608–618.

Blau, P. 1964. *Exchange and Power in Social Life*. New York: Wiley.

Collins, R. 1981. "On the Microfoundations of Macrosociology." *American Journal of Sociology* 86: 984–1014.

Coser, R. 1966. "Role Distance, Sociological Ambivalence, and Traditional Status Systems." *American Journal of Sociology* 72: 173–187.

Frey, D. 1978. "Reactions to Success and Failure in Public and Private Conditions." *Journal of Experimental Social Psychology* 14: 172–179.

Frey, W. 1968. *Sweet Madness: A Study of Humor.* Palo Alto, Cal.: Pacific Books.

Goffman, E. 1959. *The Presentation of Self in Everyday Life*. New York: Anchor.

———. 1961. *Encounters: Two Studies in the Sociology of Interaction.* Indianapolis: Bobbs-Merrill.

———. 1967. *Interaction Ritual: Essays on Face-to-Face Behavior.* New York: Anchor.

———. 1974. *Frame Analysis*. New York: Harper.

Handel, W. 1979. "Normative Expectations and the Emergence of Meanings as Solutions to Problems: A Convergence of Structural and Interactional Views." *American Journal of Sociology* 84: 858–881.

Klapp, O. 1962. *Heroes, Villains and Fools: The Changing American Character*. Englewood Cliffs, N.J.: Prentice-Hall.

Langer, E. and L. Imber. 1980. "Role of Mindlessness in the Perception of Deviance." *Journal of Personality and Social Psychology* 39: 360–367.

Lyman, S. and M. Scott. 1970. *A Sociology of the Absurd*. New York: Appleton-Century-Crofts.

Messinger, S., H. Sampson, and R. Towne. 1962. "Life as Theater: Some Notes on the Dramaturgical Approach to Interaction." *Sociometry* 25: 98–110.

Rosnow, R. and G. Fine. 1976. *Rumor and Gossip: The Sociology of Hearsay*. New York: Elsevier.

Schlenker, B. 1975. "Self-Presentation: Managing the Impression of Consistency When Reality Interferes with Self-Enhancement." *Journal of Personality and Social Psychology* 32: 46–62.

———. 1980. *Impression Management: The Self Concept, Social Identity, and Interpersonal Relations*. Belmont, Cal.: Wadsworth.

Schneider, D. 1969. "Tactical Self-Presentation After Success and Failure." *Journal of Personality and Social Psychology* 13: 262–268.

Scott, M. and S. Lyman. 1968. "Accounts." *American Sociological Review* 33: 46–62.

Stebbins, R. 1969. "Role Distance, Role Distance Behavior and Jazz Musicians." *British Journal of Sociology* 20: 406–415.

Stokes, R. and J. Hewitt. 1976. "Aligning Actions." *American Sociological Review* 41: 838–849.

Ungar, S. 1980. "The Effects of the Certainty of Self-Perceptions on Self-Presentation Behaviors: A Test of the Strength of Self-Enhancement Motives." *Social Psychology Quarterly* 43: 165–172.

———. 1981. "The Effects of Others' Expectancies on the Fabrication of Opinions." *Journal of Social Psychology* 114: 173–185.

Welsford, E. 1961. *The Fools: His Social and Literary History.* New York: Anchor.

Pauses:
Explorations in Social Rhythm

Robert P. Snow
Arizona State University

Dennis Brissett
University of Minnesota at Duluth

Despite the ubiquity of pauses in the personal and social fabric of everyday life, sociological analysis of this phenomenon has been limited in both scope and concern. In this article it is argued that pausing should not be relegated to the status of a residual category nor should pauses merely be conceptualized as breaks in action or periods of inactivity. Rather, it is suggested that pauses are an essential element of the social rhythm that demonstrates degrees of personal and community well-being and vitality. As well, pausing may be an important, perhaps even necessary, part of the process of commitment and self-esteem. A typology of pauses is offered and the implications of pausing in establishing the rhythm of human behavior are discussed.

Ask almost anyone to characterize modern urban society in a few words and in all likelihood that characterization will express, at least in part, a sense of fast-paced action. City-dwellers almost everywhere are "doers" and "goers." In "such a society, time is a commodity to be spent, lost, invested, saved, wasted, thrown away, or employed to best advantage" (Smith, 1961: 85). This "utilitarian conception of time" has certainly expedited the development of " . . . an 'activity cult,' whereby people are expected to maximize their 'active' time and to minimize any 'empty, unaccounted-for' time periods" (Zerubavel, 1981: 56).[1] Although people's attempts to optimally utilize

Reprinted from Symbolic Interaction, 9(1):1–18.

time are most evident in the industrial sector (Zerubavel, 1981), they also characterize much of nonwork activity as well.

> Jet airliners, computers, microwave ovens, speed-reading, techniques, scientific abstracts, instant foods, Polaroid cameras and even intelligence tests are all products of the modern Western preoccupation with time saving and speed. The rise of the fast-food eatery, our extremely negative attitude toward waiting, and the business-like character of so many social encounters are all manifestations of the growing acceleration of the tempo of life in the West. (Zerubavel, 1981: 57)

What Steffan Linder (1970) characterized some time ago as a "time famine" seems increasingly to be an everyday "reality" for many people. The growing popularity of "high quality" time as a justification for not spending as much time as one would like with family or friends certainly speaks to the juxtaposition of "much to do" and "so little time to do it in." As well, instances of simultaneous consumption" (Linder, 1970) seem to be proliferating.

> ... the way many doctors today manage to see several patients within the same period of time is most suggestive of this pattern. Consider also such common combinations as doing business while having lunch, listening to music while driving, watching television while eating dinner or talking over the phone. . . . (Zerubavel, 1981: 58)

Given this cultural preoccupation, it is not surprising that both common-sense and scientific understandings of society labor under an "action" bias and that the notion of inaction, rest, or pausing is largely ignored as meaningful activity in its own right.[2]

Usually, when pauses have been analyzed in sociological literature, they have been described as time-outs or breaks in on-going activity (Felton, 1966; Lyman and Scott, 1970; Gioscia, 1974; Weigert, 1981). Curiously, this suggests that pauses are characterized by an absence of time and activity.[3] "Time ceases to pass; the present extends motionlessly" (Gioscia, 1974; Weigert, 1981). In short, pauses have been conceptualized in terms of what they are not. This bias is understandable in view of the norm in industrial/commercial society of evaluating activity in terms of time.[4] We diligently attempt to reduce or extend time spent on an activity depending on whether its quick completion may afford higher profit, such as producing piecework, or resulting in aesthetic pleasure, such as savoring a sunset. In either case, momentary halts in activity are made irrelevant to assessing an activity's value. Although rest periods may be earned and valued in their own right, pausing is deemed irrelevant to the total time spent on that activity. In turn, if time during a pause is made irrelevant to an ongoing sequence of events, then activity during a pause is also understood to be irrelevant to past or future activity. We believe this temporal, or more precisely atemporal, characterization of a pause tends to inhibit an understanding of what may actually occur.

TOWARD A REFORMULATION

To us, what is fundamentally important about pauses is that they appear as instances of stopping or ceasing action only when viewed from the perspective of that which precedes or follows them. As such, pauses are considered residual elements in everyday life. However, we both agree with and extend Barry Schwartz's comments regarding one type of pause—"waiting."

> The waiting period (pause). . . . is not merely a residual phase—a quantum of time representing default in the coordination of the end of one activity with the beginning of another; rather this phase contains its own functional justification, . . . Waiting periods (pausing) . . . represent part of the connective tissue by which interactions are held together and ordered. according to the principle that the temporal separation of engagements constitutes the very condition of their inner coherence. (Schwartz, 1975: 192–93)

A subtle but overriding implication of pausing is that activity momentarily halted will continue. As such, pausing may appear to be a relatively free period when assessing the time value of an overall activity. Yet, pausing does not necessarily impede the halted activity, abrogate future commitment, or deny potential achievement; breaks in human action rarely constitute breakdowns.

In a slightly different vein it may very well be that pausing establishes the parameters of action. If "we can create time by creating intervals in social life" (Leach, 1961: 135), isn't it also possible that we establish the very form and content of our actions by pausing in our dealings with others? At the very least, our experience of the process of action is sharpened by the very lapses in that action. Mead's argument (1929) in regard to the experiencing of a continuity of events cites the critical importance of discontinuity:

> Without this break within continuity, continuity would be inexperienceable. The content alone is blind, and the form alone is empty, and experience in either case is impossible . . . The continuity is always of some quality, but as present passes into present there is always some break in the continuity—within the continuity, not of the continuity. The break reveals the continuity. . . . (p. 239)

Similarly, we argue that pauses are necessary to the recognition of action, and, as such, the rhythm of our social and personal existence. As a taken-for-granted and even primitive, universal rhythm is the concept that imparts common-sense meaning to energy pulsations of alternating action and rest which abound in physical, biological, and social domains. Consequently, social rhythm is the flow or movement of one's life and lifestyle that is predicated on both action and inaction. As described by Peter Adler (1981) rhythmicity is fundamental to developing and maintaining momentum in goal-oriented behavior. Also, "Rhythm is . . . the very essence of time, since equal intervals of time define a sequence of events as rhythmic" (Hall, 1983: 140). While it is usually argued that biological time establishes the bedrock of our rhythmic world, it is becoming more evident that people's lives are embedded in processes of inter-locking rhythms.[5]

> ... these same interlocking rhythms are comparable to fundamental themes in a symphonic score, a keystone in the interpersonal processes between mates, co-workers and organizations of all types on the interpersonal level within as well as across cultural boundaries. (Hall, 1983: 140)

Since our contention is that the flow or rhythm of one's personal and social life is characterized by alternating action and inaction,[6] instances of briefly stopping or ceasing a course of action are as important to the personal and social vitality of an individual as are flurries of activity. In addition, what is conventionally looked upon as inaction, idleness, and doing nothing is an essential accent to action in the rhythm of social life. Intermissions, delays, silences, and hesitations of life are important in fashioning a sense of identity and personal worth as well as contributing to a sense of sociality and community. As T.S. Eliot (1963: 177) reminds us, "There is only the dance."

This is not to argue that individuals should, or must, strike some sort of parity or even balance between action–inaction. Nor is it a question of people simply being too busy. The point is that we should accord greater relevance and even dignity to those lapses in communication and action that are such common features of everyday life. Since action is not sustained indefinitely, to "give pause" in dealings with others is certainly not rare, but rarely is it given the importance it well deserves.

OBSERVATIONS AND ANALYSIS

For some time we have periodically discussed the observed tendency among American urban dwellers, especially middle-class professionals, to justify and offer excuses for periods of apparent nonproductivity. This was brought home in preparation for a recent sabbatical leave when it became necessary to justify the leave on the basis of high productivity in a specified research endeavor. In lamenting the fact that sabbaticals are no longer granted for the sake of quiet reflection and rejuvenation, we began to intensify our interest and discussion on the general nature of pausing. This led to an informal field study in which we attempted to observe more carefully what appeared to go on during pauses and determine how they fit into schemes of activity. In an unstructured manner we took note of our own behavior and the behavior of close associates and others in situations we could easily observe, such as work settings, home life, and recreational activities. From our observations and notes the following findings and analysis emerged.

TYPOLOGY

To orient our investigation we defined a pause as any interruption in the ongoing flow of interaction[7] that appears to persons in that interaction as a departure from the socially anticipated goals of that interaction. As such, pauses may appear to be individualistic departures from the concerted task at hand. In this sense pauses should be viewed as periods of apparent noninteraction rather than periods of nonaction. Therefore, we agree with Weber's (1947) observation that sociology must be concerned with social action that includes both failure to act and passive acquiescence in action. In this sense, although we may identify pauses in terms of their ostensible noninteractive quality, we can still analyze their consequences in interaction. As in many things the conditions under which we notice or identify certain behaviors has little (or no necessary) relation to an examination of the meaning of those behaviors in our lives. To this end, our typology of pausing is an organization/ordering of social-psychological consequences, not a classification based on formal criteria or rules of identification and discovery.

From our observations and survey of relevant literature we identified five separate types of pausing experience: (1) *benchmarks* for distinguishing and clarifying previous actions, relationships, and physical place; (2) periods of *taking stock* for potential realignment of self in social affairs; (3) respites for physical and mental *rejuvenation*; (4) periods of *waiting* for action to resume; and (5) moments and intervals of temporary *withdrawal*. Since pauses may or may not be preplanned, and, since an actor's reasons for behavior are established during the course of interaction, each type of pause represents an empirical event made situationally meaningful rather than a condition that precipitates particular behavior. It must also be recognized that more than one meaning can and often is established for a single pause. Taking stock can occur during a wait, a wait can be classified later as a benchmark, rejuvenation can be experienced while taking stock. However, all types of pauses have properties in common that make this phenomenon distinct and separate from what is commonly defined as on-going action.

Benchmark

As an internal interruption within a course of action, a pause's most utilitarian function is a separation of other actions into meaningful and sometimes mutually exclusive categories. For example, a coffee break not only temporarily halts work, it also divides work periods into unambiguous, manageable units. Periods of silence in conversation mark beginning, turning, and end points[8] as well as establishing emphasis or rhythmic accent. As such, the pause serves as a contrasting reference point or benchmark (Roth, 1963) for past and future experience. Since we often interpret something by contrasting it to what it is not, a pause provides clarity through contrast. In observing routine academic life, we occasionally find it difficult to define precisely what is and is not professional work. One method for reducing this ambiguity is to separate intellectual activity and professional interaction with pauses for small talk and trips to the coffee machine. Professors often complain that with all the interruptions they find it difficult to get anything accomplished at the office, and yet all of our colleagues engage in these interruptions whether they are obligatory or not. At times these interruptions serve as sharp contrasts to the mental rigors of scholarship, providing distinction to that mental activity.

As a means for making clear distinctions between events, pauses also momentarily certify the temporary completion of thought and action (Sontag, 1969). The weekend is not just a play period—it marks the end of the work week as is signified in the celebration of "TGIF." Likewise, one daily round is ended and marked by going to sleep at night (Weigert, 1981). In both examples, however, continuation of work and daily routine is assumed, making a sense of continuity implicit in the notion of temporary completion. By marking off work into distinct and completed segments, the coffee break, and even a pause for a sip of coffee while working, affords an individual the opportunity to develop a sense of continuity through a work routine. Similarly, students of all ages understand that anticipated and enacted recreation pauses, such as TV cartoon hours and institutionalized holidays, are important aids in marking progress through various school time periods. Consequently, the rhythm and apparent continuity of work, school, and other routines is in part, established through pauses of contrasting behavior. Furthermore, these pauses also provide contrasting emotional states, such as the feeling of satisfaction or relief following the recognized temporary end or turning point in a course of action.

In addition, pausing to engage in nonrequired interaction with certain individuals often serves to distinguish and clarify the meaning of those social relationships. In observing fellow workers, friends, and relatives who avoid or find it difficult to pause and make small talk, a consequence is to curtail these encounters and/or increase interpersonal formality and social distance. At the other extreme, intimacy is often constructed within the context of mutual pausing, such as the after-work happy hour, card game, or dinner date. Our observations indicate that participants in mutual pausing often feel relieved of identity validation pressure; commitments are either taken for granted or momentarily suspended. The agreement to mutually pause can be both an expressed intent toward intimacy and a context in which intimacy can develop as is dramatically demonstrated in the extramarital affair in which both parties hold the future in suspension while intensifying momentary intimacy. In fact, relationships contextualized totally within a pause appear to be a form of pure play.[9]

Finally, pauses in movement through one's social world often establish the attachment one develops toward certain places in that world, such as a favorite watering hole or TV chair. From pausing at the head of a stairway or stopping at a traffic light to routine visits for coffee at the doughnut shop or strolling on a beach, place is distinguished and contextualized in pausing. In fact, "if we think of space as that which allows movement, then place is pause; each pause in movement makes it possible for location to be transformed into place" (Tuan, 1977).

Taking Stock

Similar to benchmark pauses that mark and distinguish is the act of pausing to *take stock*. In response to a personal or external challenge, this action involves a momentary cessation of a course of action followed by a review of past events and experiences for the purpose of realignment or termination. When a parent asks a child to "stop and think," it is a request to pause and consider future consequences of previous actions. When individuals suddenly discover that they are physically lost, misplaced, or have mentally lapsed, they typically hold in place and quickly reconstruct what they were doing and where they were going. Prior commitments and involvements may be reevaluated, and at the same time there may be an assessment of whether or not, and how, actions may be aligned to meet anticipated futures. An individual may decide to continue on course with the same or better performance, or to terminate. In any case, a pause to momentarily discontinue and take stock provides the opportunity to construct a sense of personal continuity.

While taking stock may result in an assessment of prior actions as failure or even meaningless, it often leads to a strengthening of purpose and dedication. This rededication is accomplished in part by a concerted act of eliminating extraneous information from future consideration. When a coach admonishes an athlete to get his/her head in the game, the coach is accusing the player of thinking about irrelevant matters and commanding a realignment with renewed vigor. In times of national peril, a presidential address is a public request to set aside personal luxury for the sake of community resolve. In this same manner, national holidays are ritualized pauses to take stock of devotion and endeavor to the nation. And, as observed in most religions the Sabbath is a period for pious reflection and renewal of faith. As a religious ritual, prayer is a pause in which secular activity momentarily ceases for the purpose of rededication to the future through religious power and orthodoxy. Therefore, the pause to take stock may accomplish two objectives: (1) overcoming confusion and developing a sense of coherency and continuity for a series of actions and events; and (2) renewal of commitment and dedication to particular kinds of future behaviors.

Rejuvenation

Time out for rejuvenation and revitalization of one's self is easily the most enjoyable and desirable act of pausing. While pausing to take stock may occasionally result in feelings of revitalization, we speak here of those intervals that are either deliberately or unwittingly devoted to a refurbishing and/or expanding of emotional and physical life. They range in classification from brief moments of stopping to take a deep breath or gazing aimlessly off into space, to catnaps, a refreshing swim, weekend retreats, and institutionalized siestas, holidays, and vacations. Commonly understood evidence of having experienced this type of pause is the feeling of emotional and physical refreshment following any break in action. From responses we obtained, we conclude that rejuvenation pauses are instances when a cognitive sequential perspective on life (including physical exercise) is superseded by an emergent emotional one. The typical comment "It was good to get away" says it quite well. By stepping back and away from a course of action to recoup, refresh, or even relax, the linearity of one's existence is jolted and feelings of relief and freedom are experienced. Indeed, feelings of relief and freedom constitute the commonly understood emotional ingredients of rejuvenation and revitalization.

From our observations, children are without question masters at pausing to rejuvenate. Whether eagerly involved in play or reluctantly engaged in work, children periodically, and usually without asking permission, physically flop or "let go." While adults often plan for respites, children do it spontaneously—seldom offering justification for the act. Children see pauses to refresh as natural and necessary in any context. As compared to adults they are less hampered by commitment to formality, the consequences of role violations, and the work ethic of earned time off. To a child, intellectualizing about or justifying a respite is rightfully absurd.

In contrast, adults express or experience freedom during a respite. Parents schedule free time away from children. Homeowners escape the never-ending tyranny of house repair. Family members retreat to the solitude of the bathroom, basement, or garage. Workers pause to daydream, physically stretch tight muscles, take a drink of water or a deep breath, and tell jokes. There seems an underlying belief that periodic relief from a course of action must be achieved in order to continue the action and maintain a standard of performance. We feel this sense of relief implies freedom, and one's self becomes rejuvenated through the realization that we can step aside from the inevitable, relentless, and obdurate quality of everyday life. By experiencing physical refreshment we feel physically able to continue. And, to the extent that pausing establishes a sense of rhythm, we feel emotionally refreshed and existentially vigorous. Consequently pauses to rejuvenate and revitalize are not simply beneficial in the sense of refreshment, they are also essential to what is existentially basic to self and to continued action.

Waiting

The most visible and aggravating type of pause is *waiting*. "All humans wait, and in the fullest sense of the term, only humans wait" (Weigert, 1981: 227). More complex than it first appears, waiting includes anticipated and unanticipated interruptions either of which may be defined as an appropriate or inappropriate break in a course of action. Moreover, waiting may initially be a deliberate, preplanned, appropriate activity that when extended for too long a period becomes an aggravating, inappropriate delay. Common to all instances of waiting is the resumption or beginning of some course of action, as seen most clearly in instances of "deferred gratification." Unlike the pleasurable connotation associated with pauses for rejuvenation, waiting often entails a frustrating, almost onerous element. Waiting differs slightly from the pause to mark and distinguish in that it essentially involves anticipation for the future rather than distinction to past events. In addition, pausing to mark is more deliberate than waiting. Unlike the pause to take stock, waiting is not done for the sake of making definitions or providing coherency. But, since waiting threatens continuity it has disastrous potential,[10] and, to save the situation, it may be converted into another type of pause. For example, waiting for someone to make up their mind and initiate action can result in destroying a mood and terminating the encounter unless a request to take stock reestablishes commitment. Or the aggravating wait at the market check-out stand may be eased through a revitalization technique. At a future point a wait may even be redefined as a benchmark, for example, looking back on a Wyoming vacation auto repair as a humorous event.

In our discussions and observations of waiting, the type people consider most common is the inappropriate, unanticipated interruption. Examples include being placed on hold on the telephone, abnormal traffic delays, electrical failure, auto repairs, and a child's untimely entrance into the bedroom. Unanticipated, yet appropriate or at least acceptable interruptions include the fortuitous storm that closes school when an unfinished report is due and any interruption or delay, such as getting sick, which is eventually defined as welcome relief or a needed rest. Anticipated delays, such as normal rush-hour traffic, waiting for a table at a restaurant, and waiting for a plane or public transport are judged acceptable or unacceptable depending on when they occur and the length of time involved. Deliberate waits are designed to enhance a future pay-off, such as queuing for good seats or delaying dessert or sex for the sake of anticipation. But again, if the wait is too long, excitement wanes and aggravation occurs.

In a discussion of waiting as a matter of becoming side-tracked, Lyman and Scott (1970: 201–203) describe how intermissions of biding time or dead time are anxiety producing, anxious waiting for something to happen. Yet our observations indicate that people sometimes relieve and prevent anxiety by converting certain waits into activities in their own right. Teenagers have turned the wait prior to a rock concert into a carnival, enjoying the wait almost as much as the concert; football fans have created the pre-game "tail-gate" barbecue; and when placed on hold during a phone conversation, individuals may listen to soothing "elevator" music. And, in a study of subway behavior, Levine, Vinson, and Wood (1973) argue that subway riders engage in acts of civil inattention to maintain social order. While each example involves waiting, the activity is a positive, future-oriented action.

An example of the deliberate wait that has become formalized is the pause for a truce or cooling off period. Since this pause is an eleventh-hour strategy designed to avoid an irreparable break in a relationship, its purpose is to maintain a commitment until a new agreement can be reached. Taking stock may occur during a truce although its intent is usually to place matters on hold with an eye to an uncertain future. Seeing a marriage counselor often serves as a cooling-off period prior to separation, divorce or reconciliation. The military truce, although sometimes only a lull in the action, provides a pause prior to working out peace negotiations.

Temporary Withdrawal

The fifth and final type of pause is the *temporary withdrawal*. Unlike a complete withdrawal that closes out a course of action, the temporary or momentary withdrawal places the past and future concerns of a preceding course of action in temporary abeyance. Unlike waiting, the temporary withdrawal is never forced and has no specific anticipation other than an awareness of a problematic future. Unlike marking for distinction and taking stock, there is no particular distinction to the pause, and it is not deliberately used for reflection or contemplation. Compared to a rejuvenation pause, the withdrawal is always deliberate and it does not necessarily result in revitalization. The vernacular expressions "marking time" and "time out" partially capture the essence of the momentary withdrawal although nothing, including time, is actually being marked; neither is time nor some activity being suspended in order to accomplish something else. The temporary withdrawal is an interruption in the career of a particular behavior (e.g., work routine or play activity) with no intent or desire to accomplish anything except to momentarily halt a preceding action. While some might view this as flying in the face of rationality or logic, consider some rather typical behaviors: a person briefly stares glassy-eyed off into space; you forget what you were thinking about without knowing why; you seem to lose track of time without being able to recall what occurred during that period. Similarly, after making a series of errors or feeling no desire to work, a typical comment is "I need a break," or "I need to get away from all this for a while." A person may even decide spontaneously to take a vacation or "flop day" with nothing specifically in mind to accomplish. In temporarily withdrawing from family obligations a parent or spouse has been known to just disappear for several days with no justification other than "I just wanted to be alone." Quite remarkably, these periods can stretch into weeks, months, perhaps even years. A colleague once confessed that as a young adult he took off an entire year to aimlessly ride the rails. At no time during that period did he inform his parents or sweetheart of his exact whereabouts or what he was doing. He literally dropped out of his former life and rejoined it after a year.

Although temporary withdrawal is sometimes described as "wandering aimlessly off track," care must be taken to note who is making that definition—actor or other? From the other's standpoint, an individual who temporarily withdraws is confounding a commonly held assumption about the synchronicity between personal biography and biological time. Be it education, occupation, friendship, or family, "each career has its timetable which contains a schedule allocating the normal time for each individual who is 'on course' to pass through the appropriate status. . . [Likewise], there is a normal age for individuals to enter a career or exit from it" (Weigert, 1981: 220–221). However from the actor's standpoint there is only a temporary refusal to continue a course of action. The notion of being off track only makes sense from the standpoint of others attempting to reorient the errant actor. Parents often take this position when they see their teenagers withdraw from so-called responsible behavior. By contrast, the patient parent takes comfort in a belief that the troublesome teenager will eventually resume or assume adultlike responsibility. Care must also be taken to avoid confusing the dropout who rejects an ongoing commitment with the person who temporarily avoids a commitment. During the sixties, the rejection by most "hippies" of their former lives would not be characterized as temporary withdrawal even though some of the more prominent hippie leaders later committed themselves to a "straight" life. These cases, as with Patti Hearst, are more accurately described as a sequence of rejection followed by a new commitment.

A variation of withdrawal that has interesting implications is the exhausted collapse. Many performers in the popular and fine arts explain their cancellations of performances by quite accurately admitting to exhaustion. This makes sense in that performers feel that even a short absence from the public eye could result in declining popularity. Since these performers drive themselves until they drop from physical and mental exhaustion, there is more to the idea of "needing a rest" or "needing a break" than a general understanding suggests. We believe that pausing is so fundamental to ongoing social activity that individuals even trick themselves into pausing when it seems inappropriate. At the extreme people can make themselves sick or drop from exhaustion while at the same time attempting to show others that a pause is not needed.

Social-Psychological Implications

From our observations and analysis, pausing has important social-psychological consequences in the establishment and maintenance of one's self and world view. In pausing to "mark and distinguish," individuals construct a sense of order in their social life. Here *pausing demarcates the flow of life by providing social reference points* along the way. Working definitions of society, situation and others emerge, and a sense that the world is, or can be orderly, evolves. Pausing helps establish the distinctions and categorization of activity within which an individual acts. The creation of social objects (Blumer, 1962) and our identifications of and with others (Stone, 1962) often emerges in the ebb rather than flow of human action. In any case, the social arena becomes manageable and the inexorable passage and pace of life is made discontinuous. Pausing also highlights certain facets of one's life not only by marking and separating but by distinguishing the relevant and the distinctive in social activity. In this sense, pausing not only reduces the ambiguity inherent in human relations, it also elevates and even enables certain of the activities contrasted.

In comparison, pauses to take stock seem more an affirmation of continuity than separation. Here an individual constructs a sense of identity and personal continuity; current commitments and involvements are evaluated, and a future is staked out. Matters of personal career, occupational career and even life course are often adjudicated in pausing to take stock. These pauses occasion a reconstruction of the past, an adjustment of biography in terms of one's present situation.[11] As an arena for the assessment of self-worth an individual steps away from the ongoing expectations and evaluation made by others and pauses to examine his/her own expectations of self. An individual's sense of personal competence and mastery often emerges from such a comparison of self-concept and behavior (Smith, 1968). It is not only a matter of noting where one has been and where one is going but, most importantly, distinguishing where one is and how well one is doing in light of one's conception of self. An individual may emerge from taking stock with renewed purpose or with a strong resolution for personal change, but, in any case, self-worth is established and adjusted. A sense of who one is, be it good, bad, or indifferent is constructed in the context of biography and anticipated futures.

On the other hand, stepping away from a course of action may result in feelings of relief and the excitement of anticipation. As one of the most common forms of hesitation, pausing to rejuvenate often involves entering a different social world, a world some observers have labeled *play* (Huizinga, 1955). What seems most important about these pauses is that people involved in them feel they have exercised personal choice rather than social obligation. This existential quality serves to highlight personal viability and promote personal style as contrasted to the social proscriptions and prescriptions of everyday routines. Much like the pauses that mark and distinguish social life, pauses that revitalize enable an accenting of personal life; a sense of mental and often physical capability and energy occurs, which sharpens the experience of self.[12] That most efforts to step back from everyday routine involve nonlinear, noncognitive and nonsequential types of behavior is a redundant but too-little-analyzed observation of modern life. It is our contention that such interludes of revitalization and rejuvenation are a necessary context for the development and nurturing of emotional life. Of particular importance is the establishment of what Cooley (1902) termed the self as sentiment, the feeling of self that is so infrequently encountered in the ordinary business of everyday life. Likewise, a sense of personal vitality rests not only on an individual's ability to synchronize with the ongoing nature of the social order. Those occasions where individuals feel they are avoiding, escaping from, or playing with the structure of everyday life (Berger, 1963: 139–141), are also the tonic of personal effervescence and spirit.

By contrast, the pause involved in waiting serves primarily as an affirmation of the social order.[13] Whether serving as a role-transition mechanism for shifts in role playing (Schwartz, 1975), or simply a needless delay in getting on with what one wants to do, it often is an unpleasant reminder that as individuals we must play according to other people's rules. In one sense waiting reaffirms the interactive[14] nature of human life as it stands in stark contrast to the "do your own thing" ethic of psychological reductionism. It underlies the hard, social fact that sometimes you must take others into account when acting. Since, in a larger sense, waiting often establishes the structure of social life itself, it makes clear that parameters of time and place are involved in much human activity. That delays in social life are often viewed as personally irksome speaks to their role in defining the nature of interpersonal bonds.

As well as articulating the social nature of human action, waiting also establishes a hierarchy in human action.[15] Whether "instrumental or ceremonial" (Schwartz, 1975), the very act of waiting imbues that which one is waiting for with a certain importance. At the very least, social distance between individuals is established (Schwartz, 1975). That some things and some people are said to be worth waiting for and others are not attests to the evaluative component of waiting. Whether waiting is experienced as annoying or pleasant can also be used as an expression of the importance of that which is awaited as can the length of time that an individual waits. In this sense, it could also be argued that waiting helps establish a personal priority of institutional commitments and a profile of one's social contingencies.

In contrast to waiting, temporary withdrawal turns the tables on society. In effect, the individual puts society on hold, ignoring the temporal as well as the spatial parameters of community life.[16] Here the individual seems to concentrate on matters other than the task or progression of tasks at hand. This withdrawal can be relatively fleeting as in what Goffman (1967: 133) describes as "aways" and hypnotists commonly understand as everyday trance states, or it can be more enduring. In either instance, individuals are declaring that, at the moment, the typical norms and rules of social life do not apply to them. It is not surprising that individuals who temporarily withdraw are socially censured by their peers as threats to the viability of the social structure. And, if these drop-outs seem satisfied and reasonably content, they raise the disturbing possibility that perhaps social life as currently constituted is flawed, or at the very least, precarious. But this is precisely the point. Temporary withdrawal does promote feelings of willfulness and personal choice. It is an affirmation of personal over social control and, as it suspends the illusion that people must always play by the rules, it is a demonstration that within the social order there is room to maneuver. More importantly it highlights the existential possibility that the social order as we know it emerges from the ongoing actions of people within it. Acting in accordance with social dictates may not be as much a matter of personal acquiescence as it is a matter of socially establishing the very contingencies that we take into account when acting.[17]

Rhythm

To us, the most far-reaching consequence of pauses is that they are essential in establishing a rhythm[18] in one's personal and social existence. The fact that rhythm is ubiquitous in all life forms may belie its importance. At the very least we feel that pausing provides the contrast, emphasis, and energy that aid in developing and sustaining meaning in any arena. And, in socially constructed rhythm, the beat, accent, inflection, gait, and meter of various activities is achieved through pauses which, if lengthened, shortened, increased, decreased, or withdrawn, fundamentally alter the overall activity and attending meaning. Each of the five pauses described in the typology contributes to establishing rhythm in an individual's life. Benchmark pauses provide accent or emphasis and also order—hence the contrasts that give rhythm its zest. Taking stock and rejuvenation are halts and rests breaking sustained action and overcoming monotony. When anticipated, waiting is an anxious hesitation or stimulating off-beat; when deliberate, it is the savored, elongated period prior to the downbeat of an activity. Similar to taking stock, the withdrawal is a halt and often a search for a new rhythm and pattern to life itself.

It may well be that social psychologists could learn much from a closer examination of the rhythmic nature of everyday life. Edward Hall's (1983) distinction between polychronic time where "people do many things at once" and monochronic time where "doing one thing at a time" is the rule, provides an intriguing context for not only understanding different cultures or subculture, but also different everyday interactions. Many of the disappointments but also the surprises of one's personal life seem often a consequence of individuals using different rhythmic models of time in their dealings with one another.

Interaction itself may be construed as primarily a matter of rhythm.[19] We refer here not only to the nonverbal synchronization of behavior (Condon, 1978), but also to the very nature of interaction itself. When social psychologists speak of organized directed activity, goal-directed behavior, networking, mutual interdependence, cooperative goal-directed behavior, coordinated activity, cooperative goal achievement, adaptation, and the like are they not implying the underlying rhythm of social encounters? While taking the attitude or role of the other enables communication, is it not also the initial timing and consequent adjustments in role-taking that enable the communication to continue and become meaningful? Is it not the chords and dischords that we strike in interaction that often key us to the existence of such phenomena as role conflict, interpersonal attractiveness, role consensus, love and enmity? In other words, it is not just what people do in relationships with others, but it is also when they do it, how consistently (or inconsistently) they do it, how intensely they do it, and how often they do it that contributes to the meaning—if not the fate—of that interaction. Rhythm, which implies pausings, seems a crucial basis for both understanding and living our interactions with others.

Just as the importance of rhythm is indicated by interactional synchronization, individuals must also be in synch with themselves and their own behavior. Whether this be the "inner forum" or "internal conversation" of which Mead (1934) so eloquently wrote or the abused everyday expression of "getting in touch with oneself," the idea of personal (maybe even intrapersonal) harmony has been a consistent theme in both the observations and conceptualizations of social psychologists. Clearly, the idea of personal and interpersonal competence, executive control, and mastery over one's life all imply a rhythmic interplay of action and self-conception. The synchrony of identity with identity performance provides a powerful measure of one's self-image and self-worth whether it be episodic or embedded in an enduring career. Again, it is not just self-concept and actions that are at stake, it is the very timing, meter and pace of their coexistence upon which one's sense of self and personal powers often rest. In his theory of momentum, Peter Adler (1981) addresses these points, noting how momentum elevates performance to a level "over the heads" of the actors involved.

> The regular symmetry of this cyclical pulsation promotes a continuing acceleration of force, because the ongoing harmonious beat prevents accumulated power from dissipating and guides the individual or group along an escalating track. (p. 32)

Finally, it is in the forum of establishing individuality that the importance of rhythm seems clearest. It is in the synchronization of an individual's performance and the audience reaction that the social self is established and maintained (Goffman, 1959). The rhetoric of self-presentation demands a consideration of rhythm be it in the guise of strategic interaction, face work or simply putting one's "best foot forward." An individual's personal, and public lifestyle is established by the tempo, pace, and counterpoint of one's interaction with others. Both the timing and rhythm of an overall situation and within a particular situation establishes who one is in social interaction. In fact, that individuals control the pace of interaction not only establishes their distinctiveness but also underscores the social-psychological metaphor of people as social actors. Even in those instances where one's behavior, and by implication one's self, is called into question, it seems not a matter of behavior gone awry as much as an interruption in the rhythm of the interaction. Both the proferring and imputation of motives reestablish interactional rhythm more than they repair breakdowns in interactional content. Doing or saying something in the company of others is nearly inevitable. However, the rhythm of such exchanges is often problematic. As social psychologists, we need to develop a vocabulary that better expresses the rhythmic score[20] as well as the act, scene, agent, agency, purpose (Burke, 1962) and audience (Goffman, 1959; Stone, 1962) of human behavior.

Still, the importance of pausing may be far wider than its implications for interaction. The very apposition of life process and substance may be realized in the discontinuities of life. As only Simmel (1971) could put it:

> In general, only youth knows [the] . . . predominance of the process of life over its substance, whereas in old age, when the process begins to slow up and coagulate, substance becomes crucial; it then proceeds or perseveres in a certain timeless manner, indifferent to the tempo and passion of its being experienced. The old person usually lives either in a wholly centralized fashion, peripheral interests having fallen off and being unconnected with his essential life and its inner necessity; or his center atrophies and existence runs its course only in isolated petty details, accenting mere externals and accidentals. Neither case makes possible the relation between the outer fate and the inner springs of life in which the adventure consists; clearly, neither permits the perceptions of contrast characteristic of adventure, viz., that an action is completely torn out of the inclusive context of life and that simultaneously the whole strength and intensity of life stream into it . . . only when a stream flowing between the minutest externalities of life and the central source of strength drags them into itself . . . [does] the peculiar color, ardor, and rhythm of the life-process become decisive. . . . (pp. 197–198)

ACKNOWLEDGMENTS

This article was a joint endeavor in every respect. We thank everyone who made suggestions on earlier drafts, especially Beverley Hainge Cuthbertson, Charles Edgely, and the *SI* reviewers.

NOTES

1. In a classical discussion of the problematics of the ascendence of mathematical time over experiential time ("duree reele") see Henri Bergson (1910). For a contemporary discussion of the varieties of time see Edward T. Hall (1983).

2. Our judgment of the underexamination of pauses in the scholarly literature is certainly debatable particularly if one takes into account the vast array of different types of investigators who have included pauses as part of their analysis of human behavior. One can find reference to pauses in the work of cognitive anthropology, ethology, psycholinguistics, kinesics, network analysis, exchange theories, and particularly in conversational analysis. However, with the minor exceptions that will be discussed in this article, the examination of pauses in this vast literature seems always secondary to a preoccupation with "what is going on" whether that be the "social organization of communicative codes," the "social organization of the body, or the social organization of the vocal chords" (McDermott and Roth, 1978). In other words, the incidence, and in some cases the relevance of pauses have been duly recognized. However, we feel that the implications of pausing as a human behavior in its own right has been given short shrift. Action, not inaction, has been the primary concern.

3. The ethnomethodologists of communication (see Psathas, 1979) are exceptions. However, their analyses of pauses, gaps, and overlaps in conversation have consistently established the pause as simply another element in the sequential structure or organization of human discourse. Silence serves talk, not the other way around.

4. In *Queing and Waiting*, Barry Schwartz (1975) creatively examined waiting in terms of a resource-availability perspective. However, it is important to note that Schwartz only devotes 8 out of 194 pages to a discussion of "how waiting adds to our satisfaction and how it is essential to a social order"(p. 188).

5. See the discussion of biological time, kinesic and proxemics research in Edward Hall (1983). For a consideration of the importance of rhythm, timing, and tempo in Human Ecology see Engel-Frisch (1943) and Hawley (1950). On timing as an interactional necessity, see Couch (1975).

6. As Schwartz (1975) has written about waiting; "if waiting were not inherent in those unpredictable contingencies which are central to the nature of modern life, some functional equivalent for it would have to be devised and institutionalized. For without frequent delays, our daily affairs would require continual interaction, with no remission save that of physical movement from one situation to the next" (p. 191).

7. For the most part, this article will not deal specifically with pauses or silences in verbal communication. Such matters as the pause in humor, the deadly pause as after "Honey, don't you love me anymore?", the reverent pause, the pregnant pause (Oldenburg, private communication) surely speak to the importance of communication pauses in defining the situation. Likewise we recognize that "there are kinds of silent listening that are so empathic and active as to be evocative as any words; there are kinds which are unpenetrable; there are kinds which appear as criticism to vulnerable talkers" (Reisman, Potter, and Watson, 1960: 333).

8. The rich literature of linguistic analysis has documented the function of pauses in human discourse. See for instance Sacks and Schegloffs (1979) discussion of "tie-makers," Osgood and Sebeok (1965) on "juncture pauses," and "hesitation pauses," and particularly Phillips's (1983) analysis of classroom and community conversation on the Warm Springs Indian Reservation and Cahir and Kovac's (1981) exploration of what typically has been thought to be "down time" in the classroom.

9. Stanford Lyman and Marvin Scott (1975) note parallels in the time, space, and play dimensions of the "adventure." Adventurers, such as participants in an extramarital affair, "live in an external present cut off from past and future" (p. 150).

10. An excellent illustration is provided by Peter Adler (1981) in his description of momentum breakers in organized athletics.

11. Two classic renditions of this reconstructive process are Berger (1963: 54–65) and Goffman (1959).

12. The significance of periods of revitalization has also been acknowledged in the creativity process often referred to as *incubation* (Lazarus, Kanner, and Folkman, 1980).

13. The many nuances of this affirmation are discussed in Schwartz (1975).

14. Waiting also underscores the dramaturgical significance of interaction. As modern society involves so much waiting in the presence of others, people come to serve as captive audiences for each other's performances. Waiting, watching and performance often seems coincidental (Edgley, 1985)

15. In confronting the mechanistic and technological dimension of our everyday lives, waiting can also be democratizing as in waiting for computer output, or traffic lights to change, or even a cup of coffee. "The poorest pauper and the most powerful politician must each wait for the coffee to brew"(Weigert, 1981: 227).

16. Susan Sontag's (1969) observations on silence point to yet another consequence of temporary withdrawal, that of "providing time for the continuing or exploring of thought. Notably speech [and we would add, action] closes off thought.... Silence keeps things open" (pp. 19–20).

17. Simmel's (1971) analysis of the adventure as one of life's relevant discontinuities describes the reciprocal tension between the social and personal in far more metaphysical terms.

18. For an explanation of the rhythm of our minds in cognitive terms see Allan Teger— "The rhythm, if you will, of our experience or stream of consciousness" (1976: 4). And, the import of pause in establishing the rhythm of one's speech is examined in James Deese (1984).

19. The notion of entrainment has been utilized to describe the rhythms of relationships in a pause-locking oscillation model of behavior (see Leonard, 1978; Condon, 1978; Hall, 1983).

20. For a diffuse but intriguing commentary on scores in human communities see Halprin (1969). Also, see Robert Lauer's discussion of the temporal pattern of any social phenomenon (Lauer, 1981: 28–41).

REFERENCES

Adler, P. 1981. *Momentum: A Theory of Social Action*. Beverly Hills: Sage.

Berger, P. 1963. *Invitation to Sociology*. Garden City, N.Y.: Doubleday.

Bergson, H. 1910. *Time and Free Will*. Trans. F.O. Pogson. New York: Macmillan.

Blumer, H. 1962. "Society as Symbolic Interaction." Pp. 179–192 in A. Rose (ed.) *Human Behavior and Social Processes*. Boston: Houghton Mifflin.

Burke, K. 1962. *A Grammar of Motives and A Rhetoric of Motives*. New York: The World Publishing Co.

Cahir, S.R. and C. Kovac. 1981. *Transitions: Activity Between Activity*. Washington, D.C.: Center for Applied Linguistics.

Condon, W.S. 1978. "An analysis of behavioral organization." *Sign Language Studies* 13: 285–318.

Cooley, C.H. 1902. *Human Nature and the Social Order*. New York: Scribner & Sons.

Cottle, T. 1976. *Perceiving Time*. New York: Wiley.

Couch, C.J. et al. 1975. "Time and Social Life." Pp. 120–138 in C. Couch (ed.) *Constructing Social Life*. Champaign, IL: Stipes.

Deese, J. 1984. *Thought Into Speech: The Psychology of Language*. Englewood Cliffs, N.J.: Prentice Hall.

Duncan, Jr., S. 1982 "Quantitative Studies of Interaction Structure and Strategy." *Sociological Methods and Research* 11(2): 175–194.

Edgley, C. 1985. "The Dramas of Time." Paper presented at the 1985 Midwest Society Meeting, St. Louis, Missouri.

Eliot, T.S. 1963. "Four Quartets: Burnt Norton." Pp. 175–181 in *The Collected Poems 1900–1962*. New York: Harcourt, Brace, and World.

Engle-Frisch, G. 1943. "Some Neglected Temporal Aspects of Human Ecology." *Social Forces* 22:43–47.

Felton, G.S. 1974. "Psychosocial Implications of the Coffee Break." *Journal of Human Relations* 14(3): 434–449. (Also pp. 18–30 in Marcelo Truzzi (ed.) *Sociology for Pleasure*. Englewood Cliffs, N.J.: Prentice-Hall, 1974)

Gioscia, V. 1974. *Times Forms*. New York: Gordon & Breech.

Goffman, E. 1959. *The Presentation of Self in Everyday Life*. Garden City, N.Y.: Doubleday

———. 1961. "The Moral Career of the Mental Patient." Pp. 127–169 in E. Goffman (ed.), *Asylums*. Garden City, N.Y.: Doubleday.

———. 1967 *Interaction Ritual*. Garden City, N.Y.: Alvelro Books.

Hall, E.T. 1983. *The Dance of Life*, Garden City, N.Y.: Anchor Press.

Halprin, L. 1969. *The RSVP Cycles: Creative Processes in the Human Environment.* New York: Braziller.

Hawley, A. 1950. *Human Ecology.* New York: Ronald Press.

Huizinga, J. 1955. *Homo Ludens.* Boston: Beacon.

Lauer, R.H. 1981. *Temporal Man: The Meaning and Uses of Social Time.* New York: Praeger.

Lazarus, R., A. Kanner, and S. Folkman. 1980. "Emotions: A Cognitive-Phenomenological Analysis." Pp. 189–217 in R. Plutchik and H. Kellerman (eds.) *Emotion: Theory Research and Experience, Vol. 1.* New York: Academic.

Leach, E. 1961. *Rethinking Anthropology.* London: Athlone.

Leonard, G. 1978. "The Rhythms of Relationships." Pp. 13–29 in G. Leonard (ed.) *The Silent Pulse.* New York: E.P. Dutton.

Levine, J., A. Vinson, and D. Wood. 1973. "Subway Behavior." Pp. 208–216 in A. Birenbaum and E. Sagarin (eds.) *People in Places.* New York: Praeger.

Linder, S. 1970. *The Harried Leisure Class.* New York: Columbia University Press.

Lyman, S.M. and M.B. Scott. 1970. *A Sociology of the Absurd.* New York: Appleton-Century-Crofts

————. 1975. *The Drama of Social Reality.* New York: Oxford.

McDermott, R. and D.R. Roth. 1978. "The Social Organization of Behavior: Interactional Approaches." *Annual Review of Anthropology* 7: 321–345.

Mead, G. H. 1929. "The Nature of the Past. "Pp.235–242 in J. Coss (ed.), *Essays in Honor of John Dewey* New York: Henry Hall.

————. 1934. *Mind, Self, and Society.* Chicago: University of Chicago Press.

Melbin, M. 1978. "City Rhythms." Pp. 444–465 in J.T. Fraser et al. (eds.) *The Study of Time III.* New York: Springer-Verlag.

Osgood, C.E., and T. Sebeok. 1965. *Psycholinguistics.* Bloomington: Indiana University Press.

Phillips, S. 1983. *The Invisible Culture.* New York: Longman.

Psathas, G. 1979. *Everyday Language.* New York: Irvington Publisher.

Reisman, D., R. Potter, and J. Watson. 1960. "Sociability, Permissiveness and Equality: A Preliminary Formulation." *Psychiatry* 22: 323–340.

Roth, J.A. 1963. *Timetables.* Indianapolis: Bobbs-Merrill.

Sacks, H. and E. Schegloff. 1979 "Two Preferences in the Organization of Reference to Persons in Conversation and Their Interaction." Pp. 15–20 in G. Psathas (ed.), *Everyday Language.* New York: Irvington.

Schwartz, B. 1975. *Queuing and Waiting.* Chicago: University of Chicago Press.

Simmel, G. 1971. "The Adventurer." Pp. 187–198 in D. Levine (ed.). *Georg Simmel on Individuality and Social Forms.* Chicago: University of Chicago Press.

Smith, M.B. 1968. "Competence and Socialization." Pp. 270–320 in J. Clausen (ed.) *Socialization and Society.* Boston: Little, Brown.

Smith, R.J. 1961. "Cultural Differences in the Life Cycle and the Concept of Time." Pp. 83–112 in R.W. Kleemeier (ed.) *Aging and Leisure.* New York: Farrar, Straus and Giroux.

Sontag, S. 1969. "The Aesthetics of Silence." Pp. 3–34 in S. Sontag (ed.) *Styles of Radical Will.* New York: Farrar, Straus and Giroux.

Sorokin, P. and R. Merton. 1937. "Social Time: A Methodological and Functional Analysis." *American Journal of Sociology* 42(5): 615–629.

Stone, G. 1962. "Appearance and the Self." Pp. 86–118 in A. Rose (ed.) *Human Behavior and Social Processes.* Boston: Houghton-Mifflin.

Teger, A.I. 1976. "Rhythm in Interaction as a Construction of Social Reality." Paper presented at the Symposium on the Biological and Social Aspects of Rhythm in Interaction, State University College at Buffalo, New York.

Tuan, I-fu. 1977. *Space and Place: The Perspective of Experience*. Minneapolis: University of Minnesota Press.

Weber, M. 1947. *The Theory of Social and Economic Organization*. Glencoe. Ill.: The Free Press.

Weigert, A.J. 1981. *Sociology of Everyday Life*. New York: Longman.

Zerubavel, E. 1981. *Hidden Rhythms: Schedules and Calendars in Social Life*. Chicago: University of Chicago Press.

Working for Television:
The Social Organization of TV Drama

Sharon Mast
Victoria University of Wellington

Data collected in a case study of a British TV play provide the basis for an analysis of the social organization of TV drama production. The perceived needs of mass audiences and the ways in which the technical requirements of television are interpreted and acted upon set the preconditions for the ongoing interaction between actors, directors and technicians. The conventions of TV production are upheld and reinforced by continued use, though subject to renegotiation by all participants.

INTRODUCTION

The production of television drama requires the coordinated efforts of numerous artistic, technical and administrative personnel. As a result of the high degree of specialization of their tasks, their different employment arrangements with the TV company and their dissimilar orientations to the ethos of commercial drama, groups of TV workers tend to develop competing perspectives through which they define and experience their work situation. This paper is concerned with the ways in which these groups of workers fit together their lines of action (Blumer, 1969: 16–17) in order to produce drama for mass audiences. More specifically, I shall examine the ways in which prevailing perceptions of the aesthetic and technical requirements of TV drama production conventionalize and constrain TV work and the social relations arising from it.

The data presented in the present paper were gathered while doing field work on a British TV play. The play was a serialized adaptation of a novel divided into six

Reprinted from Symbolic Interaction, 6(1):71–83.

half-hour episodes. Each two episodes constituted one production unit which meant that they were rehearsed and recorded together. I observed the first production unit which spanned a period of four weeks and interviewed five of the six actors and the director during the rehearsal phase of production unit 2. All of those interviewed had previously worked for television as well as having substantial theater (and in some cases, film) experience.

The TV case study was itself part of a larger investigation of occupational socialization and the dramatic actor. As participant observer, I acquired my view of the social organization of TV drama by taking the role of the actor, rather than any other organizational employee. I therefore focus on the social relations among the TV workers who *directly* interact with the actors (e.g., the director, technicians, co-actors) excluding from examination the numerous participants whose contribution to the production either precedes or follows the rehearsal period. Similarly, I shall discuss the aesthetics and technology of TV drama in terms of their impact on acting, although their influence on other facets of production will be evident. Wherever applicable, comparisons across varieties of acting settings will be made.

DESCRIPTION OF THE CASE

Pre-production planning got under way when the producer chose the novel to be adapted, commissioned a writer and director, and met with them and the script editors. Production assistants booked rehearsal space, the studio and technicians for the taping of the play; the casting director selected the actors. Once this pre-planning was completed, the actors attended a read-through of the entire six-episode script, after which the first rehearsal was scheduled.

The stage manager opened the first rehearsal by informing the cast of amendments to the script. The director and actors discussed the physical staging of the play on the sets and did a sketchy rehearsal of the first few scenes with scripts in hand. Because the rehearsal period would be short, they made rapid progress. By the third rehearsal the actors had learned most of their lines and were discussing fairly specific points with the director. At the writer's run on the fourth day of rehearsal, the cast performed the first two episodes for the writer, who then discussed his[1] reactions to the production thus far. After several more days of rehearsal, outdoor filming and weekend breaks, the producer attended a similar run, giving the cast criticism and suggestions. During the final rehearsal outside the studio (the technicians' run), cameramen and lighting technicians jotted down the director's instructions and familiarized themselves with the movements of the actors from one set to another.

The preceding work culminated in two days of taping at the TV studios. Here the activity was divided between those on the studio floor—including actors, camera and lighting technicians and floor manager—and those in the gallery—including the producer, director, writer, production assistants, vision mixer and sound technicians. Those in the gallery viewed the activity on the floor via the TV monitors. The director communicated his notes to the actors through the floor manager, who received these through his earphones and repeated (or diplomatically rephrased) them to the actors. In this way, each scene in the first production unit was rehearsed for the last time and then recorded.

THE AESTHETICS OF TV DRAMA

Television drama is often considered a simplistic and trivial representation of real life, inferior to the high culture of theater (Shils, 1964: 328–329; Billington, 1973: 120). While it can be argued that the application of theatrical standards to television constitutes a 'misreading' of the medium (Fiske and Hartley, 1978), any tendency to dilute the complexities of character and situation can perhaps be traced to the perceived needs of a mass audience and a number of organizational and technical factors.

If, as Stuart Hood (1967) asserts, the needs of a mass audience consist of "entertainment, distraction and escape" (p. 133), then a popular format for TV drama will be one "with continuing characters to whom the viewer becomes attached, with whom he is familiar, from whom he knows he can expect certain types of action and reaction (pp. 134–135). As Novak (1975: 12) points out—in a variation of the Thomas theorem—whether or not the audience *really* requires spoon-fed drama is beside the point; if producers and sponsors perceive that they do, then the audience will get TV drama which expresses only a limited range of human emotion and motivation. Conventional ways of presenting characters on TV emerge, and such conventions which "regulate the relations between artists and audience" (Becker, 1974: 771) are reflected in the selection procedures of casting directors:

> Shayne [an American TV casting director] carefully keeps folders on which actors can play which types of roles. Following is a partial listing of types within just one category, 'Character Actors, Male': Jewish, Hungarian, floorwalker, Spanish, . . . English, tough prisoners, cops, old doctors, . . . fifties, forties, . . . leads, classical, judges, old judges. (Goldman, 1970: 211)

Along with age and ethnicity, typical constellations of personality traits are embodied in various TV characters. As a member of the TV cast explained:

> [I was chosen] because this director had worked with me before; before, I played a well brought up young man, nice boy, intelligent, but a bit stupid, like this character—but a small part, less written. Therefore, I guess, this director suggested me for this part—same character, but extended.

The supposed audience requirements are well served by the series or serials which predominate over the single play on TV. The fact that writing for serials and series is a corporate enterprise only further constrains the aesthetic potential of such drama, for contributing dramatists must work within already-established situations with already-established central characters (Williams, 1974: 60). At the same time, though, the familiarity of characters in serials and series obviates the need to establish characters with broad strokes in every episode. By contrast, the single play must make unknown characters immediately recognizable, thus tending even more so, perhaps, towards stereotypes.

The organizational setting influences the aesthetic of TV drama insofar as time pressures not usually associated with theatrical productions intrude (Billington, 1973; Cook, 1976). The formal organization of specialized and interdependent tasks demands that everyone keep to a strictly coordinated schedule. Numerous technical and production staff depend upon the artistic personnel to proceed with their work in a routine and punctual manner (Shaw, 1979). For this reason, it is unlikely that the writer will have time to revise the script in reaction to developments on the rehearsal floor; nor will the actors have much scope to explore their characters. Comparing TV drama to commercial film, Lauritzen (1981: 31) notes:

> Safe material is preferred to untried categories of writing. Improvisation is out of the question.... And set routines are allowed to replace creative experimentation.

And, if pressures of time lead the actor to develop his character on his own rather than in close consultation with the director (Billington, 1973: 137), then this also helps him to 'set' his characterization before recording begins. As we will see, this is necessary if the actor is to avoid inconsistency over a series of out-of-sequence scenes.

Becker's (1978) work on arts and crafts is useful in understanding the difference between acting for theater and acting for television. The folk definition of craft includes the idea of a person using his skills to make a product, and perhaps selling those skills to an employer who reserves the right to alter the final product (pp. 864–865). Art, on the other hand, carries with it the notion of "the relative freedom of the artist from outside interference with his work" (p. 866). The very nature of theater enables the actor to define himself (and be defined by others) as an artist, for without intermediaries between actor and audience, the director necessarily surrenders his conception of the production to the actor on stage. In contrast, the vast array of personnel and machinery which interpose themselves between the actor and the TV audience reduces the autonomy of the actor in that setting, thereby transforming his art into craft. With a shift in the locus of artistry from actor to producer or director in TV, the definition of the "quintessential artistic act" (Becker, 1974: 769) becomes problematic. Negotiation of the meaning and status of various tasks infuses the relations between TV drama personnel.

THE TECHNOLOGY OF TV DRAMA

TV drama shares with film production three characteristics which differentiate them from theater in terms of the actor's own work experience: naturalism, discontinuous acting, and the mediation of the relationship between performer and audience by technical apparatus. The consequences of these features of the technology of electronic media for the TV actor will be discussed below.

Naturalism

Casting directors differ in the range of roles they consider suitable for a particular actor, and since each TV company employs several casting directors, the actor has some scope for varied characterization. However, because the visual focus on the actor is potentially so close in TV and film, acting in these media is usually more naturalistic than acting for theater. As one actor explained:

> On television, you have to control everything and you have to have everything really real, which means that at times you literally are not acting, you're being. . . You can't be big on television. If you're on stage and you rant and roar, there's a satisfaction in that, you get rid of a lot of things, but you can't do that on television—it's too real. You couldn't scream and shout because nobody would really believe that you behave like that. Television has a reality but it doesn't have a reality.

The nearness of the TV camera can effectively limit the actor to a range of roles dictated by his physical appearance. For example, one member of the TV cast who had been repeatedly cast as policemen and other 'heavies' was a fairly dissatisfied victim of such typecasting. On the other hand, success in a particular role can limit an actor's future work options since the association between actor and character may be ineradicable. It is to the actor's benefit, therefore, to keep a low profile or, as one actor put it, not to be "in anything too stamping." The best insurance of future employment is adherence to an easily identifiable type and a rather neutral rendition of roles.

The requirement of naturalism also influences the organization of rehearsal time. The intimacy of the TV image insures that any boredom or staleness in the acting will be clearly revealed. In order to keep the performance 'fresh', rehearsals are shortened as the day of taping nears. Consequently, the actor is disengaged from his work just at the point where, in theater, his participation would increase.

Discontinuous Performance and Out-of-Sequence Acting

Discontinuous performance is the absence of a full run through the play without interruption; in out-of-sequence acting, not only are the performances interrupted, but they are not rehearsed and/or recorded in chronological sequence. These conventions are not necessary to TV drama production, but are the outcome of developments over several decades (Billington, 1973; Swift, 1976).

In the 1950's, TV plays were often filmed live and so resembled theater in this respect. They differed from theater insofar as cameramen had to follow the actors from one set to the next and try not to get their cables crossed as they moved in time with the actual dramatic changes. The script writer had to limit the number of set and costume changes. For the actor, live television could be terrifying and required enormous concentration.

The problems of continuous live filming were at the same time its challenges (the first being the view from the 50's and the second the present perspective on that period). Nevertheless, video recording and sophisticated film editing were welcomed when these techniques were developed. The writer's job became easier since sequencing problems would be resolved through editing; the director's role was augmented, as he now engineered the appearance of continuity which was lost in the writing.

As TV drama became less like theater and more like film, both technically and experientially, autonomy and responsibility for the final product also changed. If, in theater, the actor is the ultimate decision maker as he steps out on the stage before the live audience, then in TV and film, the director (or editor or producer) exercises control over the final product by selecting those 'takes' which accord with his conception of the production.

The problems of discontinuous performance and out-of-sequence acting were evident in the TV production I observed. For example, the organization of the play into episodes and units created temporal difficulties for the actors. As I mentioned earlier, each two of the six episodes were rehearsed and recorded together. Several times in the course of rehearsal, it became clear that the actors could not remember when the first episode ended and the second began. This introduced ambiguities into their acting, as the following exchange shows:

> The actor says to the director, 'Should I be going into that again?' (an explanation with the script of part of the plot). The actor says this has been described 'over there' (in another part of the set, in a different scene). The director says, 'Yes, but that was last week.' In other words, they are rehearsing two episodes together which will be shown a week apart, and the audience has to be reminded of this part of the plot in the second episode. (Observer's notes)

Some of the outdoor scenes were filmed before the cast met for a read-through of the entire play in the TV studios, i.e., before the relevance of these connecting scenes to the indoor, videotaped action may have been clear. Similarly, the read-through was not strictly continuous since silent connecting sequences cannot be 'read' through. And, in order to keep production costs down, outdoor scenes from production units 2 and 3 were shot during the scheduled filming dates for unit 1.

The way in which indoor scenes were videotaped created further discontinuity. Whereas some TV companies first rehearse the entire play and then tape it, this company used a scene-by-scene rehearse/record sequence. It was clear that the actors were simply running through the play for the benefit of the technicians, certainly in the rehearse phase and possibly in the record phase as well. In the opinion of the actors and numerous onlookers (including the producer!), discontinuity robbed the performance of much of its dramatic impact.

Reflecting on the consequences for characterization of discontinuous and out-of-sequence acting, Madsen (1973: 242) has written that the actor must interpret his role "without any sense of continuity and often without any interaction with other actors." At the same time, he must have a clear understanding of his character so that he can 'turn it on' for the cameras. This was exemplified in the following incident I observed:

At one point, the actor says to the director. 'What happens at that point, do you have the cameras on me?' The director says that he doesn't, and the actor replies, 'Then I don t have to motivate that shot, I just have to appear in that spot when the cameras get to me.'

The Performer and the Audience

One film historian has called the actor's ability to modulate a performance according to the response of the audience "the very essence of theatrical artistry" (Chanan, 1980: 270). Obviously this aspect of the actor's art is irrelevant to TV work, though not to the actor (as one remarked in interview, "immediate audience appreciation" is "always gratefully received").

Actors do not respond to bystanders during outdoor filming or to technicians during indoor taping *as audience* since these groups are not there *for the purpose* of viewing the drama. I was told that bystanders could be intrusive or "unruly" and were thus seen by actors and production staff as potentially disruptive of carefully orchestrated scenes in public places. Similarly, actors did not play to the reactions of recording technicians since the latter were primarily concerned with following scripted directions and manipulating machinery, not with watching the dramatic performance.

Nevertheless, the actor must take account of the setting in which the audience views his work in order to pitch his performance correctly. Unlike film viewers at the cinema, TV viewers may divide their attention among the drama, commercials, and domestic concerns. For these reasons, words are more important than physically registered reactions and the "emotional curves" of the TV performance tend to be shorter, "intended for a more direct and immediate effect on the viewer" (Houseman, 1979: 25).

Finally, the fact that no audience is present means that actors can neither demonstrate *team* competence (Goffman, 1959) by projecting a credible performance throughout an entire evening nor demonstrate *individual* competence by withstanding co-actors' 'playful' attempts to make them lose control over their characterization— i.e., to 'corpse' (Taylor and Williams, 1971). It is hard to delight in staying in character without an audience before whom one risks slipping out of character.

THE SOCIAL RELATIONS OF TV DRAMA

Technicians and Actors

Compared with theater, the number of technicians needed to mount a TV production is extraordinary, whereas in order to keep production costs down, casts are usually small.[2] For example, at the read-through, the ratio of all production personnel to actors was 19.7; at the technical run which took place in the rehearsal room, 11:4; and during the outdoor filming, 42:4. Although there were too many technicians present during the studio taping for me to take an accurate count, a well known TV drama producer estimates that:

> A total count of the number of those concerned with one seventy-five minute
> 'Play for Today' studio production in 1973 would probably have reached at
> least seventy, behind the cameras alone—i.e., excluding the actors (Shubik,
> 1975: 44).

The technician is a permanent member of the TV organization while the actor is
hired on a freelance basis. Discussing the consequences of permanent/temporary staff
divisions in a TV serial, Lauritzen (1981: 43) writes that:

> such working conditions would have made for an accommodating attitude to work
> among the team members and thus possibly for a less imaginative and interesting
> production than it could have been.

Not all work groups necessary to an art work's production share the same interests and
goals as the central 'artist' (Becker, 1974: 769). Given the technicians' high stakes in
the organization and low stakes in the aesthetics of the production, it is not surprising
that the actors I interviewed felt that the technicians were very job- and union-
oriented.[3] In fact, as a result of a union dispute over the job category of continuity
person, no staff member involved in this production was officially responsible for this
task, thus posing a potential threat to the credibility of the actor's performance. The
actors viewed the technicians as the people least likely to 'bend a little' for the good
of the production. As one actor said "I don't think they're awfully interested in anything
other than the job itself, the angle of the camera or the microphone."

In these various ways, the technician's role sets the conditions for the actor's loss
of autonomy in TV. The technician is the crucial link between the actor and his audience
and the actor relies upon the technician to 'make him look good.'[4] In TV, the
technicians display the frenetic activity one ordinarily associates with acting. During
taping, they create the appearance of movement by filming the actors from different
angles for varying lengths of time while the actors *place* themselves in the appropriate
positions on the set. The actor does, however, negotiate a delicate balance of power
vis-à-vis the technicians since the technicians do need the actors' cooperation in order
to make a good recording. Two interview excerpts indicate how the actor manages to
retain a sphere of influence in TV work:

> I don't know which camera is on me half the time. There are actors who know
> exactly which camera is on them, but I prefer not to know at that moment; so, if
> I'm in half profile, that's just too bad.

> The cameraman we had before was good; the one we had on Monday night, I
> didn't like. He didn't do anything nasty or anything, but he was not—I was there
> to fit into his camera, he wasn't there to photograph what I was doing, and there
> is a distinction. And I'm not surprised that it was out of focus and we're going to
> have to do it again. In fact, I'm almost pleased.

Directors and Actors

In the early stages of rehearsal, the TV director's job is very much like the theater director's in that script interpretation must precede the fine points of staging. With a shorter rehearsal period than is usual in theater, actors and directors work efficiently in a kind of shorthand representing shared meanings. The fact that freelancers hired by TV companies tend to be experienced 'mainstream' professionals insures a high degree of role taking ability which furthers the coordination of all tasks. Such shared knowledge of script interpretation was evident in exchanges between actors and the director such as the following:

> During rehearsal, the actor comments on his own performance, saying that the scene feels 'a bit vague and fuzzy.' He suggests that in the next few explanatory lines, the main message should already have been conveyed. It feels uncomfortable because it isn't linked with the appropriate action and motivation. (Observer's notes)

As rehearsals progress, however, the director becomes more engrossed in technical details and less involved with the actors. He may start to tell them what he wants to see when the camera 'goes up'; remind them to register facial expressions quickly, before they go 'off camera'; or simply demonstrate his concern with technical matters, as one actor explained:

> In rehearsal, if I see a director move to check a shot, it can have one of two effects: if I think I'm acting very well and I see him think, 'it's not going to fit over there,' I think, he's not really looking at my acting, and I get angry. If I couldn't be bothered that afternoon, I think, oh, that's okay, he's not looking anyway. I think the best directors, you don't notice when they're checking those things.

In theater, the director views the performance from the standpoint of the audience; the actor, although involved in his role, can take the role of the audience who witnesses the play in its full visual scope. In TV, the director tries to limit his perception to the partial view afforded by the TV camera (and accomplishes this during taping by watching the monitors). But since the transmitted TV image depends on the director's choice of shots, the TV actor cannot imaginatively reconstruct the image of his actions received by the director or viewer. In a literal sense, the actor and director (and audience) lack a "reciprocity of perspectives" (Schutz, 1967: 61).

This influences actor/director interaction during the taping of the play. The actor performing before the cameras cannot always know whether the director requests a retake for technical or aesthetic reasons. The possibility of disingenuous communication between actor and director arises, as I learned during taping:

> The director feels that this take was okay except for the actor's mistake (which has clearly upset the actor). The director tells the floor manager to tell the actors that he is quite happy to have the chance to do that scene again for technical

reasons, despite the mistake. Another director who is sitting in today, watching the taping from the gallery, tells me that they always tell the actors that retakes are for technical reasons, and the actors always know this isn't true. (Observer's notes)

Even if his reasons for wanting a retake are *really* technical, the director may decide to forego the possibility of a technically better take because of the effect it may have on the actors (an inferior dramatic performance). Despite his technical concerns, then, the director must be sensitive to the art of acting. Contrary to Pudovkin's (1949: 118) characterization of the film director as someone who "never sees the actor as a real human being" but only as "the future filmic appearance", I observed the TV director subordinating technical concerns to the needs of the actors:

Towards the end of the third take, the atmosphere became very tense. They had to re-do the take for technical reasons from point B, but in fact re-did it from point A because, the director said, the actors couldn't effectively act from point B without its antecedent scene. (Observer's notes)

In general, however, the relationship between the actor and director in television is mediated, if not dominated, by technical details which are only of minimal importance in theater. Although the director tried to lessen his estrangement from the actors in the studio by relying on the floor manager as little as possible and speaking directly to the actors on the floor in order "to keep the personal contact going," such efforts did not dispel the actor's feeling that:

The television director serves his cameras well. A good director will keep you fairly unaware of his technical problems, but he has to serve someone else—and once we get into the studio, the actor is forgotten, really.

The director shared this view:

Once we get into the studio, your main attention—you're watching the performance, but not wholly watching the performance; you're looking at angles and lighting, so you have to assume that you've got the performance right before then, before you get near the studio.

Actors and Co-Actors

The form in which TV drama is presented affects the quality and quantity of interaction between actors. For example, TV drama may take the form of a single play (usually $\frac{1}{2}$ to $1\frac{1}{2}$ hours in length), a serial (a play divided into different episodes, usually with one episode broadcast each week in the same time slot) or a series (a collection of dramas which are unrelated except for the continuation of main characters and the basic background situation). The single play insures the brevity of the relationship between actors while the serial allows interaction between at least the leading actors over an extended period of time. The series will have its regulars—those actors playing central roles around which each episode is written—and its guest artists who make single appearances in particular episodes. Since the producer hires the regulars who, like himself, are involved in the entire series, while the director hires the guest artists who, like himself, are involved in particular episodes, the cast may split into factions in the event of producer/director disagreement.

The actor's awareness of the technical features of TV drama alters his relationship to fellow actors. Upstaging is less of a problem in TV since the relative importance of actors is partly determined by editing. This means that TV actors need not invest time and energy in maintaining an air of friendliness (as they do in theater), to prevent others from sabotaging their performances. Moreover, the very fact that performance mistakes can be obliterated and rectified contributes to the relative absence of tension between TV actors.[5] One member of the cast told me that, although he had never worked with any of these actors before, they all 'knew' each other, probably through seeing each other's work on TV. The passivity of performance dictated by the medium parallels the passive *knowledge* which co-actors have of one another. In fact, it is almost impossible to separate the lack of interaction between actors from the lack of intensive characterization in TV, as the two are mutually dependent.

If, as in TV, the meaning of the script is fairly clear and the nature of the characters is straightforward, then interpretive discussion during rehearsal will be minimal. The actors may fail to act *to* each other, or generate their roles through interaction; rather, they may engage in 'coordinated autism'[6], executing their roles automatically. This was evident on those occasions when the stage manager stood in for an absent actor to enable another actor to rehearse his role; the actor's rendition of his role did not vary with the substitution of a different other.

The simplicity of the script and its impact on social relations were described by the director who felt that relations between co-workers had been:

> very smooth. Mind you, it's not a highly complicated production; a lot of scenes are quite simple— domestic scenes, police officer scenes—it doesn't involve a lot of action or difficult technical shots, weird lighting or enormously flamboyant acting. It's kind of tight and there's not an awful lot of subtlety in the characters, for the most part, which is where you're liable to spend a lot of rehearsal time, if there are a lot of psychological things going on which could be interpreted in a dozen different ways. The interpretation, in this case, is what's written on the page; you speak the words and that's the situation, for the most part. Occasionally you can give it a bit deeper texture than that, but a lot of it is plain.

Agreeing with this, the actors said:

> I don't think close relationships will be made on this [production], because it's not the kind of demanding thing where people need to know each other well in order to do it.

> In television, [relationships] nearly always tend to be pleasant. You don't get crises where people's unpleasantness comes out. It's very smooth, we come in and we go home. Therefore, it tends to be easy and pleasant; there's no reason for anything

else to happen. Therefore, it can happen that you don't get to know people very
well and nobody wants to know you very well. . .

In TV, then, the actor can manage to do his job without becoming deeply involved with
his co-actors:

So far I've only worked with C. whom I like very much, we get on well. No, that's
all I can say, we get on well there's no problem.

And, he need not (or, perhaps, *cannot*) get very involved with his job:

I like the production. I'm enjoying it. That's about all.

Unless you're the lead, [the parts] only show one aspect of a character. You've got
to know the other aspects but you are not usually given an opportunity to explore,
so you're not absolutely concentrating.

The failure of TV to provide intensive characterization work for the actor
apparently underlay the actor's antipathy towards the extras who were involved in the
outdoor filming. The supposed difference between the actor and the extra is that the
actor assumes the role of a character different from himself while the extra is there to
permit the filming of a body which would be present were the dramatic situation real.
A manual for beginning actors warns that, "A lot of television acting is behaving"
(Swift, 1976:75). If this is so, the distinction between the TV actor and the extra is a
hazy one. The actors I observed reinforced this distinction on one occasion by laughing
loudly at two extras whose tennis playing was so bad that their volley had to be filmed
several times. On another occasion, one of the actors was indignant when a bystander
asked an *extra* for an autograph. Remembering that I was there to observe, one actor
remarked, "What does *this* tell you about acting? This isn't *acting!*" Other actors
echoed this view. The difference between the actor's self-label *(artist)* and official
designation in the TV script *(artiste)* is deceptively small. It disguises the far-reaching
consequences which discordant definitions of the situation have for the social organization of TV drama.

CONCLUDING REMARKS

From the interactionist perspective, social organization consists of "the collective
actions of minded individuals who are attempting to achieve goals through cooperative
actions in social situations that are constantly being interpreted by them" (Olsen, 1968:
243). Television represents a setting in which the balance between aesthetic and
commercial goals is renegotiated each time that actors, directors and production staff
join together to mount a dramatic production. The goals which individuals seek may
be varied; it would be foolish to assume that actors were only interested in pure art
and producers only in commercial success. Informing the interactions *between* participants is the interplay of goals *within* them.

The present case study indicated that the complex and formal organization of TV work tended to routinize the interaction between participants. The bureaucratic rationality which characterizes TV drama production is antithetical to the ideology of dramatic art, which includes notions of unpredictability, spontaneity and creative discovery. The social organization of TV drama was therefore shown to be one of strained intersection of distinct occupational cultures.

However, most of the features of TV drama production which I have discussed in this paper are neither technical nor social imperatives, but rather the result of consensually defined ways of working at a particular point in time. TV drama is sometimes theatrical or surrealistic, rather than naturalistic; some shows are filmed before live audiences in a continuous fashion. Conversely, some theater-trained actors find in television a set of different but equally satisfying rewards from theater.

Further research is needed to determine how representative is the view of TV drama offered here, to document variations in the social organization of TV drama which may exist at present, and to explore the consequences of these variations for the satisfaction of both creators and audiences.

NOTES

1.   The pronoun 'he' will be used throughout this paper to refer to males and females in order to avoid the more cumbersome 'he/she' form.

2.   The large casts in classic serials of recent years may appear to be an exception, but even here, Lauritzen (1981) found that the TV version of Jane Austen's *Emma* collapsed several characters from the novel into one.

3.   In his study of a TV documentary series, Elliott (1972: 129) also found that technicians concentrated on their "particular skills or task routines rather than on the programme".

4.   This contrasts with the final say the actor has in live performance; the same has been observed of studio musicians (Faulkner, 1971).

5.   I am indebted to Paul Rock for this idea.

6.   My thanks to Paul Rock for this phrase.

REFERENCES

Becker, H.S. 1974. "Art as Collective Action." *American Sociological Review* 39(6) : 767–776.
————. 1978. "Arts and Crafts." *American Journal of Sociology* 83(4): 862–889.
Billington, M. 1973. *The Modern Actor.* London: Hamish Hamilton.
Blumer, H. 1969. *Symbolic Interactionism: Perspective and Method.* Englewood Cliffs, N.J.: Prentice-Hall.
Chanan, M. 1980. *The Dream that Kicks: The Prehistory and Early Years of Cinema in Britain.* London: Routledge and Kegan Paul.
Cook, J. 1976. "Brand Loyalty." *The Guardian (London)* June 26: 8.
Elliott, P. 1972. *The Making of a Television Series: A Case Study in the Sociology of Culture.* London: Constable.
Faulkner, R.R. 1971. *Hollywood Studio Musicians: Their Work and Careers in the Recording Industry.* Chicago: Aldine-Atherton.
Fiske, J. and J. Hartley. 1978. *Reading Television.* London: Methuen.

Goffman, E. 1959. *The Presentation of Self in Everyday Life.* Garden City, N.Y.: Doubleday Anchor.

Goldman, W. 1970. *The Season: A Candid Look at Broadway.* New York: Harcourt, Brace and World.

Hood, S. 1967. *A Survey of Television.* London: Heinemann.

Houseman, J. 1979. "Is TV Acting Inferior?" *TV Guide* 27(35): 24–26.

Lauritzen, M. 1981. *Jane Austen's "Emma" on Television: A Study of a BBC Classic Serial.* Goteborg, Sweden: Gothenburg Studies in English Number 48.

Madsen, R.P. 1973. *The Impact of Film: How Ideas are Communicated through Cinema and Television.* New York: Macmillan.

Novak, M. 1975. "Television Shapes the Soul." Pp. 9–21 in D. Cater and R. Adler (eds.) *Television as a Social Force: New Approaches to TV Criticism.* New York: Praeger.

Olsen, M.E. 1968. *The Process of Social Organization.* New York: Holt, Rinehart and Winston.

Pudovkin, V.I. 1949. *Film Technique and Film Acting.* New York: Bonanza.

Schutz, A. 1967. *Phenomenology and the Social World.* Translated by G. Walsh and F. Lehnert. Evanston, Ill.: Northwestern University.

Shaw, E.T. 1979. "Pssst—Here's Hollywood's Last Little Secret! (Those Tardy Stars)." *TV Guide* 27(47): 35–41.

Shils, E. 1964. "The High Culture of the Age." Pp. 317–362 in R.N. Wilson (ed.) *The Arts in Society.* Englewood Cliffs, N.J.: Prentice-Hall.

Shubik, I. 1975. *Play for Today: The Evolution of Television Drama.* London: Davis Poynter.

Swift, C. 1976. *The Job of Acting: A Guide to Working in Theatre.* London: Harrap.

Taylor, L. and K. Williams. 1971. "The Actor and His World." *New Society* July 29: 188–190.

Williams, R. 1974. *Television: Technology and Cultural Form.* London: Fontana/Collins.

Good People Doing Dirty Work: A Study of Social Isolation

David S. Davis
University of California, Los Angeles

Everett Hughes (1964), in his essay "Good People and Dirty Work," implies that those who engage in dirty work may be defective in some way, a view that reflects society's perception of dirty workers. However, many of them perceive themselves to be good people *doing* dirty work. In this paper we examine the consequences of this disjunction between the audience's and the self's perception.

We examine members of a dirty work occupation: bailbondsmen. Many of these individuals are found to be socially isolated. This isolation is the result of their belief that they have been unjustly accused of corrupt and corrupting behavior and their desire to be seen and accepted as respectable. Rejected by members of respectable society and rejecting association with like others who may taint their attempts for respectability, they become socially isolated. Ironically, by proclaiming their innocence they, unlike their truly accused counterparts, find little social support or possibility of becoming integrated into respectable society.

INTRODUCTION

Everett Hughes in his essay "Good People and Dirty Work" writes of how the extermination of Jews in Nazi Germany was dirty work carried out by a small group of individuals so that the rest of German society, most of whom supported this activity, could remain distant from it and maintain a conception of themselves as good. Hughes implies the pathological and defective may be found among those who do the dirty work in society. Hughes (1964: 34) writes, "that we have a sufficient pool or fund of

Reprinted from Symbolic Interaction, 7(2):233–247.

personalities warped toward perverse punishment and cruelty to do any amount of dirty work that the good people may be inclined to countenance." Others have argued that stigmatized occupations attract certain kinds of individuals who, because of their psychological or social characteristics contribute to the occupation's reputation (see Saunders [1981] for discussion of this point). However, given that there is an "unwillingness to think about the dirty work done [and] complicated mechanisms by which the individual mind keeps unpleasant or intolerable knowledge from consciousness" (Hughes, 1964: 27) it could be argued that the definition of dirty workers as warped and perverse serves as a further distancing mechanism for the "good". Instead, perhaps, we should consider the possibility that many dirty workers are really no different from the good people; that they are good people *doing* dirty work. To strip them of their respectability by defining them as disrespectable (Ball, 1970) strengthens the respectability of others.

The theme of 'dirty work' has been picked up by those who study occupations (Blau, 1982; Goldman, 1981; Killian, 1981; Saunders, 1981; Simoni and Ball, 1977; Jabobs and Retsky, 1975). In particular, some sociologists have been interested in the "manner in which the socially deviant do the 'necessary' but unacknowledged 'dirty work' for the 'good people' whose respectability must keep them above such things" (Simoni and Ball, 1977: 361). The performance of what is perceived as dirty work plays a crucial part in an individual's self identity, since occupation has become the main determinant of status and prestige (Goldschalk, 1979; Hughes, 1951). Being a dirty worker can make claims to self worth difficult.

Ball (1970: 329) notes that "respectability is a central concern of actors in the problematic dramas of mundane life." Respectability is not a generic characteristic of an individual or group, but is a product of social relationships. Ball distinguishes between the *"unrespectable"* who agree with the audience's perception of them as not lacking meriting respect, and the *"disreputable"* who reject the way in which they are perceived. In this paper we examine a group of dirty workers, some of whom are *unrespectable* and some of whom are *disrespectable*. We show how these different perceptions of self result in different social consequences. In particular, there is a tendency for the *disrespectable to* become socially isolated.

There have been only a few sociologists who have examined social isolation. Lemert (1953), for instance, in his discussion of solitary check forgers finds that their lack of integration, "is reflected in self-attitudes in which many refer to themselves as 'black-sheep' or as a kind of Dr. Jeckyll-Mr. Hyde person" (p. 148). In prison, the check forger is marginal to and is isolated from the other prisoners. Similarly, Wulbert (1965) accounts for the lack of organized collective behavior in mental hospitals and the opposite in prisons by an absence of inmate pride in the former and its presence in the latter. Inmate pride for mental patients would require an acceptance of their inmate status. If, by attitude, we mean "a process of individual consciousness which determines activity" (Thomas and Znaniecki, 1918: 21–22) for both systematic check forgers and institutionalized mental patients the reason for their social isolation must be sought, in part, in their *self attitudes*.

Schneider and Conrad (1980) in their study of epileptics present their subjects as being isolated from one another. The authors state that the "very desire to lead conventional and stigma-free lives further separates and isolates them from each other" (p. 42). Here the authors intimate that the reason for their isolation must be sought in the epileptic's *attitude toward conventional society.*

Goffman (1963: 107–108) devotes a short discussion to the actor who finds it difficult to affiliate with like others:

> Whether closely aligned with his own kind or not, the stigmatized individual may exhibit identity ambivalence when he attains a close sight of his own kind behaving in a stereotyped way, flamboyantly or pitifully acting out the negative attributes imputed to them. The sight may repel him, since after all he supports the norms of the wider society, but his social and psychological identification with these offenders holds him to what repels him, transforming repulsion into shame, and then transforming ashamedness itself into something of which he is ashamed. In brief, he can neither embrace his group nor let it go.

While not socially isolated, this actor is somehow stuck between his tainted fellows and conventional society. He embraces the values and norms of conventional society, recognizes he violates them, but is repelled by his fellows. Part of the source of this ambivalence, for Goffman, is found in the actor's *attitude to like others.*

Faced with an inability to pass amidst conventional society and rejected by it, it would, from this work, appear that social isolation could result from a combination of three attitudes held by the discredited actor. First, a self attitude that the perception of himself as lacking in moral worth is unjustified; that he is not what he is said to be. Second, an attitude to like others that, to some extent, the attribution of stigma to the members of the group to which he belongs has at least some justification. Third, an attitude of acceptance toward conventional society's values and norms. Faced by rejection by members of conventional society, yet believing that he rightly belongs to it, it would make sense for the actor to reject affiliation with like others or other discredited actors when he believes them to lack respect. To associate with them would undermine his attempt to be seen as respectable. The crucial variable here is the actor's belief that he is unjustifiably being defined as a dirty worker, that he is being falsely accused. While this belief would not seem to necessarily result in social isolation, its presence would appear to increase the probability that social isolation will occur.

The following study examines a set of socially isolated stigmatized individuals and traces that adaptation to their consciousness of self as falsely accused. These individuals are bailbondsmen (also called bondsmen): those who work for a living by charging fees to get defendants out of jail prior to trial. They are contrasted with avowedly dishonest bailbondsmen (the unrespected), and compared as well with members of several other discredited occupations and statuses.

METHODS

Twenty-five bailbondsmen (one of whom was female), in and surrounding a county in a Northeastern state, were given unstructured interviews in sessions totalling from one to six hours. Two additional bondsmen in this area were intensively interviewed.

One set of these interviews lasted 26 hours over ten sessions and the other lasted 18 hours over seven sessions. In addition to the interviews, over 100 hours were spent in participant observation and observing bondsmen as they worked in their offices, court rooms and work related travel.

Using interview data, observations, and reputational data, bondsmen were classified as considering themselves "honest," meaning that engaging in dishonest, illegal, or unethical behavior as part of their routine work activities was seen by them to be rare and "dishonest," meaning that engaging in dishonest, illegal, or unethical behavior was seen by them to be part of and common to their work routine. For the latter, to have not engaged in those activities would have meant radically changing that routine. Among the dishonest activities observed and self reported by bondsmen were: the bribing of lawyers, judges and policemen; recommending lawyers to defendants; soliciting cases from lawyers; withholding security deposits from defendants; having foreknowledge of crimes; and failing to report cash receipts as income. As part of this classification procedure most of the bondsmen were asked the following question about each of the bondsmen interviewed: "Do you consider [name of bondsman] to be honest or dishonest?" Bailbondsmen also rated themselves as either honest or dishonest. There was a high degree of agreement between ratings based on interviews and observations, and the bondsmens' ratings of themselves and others (Davis, 1982). Twenty-one bondsmen were classified as "honest" and six bondsmen were classified as "dishonest". To obtain additional information about bondsmen, the author attended a state regulated bailbondsman course, became a bondsman and conducted a national mail survey of bondsmen.

The survey consisted of a random sample of 307 bailbondsmen in 48 communities around the United States. The sample was stratified by the number of bailbondsmen per community. The sampling frame was bailbondsmen advertisements in the telephone yellow pages, which yielded names of 3120 bailbondsmen. Thirty seven questionnaires were returned as "addressee unknown" and "not deliverable as addressed". Eighty one bondsmen responded for a 33 percent response rate. There was no follow up.

This survey should not be taken to constitute a reliable random sample of bailbondsmen. For one thing, the universe of bailbondsmen may be quite different from those who advertise in the yellow pages, although from this study it appears that most bailbondsmen do advertise in the yellow pages. The most systematic bias may arise from the low response rate. The survey was a source of data that supplemented the other data collected.

THE BAILBONDSMAN

The bailbondsman is an individual who, for a fee, will post bail for an accused defendant and thereby achieve that defendant's release from custody. In return the bailbondsman assumes the risk of forfeiting the entire bail amount should the defendant fail to appear for trial. There are approximately 4200 bailbondsmen in the United States (DeRhoda, 1979; Lazar Institute, 1981). The results of the mail survey indicate eighty-two percent of bondsmen are male (n = 66) and eighty-seven percent are white (n = 70). The mean age of the respondents was 47.8. Bondsmen are most likely to work alone. Thirty-three (89%, missing data = 44) of the respondents worked in low prestige jobs prior to becoming bondsmen, jobs only slightly higher in prestige than their fathers'. However, twenty-two percent (n = 8, missing data = 45) of the respondents had fathers who were bailbondsmen (Davis, 1982).

Bailbondsmen as Disrespected

Like many other occupations of low status in the occupational systems of which they are a part, the occupation of bailbondsmen lacks respect. An advocate of pawnbrokers describes the general problem of these low status occupations in the following passage (Levine, 1913: 14; see also, Hartnett, 1981):

> In every trade there are practitioners whose business methods react unfavorably upon their fellow tradesmen. Public opinion is very prone to condemn all in the trade as equally delinquent, making little discrimination between the honest and the dishonest. This attitude is one from which the pawnbroker has most unjustly suffered . . . Experience has taught them that the innocent as well as the guilty will suffer at the hands of an unthinking public.

The image of the "heavy-set, cigar chomping, sinister" (Wice, 1974: 50) bailbondsmen has never been a good one. In 1905 a former Police Chief of New York, William McAdoo (1905: 80–81) wrote about them:

> They threaten the destruction of honest police captains . . . they hound and prosecute an officer who interferes with their schemes or lessens their profits; they drive good and honest policemen into being bad ones; they have a price for every man on the force . . . The sergeant at the desk is often only their tool; and the Captain and his plainclothesmen and other officers have in many cases made arrests only to furnish victims and money for these unspeakable scoundrels. There should be a law against the professional bondsman.

Most of what has been written about bondsmen emerges from both a reform minded perspective and the journalistic muckraking tradition. These approaches seek to present the occupation as dysfunctional for the criminal justice system and the bailbondsman as corrupt and criminal. Goldfarb (1965: 101–102), for instance, pictures bondsmen as:

> . . . undesirable persons, former felons, and generally repugnant characters. Some bondsmen are colorful Runyonesque characters. Some are legitimate business-men. But too many are "lowlifes" whose very presence contaminates the business profession . . . (V)ery frequently, if not generally, the bailbondsman is an unap-pealing and useless member of society. He lives on the law's inadequacy and his fellowmen's troubles. He gives nothing in return, or so little as to serve no overriding utilitarian purposes.

The bailbond system is seen to be corrupted by the individuals who become bail-bondsmen. This corruption then spreads to other parts of the criminal justice system. Similar views have been echoed by investigatory committees (for instance, see U.S. Task Force on Law Enforcement, 1970), newspapers and magazines (for instance, see the recent expose in *Cleveland Plain Dealer* [1980] and other authors: see Roth, 1962; Breslin, 1963; Freed and Wald, 1964; Foote, 1966; Barnes, 1969; Smith and Ehrmann, 1974; Thomas, 1976). Bailbondsmen have been the constant object of vilifying attacks and moral crusades. Smith and Ehrmann (1974: 36, 36) wrote that, "the real evil in the [bail] situation is not the matter of easy bail, but the disreputable bondsman . . . so far as it may be impossible to eliminate the professional bondsman, his business should be regulated like that of the 'Loan Sharks' in many jurisdictions." The *Cleveland Plain Dealer* (1980) presented bailsbondsmen as "parasites who feed off the misfortunes of others." They, "feed on legal system, get fat on misery."

Bailsbondsmen possess what Saunders (1981: 43) has defined as occupational stigma.

> Occupational stigma is a discrediting attribute accorded to individuals or groups who are performing certain occupationally identifiable roles . . . by other individu-als or groups within a community, representing an actual threat to full social acceptance for the socially disgraced (by reason of their work function) who are perceived as negatively departing from the work norm of those engaged in 'respectable' occupational activities.

Awareness of Stigma

Bailbondsmen believe that conventional society perceives them as odious and they believe conventional society rejects association with them as a consequence of that perception. Both bailbondsmen who considered themselves to be respectable businessmen and those who consider themselves justly accused evinced this belief.[1] As one bondsman who considered himself to be falsely accused responded to the mail survey:

> Bailbondsmen, unlike other professionals, must start out with the opinion that they are crooks. It is a near impossibility for a bondsman, no matter how honest he is, to prove he is an honest businessman.

Another bondsman responded in an interview saying, "When people know you are a bondsman they don't want you in their house."

Workers in other dirty work occupations reveal a similar awareness. A garbage-man interviewed in Perry's (1978: 108) study of his occupation reported the following:

> People don't want to have anything to do with you. They ask you what you do. You tell them, and they right away think you make so much money. It's . . . okay, but it's not more than they get . . . Maybe it is all in my head, but it seems like they go to the other side of the street if they see you coming.

In another study of garbagemen, Saunders (1981: 32) reports one as saying, "I know chaps who change their clothes because they do not want their neighbors to know what work they do." And Bleackley (1929: xviii) describes the particular stigma of the hangman:

> (T)he necessity to perform unpleasant duties in other walks of life does not involve a social stigma. The occupations of the dentist and the dustman, the butcher, the sanitary inspector and the man midwife are frequently of an unsavory description and yet we do not ostracize these persons in consequence. The surgeon kills many more people every year than 'Jack Ketch,' but the reason we refrain from placing him beyond the pale is not because, unlike the hangman's work, it is not done on purpose. He happens to belong to a trade that is not taboo whereas 'Jack Ketch' does not.

Attitude to and Association with Like Others

Structurally, the relationship between bondsmen is primarily a competitive one, as they compete for a limited number of bailbonds within a geographically defined area. This may account, in part, for the antipathy between them. However, this antipathy is not universal. It is manifested, for the most part, by those bondsmen who consider themselves to be respectable and honest. As two of these bondsmen said:

> Ali Baba and his forty thieves would rank second to other bondsmen.

> Most bondsmen are shit. They have no morals. They are not stand up straight guys. Half of them aren't worth a damn.

Interaction between these bondsmen was limited to the requirements of their work. Indicative, was the comment of one in an interview:

> Look, I don't like to have too much to do with them [bondsmen]. I like to be around a better class of people if they'll let me.

This contrasted with the six bailbondsmen classified as "dishonest" who were interviewed and observed. They did not show antipathy to like others. Two of these six bailbondsmen were good friends. They each spoke about seeing each other socially outside the work setting. They also, upon occasion, participated in illegal activities together. An additional two of these bondsmen spoke of being friendly with other bondsmen (in other counties). None of the six bondsmen was averse to associating with other bondsmen.

Although bondsmen represent a discredited group which is the frequent object of attack by respectable society, organizations of bondsmen to counter these attacks appear to be rare, have low membership, and little commitment from most members (Davis, 1982). None of the bondsmen interviewed were members of such an organization.

The falsely accused bondsman, while recognizing individual bondsmen as respectable, attempts to separate himself from bondsmen as a whole. He sees himself as a particularly respectable businessman. Dishonest bondsmen on the other hand, tend to see themselves and other bondsmen as quite alike. One said, "We are in this boat together—all part of the swill."

Browne (1973: 58) found a similar response among used car salesmen who, "are quick to point out the difference between themselves and their kind of operation as contrasted with other used car salesmen and their less scrupulous, less honest kind of operation." This is despite the fact that Browne (p. 58) finds that "(t)hey are almost always operating well within the law. . . ." Similarly, an 18th century writer (Anonymous, 1745: 4) describes pawnbrokers as rejecting association with others. They are "a Sett of Men that never associate with any other tradesmen. . . ."

Bailbondsmen have the opportunity to affiliate with discredited individuals apart from other bondsmen; clients of bondsmen and their acquaintances. However the falsely accused bondsmen interviewed and observed distanced themselves from their clients and their world. As one of these bondsmen said:

> To me it's strictly business. I don't want to be bothered by people like that. I wouldn't want them in my home either. It happens to be a lousy business I am in.

And another remarked:

> They're [clients] the lowest of the low. I wouldn't go near them except to get their money or help them.

By contrast, five of the six avowedly dishonest bondsmen were firmly enmeshed in a social network consisting of individuals who engaged in criminal activity on a frequent basis. Their relationships with them were both of a business and social nature.

Gold (1964: 27) describes attitudes among janitors that are very similar to those of "disrespectable" bondsmen:

> Janitors are keenly aware of their occupation's lowly reputation in the community. Yet, as individuals, they develop self-conceptions of the sort that ordinarily would be found in members of established middle-class occupations. How, then, does the janitor reconcile his self conceptions with corresponding social conceptions of janitors? He uses a simple, clear-cut device. After comparing himself with occupational associates, he tends to agree that the community is right in its evaluation of *them,* but that *he* is "different." He agrees that other janitors are unprincipled, disorderly, and irresponsible. However, he, the individual janitor, belongs to the category of practitioners who are morally sound, capable, and responsible.

Attitude to and Association with Conventional Society

Bailbondsmen routinely encounter rejection from respectable society. Bailbondsmen have described how this rejection may occur in the workplace:

> Judges think bondsmen are lower than whale shit. They think we socialize with criminals. A judge would never lower himself to talk to a bondsman.

And outside the workplace:

> When people know you are a bondsman they don't want you in their house.

Pine (1977: 38), in his study of funeral directors has found a similar tendency for them to be rejected:

> Another problem for funeral directors is the occasional banning of funeral homes from certain community areas. Even in the absence of zoning regulations, funeral homes have been closed or forced to move when they were offensive to neighbors in residential areas. Also troublesome is that the funeral home ban may extend to the funeral director himself . . . (F)uneral directors have been denied membership in organizations solely because of their occupation.

The falsely accused bailbondsman is aware of how he is perceived by respectable society. Respectable society forms, in a sense, the bailbondsman's "looking glass self" (Cooley, 1964: 183–184). He believes respectable society both perceives him and judges him as dishonest and sleazy. But respectable society also forms his normative reference group. It is with them that he identifies and aspires to belong. To condemn conventional society as being as evil as the bailbondsman would be to corrupt his own aspiration to be accepted as respectable; it would bring him closer to the world of the stigmatized which he shuns. Rather he aligns himself with respectable society. The falsely accused sees respectable society as no better than he is and at the same time compares himself favorably to it. Thus he not only points to the illegal activities of respectable people, but, in addition, sees his normal work activities on an equal footing with high status occupations. As one respondent wrote to illustrate the first point that dirty workers are to be found in all occupations:

> I would suggest there are so many bad apples in other professions except a couple of educators used federal money to lobby and defame the profession (of bondsmen) because of some unethical men. There are many excellent men in the field. There are many excellent men in the field that are outstanding citizens. There are bad insurance agents, bad salesmen, bad students, just bad plain citizens, and bad politicians . . . There are many corrupt police, courts, and other enforcement people, and the percentage is fairly high from what I see.

And in demonstrating the second point, that bailbonding is not dirty work, another respondent wrote:

> It must be remembered that we are normally well educated and well versed in many professions. We, to operate successfully, must have in many respects the knowledge of attorneys, police officers, investigators, collection agencies, car salesmen, court clerks, judges and loan officers and bankers.

The falsely accused bailbondsman justifies his work as socially valuable. He sees himself as a good person *doing* dirty work. A bailbondsman said:

> I feel that having bailbondsmen are a service to the community because all persons that are locked up cannot make a bond. And we try to be selective, but be kind where there is reason, even though persons may be involved with drugs, alcohol, and other habits. We also save the taxpayer money when he does not show in court. We stand the loss and have to find the missing person, and keep a record of those that do not show, and will see that other bondsmen will not take the same person out.

The falsely accused bondsman embraces conventional values of honesty, compassion, monetary success, professionalism. In interviews falsely accused bondsmen remarked:

> I treat my business as a career and handle it with care, compassion and brains. The reason I became a bondsman was there wasn't any here. Lots of blacks were getting arrested and nobody seemed to care. I got into it as a civil thing. This was a good will thing. I made money too.

> We all know that it's for the dollars . . . You must be honest with the person, go according with the law, be honest with yourself.

Like the janitors described in Gold's (1964) study, the bailbondsman's "conceptions of himself are thoroughly wrapped up in his work. He is aware that society judges him, and that he judges himself, largely by the work he does. He is consciously trying to achieve higher status through public recognition of higher work status" (p. 21).

Social Isolation

The falsely accused bondsmen tend to lead lives of social isolation. Following Seeman's (1972) definition of social isolation, these bondsmen have a "low expectancy for inclusion and social acceptance, expressed typically in feelings of loneliness or feelings of rejection and repudiation."

These feelings have been detailed earlier in the paper. But there are other indicators of social isolation that we can point to. Only five of the twenty-one falsely accused bondsmen said they were members of community organizations, although, only two were active members. When I asked a bondsman why he was not a member of any organization he said:

> First of all, I haven't got the time for such stuff. Then I tried joining one once but they didn't like the idea of a bondsman being a member, I guess.

We find that for the falsely accused bondsman work activities are structured so that very little time is available for non-work activity:

> What social contacts do you make? A college professor meets people that is his equal or better than you. You don't have to worry about your social life. If a

bailbondsman wants to have a clean life and not associate with these people, he's limited. And then your time, you're working so many hours that you don't have time to go out and socialize. Your life passes you by and what do you end up with?

The twenty-one falsely accused bailbondsmen studied worked a mean of 76 hours a week. The six dishonest bailbondsmen worked, as bailbondsmen, a mean of 36 hours a week.

Many of the avowedly dishonest bondsmen saw their work as bondsmen as less central to their overall activities. One individual, for instance, could be said to have become a bondsman because of his involvement with others in criminal activity. He was active in many illegal activities prior to becoming a bondsman (fencing cars, running numbers, and gambling). Many of his friends and associates were also engaged in these and other illegal activities. He saw becoming a bondsman as an opportunity to make money regardless of whether it was done legally. His contacts with criminals, he believed would be useful to him. Three of these bondsmen professed to have grown up with others who routinely engaged in criminal activity. The first job of one of these individuals prior to becoming a bondsman was to pay off bondsmen and lawyers for professional criminals who wanted cases fixed and for other services. Another commented, "The only people I knew were criminals."[2] As bondsmen, except for social isolation, immersion in a stigmatized subculture remained their most viable option. As one of these bondsmen commented during an interview:

> You know, I got my friends: car thieves, robbers, bad guys. But that's all I got. I'm stuck with them and they're stuck with me.

Unlike the falsely accused bondsmen, it is not respectable society that is their reference group, but the world peopled by professional and petty criminals. The falsely accused bondsman finds it difficult to join or embrace the straight world because it often will not have him. Yet to embrace the world of the stigmatized is not a solution either. To associate with his fellow bondsmen (some of whom are dishonest and all of whom are generally believed to be dishonest) would be to confirm and strengthen, in the eyes of his audience, their original evaluation of him, thus furthering the difficulty of becoming respectable. The falsely accused bondsman does not feel he is doing anything wrong. Rather, he feels wronged. The image he presents of himself as respectable clashes with the way he believes he is viewed by respectable society. Rather than immersing himself in a stigmatized subculture or forming, with other bondsmen, a subculture of the stigmatized or an organization of the stigmatized (solutions that would belie his self image of respectability) he often chooses social isolation.

Occupants of similarly disparaged work roles also report feelings of social isolation. Sanson the executioner (1881: xii, 19) describes his life in Paris:

> I have lived for twelve years under a name which is not mine, reaping with something like shame the friendship and good will which I constantly fear to be dispelled by the discovery of my former avocations. . . . A glance at (my ancestor)

was sufficient to identify him as the executioner; men, women, and children recoiled from him.

In an 1924 pamphlet an anonymous writer describes the plight of the pawnbroker (Anonymous, 1824):

> Perhaps no class of men ever were greater sufferers from this cause (that honorable people dislike them) than the persons I am advocating. Owing to it, their personal intercourse, and friendly communication with society have been interrupted; clouds of suspicion have been raised without any cause, and evils believed which never existed.
>
> Their profession has been deemed dishonorable—their hearts callous—their sentiments illiberal; and, though I may be bold to say, many of them, in their walk of life, have been and are, considered persons of the most irreproachable character, yet the excellency of their conduct scarcely ever did more than remove the odium from themselves in the general circle to which they are confined, while the general prejudice has grown stronger from age, and more inveterate by repetition.

Similarly, Saunders (1981) in his study of lower grade workers in service organizations found that janitors and nightwatchmen are often isolates.

There were good reasons why many of the falsely accused bondsmen became socially isolated. Some of these reasons arise from the structure of the occupation itself which limits available options. Because bondsmen constantly have clients "out on the street" it is difficult to stop being a bondsman once one has become established in the occupation. Thus, it is difficult to resume or assume the role of the conformist.[3] At the same time, to pursue a livelihood as a bondsman, the individual must make it known that he is one; to advertise himself. This makes "passing" a difficult option to pursue. In addition, although there is some degree of cooperation between bondsmen, it is essentially a highly competitive business. Often resources are scarce and demand is low. Bondsmen also often work alone or in small partnerships. This may be less a result of animosity than economic rationality. As Robinson (1935: 50) has argued, in conditions where there is a high degree of uncertainty, small firms are likely to be more successful than large ones. Organizational alliances become difficult to forge under these circumstances. However, these structural reasons cannot be seen as sufficient explanations for the social isolation of the falsely accused bondsman. As we pointed out, there are good reasons why we should expect organizations of bondsmen to form. In addition, we have seen that their dishonest counterparts are not socially isolated. The social isolation of the falsely accused is an adaptation to their dilemma of believing themselves to be respectable, desiring to be perceived and accepted as respectable, and encountering rejection from respectable society.

CONCLUSION

The social categories to which bailbondsmen, janitors, garbagemen, the mentally ill, and others belong are stigmatized. That is, these individuals by virtue of their embership in these social categories are perceived as blemished and defective. Further, as a result of this perception, they encounter rejection by conventional society. Rather than accept this view of themselves some of them attempt to be and define themselves as respectable and conformist. The falsely accused's knowledge and perception that like others may be engaged in discrediting behavior may make him wary of association with other members he believes may bring ill repute upon him in his quest for respectability. Given structural conditions that make other forms of adaptation (neutralization, passing, and "rehabilitation") difficult, this may result in his social isolation between conventional and stigmatized worlds.

Stonequist (1942: 297), in his discussion of the marginal man, alludes to a similar phenomenon:

> The marginal man is the individual who lives in, or has ties of kinship with, two or more interacting societies between which there exists sufficient incompatibility to render his own adjustment to them difficult or impossible.

The social isolate is this marginal man. His isolation is made possible by three elements: 1) rejection or hostility from conventional society; 2) a belief on the part of the actor that he is being unjustly excluded from that society; and 3) an attitude toward like others and other stigmatized individuals that sees them as rightfully rejected.

We can see that if the actor can see like others as sharing in what he sees as his injustice that he may likely affiliate with them. One has only to point to the many organizations of discredited groups. But for each of these groups there are probably individuals who lie outside and isolated from them. While among Jews there are countless organizations and subcultural supports there is still the Wandering Jew (Stonequist, 1942: 307):

> They (the individual marginal Jew) . . . are divided in their social allegiance, drawn forward by the Gentile world but uncertain of its hospitality, restrained by sentiments of loyalty to the Jewish world but repelled by its restrictions. They are self-conscious and feel inferior because their social status is in question. They are the partly assimilated, the partly accepted, the real Wandering Jews, at home neither in the ghetto nor in the world outside the ghetto.

Believing oneself to be falsely accused and isolating oneself from like others and discredited others results in a paradoxical and ironic situation. If being truly accused is likely to result in affiliation with stigmatized others in a situation where one is provided with social support, believing oneself to be falsely accused may result in a social role that lacks social support. The actor who considers himself "innocent" may suffer isolation as a result. The actor who considers himself correctly stigmatized may find himself in a more positive social position. Further, this social isolation makes it more difficult to neutralize the stigma and, at the same time, makes it easier to stigmatize the actor. The inability of the falsely accused bailbondsmen to organize and protest the attributions made against them in turn, made it easier for the attributions to be made regardless of their validity.

This conception of self and its relationship to others can be seen to have a direct bearing on the very creation of stigma; who, how, and why some individuals and groups are successfully discredited. Under some circumstances (for instance when members of a group are competing with one another) it may be easier to discredit certain groups of individuals when those individuals *deny* the validity of that definition. Denial of stigma may then result in increased difficulty in neutralizing the stigma.

ACKNOWLEDGMENTS

I would like to acknowledge the substantive comments of Robert Scott as well as the comments and editorial suggestions of Gary Alan Fine, Michael Radelet, and Harold Finestone. This study was prepared with the partial support of the National Institute of Mental Health (USPHS-MH14538) and the National Institute of Handicapped Research (NIHR-G00806802) although neither agency is responsible for the views presented.

NOTES

1.   While most members of the public may have only a superficial knowledge of bailbondsmen, the bailbondsman is in daily association with those individuals in part responsible for creating their disparaged image.

2.   These bondsmen can be seen in one way as the archetypal deviant who is immersed in a subculture. However, they also illustrate the problem with that literature: the difficulty in determining whether their immersion in a deviant subculture was an adaptation to social reaction or a factor in producing their initial rule breaking.

3.   Gold (1964: 43) found that for similar reasons janitors who see retirement "as the termination of distasteful work . . . rarely reach their goal."

REFERENCES

Anonymous. 1745. *A Plain Answer To a late Pamphlet, Entitled The Business of Pawnbroking Stated and Defended.* London: George Woodfall.

Anonymous. 1824. *An Apology for the Pawnbrokers Most Respectfully Addressed to the Members of Both Houses of Parliament, the Judges of the Land and the Justices of the Peace Throughout the Kingdom.* Leadenhall Street: S. McDowell.

Ball. D.W. 1970. "The Problematics of Respectability." Pp. 326–371 in J.D. Douglas (ed.) *Deviance and Respectability: The Social Construction of Moral Meanings.* New York: Basic.

Barnes, F. 1969. "The Professional Bondsman: Life Isn't What It Used To Be." *Sunday Magazine, Washington Star,* August 17.

Blau, J. 1982. "Prominence in a Network of Communication: Work Relations in a Children's Psychiatric Hospital." *Sociological Quarterly* 23: 235–251.

Bleackley, H. 1929. *The Hangmen of England.* London: Chapman and Hall.

Breslin, J. 1963. "Best Bet for Bail: A Good Crook." *Life* (March 23): 15–16

Browne, J. 1973. *The Used-Car Game: A Sociology of the Bargain.* Lexington, Mass.: Heath.

Cooley, C.H. 1964. *Human Nature and the Social Order.* New York: Schocken Books.

Cleveland Plain Dealer. 1980. "Bailbondsmen Here Feed on Legal System, Get Fat on Misery." August 3, Section A: I.

Davis, D.S. 1982. *Deviance and Social Isolation: The Case of the Falsely Accused.* Unpublished Ph.D. dissertation, Princeton University.

DeRhoda. 1979. "Whither the Bailbondsman." *Law Journal* 1: 19.

Foote, C. (ed.) 1966. *Studies in Bail.* Philadelphia: University of Pennsylvania Press.

Freed, D. and P. Wald. 1964. "Bail in the United States: 1964." Working Papers for the National Conference on Bail and Criminal Justice, Washington, D.C.

Goffman, E. 1963. *Stigma.* Englewood Cliffs, N.J.: Prentice-Hall.

Gold, R.L. 1964. "In the Basement—The Apartment-building Janitor." Pp. 1–49 in P. Berger (ed.) *The Human Shape of Work.* New York: McMillan.

Goldfarb, R. 1965. *Ransom: A Critique of the American Bail System.* New York: Harper and Row.

Goldman, M.S. 1981. "Book Review of Robert Prus and Styllianos Irini, Hookers; Rounders, and Desk Clerks: The Social Organization of a Motel Community." *Sociology of Work and Occupations* 8: 381–384.

Goldschalk, J.J. 1979. "Foreign Labour and Dirty Work." *The Netherlands' Journal of Sociology* 15: 1–11.

Harnett, C. 1981. "The Pawnbroker: Banker of the Poor?" Pp. 149–155 in I.L. Barak-Glantz and C. Ronald Huff (eds.) *The Mad, the Bad, and the Different: Essays in Honor of Simon Dinitz.* Lexington, Mass.: Lexington Books.

Hughes, E.C. 1951. "Work and Self. "Pp. 313–323 in J.H. Rohrer and M. Sherif (eds.) *Social Psychology at the Crossroads.* New York: Harper.

———. 1964. "Good People and Dirty Work." Pp. 23–26 in H. Becker (ed.) *The Other Side.* New York: Free Press.

Jacobs, J.B. and H.C. Retsky. 1975. "Prison Guard." *Urban Life* 4: 5–29.

Killian, L.M. 1981. "The Sociologists Look at the Cuckoo's Nest: The Misuse of Ideal Types." *The American Sociologist* 16: 230–239.

Lazar Institute. 1981. Advisory Panel Meeting on Bail Bonding Study. Washington, D.C., April 10.

Lemert, E. 1953, "An Isolation Closure Theory of Check Forgery." *Journal of Criminal Law, Criminology, and Public Science* 44(3): 296–307.

Levine, S. 1913. *The Business of Pawnbroking: A Guide and a Defense.* New York: D. Halpern.

McAdoo, W. 1905. *Guarding a Great City.* New York: Harper.

Perry, S.E. 1978. *San Francisco Scavengers: Dirty Work and the Pride of Ownership.* Berkeley: University of California Press.

Pine, V. 1977. *Caretaker of the Dead: The American Funeral Director.* New York: Irvington.

Robinson, E. 1935. *The Structure of Competitive Industry.* London: Nisbet.

Roth, J. 1962. "Bondsman Looks Back Wistfully to Days of Reliable Criminals." *New York Times* (September 20): 35.

Sanson, Henry (ed.) 1881. *Memoirs of the Sansons.* Picadilly: Chatto and Windus.

Saunders, C. 1981. *Social Stigma of Occupations: The Lower Grade Worker in Service Organizations.* Westmead: Gower.

Schneider, J. and P. Conrad. 1980. "In the Closet with Illness: Epilepsy, Stigma Potential and Information Control." *Social Problems* 28(1): 32–44.

Seeman, M. 1972. "Alienation and Engagement." Pp. 467–527 in A. Campbell and P.E. Converse (eds.) *The Human Meaning of Social Change.* New York. Russell Sage.

Simoni, J.J. and R.A. Ball. 1977. "The Mexican Medicine Huckster: He Must Be Doing Something Right." *Sociology of Work and Occupations* 4: 343–365.

Smith, R.H. and H.B. Ehrmann. 1974. "The Municipal Court in Cleveland." Pp 26–59 in J. Robertson (ed.) *Rough Justice: Perspectives on Lower Criminal Courts.* Boston: Little Brown.

Stonequist, E. 1942. "The Marginal Character of the Jews." in I. Graeber and S. Brett (eds.) *Jews in a Gentile World: The Problems of Anti-Semitism.* Westport, Conn.: Greenwood.

Thomas, W. 1976. *Bail Reform in America.* Berkeley: University of California Press.

Thomas. W.I. and F. Znaniecki. 1918. *The Polish Peasant in Europe and America, Vol 1.* Chicago: University of Chicago Press.

U.S Task Force on Law and Law Enforcement. 1970. *The Rule of Law: An Alternative to Violence.* Nashville: Aurora Publishers.

Wice, P. 1974. *Freedom for Sale: A National Study of Pretrial Release.* Lexington, Mass.: Lexington Books.

Wulbert, R. 1965. "Inmate Pride in Total Institutions." *American Journal of Sociology* 71(1): 1–9.

Actors in Search of a Character: Student Social Workers' Quest For Professional Identity

Donileen R. Loseke
Spencer E. Cahill
Skidmore College

This article presents a case study of the professional socialization of neophyte social workers. Drawing primarily upon interviews of the 14 members of a senior class in an accredited social work program, the article presents an analysis of student interns' attempts to dramatically realize the occupational identity of social worker. Contrasts between their experiences and the experiences of student doctors are stressed in order to illustrate the reflexive relationship between the historical and the biographical processes of professionalization.

> . . . a status, a position, a social place is not a material thing to be
> possessed and then displayed . . . it is. . . something that must be
> enacted and portrayed, something that must be realized.
>
> Erving Goffman (1959, p. 74)

Professional socialization involves somewhat more than the acquisition of specialized knowledge and the internalization of professional values. In their studies of medical students, Jack Haas and William Shaffir (1977, 1982b) have empirically demonstrated that professionalization is a type of activity in which the management of impressions is basic. In order for neophytes to realize the occupational identity to which they aspire, they must "become good and self-confident actors by mastering increasingly difficult performance situations" (Haas and Shaffir, 1982b, p. 187). In other words, they must

Reprinted from Symbolic Interaction, 9(2):245–258.
Copyright © 1986, 1992 by JAI Press Inc. All rights of reproduction in any form reserved.
ISBN: 1-55938-551-0

dramatically convince both others and themselves that they possess the expertise and the personal qualities that are the defining characteristics of occupational incumbents' official image of themselves. The result of this process might best be described as a "conversion" to a new view of self (Haas and Shaffir, 1977).

Although neophytes' attempts to realize an occupational identity are seldom pursued without trauma and perils, they no doubt face qualitatively different challenges depending on the particular occupational identity to which they aspire. This article analyzes student social workers' attempts to realize the identity of "social worker" and contrasts their experiences to those of medical students (Becker and Geer, 1958; Becker et al., 1961; Haas and Shaffir, 1977, 1982a, b). Whereas medical students attempt to realize the occupational identity to which they aspire by self-consciously managing impressions, social workers' official image of themselves is antithetical to the idea of dramaturgy. Thus, unlike medical students, neophyte social workers must attempt to dramatically realize an occupational identity without self-consciously doing so. In addition, this contrast suggests that the historical and biographical processes of "professionalization" are reflexively related. The difficulties faced by these students in realizing the identity of social worker reflect the difficulties that the occupation itself has encountered in claiming the status of a profession.

DRAMATURGICAL BACKGROUND

Since the emergence of social work as a paid occupation in the early 1900s, there has been considerable debate over whether this occupation qualifies as a profession. In the United States, the Council on Social Work Education has gained the authority to certify programs of study leading to the Bachelor's (BSW), Master's (MSW), and Doctor (DSW) of Social Work degrees,[1] but social workers have had little success in restricting access to social work practice to those who hold degrees from such accredited programs of study. In stark contrast to the more established professions, which require practitioners to hold specific educational credentials, the majority of practicing social workers do not hold social work degrees (Bell, 1983; Ruzak, 1973).

Another reason for the continuing debate about whether social work qualifies as a profession is that social workers have never effectively claimed a distinctive area of expertise or practice. Among other things, the theoretical foundation of social work practice has been described as "rules of thumb" (Wilensky and Lebeaux, 1965), a "patchwork borrowed from the social sciences" (Greenwood, 1981), and "intellectually hollow" (Richan and Mendelsohn, 1973). In the words of two sympathetic critics, "in every area where social workers claim some expertise, there are others who are more expert" (Richan and Mendelsohn, 1973, pp. 46–47). Moreover, practicing social workers are employed by a wide variety of both public and private organizations, they serve clientele as different as public school students and prison inmates, and they are engaged in such diverse activities as "individual counseling," "community organizing," and "public policy planning" (Gurin and Williams, 1973). In other words, practicing social workers do not share common educational backgrounds, distinct world views, set of skills, type of clientele, or similar occupational environments. It is hardly surprising that public conceptions of social work are "foggy" at best (Condie et al., 1978). Indeed, even the *Encyclopedia of Social Work* fails to provide a definition of its topic.

In any case, social workers are accorded less respect and prestige than are members of the more established professions.[2] For example, many laypersons consider practicing social workers "do-gooders," "bleeding hearts," "meddlers" (Clearfield, 1977; Ruzak, 1973) or unattractive women with their heads in the clouds and their hands in the public purse (Condie et al., 1978). When given a choice, most individuals say that they would prefer to discuss their problems with someone other than a social worker (Condie et al., 1978). In brief, unlike those who are preparing for careers in the more established professions, neophyte social workers must attempt to realize an occupational identity that is neither clearly defined nor generally respected.

The Players

This study draws upon the experiences of undergraduate student interns in social work. More specifically, it is based on interviews and essays written by a 14-member senior class in an accredited BSW program at a small, private liberal arts college. The members of this class were formally interviewed near the end of the first semester of their senior year. Their responses to a series of open-ended questions such as "do you consider yourself a social worker" and "what does it take to be a social worker" were tape-recorded. In addition, some of these students were also informally interviewed, and a number of essays written by them were obtained.

In many important respects, these students were similar to students enrolled in other BSW programs. For example, they were young (21–23 years old), primarily female (85%), and four of the 14 (31%) were members of minority groups (three blacks and one Hispanic). In papers written during their junior year, all of these students wrote of being drawn to social work because of their desires to "positively touch the lives of others," to "help people feel good" or to "help people achieve their full potential." As previous research has shown, individuals are typically drawn to careers in social work for similar reasons (e.g., Gartner, 1976; Gertzel, 1983; Rosenberg, 1957). Like others who pursue such a career, however, these students' motives were not totally altruistic (Lubove, 1965). Without exception, they noted that they expected to achieve "personal growth," "self-understanding," "self-fulfillment," or "personal happiness" through helping others. Indeed, some of these students noted that such intangible rewards would compensate for the low pay and prestige they fully expected to receive from their chosen career.

Finally, like those who pursue careers in a variety of "semiprofessions," social work was not the first career choice for many of these students.[3] For example, one student said she wanted to be a doctor but failed an introductory biology course, whereas another said she chose a major in social work because it seemed to provide an "easier route" to a professional status than did a major in psychology.

The Stages

Like other accredited BSW programs, the particular program in which these students were enrolled required senior students to participate in an internship program for which they received academic credit, the so-called field practicum. According to most social work educators, the field practicum is the most important component of social work education. It is this experience that is supposed to complete the process whereby students are transformed into the type of persons social work practitioners are expected to be.

> [T]he students are to be purged of feelings, attitudes, biases and prejudices inappropriate to the social work profession.... The supervisor performs casework functions vis-à-vis the trainees. . . . enabling them to develop skills, but more importantly, to influence attitudes, affect philosophies and develop maturity. (Gardner, 1976, p. 152)

In other words, the field instructor—a practicing social worker—is expected to do more than help students acquire technical skills. His/her primary responsibility is to "purge" the student of those beliefs, feelings, and patterns of behavior that are inconsistent with social workers' official image of themselves and thereby transform the student into a professional social worker.

In accordance with the guidelines established by the Council on Social Work Education, each of the students on which this study is focused was required to work 14 hours a week during the fall and 21 hours a week during the spring semester at an assigned agency without pay. During the junior year each student had submitted a resume and an essay concerning the types of social work practice he/she would prefer to the "field coordinator," a member of the social work faculty. The field coordinator then assigned each student to a local service agency. For a variety of reasons, students were not always pleased with their field assignment.[4] The 12 agencies to which these 14 students were assigned, however, reflected the diversity of stages on which practicing social workers typically perform their occupational identity. These included a hospital, an elementary school, a medium-security prison, a psychiatric halfway house, a juvenile detention center, a home for the elderly, community outreach programs, and counseling centers. Like veteran social workers, these interns were participating in a variety of situated activity systems (Goffman, 1961) and were performing a number of specific roles. For example, they were engaged in such diverse activities as community organizing, client advocacy, educational testing, dispute mediation, and various types of "counseling." They also served a variety of different types of clients such as the elderly, single mothers, public school students, prisoners, hospital patients, and so-called drug and alcohol abusers.

The diversity of stages, parts, and audiences encountered by these students produced two immediate consequences. First, the common identity of "social work student" that they had developed over the course of their prior academic training quickly dissolved during the field practicum. In contrast to student doctors who tend to accumulate similar experiences in the course of their professional socialization, these student social workers found that their individual experiences were too dissimilar to sustain a common identity. Indeed, many of these student interns complained that they no longer even spoke the same language.

> I've tried to talk to students . . . most people don't understand what I'm talking about. They don't understand the terms.

> Sometimes people use terminology that they have to explain because you don't know what they're talking about.

As a result, these students did not have the benefit of a "collegial performance team" (Goffman, 1959, pp. 162–166) to which they could turn for guidance and support in their individual efforts to dramatically realize the identity of social worker.

Second, many students complained that the characteristics of their particular field assignments did not provide them with opportunities to realize the identity of social worker. For example, one student described her work as a community organizer as similar to arranging a church social, and "since anyone can do that," she maintained that it was not social work. Another who worked with involuntary clients maintained that because social work depended on "open lines of communication with clients," she too was not engaged in actual social work. Similarly, another student considered "one-on-one counseling" an essential component of social work, and so her work as a client advocate did not qualify. Yet another complained that all she did in her capacity as a student intern was "really" bureaucratic record keeping and not social work. In brief, most of these students considered their particular field assignments inappropriate in that, for one reason or another, they felt that they were not engaged in "real" social work. It is clear that these students' assessments of their internships suggest that they had at least some vague conception of what constituted "real" social work or, in more dramaturgical language, of what constituted an effective portrayal of the occupational identity to which they aspired.

Preparation for the Part

Whatever the source of these students' conceptions of "real" social work, it is doubtful that it was based on direct experience. With only one exception, each of these students had previously held only one or two summer jobs that bore any resemblance to social work practice, most often as either a "camp counselor" or a clerical worker in a social service agency. In other words, these students had little direct knowledge of social work practice prior to the fieldwork practicum.[5]

Like other social work students (Mahler, 1982), the students in this study also found that their prior academic training was of little use to them in their capacity as neophyte social workers.

> I think I'm still realizing that both the content and process that I've learned are totally unrelated to both the process and content of being good at the field placement.

Even the few students who found their prior coursework of some use could not draw direct guidance from it.

> I'm sure I'm using things that come from the textbooks but if someone asked me to write it down, take from my classes, put into words what I'm using I don't think I could.

In any case, these neophyte social workers found that their prior academic training was not a source of clear guidelines upon which they could draw in their attempts to realize the identity of social worker. Of course, in this respect, neophyte social workers are similar to those who embark on careers in the more established professions such as law (Ritzer, 1977) and medicine (Becker and Geer, 1958). Social work students, however, would probably find more support than law or medical students for their evaluations of the practical utility of their academic training. For example, there is little evidence that accredited programs of study in social work benefit future practitioners (e.g., Brennan and Khinduka, 1970; Wasserman, 1970), and even practicing social workers question the necessity of formal academic preparation for this career (Clearfield, 1977).

Moreover, social work students are not typically subjected to as many or as demanding "ritual evaluations of competence" (Haas and Shaffir, 1982a) as are law and medical students. As Haas and Shaffir (1982a, p. 149) have demonstrated in the case of medical students, the successful negotiation of ritual ordeals such as standardized assessments of specialized skill or examinations help to foster the impression that the neophyte is "achieving special and trustworthy competence." In comparison to law and medical students, social work students are provided with few opportunities to convince others and thereby themselves that they are being transformed into the types of persons occupational incumbents are expected to be. Their first notable opportunity to do so is often provided by the fieldwork practicum during which they are expected to enact the identity of social worker.

Identifying Props

Neophyte social workers must also attempt to realize the occupational identity to which they aspire without the benefit of unambiguous symbols of that identity. Unlike doctors, there is no standard uniform for social workers. Some of the students in this study attempted to dress "professionally," whereas others imitated the costumes of their clients. Needless to say, neither strategy served to display effectively the distinctive identity of social worker. Moreover, in contrast to medical students, these social work students did not possess a distinctive occupational dialect that served to display the specific identity that they were attempting to realize. Although many of these students used such expressions as "reflective listening," "processing information through my channels," and "targeting," these and similar expressions are also used by members of other "helping professions" as well as by a growing segment of the lay public. Indeed, there are apparently no symbols such as white laboratory coats, stethoscopes, or a distinctive occupational dialect through which the identity of social worker can be unambiguously announced.

In addition, most of the students on which this study is focused were implicitly aware that the effective portrayal of an occupational identity involves the employment of such "expressive equipment" (Goffman, 1959, p. 24). This was apparent in some students' responses to the question: "How can one be recognized as a social worker?"

> Well, you know, you have to . . . carry around your appointment book, have your nine cups of coffee . . . and, you know, not smile a lot.

Another student spoke of the "tricks of the trade," which she defined as an office, phone, and clipboard to hold documents, whereas yet another described the identifying significance of her "official" name badge. It is clear that the symbols and expressions that these students associated with the identity of social worker are also associated with a variety of other occupational identities. In other words, these neophyte social workers were unable to find any symbols through which they could display the specific occupational identity that they were attempting to realize.

Audiences

In the course of the field practicum, these neophyte social workers also discovered that they could not evaluate the effectiveness of their identity portrayals on the basis of audiences' reactions to their occupational performances. Although they had been warned that social work was a "low status" profession, they now confronted the reality underlying that abstraction. For example, students often complained about the treatment of social workers by other "professionals" such as teachers, corrections officers, psychologists, and doctors.

> Sometimes I feel she is the low man on the totem pole as a social worker. . . . What she says is not taken as seriously as I would like.

> They call social work something for liberal-minded, bleeding hearts. . . . They're always wary of new people who come in under the heading of social work.

> They blame the social workers for what's happening, but the problem isn't there.

Like veteran social workers (Clearfield, 1977), these neophytes attributed such lack of regard for their chosen occupation to ignorance and prejudice. Nevertheless, they became painfully aware that social workers' official image of themselves was not always shared by those with whom they worked.

For social workers, though, clients are the most crucial audience for their occupational performances. According to their official image of themselves, a social worker's claim to a professional status rests on an uncommon ability to "help" clients in myriad ways. By implication, thankful clients can provide a practicing social worker with convincing evidence that he/she has successfully realized the identity of social worker despite negative reviews from his/her coworkers. These neophyte social workers found, however, that such convincing evidence was often difficult to obtain.

> At times, I question what [we're] doing because sometimes people can't really be helped or it takes so long. It's very discouraging.

> Some of these people really don't recognize their problems, really have no interest in dealing with it, no interest in wellness.

Indeed, one student observed that the identity of social worker was a liability in obtaining good reviews from clients.

> Q: So you think of yourself as a social worker?
> A: No, a friend.
> Q: But not a social worker?
> A: The difference is that when I come up to someone and say "I'm a social worker" I can pretty much know what they're thinking, social workers are this, that and the other thing.
> Q: What's that?
> A: Mostly negative, usually "oh, my goodness, a social worker, maybe I ought to back off." But if I say "I work for staff development" then it's "okay, staff development."

In brief, unlike medical students who rehearse their occupational identity in front of relatively receptive client audiences (Haas and Shaffir, 1982b), these students rehearsed the identity of social worker in front of audiences who were reluctant to applaud *any* performance of that identity.

CHARACTER ACTING

Although neophyte social workers do not have the benefit of clear directorial cues, a distinctive set of identifying symbols, or receptive audiences for their occupational performances, these dramaturgical handicaps merely reflect a more fundamental problem involved in realizing the identity of social worker. Indeed, the students on which this study is focused did not believe that realization of that identity depended on receptive audiences, displays of identifying symbols, or the enactment of a specific, predefined part. From their points of view, a certain constellation of personal qualities was the defining characteristic of an "authentic" social worker.

The Social Worker as Character Type

When asked to describe the veteran social workers whom they admired, these students described such model social workers as emotionally controlled, hardworking, "nice persons," "extremely personable," having an "incredible respect for the people who come in there," and "caring—there's a real warmth." Similarly, practicing social workers who hold degrees from accredited social work programs characterize their colleagues as "responsible," "pleasant," "patient," and "optimistic" (Clearfield, 1977, p. 26). The similarity between these students' and veteran social workers' characterizations of practicing social workers suggests that the image of social workers to which these students subscribed was not one of their own creation, as one student clearly revealed.

> In the coursework we always read about what a social worker is and I've found (my field instructor) to be just that.

In other words, accredited programs of study in social work apparently transmit an image of the authentic social worker as a recognizable character type.

Indeed, many social work educators argue that the *primary* goal of social work education should be the "fostering of personal growth" (e.g., Lubove, 1965) or, in somewhat different terms, the development of a particular type of character. In their view, accredited programs of study in social work should transmit certain "fundamental values" to students as well as knowledge and skills. Although there is no generally accepted statement of these fundamental values (Morales and Sheafor, 1983, p. 199), they have been variously described as a belief in "the inherent dignity and worth of every human being" (Pilsecker, 1978), the "right of clients to self-determination" (Richan and Mendelsohn, 1973), "positive views of human nature" (Cryns, 1977), and "equal rights, service, psychodynamicmindedness and universalism" (Judah, 1979; Varley, 1963). In any case, the image of the social worker conveyed by these descriptions is not one that can be realized by self-consciously enacting a specific role. Indeed, this official image of the social worker is antithetical to the very idea of dramaturgy.

Character Models

Despite social work educators' conception of their mission, research evidence indicates that accredited programs of study in social work are not very effective in transforming students into the types of persons that both social work educators and their students believe that social workers should be (Cryns, 1977; Judah, 1979; Pilsecker, 1978; Varley, 1963). It was predictable that on the basis of their observations of practicing social workers, the students in this study would conclude that social work education was neither sufficient nor necessary to produce the type of personal character that practitioners who held social work degrees were more competitive than social workers should be. Other students were shocked by the apparent cynicism of such practitioners.

> He said that he will start to not like someone before he'd met them, and I said "but that's not what you're taught as a social worker, you know. Your values are lost." And, he said "well, yeah," and they laugh about it.

In addition, these students also learned that some of those who were identified by their job titles as "social workers" did not hold social work degrees, and, as one student noted, those without such a degree are sometimes the "best" social workers. In other words, these students learned that a degree from an accredited social work program was not a reliable predictor of how closely an individual conformed to social workers' official image of themselves.

Many of these students also implicitly recognized that the configuration of personal qualities that they considered the defining characteristic of "authentic" social workers is not unique to those who claim such an identity. Of course the members of other "helping professions" maintain that they are also committed to the same moral program to which authentic social workers are supposedly committed (Morales and Sheafor, 1983) Many of these student social workers believed that such a commitment was even more widely distributed. This was apparent in some students' responses to the question: "What is a social worker?"

> A person who is going to aid you in doing something you don't know how to do, someone to sound off to, someone to bail you out because you're freaked out, or just a friend.

> Working with people and if you do that you can take on anything, work in any role. A mother is a social worker. She has to be.

> If you're teaching and caring about people and seeing them as whole beings, you're doing more than teaching. You're doing social work.

As these comments suggest, at least some students seemed to believe that caring teachers, loving mothers, and good friends possess the same constellation of personal qualities that is the defining characteristic of an authentic social worker.

Character Development

As an apparent consequence of their belief that such a configuration of personal qualities is neither unique to social workers nor a product of social work education, these students seemed to conclude that the defining characteristics of an authentic social worker were not acquired but developed "naturally." For example, in the course of describing a practicing social worker whom she admired, one student observed that perhaps "it's just her personality." Another characterized her field instructor's commitment to her occupation as "just her thing." These students apparently believed that the character of the ideal-typical social worker simply evolved.

In any case, these students did not believe that they could simply enact such a character. This was apparent in their responses to the question: "What makes a good social worker?"

> [D]eveloping a self which can only come from within. . . . Such a professional self includes a set of skills, a style of presentation and an integration of one's native personality.

> The little things, by that I mean inside you. How much you're willing to give . . .
> of what you feel.

In other words, unlike neophyte doctors who self-consciously manage impressions in their attempts to realize the occupational identity to which they aspire (Haas and Shaffir, 1977, 1982b), these students did not believe that they could realize the identity of social worker by doing so.

In Search of the Character

Like social work educators who argue that being a social worker requires that one not only act but also "think and feel" like a social worker (Varley, 1963, p. 109), these students believed that realization of the occupational identity to which they aspired required management of the feelings from which behavioral expressions follow.

> Before I can help others I must understand and be able to control the way I think,
> feel, communicate and relate to others.

In other words, these students believed that effective enactment of the identity of social worker required what Arlie Hochschild (1979, p. 558) has termed "depth-acting" rather than mere "surface-acting." They believed that such a person must be sincere; that is, he/she must not only perform his/her occupational role but must also believe in the impressions which that performance fosters (Goffman, 1959, p. 18).

> A quality that I hope to continue to develop is a sincere interest in the people
> that I serve whether I like them personally or not. In my opinion, a social
> worker should care for the people that she works with in order to truly care if
> they are helped.

By implication, every time these social work students self-consciously managed their behavioral expressions, they were reminded that they had not yet been transformed into the kinds of persons they believed social workers should be.

In their capacity as neophyte social workers, however, they often resorted to surface acting. Some admitted that they self-consciously had to conceal their anger toward clients.

> Several times the tone of a client's voice or the response gets me so angry that I
> really have to bite my tongue or I would say things in relation to how thankful
> they should feel.

Others admitted that they self-consciously had to conceal their sympathy for clients.

> I get frustrated with myself because sometimes I think "I don't blame you." Like,
> I don't say it, I don't put that attitude across, but it's frustrating because I feel
> hypocritical when I say to clients "now do this, do that."

In either case, their dependence on the self-conscious management of behavioral expressions was inconsistent with the image of the authentic social worker to which they subscribed.

Not surprisingly, few of these students identified themselves as social workers. For example, when asked if they considered themselves social workers, most of these neophytes said that they continued to think of themselves as students.

> I still identify myself as a student, as a person who's been put in this frustrating situation of supposing to be something which you're not really.
>
> I thought I was going to feel more like a professional. I still feel like a student. . . . I'm still me. I haven't changed. Rats.

While some students did use specific job titles such as "community organizer," "corrections counselor," or "drug therapist" to refer to themselves, in each instance they contrasted such identities to that of social worker.

Although some of these students continued to believe that they would eventually realize the occupational identity to which they aspired, others feared that they would never do so.

> I don't know what it takes to make you feel part of the profession. . . . I don't know. I don't know if I ever will.
>
> I know that I'll never be a social worker. It's a process. I'll always be working on it.

It is clear that the realization of the identity of professional social worker remained an elusive goal for most of the students despite their sometimes valiant efforts to achieve that goal. They were truly actors in search of a character.

CONCLUSIONS

As the preceding case study illustrates, in at least one important respect neophyte social workers are engaged in a more difficult undertaking than are those who embark on careers in the more established professions. Student doctors can wrap themselves in a "cloak of competence" by adopting commonly recognized symbols of their chosen occupation, convince relatively receptive audiences of their authority over their role, and thereby convince themselves that they have realized the occupational identity to which they aspire. In contrast, neophyte social workers are not provided with commonly recognized symbols of their chosen occupation, and they seldom perform their occupational role in front of receptive audiences. Furthermore, neophyte social workers' academic training tends to convince them that the identity of social worker cannot be effectively enacted by self-consciously managing impressions.

Neophyte social workers, however, are not unique in this regard. Sherryl Kleinman (1984) has shown that contemporary seminarians are engaged in a similar undertaking. Because a growing segment of both the clergy and the lay public no longer considers ministers to be experts on matters of faith and morality, contemporary seminarians cannot realize their chosen occupational identity by displaying specialized knowledge or skills. Instead, like social workers, they must now demonstrate that they are the "right kind of people." In other words, social workers' failure to claim a recognized area of occupational expertise and the ministry's loss of such a claim have had similar consequences for occupational neophytes.

Claims that an occupation qualifies as a profession are based in part upon what Goffman (1959, p. 46) once termed "a kind of 'rhetoric of training,'" that is, occupational neophytes are required to "absorb a mystical range and period of training" in order to foster the impression that they have been reconstituted by their learning and are now set apart from others. Yet when a configuration of personal qualities rather than specialized knowledge and skills supposedly sets occupational incumbents apart from others, a required range and period of training may not effectively foster such an impression. Indeed, as the examples of both the ministry and social work indicate, a required range and period of training may even fail to foster such an impression among those who receive it.[6]

Although Haas and Shaffir (1982a, p. 151) have observed that the biographical and historical processes of professionalization are "strikingly analogous," this case study indicates that these two processes are also reflexively related. The problems neophyte social workers encounter in their attempts to realize the identity of social worker reflect their chosen occupation's difficulties in gaining public recognition as a profession. Social workers' official image of themselves and consequent failure to claim a distinct area of expertise and practice are the conditions under which neophytes attempt to realize their occupational identity. Because dramatic realization of a distinctive occupational identity is difficult under such conditions, many neophytes are not converted to a new view of self. Moreover, if occupational incumbents are not persuaded that they are set apart from others, then they will not effectively counter the public's cloudy and unflattering image of that occupation. In other words, the history of an occupation supplies the resources with which recruits attempt to realize a distinctive and valued occupational identity, and their effectiveness in doing so shapes the occupation's future. Indeed, the relationship between the historical and biographical processes of professionalization "goes right to the heart of sociology"(Ritzer 1973, p. 62). History provides the resources out of which individuals must fashion their biographies, and in fashioning their biographies, individuals make history.

ACKNOWLEDGMENTS

This article is a revised version of a paper presented at the 1985 annual meetings of the Society for the Study of Symbolic Interaction. We are indebted to Sherryl Kleinman, John Johnson, and the anonymous reviewers of *Symbolic Interaction* for their insightful comments and suggestions.

NOTES

1. Several hundred colleges and universities throughout the United States now have such accredited programs, and in 1981 more than 17,000 graduate and almost 27,000 undergraduate students were enrolled in these programs (Council on Social Work Education, 1981).

2. There are many explanations for why social workers are accorded little respect and prestige. The association of social work with public welfare and a socially undesirable clientele (Richan and Mendelsohn, 1973), low pay and poor working conditions (Condie et al., 1978), and the predominance of female practitioners (Toren, 1969) have all been advanced as explanations for social work's low status. These characteristics of social work, however, are as much effects as they are causes of low status. Social work may be accorded little prestige because the majority of practitioners are women, but the majority are women perhaps because men have more employment opportunities and are not attracted to an occupation with such low prestige. Low pay might bring low prestige, but low prestige just as certainly brings low pay. A socially undesirable clientele may bring low status, but low status service providers do not attract a socially desirable clientele.

3. Previous research indicates that many students who pursue careers in other semiprofessions do so for similar reasons. For example, both physiology (Becker and Carper, 1956) and chiropractic (Wardell, 1952) students often pursued careers in these occupations only after failing to gain entry into medical school, and many males who pursued careers in nursing (Segal, 1962) also did so because medical school was not a realistic alternative. As Simpson and Simpson (1969) have argued; the fact that many students declare majors in social work and education relatively late in their academic careers suggests that at least some of these students pursue careers in these fields for similar reasons.

4. For example, the agencies to which students were assigned had to have sufficient hours of operation to allow students to work the required number of hours. They also had to employ "professional" workers who were willing to supervise student interns. Moreover, many students did not have an automobile and, consequently, had to be assigned to one of the few agencies in the local community.

5. Although there is no available information regarding the previous social work experience of students enrolled in other accredited BSW programs in the United States, previous research does indicate that social work practitioners who hold only BSW degrees are typically younger and less occupationally experienced than those with either BA or MSW degrees (Biggerstaff and Kolevzon, 1980; Kolevzon and Biggerstaff, 1983). It seems unlikely, therefore, that the students on which this study is focused differed significantly from other BSW students in this respect.

6. At least one social work educator has suggested that instead of attempting to reconstitute students through education, "admissions procedures should systematically appraise students' values" (Judah, 1979, p 85). If prospective social workers were selected on the basis of their personal qualities, then the claim that social work qualifies as a profession could be based upon a "rhetoric of election" rather than a "rhetoric of training," and, as was the case in the not so distant past, there would be little need for social work education. Such a method of occupational recruitment might assure occupational neophytes that they were set apart from others, but it is doubtful that the public would be similarly impressed.

REFERENCES

Becker, H. and J. Carper. 1956. "The Development of Identification With an Occupation." *American Journal of Sociology* 61 (January): 289–298.

Becker, H. and B. Geer. 1958. "The Fate of Idealism in Medical School." *American Sociological Review* 23(February): 50–56.

Becker, H., B. Geer, E. Hughes, and A. Strauss. 1961. *Boys in White: Student Culture in Medical School.* Chicago: University of Chicago Press.

Bell, W. 1983. *Contemporary Social Welfare.* New York: Macmillan.

Biggerstaff, M. and M. Kolevzon. 1980. "Differential Use of Social Work Knowledge, Skills and Techniques by MSW, BSW and BA Level Practitioners." *Journal of Education for Social Work* 16(Fall): 67–74.

Brennan, W. and S. Khinduka. 1970. "Role Discrepancies and Professional Socialization: The Case of the Juvenile Probation Officer." *Social Work* 15(April): 87–94.

Clearfield, S. 1977. "Professional Self-image of the Social Worker: Implications for Social Work Education." *Journal of Education for Social Work* 13(Winter): 23–30.

Condie, C.D., J. Hanson, N. Lang, D. Moss, and R. Kane. 1978. "How the Public Views Social Work." *Social Work* 23(January): 47–53.

Council on Social Work Education. 1981. *Statistics on Social Work Education in the United States.* New York: Council on Social Work Education.

Cryns, A. 1977. "Social Work Education and Student Ideology: A Multivariate Study of Professional Socialization." *Journal of Education for Social Work* 13(Winter): 44–51

Gartner, A. 1976. *The Preparation of Human Service Professionals.* New York: Human Science Press.

Getzel, G. 1983. "Speculations on the Crisis in Social Work Recruitment: Some Modest Proposals." *Social Work* 28(May/June): 235–237.

Goffman, E. 1959. *The Presentation of Self in Everyday Life.* Garden City, NY: Doubleday.

———. 1961. "Role Distance." Pp. 83–152 in *Encounters.* New York: Bobbs-Merrill.

Greenwood, E. 1981. "Attributes of a Profession Revisited." Pp. 255–276 in N. Gilbert and H. Specht (eds.) *The Emergence of Social Welfare and Social Work,* 2d ed. Itasca, IL: F. E. Peacock.

Gurin, A. and D. Williams. 1973. "Social Work Education." Pp. 201–248 in E. Hughes, B. Thorne, A. DeBaggis, A. Gurin and D. Williams (eds.) *Education for the Professions of Medicine, Law, Theology and Social Welfare.* New York: McGraw-Hill.

Haas, J. and W. Shaffir. 1977. "The Professionalization of Medical Students: Developing Competence and a Cloak of Competence." *Symbolic Interaction* 1(Fall): 71–88.

———. 1982a. "Ritual Evaluation of Competence: The Hidden Curriculum of Professionalization in an Innovative Medical School Program." *Work and Occupations* 9(May): 131–154.

———. 1982b. "Taking on the Role of Doctor: A Dramaturgical Analysis of Professionalization." *Symbolic Interaction* 5(Fall): 187–203.

Hochschild, A. 1979. "Emotion Work, Feeling Rules and Social Structure." *American Journal of Sociology* 85(November): 551–575.

Judah, E. 1979. "Values: The Uncertain Component in Social Work." *Social Work* 15(Spring): 79–86.

Kleinman, S. 1984. *Equals Before God: Seminarians as Humanistic Professionals.* Chicago: University of Chicago Press.

Kolevzon, M. and M. Biggerstaff. 1983. "Functional Differentiation of Job Demands: Dilemmas

Confronting the Continuum in Social Work Education." *Journal of Education for Social Work* 19(Spring): 26–33.

Lubove, R. 1965. *The Professional Altruist: The Emergence of Social Work as a Career 1880–1930.* Cambridge: Harvard University Press.

Mahler, R. 1982. "Baccalaureate Social Work Graduates: Reflections on Employment, Professional Identification and Educational Preparedness." *Journal of Education for Social Work* 18(November): 80–85.

Morales, A. and B. Sheafor. 1983. *Social Work: A Profession of Many Faces.* 3d ed. Boston: Allyn and Bacon.

Pilsecker, C. 1978. "Values: A Problem for Everyone." *Social Work* 23(January): 54–57.

Richan, W. and A. Mendelsohn. 1973. *Social Work: The Unloved Profession.* New York: New Viewpoints.

Ritzer, G. 1973. "Professionalism and the Individual." Pp. 59–73 in E. Freidson (ed.) *The Profession and Their Prospects.* Beverly Hills: Sage.

———. 1977. *Working: Conflict and Change.* Englewood Cliffs, NJ: Prentice-Hall.

Rosenberg, M. 1957. *Occupations and Values.* Glencoe, IL: Free Press.

Ruzak, S. 1973. "Making Social Work Accountable." Pp. 217–244 in E. Freidson (ed.) *The Professions and Their Prospects.* Beverly Hills: Sage.

Segal, B. 1962. "Male Nurses: A Case Study in Status Contradiction and Prestige Loss." *Social Forces* 41(October): 31–38.

Simpson, R. and I.H. Simpson. 1969. "Women and Bureaucracy in the Semi-professions." Pp. 199–265 in A. Etzioni (ed.) *The Semi-Professions and Their Organization.* New York: Free Press.

Toren, N. 1969. "Semi-Professionalism and Social Work: A Theoretical Perspective." Pp. 141–195 in A. Etzioni (ed.) *The Semi-Professions and Their Organization.* New York: Free Press.

Varley, B. 1963. "Socialization in Social Work Education." *Social Work* 8(July): 102–109.

Wardell, W. 1952. "A Marginal Professional Role: The Chiropractor." *Social Forces* 30(March): 339–348.

Wasserman, H. 1970. "Early Careers of Professional Social Workers in a Public Child Welfare Agency," *Social Work* 15(July): 93–101.

Wilensky, H. and C. Lebeaux. 1965. *Industrial Society and Social Welfare.* New York: Free Press.

Legitimation of Oppression: Response and Reflexivity

Charlotte Wolf
Memphis State University

The basic question addressed in this article is why people in inferior and devalued strata submit to oppression. It is my thesis that the legitimation of oppression is one of the key issues for subordinate people and that the study of the creation and processes of legitimation among such groups will shed light on the phenomenon of human obedience or of resistance to oppressive rule. The core of the study consists of (1) the development of a model of the legitimation process and (2) the use of examples from the experiences of oppressed groups to illustrate dimensions of this process.

Servility and submission are hardly new: these responses thread through history, deeply incised, though shadowed by the claims and power of domination. Changes in the status of subject peoples historically have been slow, and the treatment of the powerless often has been harsh and oppressive. Yet we find revolution against oppression exceedingly rare. Meakness, the inability to resist, and even willing subservience more frequently have been the cornerstones of human response.

Many have observed this and have commented on its purpose, its morality, or its injustice. But the issue of human obedience, which slices to the heart of the matter, was posed some years ago by Max Weber (1958, p. 78), when he asked: "When and how do men obey? Under what inner justifications and upon what external means does this domination rest?" The question has lost none of its insistency; and in recent years, as we have become more aware that resistance to oppression is uncertain, focused

Reprinted from Symbolic Interaction, 9(2):217–234.
ISBN: 1-55938-551-0

variations have been added such as: why do people in inferior and devalued strata submit? and why do oppressed groups so seldom revolt against their oppressors?[1]

Numerous explanations for acquiescence to domination have been suggested. Among them are coercion, fear, custom, expedience, reverence, mystification, and so on. And these have explanatory value. It is my thesis, however, that the *legitimation of oppression* is one of the key issues for subordinate people, and that the study of the creation and processes of legitimation among such groups will shed light on the age-old questions of human obedience and of resistance to oppressive rule.

Within the frameworks of legitimation theory and symbolic interactionist theory, it is proposed that acceptance or even moral approval of a powerful ruler or inequitable social order can develop over time and that compliance in the face of coercive domination can become voluntary, supported by an emergent sense of consent or approbation or both. It is further suggested that the counterpart to an oppressed people's accordance of legitimacy to a power-holder or a social order is that of their accordance of legitimacy to their own status of subordinance, which I will call here *reflexive legitimation*. This, it is surmised, is not only an integral dimension but very likely *the axis of the legitimation process*. In line with this, it is possible that such attribution of legitimacy and the continuing justification of rule, although indeed apt strategies for adapting to oppression, could be major reasons why oppressed groups have found resistance to oppression so difficult to muster.

ANALYTICAL DIRECTIONS AND PROBLEMS

My primary objective in this article is to focus on the experience of oppression and the meaning it has for individuals and groups. I will use examples, mostly from the lives of three oppressed groups: Japanese-Americans, 1941–1945; black American slaves, 1800–1865; and American women, 1800–1860s. Although extensive discussion and details of each group's history are beyond the scope of this article, my data and ideas are essentially based on their views, coming from their diaries, journals, testimonials, interviews, autobiographies, and letters. Barney Glaser and Anselm Strauss's (1967) work on grounded theory, in particular,[2] has provided methodological guidelines:

> In discovering theory, one generates conceptual categories or their properties from evidence; then the evidence from which the category emerges is used to illustrate the concept. The evidence may not necessarily be accurate beyond a doubt (nor is it even in studies concerned only with accuracy), but the concept is undoubtedly a relevant theoretical abstraction about what is going on in the area. (p. 23)

Thus this method used as orientation implies the possibility of grasping the meaning of people's oppression in the crucible of *their* experiences.

As with all historic data of these sorts, however, there are some very basic problems. The oppressed have too often slipped quietly through history, leaving us with few or at best fragmentary accounts of their lives. We are faced with what Paolo Freire (1974, p. 10) has called "the culture of silence." We are told by various historians and sociologists (e.g., Stampp, 1971, p. 367; Blassingame, 1972,1978; Yetman, 1970, p. 5; Litwack, 1980, p. xviii; Lebsock, 1984, p. xiv; Ryan, 1981, p. 129; Jeffrey, 1978, p. xv; Kashima, 1980; Tateishi, 1984, p. vii) that there are few first-hand materials, and these must be studied with caution. The insights gained from their study then should be seen in this light. Before going further, the concepts of oppressed groups and legitimation will be defined, and relevant theoretical frameworks will be discussed.

Oppression

Oppression is a term from the classical Latin word *oppressus*, meaning a pressing down. It implies power and more precisely the configurations of power between those who are pressed down and those who press down. This relationship, in the words of Karl Marx (1973, p. 326) a "relation of domination,"[3] is critical to the understanding of oppressed people. As a working definition, the phrase *oppressed group* refers to those who, consequent to subjection, share with others of their kind conditions of low status, low power, low autonomy and mobility, restricted access to the material resources of a society,[4] and ascriptive disadvantages[5] relative to a group of dominant others. Of course there are degrees of oppression, and variance can be in accord with group position, culture, time, and place.

In the bulk of history the numbers of oppressed people have been legion: slaves, women, Jews, pagans, colonials, peasants, poor people, hapless minorities of all sorts—any and all groups subjugated by powerholders and defined by them as being of lesser or inferior nature and accorded unequal treatment. Furthermore, in any given society, depending on its history and on the complexity of its stratification system, there might be one or several differentially located oppressed groups of people.[6]

Legitimation

Much of contemporary sociology has based its understanding of legitimation on the work of Max Weber. Simply put, Weber tells us that the core of legitimation lies in the dynamic relationship between powerholders who demand obedience and lower ranking participants who respond with support and compliance. It must be stressed that legitimacy might be *claimed* by a powerholder, but *only if the subjects acknowledge the validity of those claims* could they be considered legitimate (Weber, 1978 [1], p. 214; 1947, pp. 126–127). In his discussion of the relationship of ruler and subordinate, Weber makes it very clear that rulers might issue commands and expect them to be obeyed and can perhaps force people to obey them, but at bedrock, legitimacy springs from what a sufficient number of followers believe and honor with their voluntary compliance. By emphasizing the underlying motivational patterns supporting social and political power and the meanings attached to the authority relationship, Weber bares the social psychological bones of legitimation.

A great deal of critical thought has been expended in the analysis of Weber's theory. Two major points are salient for this article. A number of people have criticized the clarity of his ideas. Joseph Bensman (1979), for example, states that Weber has presented two separate concepts of legitimacy, *"legitimacy as claimed and legitimacy as believed"* (p. 19). Although legitimation provides "grounds for obedience by the powerless and justification for the fact that they enjoy less than a proportionate share of the goods of this world" (p. 40), he contends that Weber has focused his work on the "formal presentation of claims, promises, and justifications as presented but not received" (p. 32). Similar criticisms have been made by David Easton (1958), Dennis Wrong (1970), Jose Merquior (1980), and Frank Parkin (1982). Parkin, in particular, argues that Weber neglected the study of acceptance and obedience patterns of subordinate groups, and although he constructed a typology of powerholder claims for obedience, he ignored the need for a typology of subordinate responses to those claims. A line of research has been generated in recognition of these problems. For example, S.M. Dornbusch and W.R. Scott (1975), H. Andrew Michener and Martha R. Burt (1975a, b), and Henry A. Walker et al. (1986) have constructed models involving typologies of objects of legitimation, assessors of legitimation, and responses. Thus the trend is toward a more richly complex conceptualization of legitimation relations.

The second knotty question is whether it is possible for oppressed people to legitimate coercion or force, even violence. The denial that coercion and legitimation could be bedfellows has a long and venerable history that includes such adherents as the Socratics, Plato, Jean-Jacques Rousseau, Bertrand Russell, R.M. MacIver, to mention only a few. On the other hand, Seymour Martin Lipset (1963), Dennis H. Wrong (1979), Joseph Bensman (1979), Paul Rosen (1979), and Edward Shils (1981) have suggested that legitimation of even the most brutal power might eventually emerge as a response from the oppressed.[7] Barrington Moore (1978) bluntly sums this up, saying that "in real life oppressed groups generally accept in some degree the legitimacy of their oppressors" (p. 96).

Critical theorists take a different structural tack, conceiving authority as initially *imposed from above*[8] by the ruling system, not as emerging from below as validation of power. The imposition of domination occurs through either direct control over subjected peoples or through dependency relationships forced upon them (Shroyer, 1973; Agger, 1978). Jürgen Habermas's analysis goes further, conceiving of legitimation as the set of ideas successfully generated by a repressive political system as justification for the status quo of privilege and oppression. He specifies that the ruling system's power over populations is based both on structural force and on its capacity to shape ideology and "systematically distort communication." This "pseudo communication" (Habermas, 1970a,b), in becoming a property of the normative structure, pervades the innermost self of subject members, resulting in a "willingness to consent" (Habermas 1973, 1976); and people thereby come to oppress themselves in the name of the larger social structure.

Explanations

The underlying question is how does this linkage between structural power and consciousness, or between macrosocial phenomena and individual interpretation and response occur? The work of symbolic interactionists and phenomenologists provides theoretical suggestions. Elemental to this are Charles H. Cooley's (1912) idea of the "looking glass self" and George Herbert Mead's (1962) concepts of the generalized other, taking the role of the other, and of reflexivity. Emphasizing that the self is a social product generated from the interactive fabric of communication, Mead tells us that by taking the viewpoint of the generalized other or of significant others (Sullivan, 1953), the individual both gains a self and participates in a common world of meaning. A crucial phase of this process lies in the reflexive dynamism of the self. As Mead (1962) writes:

> It is by means of reflexiveness—the turning-back of the experience of the individual upon himself—that the whole social process is thus brought into the experience of the individuals involved in it; it is by such means, which enable the individual to take the attitude of the other toward himself, that the individual is able consciously to adjust himself to that process, and to modify the resultant of that process in any given social act in terms of his adjustment to it. (p. 134)

Herbert Blumer (1969) further clarifies the reflexive process by emphasizing that it is one of interpretation and of determining the significance of things for the individual's "line of action" (pp. 63–64).

The possibility of bridging from interpreted experience to an external and coercive social reality is presented to us in the phenomenological views of Peter Berger and Thomas Luckmann (1967). Against their conceptual background of objectivation, as the process by which human products are externalized and objectified (p. 60), and of symbolic universe or the dominant order of society (p. 96), they posit that legitimation is a second order objectivation of meaning, or productive of new meanings that serve to integrate the meanings already attached to institutional processes, and, as such, a crucial dimension of the relationship between intersubjectivity and the social world.

LEGITIMATION OF OPPRESSION: A MODEL

Legitimation, as the concept used in this article, is the process by which an oppressed group comes to accept the dominant–subordinate relationship. Thus it implies validation by the oppressed of both sides of the nexus: the right of domination for the ruler and the acceptance of subordination by the inferior. Witness Elie Cohen's (1954) description of the power relationship in a concentration camp:

> The SS man was all-powerful in the camp, he was the lord and master of the prisoner's life. As a cruel father he could, without fear of punishment, even kill the prisoner and as a gentle father he could scatter largess and afford the prisoner his protection. The result was that for nearly all the prisoners the SS became a father image. (pp. 176–177)

The problem of an SS man being seen as a father to his victims is a curious one, casting up in tragic relief the antipodal emotions of the ruled against the starkness of brutal coercion. How can this be understood? It is assumed in this study that coercive power is not necessarily antithetical to legitimated power; indeed, it can become one and the same thing, and at the same time it can become internalized as part of an oppressed person's very self.

It is likely that the emergence of the legitimation process must come from the fallow ground of closed circumstances for the oppressed, circumstances that are both generative and supportive of legitimation and that predispose people to acknowledge the oppressive system as valid. It is suggested that the bases of relationship with the oppressor, which might eventually lead to conformity and the legitimation of an oppressive order, are those of habituation (including socialization), accommodation, and dependency relations. Habituation takes place primarily through the passage of time and the imposition of coercive routine. People become accustomed to the way things are; and the life pattern and relations between superior and subordinate come to seem normal, even inevitable. Other factors that figure prominently in the degree of habituation are those of isolation, both geographic and social structural, and imposed ignorance or knowledge deprivation.

The lack of perceived alternatives or options in the closed world of deprivation is of basic cognitive importance to the growth of both habituation and accommodation. People tend to accommodate rather rapidly to small, limited worlds when they are forced to. In accommodating, discrepant behavior must be at least overtly clipped and shaped to conform. Within narrowed confines of life, people can tend to become obliging and disposed to comply; they can learn to accept that the required behavior is necessary. Two factors that operate to support accommodation are those of relative advantage and group conservatism. Relative advantage[9] is the belief that, in comparison with other disadvantaged people, one's self or one's immediate group is doing better.[10] It is a selective assessment of one's situation and an intraoppressed population phenomenon. The sense of relative advantage limits the sense of deprivation, and thus the oppressive system as it is felt or as it envelops group life is used as a positive frame of reference. Conservatism characterizes the interest in clinging to what the oppressed group has, little as it might be, and in preserving their situation as known and manageable. It expresses itself in an unwillingness to take risks. Members who take chances, who speak out, who behave independently can bring down wrath and censure upon the entire group (for example, Bettelheim, 1960, pp. 170–171; Douglass, 1970, p. 222), and thus pressure is brought by the group to suppress forms of nonaccommodative behavior. These factors can be briefly expressed as: Bad as it is, it could be worse; and don't rock the boat. Working in tandem, they undercut change and encourage accommodation.

Dependency is a third variable contributing to this type of legitimation.[11] Stemming from the relative powerlessness of subject people, it issues forth as a tie between the oppressor and the oppressed. Moreover, this relationship can come to be seen by the oppressed as one in which the powerholder has a responsibility to care for, provide for, and protect the subordinate in exchange for compliance, deference, or whatever exchange is perceived as required.

Legitimation of oppression is a multidimensional phenomenon, rooted in the perspectives of the oppressed group. The model of subordinate legitimation involves:

the acknowledgment of the social order of powerholder as legitimate; the responses consequent to this acceptance, such as obedience, explanations and justifications,[12] and so on; and an ongoing negotiation of obligations and rights between the powerless and the powerful. The results of this, although always fluid, will of course be influenced and shaped by the counters held by the oppressed and the constraints of their situation (Strauss, 1978). Obviously, the more severe the repression and the less power the oppressed have, the less likely they will be able to wangle favorable concessions. Given some leeway, however, they do have important bargaining chips on their side—those of their compliance and of their power of legitimation. Through this process, the boundaries of expectations and the normative parameters of their relationships with superordinates and of the system tend to become defined. Privileges, duties, appropriate social locations, even identities are worked out in some measure in these transactions. But subordinate life is chancy, and because of the lack of power, the outcomes are fragile and always contingent (Goffman, 1969).

The model of subordinate legitimation also involves reflexive legitimation. As the fourth dimension of this schematic outline, it is the core explanatory concept that refers back to the individual. It implies the acceptance of the status and characteristics inherent in being subject to an oppressive social order. Acceptance lies in the realm of identity conception and involves either the internalization of inferiority vis-à-vis the dominant group or the internalization of one's place in the system as appropriate or both.

The last three components are essential and related processes by which the oppressed acknowledge a commitment to this dominant-subordinate relationship and ultimately acknowledge the legitimacy of their own subordinate status. They are the critical counterparts of according legitimacy to any social order, and they represent in effect the social-psychological bonds of the oppressed to the oppressor. Taken together, the dimensions of this model constitute a generalized commitment to a social order. It should be emphasized, however, that in principle all of the dimensions are both analytically and in reality separable and that each varies in degree and can be independent of the others. There is no reason to believe, and the empirical evidence bears this out, that people who acknowledge the legitimacy of a power structure will internalize the implied obligations of obedience[13] or that the individual will internalize characteristics appropriate to inferior status. The extent of the discrepancy between acceptance or rejection in any of these dimensions, given similar oppressive conditions, might help us to understand why some oppressed people have managed to keep the total effects of psychic oppression at arm's length, whereas others have not. I will, however, explore each of these dimensions of the legitimation process in greater detail and will provide some illustrations.

Legitimation of Oppression

A dominance relationship is defined as legitimate as long as the subordinate members regard this domination as proper and justified and are willing to support it. The more this is the case, the less likely they are to believe that they are oppressed.

Attend to the remarks of Nicey Kinney of Georgia, an old black woman who had been a slave and who in the 1930s reminisced with a Federal Writers Project interviewer about the old days:

> Marse Gerald Sharp and his wife, Miss Annie, owned us and, child, they was grand folks. Their old home . . . that big old plantation run plumb back down to the Oconee River. Yes, ma'am, all of them rich river bottoms was Marse Gerald's. . . . Oh! if I could just see 'em one more time! But they can look down from the glory land and see that I's trying to follow the road that leads to where they is, and when I gits to that good and better world I just knows the Good Lord will let this aged woman be with her dear master and mistress all through the time to come. . . . (as quoted in Botkin 1945, pp. 79–80)

Less identification with the powerholder and a more distanced evaluation was made by Alan V. Manning in his interview:

> I was born in slavery, and I belonged to a Baptist preacher. Until I was fifteen yers old I was taught that I was his own chattel-property and he could do with me like he wanted to, but he had been taught that way, too, and we both believed it. I never did hold nothing against him for being hard on Negroes sometimes, and I don't think I ever would of had any trouble even if I had growed up and died in slavery. (as quoted in Botkin 1945, pp. 93–94)

Of course not all slaves felt this way. However, many—even runaways—acknowledged the validity of the property relationship. Lewis Clarke, who had escaped to Canada from the South, said in his narrative that there were black fugitives who had been tortured by a sense of obligation and guilt and had returned from Canada to their masters, seeking their forgiveness (Clarke and Clarke 1969, p. 117). Nathan Huggins (1979), in his book *Black Odyssey,* mentions his surprise at finding "among the many letters from blacks who managed to escape notes of apology to their former owners. They would say they were sorry they had had to run away, and they often offered to compensate their masters with money. Surprising, but it was a frequent occurrence" (p. 236).

There are many examples of women in the nineteenth century who believed that men should be obeyed as the superior member of the family. Mary Richardson Walker, while going west to Oregon, wrote in her diary on June 10, 1838: "I regard my husband as a special blessing conferred by Heaven and I am determined if possible that my life shall evince my gratitude" (Luchetti, 1982, p. 63). And Mrs. Sandford, during the first half of the nineteenth century, proclaimed: "A really sensible woman feels her dependence. She does what she can, but she is conscious of inferiority, and therefore grateful for support" (quoted in Welter, 1978, p. 318).

Although severe oppression was of much shorter duration for them, some Japanese-Americans also began to express acceptance of and justification for oppression. An insurance agent, a male Issei of 43 years of age, stated: "I had not any bad feeling against evacuation, because the authority tried to protect us. I have lost my setup but can't help it under the circumstance. We should feel that it is a good experience to learn lots of things" (Brown 1945, pp. 19–20).

It is obvious of course that legitimation might be granted, but very often it is neither granted on the precise grounds nor to the extent claimed by powerholders, and for that matter the individual powerholder might not be seen as legitimate at all, authority being derived from and upheld by the system and by a subject people's generalized legitimation of that system. Moreover, legitimation can be selective so that there is acceptance of authority in certain areas of life but not in others; it will vary in intensity; it will rarely be consensual; and the social location of its supporters will influence their responses.

Legitimation is often backed up by ideological statements of why the ruler or the rule has been accepted as valid. These understandings can be categorized on the basis of whether they explain or justify (Berger and Luckmann 1967, p. 93), although the distinction between the two is often blurred. Statements that explain why legitimacy has been conferred have been that the ruler is superior on such grounds as competence or education or strength or power or inherently so or that the ruler is able to provide much-needed security and protection, whereas justifications for oppression have been that it was God's will or destiny or that an individual's or group's sins have brought this down on them.

Obedience to the powerholder, although it might be claimed and was thought by Weber (1958, p. 79) to be inherent in the legitimation process, was often given reluctantly, sparingly, and sometimes not at all. Yet in some instances, we find a person like Daddy June, a former slave in South Carolina, who, when interviewed in 1930 at the age of 85 years by J. Brewton Berry (1935), said:

> Massa didn't had to tell me a t'ing but once. W'en he tell me to do sumpin ah come widin ninety-nine cents o' doin' it. If he hada tol me to bus' my head on a brick wall ah woulda done it. Ah woulda even t'ought it a fine t'ing to do, ah had dat much confidence in Massa. (p. 75)

Sarah Katherine (Stone) Holmes (1955), a white woman of the Antebellum South, although not enthusiastic, nonetheless obeyed the male members of her family, voicing little protestation:

> The Nutt family we found the most pleasant of all, and they added most to our entertainment. Such bright, intelligent women. We visited and received them frequently, and they were just as kind as they could be. We were great friends for some months. But they talked too freely and too emphatically, and My Brother put his veto on our going there again. We regretted it so and could never explain what to them could only seem heartless caprice. They had been unvaryingly kind and polite to us and how I hated to make such a return. (p. 370)

When Mary Chesnut, an older and sophisticated woman, was told by her husband during the period of the Civil War that there had been enough feasting and merrymaking in the house, she accepted his decision, for "he is the master of the house. To hear is to obey" (Wiley 1975, p. 34).

And Minoru Yasui, in recollecting the relocation experience of Japanese-Americans during the early 1940s, said:

> I'm personally convinced that the Nikkei in 1942 would have gone dociley to the gas chambers if ordered to do so by competent authority. That's a terrible thing to say, but remembering the quiet obedience of the Japanese Americans in 1942, their almost pathetic eagerness to please, the lack of anger or overwhelming feelings of injustice, I'm not convinced that any large numbers of Nikkei now would take up arms to resist the U.S. government. I don't believe that Japanese Americans would fight back with violence. (as quoted in Tateishi 1984, p. 92)

Obedience as a norm of conduct can involve overt conformity such as performing required tasks and the display of proper attitudes of submission, including demonstrations of both deference and the willingness to comply. The range of responses then is from minimal or noncompliance to total obedience, as professed by Daddy June.

Negotiation

Whatever amount of obedience is proffered, it is only part of the bundle of obligations and rights that are hammered out between the powerholder and the subordinate. As Georg Simmel (1950, pp. 182–183) has told us: "Even in the most oppressive and cruel cases of subordination, there is still a considerable measure of personal freedom. . . . the fact [is] that interaction, that is, action which is mutually determined, action which stems exclusively from personal origins, prevails even where it often is not noted." The limits of power and the limits of response are to some extent reciprocally defined. Expectations by the oppressed of what the powerholder should do often involve protection, security, and at least minimal food, shelter, and rest or the means to procure them. In 1855 a women who lived near Augusta, Georgia, in writing these words in her diary, suggests the exchange situation between herself and her husband:

> I thank thee oh my Heavenly Father for thy many mercies, but for none do I sincerely thank thee as for *my husband,* combining such moral quality, such an affectionate heart, with just such a master will as suits my woman's nature, for true to my sex I delight *in looking up* and love to feel my woman's weakness protected by man's superior strength. (as quoted in Scott 1970, p. 96, emphasis in original)

More graphic and direct is the statement made by Ellen Betts while telling of her slave days in the South:

> [t]hen was the really happy days for us niggers, course we didn't have the 'vantages that we has now, but there was something back there that we aint got now, and that's security. Yes sir, we had somebody to go to when we was in trouble We had a massa that would fight for us and help us and laugh with us and cry with us. We

had a mistress that would nurse us when we was sick and comfort us when we had
to be punished. (as quoted in Botkin 1945, p. 152)

Elige Davison, an old freed slave, in a less sentimental fashion, believed his property
status to be advantageous in the negotiation:

Massa, he look after us slaves when us sick, 'cause us worth too much money to
let die, just like you do a mule. (as quoted in Yetman 1970, p. 91)

Moreover, it often appears that the powerholder is believed to be morally obligated to
comply with certain types of their demands if they give this person or group their
obedience, to say nothing of their validation of the right to power. It has been suggested
by several sociologists (Simmel, 1950, pp. 181–189; Emerson, 1962, pp. 31–41;
Wrong, 1968, pp. 673–681) that the power to legitimate serves to control and to limit
the arbitrariness or capriciousness of the ruler, permitting the oppressed to carve out
some living space for themselves. This is borne out in these studies. In time, a
normative structure emerges, defining the mutual rights and obligations, what is owed
to the ruler, and what is owed to the oppressed. Although the situations of the three
groups—black slaves, nineteenth-century women, and Japanese-Americans—were
quite different and in the case of the Japanese-Americans was of shorter duration, even
among the last group we begin to see incipient similarities. For example, a young
Japanese-American evacuee at one center in the 1940s wrote:

The biggest thing that has come up [in the block] was the Vegetable Committee.
That started back in July, I wasn't on the Block Council then, but I thought that it
wasn't the right thing for us to grow vegetables. The way I figured it then was that
the Government had agreed to give us certain things like food, clothing, and shelter
in return for which we agreed to abide by certain rules. I thought that the
Government should live up to its agreement, and why should we be expected to
furnish food for ourselves? (as quoted in Spicer et al., 1946, p. 57)

Definitions of relationships do not remain untested, however. Zones of toleration
are pushed. Concessions are asked for, argued over, and sometimes gained. Charles
Ball (1859), a slave, tells us in his narrative how he managed to negotiate an extra
half-day off:

I now, for the first time in my life, became a hunter, in the proper sense of the
word; and generally managed my affairs in such a way to get the half of Saturday
to myself. This I did by prevailing on my master to set my task for the work on
Monday morning. Saturday was appropriated to hunting. . . . (pp. 278–279)

Most of the terms of these agreements were largely unstated, perhaps only vaguely
known by one of the parties, but violations by the ruler might bring on revolt. Slave
annals are replete with stories of how blacks took to the woods until they got their
expected Sundays or holidays off and of slaves who ran away when the master did not
perform as expected. Japanese-Americans in the relocation centers, working under the

direction of Caucasian foremen, managed with perseverance to work out acceptable
term of work:

> However, all foremen were themselves up against the standards of the Government
> agency of a maximum work output for an eight hour day, and moreover were faced
> with getting specific jobs done.... As a result, there was persistent trouble as the
> evacuee standard of "let us work, but let us not work too hard" came into conflict
> with the standards which foremen and supervisors were attempting to live up to.
> Rigorous foremen found themselves up against a sort of passive resistance, as
> evacuee work crews quietly developed their system of rest periods and early
> quitting times. They found a general tendency on the part of evacuees never to
> allow themselves to be pushed too hard and to balk at any signs of inconsiderate
> handling or evidences of racial prejudice. Some foremen, accustomed to work
> situations where a man could be hired and fired, exploded and found that their
> crews walked out on them. Friction between work crews and foremen was
> persistent throughout the early months in the centers. Most foremen, however,
> found themselves compromising gradually with the standards set by the evacuees,
> and slowly the evacuee standard dominated the centers. (Spicer et al. 1946, p. 95)

Even in cases of flagrant disobedience by the oppressed, violation of the rules
does not always imply that there is a disavowal of the validity of the social order. Some
types of disobedience actually support or reinforce the oppressive system. They do not
challenge it if such deviation is tailored by considerations of adjusting to the status
quo. Thus, in effect, some types of circumventing the system represent an accommodation to it. For example, stealing by slaves often seemed to be a case of this sort.
Frederick Douglass (1970) explained:

> Considering that my labor and person were the property of Master Thomas, and
> that I was by him deprived of the necessaries of life—necessaries obtained by my
> own labor—it was easy to deduce the right to supply myself with what was my
> own.... In the case of my master, it was only a question of removal—the taking
> his meat out of one tub, and putting it into another; the ownership of the meat was
> not affected by the transaction. At first, he owned it in the *tub*, and last he owned
> it in *me*. (p. 147 emphasis in original)

Reflexive Legitimation

Compliance is neither a simple response, nor a simple set of reactions. The
wellsprings of the dominant-subordinate relationship lie in its meaning for individuals.
Shrugging into the cloak of submission means to accept that one has acquired a station
in life, it means accepting not only what one's actions might have to be but what kind
of person one must be or has become. Reflexive legitimation provides the subjectively
meaningful grounds for compliance. It is ultimately the acceptance of the identity of
a subordinate person.

Reflexivity is both the mirrored image of how relevant superior others are
perceived as seeing the subordinate[14] and how this is reflected upon and interpreted
by the individual. In the case of reflexive legitimation, while recognizing the superior

power of the superordinate, the individual comes to ground with the further recognition of his or her correspondingly inferior power and reflexively regards these and their meaning for the self. Reflexive legitimation involves not only seeing one's self from the standpoint of significant and powerful others, but it also involves seeing one's self from the standpoint of the structure of domination as an inferior and relatively powerless member of this relationship. Thus as legitimation is to the dominant individual or group, reflexive legitimation is to the subordinate, bringing the relationship full circle, an encompassing ring of oppression. The individual reflexively responds to the self as a person or an object that has a specific station in life. Just as directly, that individual responds to the superior as being the incumbent of a higher station in life. Further, reflexive legitimation is not only a matter of adjusting one's role and identity to those of relevant and powerful others or even to those of like-situated, oppressed others; it is also a matter of hewing out from an oppressive context a "realistic" or possible sense of self. To the extent that this corresponds to the role of the subordinate, insofar as the constraints are directed toward playing that role, we can say that oppression and the oppressive relationship more nearly achieve totality.

Reflexive legitimation is a process by which the external structure of oppression is internalized. People respond to a social environment on the basis of the meanings that perceived or salient elements have for them as individuals and members of groups: In the case of oppression, they selectively attend to the actions and expressed attitudes of the oppressor. That there is heightened sensitivity to those who have power over one's life or welfare is hardly surprising. It has been noted before by sociologists, for example, Jerry D. Rose (1969), D.L. Thomas, D.D. Franks, and J.M. Calonica (1972), whose research has suggested that lower status people are sensitized to the responses of the dominant group or person and more adept at taking the role of the particular other, thus gaining that perspective and seeing themselves as they are seen.

Components of this process are, first, to some extent, the individual's conception of him- or herself grows out of this social interaction with significant and powerful others and the reflection of how they are appraised; the second element is that of the objectification of self. This objectification of self is the reflexive experiencing of the self, the seeing of self as a thing but as a thing that has been patronizingly or pejoratively defined by the powerful. For example, Japanese-Americans, after a time in the relocation centers during World War II, came to see themselves to an even greater extent than previously through the eyes of prejudiced Caucasians. They leveled such pejorative terms as "Jap," "bootchie," and "Buddha-head" at one another and at themselves with thinly veiled hostility. Slaves were legally defined by whites as chattels, property who could be sold or leased, and were discussed as to "what they were worth" in dollars or in other negotiable objects. Many black slaves came to accept and to use these quantitative evaluations to define themselves. One commented that he was worth "fifteen mules"(Drew, 1968, p. 257); another said his sister had been sold for fifteen bales of cotton (Botkin, 1945, p. 231). Their value in dollars was discussed frequently by them, often proudly; the higher the figure, the greater the expressed sense of worth and recognition. For instance:

They would drive slaves off just like they do hogs now. A great big nigger like me would bring four or five thousand dollars but a little nigger wouldn't bring nothing hardly. Nobody wanted a puny nigger. (as quoted in Fisk University 1945, p. 350).

Rosa Starke, after more than seventy years had passed, still vividly remembered the occasion of her master's death and the subsequent sale of the plantation, the stock, and the slaves as one of the greatest events of her life.

Old marster die. De 'praisers of de State come and figure dat his mules, niggers, cows, hogs, and things was worth $200,000. Land and house I dis-remember about. They anyhow, say de property was over a million dollars. They put a price of $1,600 on mammy and $1,800 on pappy. I 'member they say I was worth $400.00. Young Marse Nick tells us dat the personal property of the estate 'praised at $288,168.78 (as quoted in Federal Writers' Project [S. Carolina III] 1972, p. 149)

Women were objectified as the opposite sex or according to Lucy Lee Pleasants (1916) "the sex":

Men took pride in their devotion to "the sex" and thought it no shame to offer themselves to be rejected. . . . This temperament on the part of the men developed a species of belle which, I believe, has never been equalled elsewhere. (p. 95)

The third component of this process is that of forming a conception of self in regard to one's placement in a social universe. In discussing Mead's use of the "game" to illustrate the mental images that the individual holds of all the other players, Ralph Turner (1956, p. 320) suggests: "The manner in which the actor relates his own role to the others is in terms of their interactive effect rather than simply in terms of accepting their direction." This might be extended to include the linkage of the subordinate both to the superordinate and to others of his or her kind, classified by similar station and roles in life. The sense of esteem and worth tends to be tied to this narrow world. One's sense of who one is and how worthy one is thus is oriented and legitimated by reflexive reference to the authority-subordinate relationship and how this works out in interactive patterns. Mary Orne Tucker, a New England wife, in her diary entry of May 1, 1802, illustrates what four years of marriage, centuries of female accommodation, and the process of reflexive legitimation had impressed upon her:

[t]o shine as a good wife, is an object of my highest ambition, there are many humble duties to fulfill and to fulfill them with honor and chearfulness [sic]is a consideration which ought not to be beneath the notice of every reflecting woman. I am every day amply repaid for all my endeavors to please, every look from my master is a certificate of my success; and the plaudit of my own conscience affords sweet peace. (as quoted in Cott, 1977, p. 72)

Some years later, Jane Swisshelm (1880), a writer of the mid-1800s, told of how she as a married woman had felt it her duty to give up painting:

Housekeeping was "woman's sphere," although I had never then heard the words, for *no woman* had gotten out of it to be hounded back; but I knew my place and scorned to leave it. . . . I put away my brushes, resolutely crucified my divine gift, and while it hung writhing on the cross, spent my best years and powers cooking cabbage. . . . (pp. 48-49, emphasis in original)

The final stage of this process is that of reflexive legitimation. Disprivileged people know they are inferiors; reflexivity signals to them what they are expected to do, what they have become, and the propriety and rightness of their station. This affirmation of one's place in life is illustrated by the problem that Ellen Bett's sisters, all of whom were slaves, faced in the antebellum South:

Old Man Denman's boy gits kilt, and two my sisters he property, and they don't know what to do, 'cause they has to be somebody's property and they ain't no one to 'heritance 'em. . . . (as quoted in Botkin 1945, p. 154)

It might be said that if primary oppression is that which the oppressor exerts against subordinates, *secondary oppression,* or reflexive legitimation, is the true bite of meaning that oppression holds for the oppressed.

CONCLUSION

It is probably rare that subject people are kept in check for any period of time without a measure of their cooperation. Based on primary source materials from three oppressed groups, I have suggested in this article that this is the case and that oppressed people come to legitimate the oppressive order. Legitimation of oppression is a response to narrowed and harrowing circumstances. It is not congruent with the inception of oppression; rather, it emerges as a normative reaction.

The process of legitimation involves four interrelated parts: acknowledgment of the right of the ruler to dominate; subordinate response of obedience or whatever action and rationales are deemed appropriate; a continuing negotiation with superordinates of the ground rules of the relationship; and reflexive legitimation. It is this last phase, reflexive legitimation, that is crucial to the molding of the oppressed self, that speaks of the internalization of oppression, for it is here that the person validates his or her own subordination. Moreover, implied in this model is the point that the individual or group in oppressive circumstances becomes an active participant in the dominant-subordinate relationship; and although legitimation by the oppressed of a ruler or dominant order might permit a more stable and manageable situation, possibly operating to some degree as a brake of control over the arbitrariness and excessiveness of superordinate power and over the restiveness of the subordinate, it is likely that it also contributes to the perpetuation of the system.

Finally and more generally speaking, it is possible that the ideas of legitimation of oppression and of reflexive legitimation might provide an explanatory linkage between microinteractionist and macrostructural contexts in minority group study. Certainly, no matter what we call these concepts, the histories of the oppressed starkly illustrate for us that the experiences they undergo are both incorporated and reinterpreted by these people in the construction of their *oppressed* lives and *oppressed* selves.

ACKNOWLEDGMENT

This is a revised version of a paper "Reflexivity in the Legitimation of Oppression," given at the Annual Symposium of the Society for the Study of Symbolic Interaction, University of Georgia, April 14, 1983. It is also part of a larger work on oppressed groups (in progress).

NOTES

1.   For recent and provocative studies centering on these questions, see Barrington Moore (1978), Barry D. Adam (1978), and L. Richard Della Fava (1980).

2.   For discussions of analytic induction, which is a similar methodology to that of grounded theory and preceding it, see the following: Florian Znaniecki (1934), Alfred R. Lindsmith (1947, esp. pp. 5–20; 1953, pp, 604–611), and Howard S. Becker (1953, p. 45).

3.   In this selection from *Grundrisse,* Marx is discussing with robust amusement an article from *The Times* of November 1857 on the Quashees, or free black workers of Jamaica. The article included a letter from a white West-Indian plantation owner, who advocated the reintroduction of black slavery and voiced outrage that free blacks refused to work a whole day when half a day would suffice for subsistence. In reference to this, Marx says: "Wealth confronts direct forced labour not as capital, but rather as *relation* of *domination* . . .; thus, the relation of domination is the only thing which is reproduced on this basis, for which wealth itself has value only as gratification, not as wealth itself, and which therefore can never create general industriousness" (1973: 325–326, emphasis in the original).

4.   Louis Wirth's definition of minority group (1964, p. 245) remains a classic in the field and is reflected in my definition of oppressed group.

5.   For a sophisticated discussion of ascription, see Theodore D. Kemper (1974).

6.   For a work that is basic to the area of the social psychology of minority groups, see Tamotsu Shibutani and Kian M. Kwan (1965).

7.   One of the most stark examples of the legitimation of violence and oppression is recounted by E. V. Walters (1969) in his study of the Shaka regime in Zululand in the early nineteenth century. Although Shaka's rule was dependent on the use of terror and brutality, the submission of his subjects was a curious admixture of fear, respect, enthusiastic conformity, and legitimation of rule.

8.   The Frankfurt School's work primarily has addressed these problems as relevant to late capitalistic societies. Nonetheless, it is suggested that critical theory might also be enlisted to explain the structural relationships of power groups and subject populations in other historic time frames (see Max Horkheimer, 1972).

9.   Because relative advantage is conceived by me to be antithetic to the concept of relative deprivation, a mention of work involving the latter is probably appropriate. See, in particular, W.C. Runciman (1966) and J.A. Davis (1959).

10.   Status borrowing (Charlotte Wolf, 1969, p. 103; 1978) could be part of this mechanism of relative advantage insofar as people, in deriving their status from superior others, flaunt or

use it as comparative capital wlth other oppressed people or groups in defining social distance or in gaining deference.

11. Insightful studies of the dependency relationship must include those of Richard M. Emerson (1962), O. Mannoni (1968), and Albert Memmi (1965, 1984).

12. Peter Berger and Thomas Luckmann (1967, p. 93) tell us that "legitimation is the process of 'explaining' and 'justifying.'" However, Sandra J. Ball-Rokeach, in her discussion of the legitimation of violence (1972), questions that in such cases justifications are either necessary or likely to occur. In my work, however there seems to be a felt need on the part of many of the oppressed to believe in the benevolence of the oppressor and to justify their position and their acquiescence to it.

13. Gresham Sykes (1966, p. 48) has pointed out that in the maximum security prisons he studied there was no question that the inmates accepted the right of the warden and the guards to control them but that this was not accompanied by any sense of obligation to obey.

14. Guilt, I suggest, might also be an expression of this aspect of reflexive legitimation. For example, there is quite a bit of evidence that Japanese-Americans were overwhelmed with feelings of guilt when they were sent to the relocation centers. It was as if the following were the case: We must be the people they say we are otherwise why would they be treating us in this way? Frantz Fanon (1968, p. 139) grimly describes this in an austere paragraph: "All those white men in a group, guns in their hands, cannot be wrong. I am guilty. I do not know of what, but I know that I am no good." The ideas of Anna Freud on identification with the aggressor and of Karl Marx on false consciousness might also be explored within the notion of reflexive legitimation.

REFERENCES

Adam, B.D. 1978. *The Survival of Domination: Inferiorization and Everyday Life.* New York: Elsevier.

Aggar, B. (ed.) 1978. *Western Marxism: An Introduction.* Santa Monica, CA: Goodyear.

Ball, C. 1859. *Fifty Years in Chains: Or, The Life of an American Slave.* New York: H. Dayton.

Ball-Rokeach, S.J. 1972. "The Legitimation of Violence." Pp. 100–118 in J.F. Shon, Jr. and M.E. Wolfgang (eds.) *Collective Violence.* Chicago: Aldine-Atherton.

Becker, H.S. 1963. *Outsiders. Studies in the Sociology of Deviance.* New York: Free Press.

Bensman, J. 1979. "Max Weber's Concept of Legitimacy: An Evaluation." Pp. 17–48 in A.J. Vidich and R.M. Gassman (eds.) *Conflict and Control. Challenge to Legitimacy of Modern Governments.* Beverly Hills: Sage.

Berger, P. and T. Luckmann. 1967. *The Social Construction of Reality.* New York: Doubleday Anchor.

Berry, J.B. 1935. "Silver Spoon: The Autobiography of Daddy June." *Story* (August): 65–79.

Bettelheim, B. 1960. *The Informed Heart.* New York: Avon.

Blassingame, J.W. 1972. *The Slave Community: Plantation Life in the Antebellum South.* Oxford: Oxford University Press.

———. 1978. "Using the Testimony of Ex-slaves: Approaches and Problems." Pp. 169–193 in A-T. Gilmore (ed.) *Revisiting Blassingame's The Slave Community,* Westport, CT: Greenwood Press.

Blumer, H. 1969. *Symbolic Interactionism: Perspectives and Method.* Englewood Cliffs, NJ: Prentice-Hall.

Botkin, B.A. 1945. *Lay My Burden Down: A Folk History of Slavery.* Chicago: University of Chicago Press.

Brown, G.G. 1945. "War Relocation Authority: Gila River Project; Rivers, Arizona; Community Analysis Section. May 12 to July 1945. Final Report." *Applied Anthropology* 4: 1–48.

Clarke, L. and M. Clarke. 1969. *Sufferings of Lewis and Milton Clarke, Sons of a Soldier of the Revolution During a Captivity of More Than Twenty Years Among Slaveholders of Kentucky, One of the So-Called Christian States of North America.* New York: Arno Press.

Cohen, E. 1954. *Human Behavior in the Concentration Camp.* London: Jonathan Cape.

Cooley, C.H. 1912. *Human Nature and the Social Order.* New York: Scribner.

Cott, N.F. 1977. *The Bonds of Womanhood: "Woman's Sphere" in New England, 1780–1835.* New Haven: Yale University Press.

Davis, J.A. 1959. "A Formal Interpretation of the Theory of Relative Deprivation." *Sociometry* 22: 280–296.

Della Fava, L.R. 1980. "The Meek Shall Not Inherit the Earth: Self-evaluations and the Legitimacy of Stratification." *American Sociological Review* 45: 955–971.

Dornbusch, S.M. and W.R. Scott. 1975. *Evaluation and the Exercise of Authority.* San Francisco: Jossey-Bass.

Douglass, F. 1970. *My Bondage and My Freedom.* Chicago: Johnson.

Drew, B. 1968. *The Refugee: Or the Narratives of Fugitive Slaves in Canada, Related by Themselves.* New York: Negro Universities Press.

Easton, D. 1958. "The Perception of Authority and Political Change." Pp. 170–196 in C.J. Friedrich (ed.) *Authority [Nomos I],* Cambridge: Harvard University Press.

Emerson, R.M. 1962. "Power-dependence Relations." *American Sociological Review* 27: 31–41.

Fanon, F. 1968. *Black Skin, White Masks.* New York: Grove Press.

Federal Writers' Project. 1972. in George P. Rawick (ed.) *The American Slave: A Composite Autobiography,* 17 vols. Westport. CT: Greenwood Press.

Fisk University. Social Science Institute. 1945. *Social Science Source Documents, No. 1: Unwritten History of Slavery. Autobiographical Account of Negro Ex-Slaves.* Nashville, TN: Fisk University, Social Science Institute.

Freire, P. 1974. *Pedagogy of The Oppressed.* New York: Seabury Press.

Glaser, B.G. and A.L. Strauss. 1967. *The Discovery of Grounded Theory: Strategies for Qualitative Research.* Chicago: Aldine.

Goffman, E. 1969. *Strategic Interaction.* Philadelphia: University of Pennsylvania Press.

Habermas, J. 1970a. "On Systematically Distorted Communication." *Inquiry* 13: 205–218.

———. 1970b. "Towards a Theory of Communicative Competence." *Inquiry* 13: 360–375.

———. 1973a. *Legitimation Crisis.* Boston: Beacon Press.

———. 1973b. *Theory and Practice.* Boston: Beacon Press.

———. 1976. "Problems of Legitimation in Late Capitalism." Pp. 363–387 in P. Connerton (ed.) *Critical Sociology: Selected Readings.* New York: Penguin.

Holmes, S.K. (Stone). 1955. *Brokenburn. The Journal of Kate Stone. 1861–1868.* Baton Rouge: Louisiana State University Press.

Horkheimer, M. 1972. *Critical Theory: Selected Essays.* New York: Herder and Herder.

Huggins, N.I. 1979. *Black Odyssey: The Afro-American Ordeal in Slavery.* New York: Vintage.

Jeffrey, J.R. 1978. *Frontier Women: The Trans-Mississippi West 1840–1880.* New York: Hill and Wang.

Kashima, T. 1980. "Japanese American Internees Return, 1945–1955: Readjustment and Social Amnesia." *Phylon* 41: 102–115.

Kemper, T. 1974. "On the Nature and Purpose of Ascription." *American Sociological Review* 39: 844–853.

Lebsock, S. 1984. *The Free Women in Petersburg: Status and Culture in a Southern Town, 1784–1860.* New York: W.W. Norton.

Lindsmith, A.R. 1947. *Opiate Addiction.* Bloomington, IN: Principia Press.

————. 1953. "Comment on W.S. Robinson's 'The Logical Structure of Analytic Induction.'" *American Sociological Review* 18: 604–611.

Lipset, S.M. 1963. *Political Man: The Social Bases of Politics.* New York: Anchor Books.

Litwack, L.F. 1980. *Been in the Storm so Long. The Aftermath of Slavery.* New York: Vintage.

Luchetti, C. 1982. *Women of the West.* St. George, UT: Antelope Island Press.

Mannoni, O. 1968. *Prospero and Caliban. The Psychology of Colonization.* New York: Praeger.

Marx, K. 1973. *Gundrisse.* New York: Vintage.

Mead, G.H. 1962. *Mind, Self, and Society.* Chicago: University of Chicago Press.

Memmi, A. 1965. *The Colonizer and the Colonized.* New York: Orion Press.

————. 1984. *Dependence.* Boston: Beacon Press.

Merquior, J. 1980. *Rousseau and Weber: Two Studies in the Theory of Legitimacy.* London: Routledge and Kegan Paul.

Michener, H.A. and M.R. Burt. 1975a. "Components of 'Authority' as Determinants of Compliance." *Journal of Personality and Social Psychology* 31: 606–614.

————. 1975b. "Use of Social Influence Under Varying Conditions of Legitimacy." *Journal of Personality and Social Psychology* 32: 398–407.

Moore, B., Jr. 1978. *Injustice: The Social Bases of Obedience and Revolt.* White Plains, NY: M.E. Sharpe.

Parkin, F. 1982. *Max Weber.* London: Tavistock.

Pleasants, L.L. 1916. *Old Virginia Days and Ways: Reminiscences of Mrs. Sally McCarty Pleasants.* Monaska, WI: George Banta Publishing Co.

Rose, J.D. 1969. "The Role of the Other in Self-Evaluation." *Sociological Quarterly* 10: 470–479.

Rosen, P.L. 1979. "Legitimacy, Domination, and Ego Displacement." Pp. 75–95 in A.J. Vidich and R.M. Glassman (eds.) *Conflict and Control, Challenge to Legitimacy of Modern Governments.* Beverly Hills: Sage.

Runciman, W.G. 1966. *Relative Deprivation and Social Justice.* London: Routledge & Kegan Paul.

Ryan, M. 1981. *Cradle of the Middle Class: The Family in Oneida County, New York, 1790–1865.* Cambridge: Cambridge University Press.

Schutz, A. 1970. in H.R. Wagner (ed.) *On Phenomenology and Social Relations.* Chicago: University of Chicago Press.

Scott; A. 1970. *The Southern Lady: From Pedestal to Politics 1830–1930.* Chicago: University of Chicago Press.

Shibutani, T. and K.M. Kwan. 1965. *Ethnic Stratification: A Comparative Approach.* New York: Macmillan.

Shils, E. 1981. *Tradition.* Chicago: University of Chicago Press.

Shroyer, T. 1973. *The Critique of Domination: The Origins and Development of Critical Theory.* New York: George Braziller.

Simmel, G. 1950. in K.H. Wolff (trans. and ed.) *The Sociology of Georg Simmel.* Glencoe, IL: Free Press.

Spicer, E., K. Luomala, A.T. Hansen, and M. K. Opler. 1946. *Impounded People. Japanese Americans in Relocation Centers.* Washington, DC: War Relocation Authority, United States Department of the Interior.

Stampp, K. 1971. "Rebels and Sambos: The Search for the Negro's Personality in Slavery." *Journal of Southern History* 37: 367–392.

Strauss, A. 1978. *Negotiations: Varieties, Contexts, Processes, and Social Order.* San Francisco: Jossey-Bass.

Sullivan, H.S. 1953. *The Interpersonal Theory of Psychiatry.* New York: Norton.

Swisshelm, J. 1880. *Half a Century.* Chicago: Jansen. McClurg & Co.

Sykes, G.M. 1966. *The Society of Captives. A Study of a Maximum Security Prison.* New York: Atheneum.

Tateishi, J. 1984. *And Justice for All. An Oral History of the Japanese American Detention Camps.* New York: Random House.

Thomas, D.L., D.D. Franks, and J.M. Calonica. 1972. "Role-taking and Power in Social Psychology." *American Sociological Review* 37: 605–614.

Turner, R.H. 1956. "Role-taking, Role Standpoint, and Reference Group Behavior." *American Journal of Sociology* 61: 316–328.

Walker, H., G.M. Thomas, and M. Zelditch, Jr. 1986. "Legitimation, Endorsement, and Stability." *Social Forces* 64: 620–643.

Walters, E.V. 1969. *Terror and Resistance: A Study of Political Violence.* New York: Oxford.

Weber, M. 1947. in A.M. Henderson and T. Parsons (trans.) *The Theory of Social and Economic Organization.* Oxford: Oxford University Press.

———. 1958. in H.H. Gerth and C. Wright Mills (trans. and eds.) *From Max Weber: Essays in Sociology.* Oxford: Oxford University Press.

———. 1978. in G. Roth and C. Wittich (eds.) *Economy and Society, I and II.* Berkeley: University of California Press.

Welter, B. 1978. "The Cult of True Womanhood: 1820–1860." Pp. 313–333 in M. Gordon (ed.) *The American Family in Social-Historical Perspective.* New York: St. Martin's Press.

Wiley, B.I. 1975. *Confederate Women.* Westport, CT: Greenwood Press.

Wirth L. 1964. "The Problem of Minority Groups." Pp. 244–269 in A.J. Reiss (ed.) *On Cities and Social Life.* Chicago: University of Chicago Press.

Wolf, C. 1969. *Garrison Community: A Study of an Overseas American Military Colony.* Westport, CT: Greenwood Press.

———. 1978. "Social Class, Status, and Prestige." Pp. 135–146 in J.S. Roucek (ed.) *Social Control for the 1980s.* Westport, CT: Greenwood Press.

Wrong, D.H. 1968. "Some Problems in Defining Social Power." *American Journal of Sociology* 73: 63–681.

———. 1970. *Max Weber.* Englewood Cliffs, NJ: Prentice-Hall.

———. 1979. *Power: Its Forms, Bases, and Uses.* New York: Harper.

Yetman, N. 1970. *Voices from Slavery.* New York: Holt, Rinehart and Winston.

Znaniecki, F. 1934. *The Method of Sociology.* New York. Farrart and Rinehart.

The Social Construction of Historical Events Through Public Dramas

Edward Gross
University of Washington

Medieval Corpus Christi pageants, community and royal public dramas, and French revolutionary demonstrations are examined in order to uncover the elements of their social construction. The elements are seen to be focus, engrossment, costuming, performer selection, scripting, performance effects and moods, and the presentation of symbols. These theatrical elements form a technology that is employed by elites when they collectively seek to symbolize power, present the status order, demand expressions of loyalty, symbolize tradition, emphasize solidarity, and engineer social and cultural change. It is concluded that the study of power effectiveness requires attention not only to legitimacy and interest satisfaction but also to the manner in which power is presented.

At least since the appearance of Berger and Luckman's highly popular book *The Social Construction of Reality* (1966), as well as the growth in acceptance of ethnomethodological research, the meaning of the term "social construction" has moved from an original concept to something approaching a cliché. This is not to say that the term has lost its usefulness, quite the contrary. Instead, because the implications of the term have rarely been worked out in sufficient detail, it has hardly realized its promise. The mere fact, for example, that a new or newly named disease has made its appearance, along with specialists who are ready to treat sufferers, is not sufficient evidence to conclude that a new "social construction" has taken place, for such an historical experience may involve little more than the emergence, growth, and decline of

Reprinted from Symbolic Interaction, 9(2):179–200.

occupations and professions (e.g., Krause, 1971) and shifts in the division of labor. Nor is the emergence of newly named forms of deviance sufficient for the conclusion that a new "reality" has now been constructed. In the few symbolic interactionist studies in which attempts were made to describe in detail how a given reality is constructed (such as Ball's [1967] description of an abortion clinic, the battle between competing definitions of reality [Emerson, 1970], or Goffman's pictures of various "frames" [1974]), we were given hints of how difficult and painstaking a job it is to describe and account for a separate reality (cf. Weick, 1977).

If social construction as a concept is to have theoretical value, it would seem desirable to restrict its use to situations in which we have evidence that persons have set about putting something together with some degree of deliberateness, following a plan or image. Ruled out would be norms or practices that grew up crescively, with little awareness other than adding to or tinkering with tradition. Of course even there each addition may be "constructed" or thought through to some degree, but to call all such acts "social constructions" would give the term little usefulness.

One would look, instead, for evidence that men and women are at work on their own or with staffs, experts, materials, and equipment, along with plans, collaborators, and directors. A social construction would show some degree of originality—even artistry—modifications, feedback, evaluations, inspections, payments, and sanctions. There is no assumption that persons always act rationally or know clearly what they are about. Sometimes persons end up with constructions that they had not intended or that are different from what was hoped for. But constructions they are as long as there were minimal plans, a program, a division of labor, and some product or envisioned outcome.

The task of this article is that of identifying the chief elements that enter into social constructions. One reason the task has proved difficult is that analysts have tended to focus on constructions that are subtle or not clearly seen by the participants, perhaps even naively being unaware that a construction was taking place. Thus in discussing the *discovery* (author's italics) of child abuse, Pfohl (1977) argues that a certain behavior (striking children to the point of producing tissue damage) was in existence for many years, perhaps centuries. Physicians were aware of it but did not raise any questions, partly because they did not see it as part of their clinical responsibility to probe legal and moral aspects of the matter. Instead, pediatric radiologists who did not directly face parents as clients were the first (aided by pediatricians and psychiatrists) to "blow the whistle" on what they saw as a serious moral or legal problem. In turn, the more direct "construction" became visible when the term "child-abuse syndrome" was invented, thus letting parents or other perpetrators off the moral or legal hook because they were now treatable as sick people. But those who invented the term "child-abuse syndrome" were not (it is believed) deliberately constructing something to generate therapeutic business for themselves. They really believed there was such an illness. A similar argument can be made for many kinds of medicalized problems as well as other social problems.[1]

Such social constructions are difficult to penetrate because they are surrounded by disclaimers of intent as well as by defenses offered when critics accuse them of being "moral entrepreneurs" (Becker, 1963) who now have a stake in the condition or problem they have created by their own activities.

In order to bypass the problem of penetrating those defenses, we turn attention to historical *public dramas* as a model for exploring the elements of social constructions. Such dramas had as their central and clearly recognized purpose the realization of a consensual image, whether of a religious order, a community, or a nation. Further, the attempt was often made in the face of indifference or even outright hostility from the population on whom the image was being imposed. This combination of deliberate intent in the face of indifference or opposition made it difficult for those carrying out the drama to hide either the intent or, what is more to our purpose, the details of the processes whereby the image was constructed. By seeking to identify the major techniques thus revealed, we gain hints of the elements of social construction that may be present in other realities in which they are more likely to be hidden.

PUBLIC DRAMA FORMS

Public dramas are large-scale performances intended to celebrate an important occasion or to affirm a collective purpose and are usually presented in the open air to mass audiences. Their purpose is partly didactic—to transmit some belief, restage historical events, or communicate some message—and partly to mobilize emotion and reinforce sentiments of attachment to group, tribe, class, or nation.

Public dramas appear to be universal. Peasant and preliterate societies regularly conduct processions in which practically all able-bodied members of a village or settlement participate. Some of these celebrations have purely local significance, whereas others are part of occasions of national rejoicing such as religious feasts, patriotic celebrations, or carnival processions derived in Europe from Roman feasts. Many forms, as we note below, developed from religious ceremonies that came to be elaborated and secularized as dramatic elements were added to them partly to serve as ways of teaching gospel truths and partly to celebrate those truths themselves in vivid form. Other occasions included contests such as races, fights, or tournaments in which the outcome was held to be determined by supernatural forces. In more modern times pageants came to be associated directly with dramatic performances, for example, when Ben Jonson and Inigo Jones wrote and staged court masques during the reigns of the Stuarts (Jones, 1966). Molière wrote one of the most elaborate fetes in 1664 for Louis XIV (Matthews, 1916), and T.S. Eliot wrote the choruses of a religious pageant staged in England in 1934 (Eliot, 1934). More commonly, however, and especially in recent times, pageants have been written and staged by amateur members of a community, the participation itself being an important element of a collective enterprise. Talent is required, as we shall see, but it need not be of genius level.

We shall focus mainly on three kinds of public dramas:

1. *The Corpus Christi or "Cycle" Pageants of England from the Fourteenth to the Sixteenth Centuries.* These were plays dramatizing various events revolving about the life of Christ as well as other biblical scenes.[2]

2. *Community Pageants.* These were historical (such as centennial celebrations) or thematic (celebrating "freedom," "liberty," or other ideologies).[3] The form reached spectacular proportions in the displays associated with medieval chivalry and with the royal and absolutist courts.
3. *Pageants of the French Revolution.* These pageants were enacted (often under the direction of Jacques Louis David, the famous painter) to develop revolutionary solidarity as well as patriotic fraternity in the French population.[4]

These three kinds of public dramas were selected partly because of the availability of data and partly because they provide widely varying samples of drama-types, giving us some confidence in the generality of our conclusions. The Corpus Christi pageants assumed that a consensus in values was present but also sought to provide moral lessons for the wavering, the backsliders, and other deviants. Community pageants reveal the technology in more self-conscious fashion. Although often employed as backdrops to commercial enterprises as well as for the celebration of consensus, they could be and were used by political authorities to provide displays of intimidating power when that power was open to possible challenge. The French Revolution pageants were chosen to show how the pageant form can be employed not only to celebrate or affirm an already existing symbolic theme or power but also to introduce wholly new even revolutionary themes and thus to engineer the process of social change directly.

THEATER AS A TECHNOLOGY OF SOCIAL CONSTRUCTION

It will be recalled that one of Durkheim's central claims was that the unity of societies required periodic collective rituals and ceremonies that functioned to reaffirm solidarity and common sentiments. Durkheim (1915) wrote that such unity or solidarity " . . . cannot be achieved except by means of reunions, assemblies and meetings where the individuals, being closely united to one another, reaffirm in common their common sentiments" (p. 427). Such rituals and meetings were essentially religious even when they were applied to secular occasions.

Those whom Lukes (1975, p. 293) calls neo-Durkheimians apply Durkheim's views to secular occasions, for example, when Shils and Young (1975) describe the coronation of Queen Elizabeth as "a great act of national communion"(p. 80), when Warner (1962, p. 8) sees Memorial Day in the United States as acting to unify a local community with its "conflicting symbols and opposing autonomous churches and association," when Verba (1965) examines the funeral of President Kennedy, or when Bellah (1967) describes the "civil religion" of the United States.

Lukes (1975) quarrels with the identification of "unity" with "consensus," pointing out that members of a society may work together yet exhibit little agreement on values, ceremonies, and rituals and that such settings do not necessarily provide evidence of consensus but rather seek to "define as authoritative certain ways of seeing society" (p. 301). Lukes provides, as an example, the parade of Orangemen in Ulster on the anniversary of the Battle of the Boyne. Such a demonstration carried out before sullen Catholic onlookers hardly connotes consensus, he points out, but is clearly a symbolic statement made up of primarily cognitive dimensions. One might agree with Lukes while noting that the demonstration does make clear (and is meant to make clear) that there is consensus *among the Orangemen* on the values they are proclaiming, although those values are not shared by the Catholics. But the question left unanswered by Lukes is why the Orangemen choose to make clear their "way of seeing society" through the means of a parade.

The neo-Durkheimians do not account for the use of the means they discuss such as a coronation or the Kennedy funeral that made it apt for the celebration of consensus. Durkheim himself did not explore the question of why "reunions, assemblies, and meetings" should be so widely employed for collective affirmation.

The problem, then, is to identify the elements of those technologies that make them especially effective and account for the popularity. It is here that public dramas can serve because they are employed not only in situations in which a collective sentiment is being affirmed but also, as noted earlier, in which one cannot assume that there is any collective sentiment but the attempt is being made to impose such a sentiment on an audience, even a hostile one. Because the sentiment cannot be assumed, it must be constructed. But constructed of what? That is the question.

The clue that public dramas provide, as implied in their name, is that the technology turns out to be one that makes use of theater. For example, Bellah (1967), in describing the origins of the American civil religion in the American Revolution, calls attention to the sacred symbol of "liberty." But he does not consider the question of how "liberty," which is after all an abstract concept, was communicated other than through literary statements or speeches. In contrast, historian Albanese (1976) quotes an early account of an event in one city that was repeated in several others.

> At Portsmouth, in New Hampshire, the morning was ushered in, with tolling all the bells in town. In the course of the day, notice was given to the friends of liberty, to attend her funeral. A coffin, neatly ornamented inscribed with the word *Liberty* in large letters, was carried to the grave. The funeral procession began from the state-house, attended with two unbraced drums. While the inhabitants who followed the coffin were in motion, minute guns were fired, and continued till the corpse arrived at the place of interment. Then an oration in favour of the deceased was pronounced. It was scarcely ended before the corpse was taken up, it having been perceived that some remains of life were left, at which the inscription was immediately altered to "Liberty revived." The bells immediately exchanged their melancholy, for a more joyful sound, and satisfaction appeared in every countenance. (p. 70)

A modern writer might amend the "satisfaction in every countenance" to a note that the performance was "greeted with applause," for this is more than mere audience participation in a collective ritual; it is plainly theater itself. We generally find public dramas employing a theatrical technology to express and communicate ideas as well as mobilize feelings, in short, to produce powerful effects on an audience who may themselves be coparticipants as well.

Theater can of course be brought privately to select audiences for their amusement and distraction, but those who have sought to generate or proclaim collective values have found it useful to turn to public dramas performed before as wide an audience as possible.[5] In historical cases, this has meant staging on available streets or open places.[6]

As a consequence, those who wished—as fourteenth-century English churchmen did—to ensure belief in Christianity, those who wished to bind together the members of a nineteenth-century American village, or those who sought to substitute for a set of traditional ideas some revolutionary ideas have all found it useful, perhaps essential, to conduct public theatrical performances. There may be other technologies that would work as well, but so far none have appeared to challenge seriously the power of theater in the construction of values.

We will first examine the elements of the theatrical form that account for its effectiveness as a technology and then turn to the conditions under which theatrical forms are employed.

PUBLIC DRAMA AS THEATER

The major theatrical elements in public dramas can be identified as focus, engrossment, costumes, the performers, scripts, the performance, and symbols.

Focus

The first and most obvious feature of theatrical performance that recommends itself to those seeking to construct public images or collective sentiments is that it gets people's attention. Persons are invited to view a play—a drama of limited duration—carried out before their eyes on a public stage. These are defined as "occasions" (Faris, 1973), that is, as special times in which there is sanctioned deviance. Persons are allowed, even required, to put aside normal everyday activities and obligations and come together to view a set of activities that are unusual (even in "realistic" drama), requiring imagination and what Coleridge spoke of as a "willing suspension of disbelief."[7] Persons talk about the forthcoming event as an occasion, make arrangements to attend it together, often get "dressed up" in special clothes not otherwise worn, instruct children in the decorum appropriate to the occasion, and assume, on arrival, the role of spectator. Central to providing focus is the stage itself. Cycle plays were acted out on movable pageant wagons and platforms, but the performance often spilled out onto the street or adjacent spaces or "stations." This meant that the pageant had to be preceded by street cleaning and the removal of clutter or anything that might interfere with clear viewing, such preparations adding to the "glory" and anticipation of the occasion. In community pageants the question of whether to stage the event in the open or indoors engages much attention. Outdoors allows for processions and massed performances but also the possible loss of focus. Indoors allows for control of lighting and the technological devices that the proscenium offers (such as revolving stages, raked floors, easy scene-shifting, curtains, etc.) but forces the audience into a position of passivity. In the case of British coronations, as Churchill (1953) describes them, Westminster Abbey is the only possible stage and itself becomes part of the essential symbolism, as we note below). Because the coronation is accompanied by a long procession, the streets themselves form a stage.

In Revolutionary France the streets were also stages, viewed by foreigners invited to witness demonstrations and pageants as well as executions. Robespierre and his colleagues were keenly conscious of the fact that the "whole world is watching."[8] As a consequence, there was deep concern that what they were doing should not be perceived as indiscriminate butchery or mere mob violence but that it should be seen as a carefully orchestrated creation of a new society that would be a model to the world. Although it was recognized that intellectuals and critics might want time to study the written defenses and philosophical justifications at their leisure, it was felt that something more immediate and impressive was needed, for which the theatrical form seemed appropriate and thus was used repeatedly. It was not enough that the people revolt; they had to *stage* a revolution as a magnificent occasion to (they hoped) the applause of the downtrodden everywhere (Henderson, 1912).

Engrossment

In discussing the "theatrical frame," Goffman (1974) states that his major concern is "... the very remarkable capacity of viewers to engross themselves in a transcription that departs radically and systematically from an imaginable original" (p. 145). Although Goffman's interest is in calling attention to the ability of the human self to become thus engrossed, our concern is with the further question of how such engrossment is achieved. What pageants tell us is that engrossment proceeds precisely from the fact that the transcription does "depart radically" from any comparable scene in everyday life. As just noted, everyday life is full of distractions and routines that do not so much engross us as merely distract us, calling on a continuing shift of attention from work requirements to after-work obligations and to recreational excitements—each momentary—snatched as the opportunity arises. But the chance to witness a pageant is a rare experience, its rarity springing partly from the fact that it "departs radically" from anything we usually experience. The unique experience (as well as focus) is caught in Schramm's (1965) description of the central role of television in bringing to view President Kennedy's assassination and its aftermath. He writes:

> Immediacy was one striking quality of the information flow during those days of crisis; another was the pervasiveness of it. For all practical purposes there was no other news story in America during those four days, and the mass media concentrated on telling it. There were times during those days when *a majority of all Americans were apparently looking at the same events and hearing the same words from the television sets—participating together, at least to that extent, in a great national event. Nothing like this on such a scale had ever occurred before.* (p. 4, emphasis in original)

Nor was it simply the assassination, in all its morbid fascination, that engrossed persons. There was a procession—a formal ordering of events—a cortege that included hundreds of distinguished (and many immediately recognizable) figures who, like the television viewer, were witnesses to this event that departed so radically from any imaginable everyday event. It was news, yet it was also, however horrible, tragic theater.

A major clue to the power of pageants lies squarely in the ability, as in the case of all theater (Shank, 1979, Ch. 3), to create an experience that appears more real than everyday life because it is a different reality which the members of the audience, by their willingness to "suspend disbelief," help to create. In turn, the experience in which, in Langer's words (1953, p. 307), tension is created by the dramatist's ability to make a "present filled with its own future" becomes not only real but vivid and exciting. So the pageant master does not call an audience together to tell them *about* the miracle of Jesus's birth (which they have all heard many times before anyhow) but to show it to them as experienced by characters who seem as human as they. The director and the scriptwriter of a community pageant who wish to tell the members of the community that ten years have passed do not simply say so but have actors dressed up *as* people were dressed in 1971, 1972, 1973, and so forth, each in some way recalling a major event of the year in the way that he or she appears, each gracefully moving across the stage while appropriate music heralds the coming of the "big year" when something important happened. As for the French Revolutionists, they were not content to write a report stating that the monarchy was overthrown. They paraded the king himself to the guillotine and to silence forever any doubts about their seriousness, they cut off his head in full public view, a sight the viewers (and the world) could hardly ignore and would not forget.

Such engrossment was further facilitated by imaginative uses of equipment. The pageant wagon drawn in cycle plays was colorfully decorated, as seen in a description of a manger scene staged by the mercers of Chester (England):

> Of caryage I have no doubt
> Both within and without
> It shall be deckyd yt all the Rowte
> Full gladly on it shall be the loke.
> With sundry cullors it shall glime
> of velvet satten and damske fine
> Taffyta sersnett of poppyngee grene.
> (Spencer, 1911, p. 96)[9]

Particular care was given to constructing properly frightening "hell mouths" in other pageant cars, including a dragon's head with side-gaping jaws and long, sharp teeth and gleaming eyes, so exaggerated that we sense the hand of scenic designers carried away by their sense of drama. A production at Valenciennes in 1547 was described by a witness as follows (Nicoll, 1976):

> The effects associated with Heaven and Hell were veritably prodigious and might well have seemed to the audience the result of magic.... From Hell, Lucifer rose, how, one could not tell, on a dragon's back. Moses' staff, dry and withered,

suddenly burst forth with flowers and fruit; the souls of Herod and Judas were borne into the air by devils. . . . Water was seen to change into wine . . . and more than a hundred persons tasted the wine; the five loaves and two fish were multiplied and distributed to more than a thousand people, yet, notwithstanding, there were a dozen baskets (left) over. (p. 113)

Still others made use of crumbled biscuits to simulate the fall of snow, and rain was made to fall as rosewater (apparently scented "to protect noble nostrils from loyal but noisome 'stinkards'" [Wickham, 1959, p. 96]).

Costumes

Costumes generally made use of whatever was considered appropriate for the character according to accepted conventional representations. Kings always wore crowns (even in bed) as well as crimson-purple robes. For community pageants, St. Peter carried keys; St. Christopher, a child; St. John, a lamb; St. George was pictured with his foot planted on a dragon; and Justice brandished a sword. Colors had clear meanings: Yellow was not only used for the sun, for Sunday scenes, and for representing youth or springtime but also for faith and constancy. White—for the moon, October, November, and infancy—was also representative of hope and innocence; vermilion stood for Mars, Tuesday, ages 30 to 40, and charity; black stood for Saturday, crooked old age, and prudence and constancy (Wickham, 1959, p. 48).

In modern community pageants, the critical element sought was accuracy for an historical pageant and simplicity for an abstract theme. For example, in a Savannah (Georgia) reenactment of a ball held in honor of a visit by then U.S. President James Monroe, a certain William Scarborough, "a merchant prince" of the time, was shown greeting the President. The part of Scarborough was played, as stated in the program "by his great-great-nephew, John Stark,"a present-day resident of Savannah (Taft, 1921 p. 148). In addition, attempts were made to utilize any artifacts or pieces of furniture of the portrayed period (all duly noted in the printed program).

For royal pageants, equipment and costume not only had to be authentic but had to match the occasion in detail as well as splendor, as may be seen in the description of the first meeting in 1514 of King Louis XII of France and Mary Tudor, sister of Henry VIII of England, who was to become (briefly) the queen of France. The meeting was rigged outside of Abbeville, allowing King Louis to come upon Mary's procession accidentally:

He rode as jauntily as he could (he was in poor health and he suffered from gout) a beautiful Spanish horse, whose barb was of cloth of gold and black satin in chequers. (After Louis had gone) A procession was formed. It led off with fifty of Mary's esquires dressed in silks of several sorts, all wearing the inevitable gold collar and chain. Next came the Duke of Norfolk, with the ambassadors and noblemen two and two, all wearing enormous gold chains, some doubling and trebling them around their necks. . . . Garter King at Arms and Richmond Herald in their tabards followed, with eight trumpeters in crimson damask, and macers with gilt maces surmounted by a royal crown; then two grooms in short doublets of cloth of gold and black velvet, with velvet caps, each leading a palfrey, and after these, two other palfreys ridden by pages. (And so it went on until) Last of all came 200 English archers marching two and two in three divisions; the first were in doublets of green satin and surcoats and belts of black velvet, with shaggy red and white hats; the second wore black doublets and shaggy white hats; the third, black with grey hats. (Brown, 1911, pp. 113–115)

A counter-procession then met her.

The Performers

The town corporations were particularly concerned that properly qualified actors should be chosen for the Corpus Christi pageants. Chambers (1903) says: "An order at York in 1476 directed the choice of a body of 'connyng discrete, and able players' to test the quality of all those selected as actors."[10] And delinquents were chastised. For example, in 1452 a certain Henry Cowper, a "webster" (weaver) of Beverly, was fined by the town wardens for not knowing his part and on another occasion, ". . . two shillings (were) collected from 'Richard Trollop, Alderman of Payntours (painters), for that his Play of 'Les 3 Kyngs of Collyn' was played badly and disorderly, in contempt of the whole community, in the presence of many strangers'" (Spencer, 1911, p. 52).[11] The players in community pageants were not expected or required to be professionals but to look the part and given the distance of the audience from the performers, this often came down to plainly physical matters—height (for leading figures) and a minimal degree of grace of movement (often assured by simply having the performer do very little or nothing at all). If performers (especially children) were members of the local community, then the audience could be counted on to forgive any but the most inept of performances.

For courtly processions, festivals, and other occasions, the performers were those called for by the event (those to be crowned in coronations, Olympic Games participants, et al.), but it is clear that much coaching and rehearsals preceded these events—given the awareness that they were to be performed for audiences, however much official ideology might have celebrated the events as rituals or events in their own right. When an historical event was to be portrayed, there was much concern that it be carried off to be dramatically effective as well as faithful to the event. For example, in the Oberammergau Passion Play, Moses (1930) tells of the concern that the crucifixion go off without accident. A textbook of 1815 advises that the person playing the part of Christ should be bound " . . . with strips of linen around the body, hand, arms, round the breast and loins, so that, should he become unconscious, he will not fall from the cross" (Moses, 1930, p. lxxvi; see also Heaton, 1970).

Scripts

Although the scripts of the Cycle plays were highly standardized, rivalry among the guilds led to the rewriting and revising of plays as well as the renting of scripts from other towns. There was opportunity for innovation (within stylized limits), and a guild (especially a new one) might create one or develop to full length what had been treated as a minor incident (Spencer, 1911, pp. 37, 53–54).

Writers (e.g., Chubb and Associates, 1912) on amateur community pageants urged that spoken scripts be kept to a minimum of a few lines to introduce the piece, the rest being performed in pantomime because, even with amplification, large audiences cannot hear or attend to speeches or complex dialogue. Performances before mass audiences, especially those watching on television, are usually highly formalized but not only because of technical requirements. At the funeral march for President John F. Kennedy, the presence of representatives of all national institutions as well as official delegations from 93 countries *(Four Days: The Historical Record of the Death of President Kennedy* 1964, pp. 140–141) created the need to decide precisely (for reasons of protocol as well as simple order) who should march first—who to the right and who to the left—an order that was as rigid as any ballet although it might have ruffled diplomatic feathers.

Designs of the major court fetes or pageants to celebrate the entry of the Spanish Princess Katherine into London (where she was to marry Prince Arthur—the son of Henry VII); or the spectacles put on by the Duc of Anjou were so complex that there was never any question of putting the scripts and movement plans into the hands of amateurs: The leading writers, painters, and scene designers available were given specific commissions, their very luster itself contributing to the grandeur of the occasion. Given the expected emphasis on pomp in regal processions, it comes as something of a surprise that the French Revolutionary pageants were also put into the hands of leading designers. Dowd (1948) writes that these ceremonies were " . . . realized through the collaboration of leading artists of the day: Grossec for the music, J.J. Chenier for the lyrics, and above all, (Jacques Louis) David for the decorations and organization" (p. 54). The list of "credits" sounds like the advertisement for a Broadway show, which is really not surprising, for shows they were.

The Performance

Nowhere is the dramatic element more clearly in evidence than in bringing off the performance itself. Here are seen all the accoutrements and every trick of the theatrical stage. Public dramas must of course be rehearsed, although there is less of this than in conventional drama because the vastness of the spectacle often precludes overall rehearsal, leaving individual units to do their own rehearsing. Still, the performance itself must be announced. The Corpus Christi plays were heralded by "waits" who went throughout the town calling out the name and the place of the coming performance; community pageants are advertised in newspapers (as were the French Revolutionary pageants), and modern events may be proclaimed sometimes years before—as in the case of the Olympics or of political conventions.

The key figures are the directors, or pageant masters, who exercise usually dictatorial control over on-the-spot decisions although they hew to the general policy of a board of directors. But much more is required of them than mere stage managing.

Pageant masters are not only talented but must be possessed of a minimum of charisma, or the ability to inspire performers. Because performances are linear movements through time, anything can go wrong, and improvisation and originality are therefore often required. For the Corpus Christi plays, some innovations, once demonstrated were widely adopted. To avoid the necessity of exits, which took time and required awkward departures from the pageant wagon, pageant masters hit upon the device of having the actors not in the next scene simply feign sleep while the action went on around them. Another simple but effective device was used to provide a simulation of blood: a concealed leather bag (full of red vinegar or, occasionally, animal blood) was pricked, creating a vivid effect, particularly when actual murder was shown, as was done in a play performed in Canterbury, which depicted the murder of its patron saint, Thomas à Becket (Spencer, 1911, p. 205).

For community pageants, the pageant master finds himself in charge of a dispersed rather complex organization that might include an artist, costumer, musical director scenic manager, electrician, and directors of the various episodes in the pageant. Taft (1921) points out that tension between the master and those persons is ever likely especially when some get carried away with artistic originality or fail to recognize, as the music director seems most prone to, that they are there to support the pageant and not to demonstrate their own virtuosity (cf. Shank, 1979, p. 49). Still, their ingenuity may be called into play, as would happen when an impending storm would lead the master to have the music director speed up the music so that the performance can end before the rains come.

As for the French Revolutionary festivals, we have commented several times on the central role of Jacques Louis David as director and on his many innovations. One last one should be mentioned. He conceived of the simple device of printing small medallions, which were then given away to the crowd as a souvenir or memento of the occasion. To be present when history is being made is exhilarating. To be able to prove to one's grandchildren that one was there makes the medallion into a cherished heirloom of the great occasion that will never be forgotten.

Symbols

In Meadian social psychology, the meaning of a gesture is seen as the uncompleted part of an act, the completion being carried out, in imagination, by another whose thoughts in such imaginative completion match those of the individual who offers the gesture. Such a gesture then becomes a significant symbol (Blumer, 1969). In public dramas, an identical process occurs. In everyday interaction, however, previous socialization and the assumption of a working consensus (Goffman, 1959, Ch. VIII) may be sufficient to generate at least a rough correspondence of meanings among those in interaction or engaged in collective enterprises. But in public dramas, such correspondence is not assumed but is deliberately set out in such a vivid manner as to call forth a desired image and make certain that no one can possibly miss the intended meaning. All the dramatic devices heretofore discussed are mobilized to emphasize that meaning.

For the Corpus Christi cycle, meaning revolves around events in the life of Christ as well as other sacred persons or events. These are then acted out so that audiences can see the Magi arriving, Christ being crucified, and Judas hanging himself, other figures such as Abraham and Lot, Noah and the Ark, all following the Bible as script. The usual staging directions call for realism so that the identification will be unmistakable.

Community pageants, whether of royalty or of local communities, are expected to make a clear statement, which they typically do by drawing on obvious or striking imagery. Given their resources, a favorite device of royal courts was to proclaim that all was well in the regime by putting on a brilliant display.[12] In England in 1467, when there was turbulence and conflict, the installation of the Archbishop of York was seized upon as an occasion to demonstrate that all was tranquil:

> Six thousand guests are said to have been present (including many leading members of the nobility) . . . the kitchen provided among other items, 300 quarters of wheat, 300 tuns of ale, 100 tuns of wine, 104 oxen, 6 bulls, 1,000 sheep, 2,000 geese, 2,000 chickens, 4,000 pigeons, 4,000 rabbits, 2,000 hot custards, 3,000 baked cold custards, 3,000 dishes of jelly, and 4,000 cold tarts. (Myers, 1959, p. 2)

On a less grand scale, the American high school pageant has been and still is employed to make symbolic statements. For example, Taft (1921, pp. 110 ff.) describes a pageant in which the Spirit of Thanksgiving, aided by Hope, does valiant battle against Despair, and the battle is celebrated through "primitive pastoral times," including the Greeks, the Pax Romana; the confirmation of Ethelbert, King of Kent; the crowning of the Dauphin on France by Joan of Arc; and the return of Columbus, capped off with a federation of the countries of the world, all done in the Savannah, Georgia, City Auditorium by the Savannah Festival Association and the Savannah High School Parent-Teacher Association.

Through manipulation of symbolic imagery these events clearly mobilize and focus emotion for public audiences. In the case of the French Revolutionary public displays, there seems to be little question that, as we have noted, they were organized, orchestrated, and planned as public spectacles. Butwin (1975) puts it as follows:

> The notion that "all the world's a stage" is such a pervasive source of metaphor that we commonly speak of historical events as if we were speaking of a play. Historians of the French Revolution are so attached to this metaphor that it is hard to believe that the event was not performed on one vast stage. In fact, it was. (p. 141)

CONDITIONS UNDER WHICH THEATRICAL FORMS ARE EMPLOYED

The effectiveness of public dramas contributes to understanding their universal popularity. Their use, however, might easily be limited to entertainment or to purely ceremonial purposes. Such often seems the case in the rituals described by Durkheim, in which regular and periodic ceremonies are performed to symbolize births, coming of age, death, marriage, and other rites of passage. Their functions may be the reduction of anxiety on important occasions, as Malinowski (1974) suggested, or the solemnizing of important occasions, as Radcliffe-Brown (1939) pointed out. What is usually the case for such rituals is that they are standardized, enacted by professionals, understood by the celebrants, and carried out in traditional form. For such occasions, it is usually possible to assume that there is a consensus that is being reaffirmed by the ritual.

In moments of great historical change, however, neither tradition nor consensus can be assumed. Instead, a deliberate, rational, strategic process of social construction is called for to the end of inventing and proclaiming a new vision, a change of the locus of power, a change in values, or a new direction for the society. Such occasions require something quite different from the enactment of a ritual. They call for nothing less than the stage managing of history. Events cannot then simply be allowed to occur; they must be proclaimed and their significance made clear to people who would otherwise either not notice or would soon forget as they go about their everyday tasks.

Public dramas, designed and executed through theatrical devices that we have described, seem then to be widely employed. But there appear to be special conditions under which theatrical dramas are likely to be employed. Our examination of public dramas suggests that the following six conditions are of particular significance.

The Symbolization of Power

The Corpus Christi Cycle plays made vividly clear that Christian beliefs were not only unquestioned because they were rooted in history and reaffirmed through the sacrifice of martyrs but that any who dared to question those beliefs, let alone transgress them, would be devoured by the devils (portrayed on stage) who would transport the spot into vast hell holes (neatly provided on pageant wagons).

The medieval national pageants, especially those associated with royal or political leadership, employed vivid spectacle that took the following three main forms:

1. *The royal entry*, whereby a ruler would make a solemn entry into and take ceremonial possession of a city or a town. The entry was organized so that clergy, town officers, bourgeoisie, and members of the guilds would meet the royal or noble visitor at the city gates and lead him or her through the town. In anticipation, archways, tableaux, castles, genealogical trees, tabernacles, fountains, and gardens were often built and prepared.

2. *The exercise of arms or tournaments*, including the tilt (in which knights broke lances against one another across a barrier to prevent injury to their horses); the tourney (in which rival parties of knights fought in a melee); and the barriers (in which fighters on foot exchanged blows with swords across a barrier). To the winners, prizes were often presented by the ladies present.

3. *The indoor divertiseement*, or *court fete*, usually an entertainment focused on humanistic themes such as the triumph of "peace" or of "reason." Widely

used were *imprese,* or personal devices, such as the use of the crescent moon by France's Henry II (after his mistress Dianne) or England's James I's identification of himself with King Solomon, as shown by his adoption of the motto: *Beati Pacifici.* The main point, as Strong (1984) puts it, was that

> Magnificence . . . became a princely virtue. A prince must be seen to live magnificently, to dress splendidly, to furnish his palaces richly, to build sumptuously or to send grand embassies to other monarchs. (p. 72)

Or, as Meyers (1959) writes,

> If a lord did not ceaselessly strive to maintain and to enlarge his affinity (his set of dependents and followers), he might find himself in the position of a modern bank if the rumour should begin to spread that its finances were no longer sound. No more than a bank could a magnate afford to look shabby and poverty-stricken; on the contrary; in this lethally competitive society he must impress men by his ostentation and attract them by his hospitality. (p. 2)[13]

Those planning to overthrow existing elites and to proclaim new values have also found it especially desirable to express the power of the new leadership and the magnificence of the new values by a dazzling show, almost as if to demonstrate pride in the new, in case there is any lingering guilt about the rejection of the old. It is then not surprising to find the designers of processions making use of massive display during the French Revolution.

Of the festivals of the French Revolution, Dowd (1948) writes:

> First of all was the physical equipment: the stationary but temporary monuments, such as colossal statues, arches of triumph, columns, temples, altars, and even mountains which punctuated the line of march; then there were the warehouses full of movable items, such as the *chars,* floats, and litters used to transport the various emblematic devices as well as the costumes, standards, and banners which figured in the procession; finally there were the inscription, paintings, bas-reliefs, and other symbolic *decor,* inspired largely by classical antiquity, which adorned these physical objects. (pp. 128–129)

It seems clear that because of its sheer massiveness, the space it took up, and its glitter, such a procession had no other effect (if not object) than to intimidate (as well as dazzle) a vast audience. At the very least, it literally coerced attention and provided the central topic of conversation in the homes of persons of all social classes.[14]

The Presentation of the Status Order

Closely related to the demonstration of power is the capability of pageants to proclaim and to celebrate a clear status order in the sequencing of symbols. In the court fetes and tournaments of the fifteenth and sixteenth centuries, the king or nobles might have taken part in costume—masked or sometimes unmasked—in order to demonstrate their strength or skill or to seek the acclaim of the crowd (which could hardly have been denied). In the case of coronations (which have long traditions, e.g., that of Great Britain), the participants and their roles are usually clearly established. At Queen Elizabeth II's coronation, the sequence in which persons were required to declare their fealty to her after the coronation was ritually prescribed: first, the Archbishop; then the dukes of Edinburgh, Gloucester, and Kent; then the Duke of Norfolk (on behalf of all the other dukes); and so forth. Change is made from time to time, but it is not easy to accomplish. Occasionally the effectiveness of a pageant may be threatened by the unwillingness of persons to accept their positions in the status order to which they are assigned. Grimes (1976), describing the annual celebrations in Santa Fe, New Mexico, or the reconquest of Santa Fe (after its conquest by the Pueblos) by the Spanish under Don Diego de Vargas tells of how pleased local descendants of de Vargas were to participate. Not so willing were local Indian residents who began to refuse to have anything to do with the celebration, leading to the use of Hispanic children, whose skin had been darkened, to act the part of the Pueblos, resulting in embarrassment for the organizers. They tried to mute or transform the message of conquest by claiming that the:

> reconquest was not over one another but over violence and that the victor was peace and goodwill to man. . . . (p. 172)

The local Indians were not fooled, for there is no getting away from the fact that the occasion celebrates an Indian defeat and a Spanish victory. Attempts of the organizers to have it both ways resulted only in status confusion. Theatrical effect seems to require an unmistakable order.

Providing for Demonstrations of Loyalty

The fact that Henry VII of England had been proclaimed successor to Richard III on the battlefield (where the latter was slain) left room for uncertainty as to the legitimacy of the royal claim. In order to quickly reinforce that claim, as well as to formalize the end of the War of the Roses, Henry (of the house of Lancaster) not only married Elizabeth of the House of York but also moved quickly in 1486 to make a "progress"or royal tour to York in order to make sure that the citizens of York recognized his claim. This they did by holding a glorious pageant in which actors representing the previous six Henrys and the mythical founder of the city greeted their illustrious successor in grand style. Much in evidence was the symbolism of roses—the red rose of Lancaster and the white rose of York—shown entwined or as a single "union rose" to which all other flowers were shown giving obedience (Anglo, 1969, pp. 25 ff.; see also Alexander 1980, Ch. III). Similar pageants were held as the progress made its way through other cities whose loyalty was suspect. Henry did not rest content by limiting himself to these ceremonies, but they made a powerful statement that served as a signal to others and as a warning that resistance would be costly. Loyalty was a central theme in French Revolutionary pageants also, although it was of course to be paid to a new set of ideas and to a new government.[15]

To Symbolize Tradition

The fact that the Corpus Christi Cycle plays stuck to a close control of the guilds over the equipment, the scripts, and the pageant cars produced a powerful force that made innovation difficult, although it was never absent. But the force of tradition is best illustrated in the case of royal coronations, in which it is felt to be necessary to call upon the blessing of an immemorial and sacred past to beatify the new monarch and by the same token, to emphasize that the new monarch is the head of all the people. Of the British monarchy, Churchill (1953) quotes Sir Harold Nicholson as follows:

> The Monarchy is to-day regarded by the people of this island and of the Commonwealth and Empire as the magnet of loyalty, the emblem of union, the symbol of continuity and the embodiment of national, as distinct from class or party, feeling. (p. 11)

The regalia are especially well chosen in order to provide visible evidence of this continuity: the crown of St. Edward; the Orb with Cross (an ancient Christian ornament going back to the Romans); a Sceptre containing the largest part (500 carats) of the Cullinan diamond from South Africa; the Imperial State Crown, made for Queen Victoria in 1838 and containing the second-largest portion of the Cullinan diamond (300 carats); St. Edward's staff, made for the coronation of Charles II; various swords, including one presented to Henry VIII at the time he was made Defender of the Faith; and many other items to which sacred character has come to be attached, as well as those persons honored by being allowed to present the items to the newly crowned monarch.[16]

To Emphasize Solidarity

Although all the devices previously discussed help to create and affirm solidarity, solidarity as a value in its own right may provide the major focus. The ability of television to provide a stage for the viewing of worldwide audiences makes possible collective enactments that have been quite unprecedented in history. A recent example was provided by the marriage of Prince Charles and Lady Diana, in which television was able to make

> ... a Cinderella of Lady Diana and (to hold) high the symbols of marriage, family, nobility and, above all, of Britishness and communitas (all this transcending) a failing economy, the riots in London neighborhoods, and the fighting in Northern Ireland. (Katz and Dayan, 1983, pp. 10–11)

Persons seem compelled to stop whatever they are doing and view these events with some degree of reverence or at least in silence in spite of themselves. They are not merely viewing a report on an event but the event itself presented as theater for them as audience.

In view of such demonstration of the stage-managing power of the public media, one wonders what French Revolutionary leaders might have done if they had had TV. Actually, they did very well without it. Following the thoughts of the *philosophes* and other early leaders of the Revolution, the role of festivals was seen as a prime method of social control in the beginning and as a means of forming solidary values toward the end of the Revolution. The purpose was, in the words of one leader, "to form republicans." In the face of threatened famine and inflation as well as continued skepticism expressed by workers and peasants, Robespierre came to the realization that although the Revolution might do away with the power of the Church and even with Christianity, some form of religion was necessary for the masses. To that end, a Festival to the Supreme Being was designed by pageant master David and was enthusiastically approved. After a parade accompanied by martial music, the crowds marched to the Tuileries Gardens, heard a sermon by Robespierre, and then, after singing a hymn, presented a lighted torch to David. David then ignited a cardboard statue labeled Atheism, revealing underneath a "somewhat charred image of Wisdom" (Butwin, 1975, p. 141). The procession then formed and marched to the Champs de Mars. Dowd (1948) writes that

> This procession, in which classicism and emotionalism were balanced and patri-
> otic and humanitarian symbols were combined, was David's masterpiece in this
> art. At its destination the painter had constructed a huge symbolic mountain.
> Robespierre led the Convention to its lofty summit while the delegates of the
> sections occupied the slopes and the enormous crowds sang appropriate verses
> and fraternized below. Then the youths and old men re-enacted the symbolic
> rite depicted in David's *Oath of the Horatii*. The celebration ended with
> salvoes of artillery, fraternal embraces, and prolonged cries of "Vive la
> Republique!" (p. 123)

To Engineer Social and Cultural Change

Testimony to the power of drama is perhaps clearest on occasions of change. The importance of the royal regalia in emphasizing the tradition and power of the monarchy (discussed above) led England's Cromwell to destroy them, after which he set about to create symbols appropriate to a republic (Churchill, 1953, p. 36). More impressive was the campaign against iconoclasm in 1538 and early 1539, which was organized by ministers of Henry VIII after his break with Rome. Partly in fear of organized Catholic forces but also to make clear the finality of the severance from Rome—as well as to express defiance, images associated with the monasteries were publicly destroyed. One of the most famous, the Rood of Grace, an object of pilgrimage in Kent, was removed and set up in a church pulpit where the preacher

> . . . smashed its mechanism (a device which caused the eyes and lips to move)
> before consigning the mortally wounded miracle-worker to the "rude people and
> boyes" who cheerfully broke it into pieces and fed it to the flames. . . . Thereafter,
> a veritable fever of iconoclasm seized the country. (Anglo, 1969, pp. 273–274)

The efforts of Henry's father to establish the legitimacy of the new House of Tudor were as remarkable as the campaign. Not content with the purely ceremonial expressions of loyalty (discussed above), he and his wife, Elizabeth, were soon to present to the country a son, Prince Arthur, who, in his person, represented the union of the houses of Lancaster and York. There remained one last act, namely, to secure recognition from the Continent, which Henry VII sought by betrothing Arthur to Katharine, the youngest child of the King of Spain. Katharine's welcome to London in 1501 was masked by a set of six pageants, all carefully and artfully related to one another in what Anglo (1969) calls the "supreme masterpiece of English civic pageantry." Unfortunately, Prince Arthur died not long afterward but not before Europe had been made vividly aware of the brilliance of the new Tudor dynasty.

If kings of England and France could use pageantry to celebrate social change, so could the designers of the French Revolution. Robespierre was particularly concerned about where the new legislative body should meet. Because he thought that the crimes of the old regime stemmed from the fact that the Assembly and Convention carried out their deliberations in secret, he felt that the meeting place of the new legislative body would have to be accessible to the public. Furthermore, Robespierre said that the Constitution

> . . . must deny the members (of the legislature) powers of any kind to influence the composition of the audience and to restrict arbitrarily the size of the place that is to receive the people. The Constitution must insure that the legislature reside in the midst of an immense population and deliberate under the eyes (*sous les yeux*) of the greatest number of citizens possible. (Butwin, 1975, p. 144)

The acoustics and seating should allow presence, he said, in a "moment of utopian revery 'of the entire nation'" (Butwin, 1975, p. 145). Robespierre was apparently willing to settle for a "vast and majestic edifice, open to 12,000 spectators"(Butwin, 1975, p. 145). The *sous les yeux* phrase was to recur in Robespierre's speeches as evidence of a continued concern for audience effects.

Perhaps the strongest symbolic demonstration of the destruction of the monarchical regime was the manner in which participation in processions was organized. The question of who should be the participants was never in doubt: the mass of the population. Of an early procession, Dowd (1948) writes that

> . . . its most striking characteristic was popular participation. . . . Although all classes were represented, the bulk of the participants were the common people of Paris— especially those from the poorer sections. The radical popular societies were out in full force. Great numbers of National Guards unarmed and off duty, students, veterans, and market porters were included in the vast throng. . . . As Brissot expressed it, "the people were the regulator, the executor, the ornament, and the object of the celebration." (p. 60)

In modern times even the most secularist of nations, the Soviet Union, committed to abolishing all religious symbols, found itself, Lane (1981) shows, driven inexorably to the construction of new public dramas involving the

> . . . staging of life-cycle rites (by) considerable expenditure for permanent ritual halls, payment of masters of ceremony, musicians, orators, as well as . . . various ritual attributes, such as printed invitations, certificates, badges, flowers and candles. . . . (p. 52)

Marriages have changed from the early practice of simple registration before a state functionary to the use of Wedding Palaces—Palaces of Happiness or of Solemn Events (in the Ukraine)—where, Lane tells us, there are said to be 311 ritual "salons" and thirty-two "festival halls." The goal, according to the Central Committee of the Communist Party, was to "reduce religious involvement" (p. 46), but the carrying out of such a goal was felt to require " . . . the scripting and producing of a play" (p. 50) with clear messages such as (in the case of births) the transmission of socialist values and the overcoming of any "harmful tendency to put the welfare of (the family's) members above that of the larger collective" (p. 68). Whatever the goal—whether initiation into social or political collectives such as youth organizations or schools, Harvest Day, Seeing-off-of-Winter (or *Maslenitsa*), or the mass recall of the revolutionary tradition—the means employed are usually theater in the form of public dramas.

CONCLUSIONS

It is worth calling attention to the limitations of our analysis. Although we have been concerned with developing a clearer conception of elements of social constructions, we have focused on what is clearly an extreme form—the public drama. Our pointing to the centrality in such dramas of theater should not be interpreted to mean that all social constructions are theatrical. Nevertheless, insofar as they are constructions and insofar as they involve deliberate attempts to create social realities, it is a plausible hypothesis that the more effective and the more acceptable of social constructions will be those that make use of theatrical elements. It is not then surprising that the construction of the "disease of irresistible addiction" to marijuana smoking should have been stimulated by such films as *Reefer Madness* nor that the attempt to construct an image of the United States as "standing tall" should be symbolized by Rambo as the conquering hero. The latter is "merely" a movie, but its popularity suggests that it reflects motives other than those of entertainment and distraction.

On the other hand, the frequent association of public dramas with centers of power is hardly minor, making the question worth asking whether the analysis presented may not form the basis for a contribution that symbolic interactionist theory can make to the study of power. It is clear that the employment of public dramas by political actors is hardly an accident. The public character of these dramas means that they can rarely be private occasions, their scale alone often resulting in performances on public streets and in open places. Financially too their scope and the resources, stages, costumes, and professional personnel and actors used all require heavy expenditures that call for public subsidy and support, at the very least. Such requirements demonstrate that public dramas are not spontaneous affairs carried out only on recognized occasions for purely ritual purposes. They are and must be deliberately constructed, employing for effectiveness the kind of technology that we have been describing.

The requirements of governmental endorsement, at minimum—or actual connivance in such enactments—thus calls our attention to a neglected dimension in the study of power. After Weber, we have been taught to see power as being regularized and made effective through authority—the legitimation of power. Such legitimation does not necessarily imply acceptance, for as Etzioni (1975) has noted, we also need to see that power is used in the interests of the persons over whom the power is being exercised.

The examination of the social construction of public drama calls attention to a quite different element. To be effective, power must not only be legitimate (as well as used to serve the interests of those over whom it is exercised), but it must be *presented* in such form as to be accepted. Public dramas tell us that power can be attractive and can come to us in such a thrilling form that it is difficult to resist. Historic shifts in power do not simply happen; they are often staged in theatrical dress. The study of such social constructions thus provides symbolic interactionist researchers with new opportunities to illuminate social history.

NOTES

1.   I do not enter here into the theoretical issues raised by Woolgar and Pawluch (1985a, b). Their concern is more with the methodological and conceptual problems created by attempts of labeling theorists and others to distinguish any form of behavior from social constructions dealing with such behavior. My concern is with the process of social construction itself.

2.   They were often also referred to as mystery plays (after *mystere*) for "guild," although there is some question about the etymology of the term (Brockett, 1969, pp. 110 ff.). The plays were held in several cities. They began as religious processions but gradually became increasingly secularized until the occasion took on the spirit of a festival. The plays themselves were typically staged in lavishly decorated pageantwagons equipped with the levels and appropriate props. The wagons were moved around the city, stopping at various "stations" where the play was acted out. Although under the general direction of town officials, the individual episodes or plays were the responsibility of the guilds often with what Chambers (1903, vol. 2, p. 131) sees as "dramatic appropriateness" (e.g., the Last Supper play was assigned to the bakers; the "Harrowing of Hell" to the cooks; Noah to watermen, shipwrights, fishers, and mariners; and Joseph and Mary to the carpenters).

3.   Historical pageants were highly popular in the United States of the nineteenth and early twentieth centuries. They often employed the services of large numbers of a town's population, particularly living descendants of a founder or pioneers. They were favorites of grade and high schools, using original scripts that were sometimes published and made available to other schools or communities. Such pageants, more commonly called festivals, have continued of course right up to the present. Although school pageants—in the forms of commemorations of events, holiday recognitions, and science fairs, as well as recognition of achievement assemblies—are as common as ever, there seems to have been a decrease in literature associated with them since the 1930s. Wasserman et al. (1977) describe hundreds presented in various parts of the United States. These are often mere excuses for commercial promotions, but the technology reproduces that of earlier pageants.

4. After the first pageant—a procession surrounding the removal of the remains of Voltaire (who had been denied church burial) to the Pantheon (a powerful anticlerical statement)—a series of brilliant pageants continued until the death of Robespierre. A provision for such national festivals was written into the Constitution of 1791, at first as an educational device (about three-fourths of the population was estimated to be illiterate) but then expanded to include other demonstrations of solidarity such as a celebration of the recapture of Toulon from the English and the Festival of Unity and Indivisibility in the midsummer of 1793.

5. As is well known, structural-functionists claim that value consensus is developed through socialization in early childhood and by later organizational experiences. But before such individual acts can occur (such as parents teaching children "respect" for some set of values), persons must discover what those values are and it seems to me insufficient or question begging to reply: "They learned it from their parents in turn." Nor can we ignore the socializing effects that occur when children witness the spectacles we are calling attention to.

6. With television of course, worldwide audiences can be addressed (Cf. Katz, 1980; Schmid and de Graaf, 1982).

7. These include what are usually called conventions (Brooks and Heilman, 1948, Glossary, pp. 34–36) such as the acceptance of soliloquies—"asides" addressed to the audience as well as the assumption of the "fourth wall" of the room is in place. It is usually assumed further that the actors are unaware of the audience although each may be shouting in order to be heard in the rear balcony and although the members of a family group seated at a dinner table are arranged around the far side of the table, facing the audience (see also Burns, 1972, ch. 5–7; the Coleridge quotation can be found in Coleridge, 1834, p. 174).

8. In his book bearing that title, Gitlin (1980) chronicles the growth in sophistication of the Students for a Democratic Society in the 1960s as they came to recognize that they were acting on a national, even a world stage, before fascinated audiences. Leaders came to learn what was "newsworthy" and what was not and how to certify leaders that the media would accept. "Movement people started thinking like promoters—specialists in headlines" (p. 235).

9. yt = out; Rowte = route; loke = look; glime = gleam; sersnett = a soft silk.

10. connyng = skilled or knowledgeable; discrete = discerning.

11. But it must be emphasized that the actors were not professionals but received a fee not necessarily according to experience or skill but in proportion to the dignity of their parts. In various towns the actor who hanged Judas received 4 pence; actors who played the parts of souls (saved or damned) received 20 pence; Noah, 1 shilling; and God, 3 shillings, 4 pence (Chambers, 1903, vol. 2, p. 139).

12. Shils and Young (1975), writing of the coronation of Elizabeth II, quote a newspaper account of a remark made by a "philosophical Northern villager": "What people like is the sheer excess of it. We lead niggling enough lives these days. Something a bit lavish for a change is good for the soul" (pp. 146–147).

13. The comparison to a bank is more than mere metaphor. Examining the vast expenditures that England's Henry VII made for precious stones and plate, Anglo (1969, p. 105) quotes a recent economic study that sees that expense as a form of saving. But the sheer quantity and its display had impressive power in itself. The whole question of the costs of pageants deserves more space than we can give it here. When costs could not be discharged through charges for public viewing (which created its own problems, as Cooper [1974] shows in the case of public executions), then local or national governments had to assume the responsibility, thus locking in their control over these events.

14. It is clear also that processions are big business. Of the particular pageant described above, Dowd (1948) writes: "A small army of dressmakers, carpenters, painters, and other

artisans was required to fabricate and maintain this equipment at a cost of 100,000 livres per month in the spring of 1794" (p. 129).

15. Hunt (1984) describes the repeated attempts made by the revolutionary leaders to invent symbolic means for expressing such loyalties (for example, seals portraying various views of a female Liberty figure or a male Hercules) and the search for a revolutionary uniform. The matter was illustrated with striking clarity in the search for a color for the cockade (usually worn on the hat). At first, the color was green, which was then rejected because green was the color of the livery of the king's brother. Once a tricolor (red, white, and blue) was adopted, any other colors became symbolic of disloyalty. A march of women to Versailles was galvanized when word reached them that soldiers " . . . had trampled the tricolor cockade and worn in its place the white of the Bourbons or the black of the aristocratic counterrevolution" (Hunt, 1984, p. 58).

16. Other elements in coronations add further weight to the authority of tradition, as suggested in the analysis of the coronation of Elizabeth II by Shils and Young (1975). The suggestion that there might arise some dispute about whether the monarch is a true successor is provided in the office of the Queen's Champion who rode into the banquet at Whitehall in full armor during the coronation of Mary I, and pronounced the "challenge," basically daring anyone who disputed the queen's succession to step up and face him for a fight (Erickson, 1978, p. 323).

REFERENCES

Albanese, C.L. 1976. *Sons of the Fathers: The Civil Religion of the American Revolution.* Philadelphia: Temple University Press.

Alexander, M.V.C. 1980. *The First of the Tudors.* London: Croom Helm.

Anglo, S. 1969. *Spectacle Pageantry, and Early Tudor Policy.* Oxford: Clarendon Press.

Ball, D.W. 1967. "An Abortion Clinic Ethnography." *Social Problems* 14: 293–301.

Becker, H.S. 1963. *Outsiders.* New York: Free Press.

Bellah, R.N. 1967. "Civil Religion in America." *Daedalus* 96: 1–21.

Berger, P.L. and T. Luckman. 1966. *The Social Construction of Reality.* Garden City, NY: Doubleday.

Blumer, H. 1969. *Symbolic Interactionism.* Englewood Cliffs, NJ: Prentice-Hall.

Brockett, O.G. 1969. *The Theatre.* New York: Holt, Rinehart, and Winston.

Brooks, C. and R.B. Heilman. 1948. *Understanding Drama.* New York: Holt, Rinehart, and Winston.

Brown, M.C. 1911. *Mary Tudor: Queen of France.* London: Methuen.

Burns, E. 1972. *Theatricality.* New York: Harper & Row.

Butwin, J. 1975. "The French Revolution as *Theatrum Mundi.*" *Research Studies* 43: 141–152.

Chambers. E.K. 1903. *The Medieval Stage.* 2 vols. Oxford: Clarendon Press.

Chubb, P. and Assoc. 1912. *Festivals and Plays in Schools and Elsewhere.* New York: Harper.

Churchill, R.S. 1953. *The Story of the Coronation.* London: Derek Verschoyle.

Coleridge, S.T 1834. *Biographia Literaria or Biographical Sketches of My Literary Life and Opinions.* New York: Leavitt, Lord, and Co.

Cooper, D.D. 1974. *The Lesson of the Scaffold.* Athens: Ohio University Press.

Dowd, D.L. 1948. *Pageant-Master of the Republic: Jacques-Louis David and the French Revolution.* Lincoln: University of Nebraska Studies (June).

Durkheim, E. 1915. *The Elementary Forms of the Religious Life.* London: George Allen and Unwin.

Eliot, T.S. 1934. *The Rock.* New York: Harcourt-Brace.

Emerson, J.P. 1970. "Behavior in Private Places: Sustaining Definitions of Reality in Gyneco-logical Examinations." Pp. 73–97 in H.P. Dreitzel (ed.) *Recent Sociology.* New York: Macmillan.

Erickson, C. 1978. *Bloody Mary.* Garden City, NY: Doubleday.

Etzioni, A. 1975. A *Comparative Analysis of Complex Organizations.* New York: Free Press.

Faris, J.C. (1968) 1973. "'Occasions' and 'Nonoccasions.'" in M. Douglas (ed.) *Rules and Meanings: The Anthropology of Everyday Knowledge.* London: Penguin.

Four Days: The Historical Record of the Death of President Kennedy. 1964. American Heritage Publishing Co.

Gitlin, T. 1980. *The Whole World Is Watching.* Berkeley: University of California Press.

Goffman, E. 1959. *The Presentation of Self in Everyday Life.* Garden City. NY: Doubleday.

———. *Frame Analysis.* New York: Harper & Row.

Grimes, R.L. 1976. *Symbol and Conquest: Public Ritual and Drama in Santa Fe, New Mexico.* Ithaca, NY: Cornell University Press.

Heaton, V. 1970. *The Oberammergau Passion Play.* London: Robert Hale.

Henderson, E.F. 1912. *Symbol and Satire in the French Revolution.* New York: Putnam's.

Hunt, L. 1984. *Politics, Culture and Class in the French Revolution.* Berkeley: University of California Press.

Jones, I. 1966. *Designs by Inigo Jones for Court Masques and Plays at Court.* New York: Russell and Russell.

Katz, E. 1980. "Media Events: The Sense of Occasion." *Studies in Visual Communication* 6: 84–89.

Katz, E. and D. Dayan. 1983. "Contest, Conquests, Coronations: On Media Events and Their Heroes." Unpublished paper, Annenberg School of Communications, University of Southern California.

Krause, E.A. 1971. *The Sociology of Occupations.* Boston: Little, Brown.

Lane, C. 1981. *The Rites of Rulers: Ritual in Industrial Society—The Soviet Case.* Cambridge: Cambridge University Press.

Langer, S.K. 1953. *Feeling and Form.* New York: Scribner's.

Lukes, S. 1975. "Political Ritual and Social Integration." *Sociology* 9: 289–308.

Malinowski, B. 1974. *Magic, Science, and Religion and Other Essays.* London: Souvenir Press.

Matthews, B. 1916. *Moliere: His Life and Work.* New York: Scribner's.

Moses, M.J. 1930. *The Passion Play of Oberammergau.* New York: Doubleday.

Myers, A.R. 1959. *The Household of Edward IV: The Black Book and the Ordinance of 1478.* Manchester: Manchester University Press.

Nicoll, A. 1976. *World Drama.* New York: Barnes and Noble.

Pfohl, S. 1977. "The Discovery of Child Abuse." *Social Problems* 24: 310–324.

Radcliffe-Brown, A.R. 1939. *Taboo.* Cambridge: The University Press.

Schmid, A.P. and J. de Graaf. 1982. *Violence as Communication.* Beverly Hills, CA: Sage.

Schramm, W. 1965. "Communication in Crisis." Pp. 1–25 in B.S. Greenberg and E.B. Parker (eds.) *The Kennedy Assassination and the American Public.* Stanford, CA: Stanford University Press.

Shank, T. 1979. *The Art of Dramatic Art.* Belmont, CA: Dickenson.

Shils, E. and M. Young. 1975. "The Meaning of the Coronation." Pp. 63–82 in E. Shils (ed.) *Center and Periphery: Essays in Macrosociology* vol. 1. Chicago: University of Chicago Press.

Spencer, M.L. 1911. *Corpus Christi Pageants in England.* New York: Baker and Taylor.

Strong, R. 1984. *Art and Power: Renaissance Festivals 1450–1650.* Great Britain: Boydell.

Taft, L. 1921. *The Technique of Pageantry.* New York: Barnes.

Verba, S. 1965. "The Kennedy Assassination and the Nature of Political Commitment." in B.S. Greenberg and E.B. Parker (eds.) *The Kennedy Assassination and the American Public: Social Communication in Crisis.* Stanford, CA: Stanford University Press.

Warner, W.L. 1962. *American Life.* Chicago: University of Chicago Press.

Wasserman, P. et al. (eds.). 1977. *Festivals Sourcebook.* Detroit: Gale Research.

Weick, K.E. 1977. "Enactment Processes in Organizations." Chapter 8 in B.M. Staw and G.R. Salancik (eds.) *New Directions in Organizational Behavior.* Chicago: St. Clair Press.

Wickham, G. 1959–1972. *Early English Stages 1300–1660.* New York: Columbia University Press.

Woolgar, S. and D. Pawluch. 1985a. "Ontological Gerrymandering: The Anatomy of Social Problems' Explanations." *Social Problems* 32: 214–227.

———. 1985b. "How Shall We Move Beyond Constructivism?" *Social Problems* 33: 159–162.

Fighting Words:
What We Can Learn from
Hitler's Hyperbole

Michael Blain
Boise State University

The question of why human beings fight wars continues to stalk modern thought. This article treats Hitler's national socialist discourse as an extreme example of the social construction of a social problem, a cultural paradigm of how to talk people into fighting revolutions and wars. Drawing upon recent work in rhetorical studies by Gusfield and others, I show how political agents concoct a rhetoric of motives which they use to incite their followers to fight their enemies. The formal and poetic features of this system of discourse are identified and explicated. We can learn many things from Hitler. By identifying his technique, we can recognize when political agents are using the same technique and counter its seductive effects. We learn that the main effect of war rhetoric is social integration through the constitution of common enemies. And finally, we realize that wars are made to happen through the calculated use of symbolic practices. War is not, as many have argued, a fall into a latent animality, but an expression of our symbol-mindedness—our capacity to make and use hyperboles.

Tens of millions of people were killed in World War II. A disproportionate number of the casualties came in eastern Europe and Russia, areas containing large Slavic and Jewish populations. Six of the nine million Jews in Europe in 1939 fell victim to the war. We need to know how political leaders like Hitler are able to get their followers to wage war and to slaughter millions of non-combatants. As Kenneth Burke (1941, p. 191) urged, we need "to discover what kind of 'medicine' this medicine-man . . .

Reprinted from Symbolic Interaction, 11(2):257–276.

concocted, that we may know, with greater accuracy, exactly what to guard against, if we are to forestall the concocting of similar medicine in America" (1941, p. 191), or, for that matter, anywhere else."

Let me introduce my approach to Hitler's discourse through a consideration of one of Friedrich Nietzsche's aphorisms:

> Whoever fights monsters should see to it that in the process he does not become a monster. If you look too deeply into the abyss, the abyss will look into you.

Nietzsche's use of aphorisms is a manifestation of his hyperbolic style of writing (Nehemas, 1985, pp. 13–14). An aphorism is an isolated sentence or short text, while hyperbole refers to the figurative language of exaggeration and overstatement. Aphorisms often contain hyperboles to attract attention and suggest hidden implications. This one contains two: monsters and abyss. Hyperboles may be used to emphasize a point. This one warns us to not become like those we fight. Nietzsche cultivated the hyperbolic for explicitly rhetorical reasons. It was his means to gain the reader's attention, to counter the dominance of literalism in philosophical discourse, and to make himself unforgettable. Who can forget Nietzsche's parable of the Madmen who ran into the market place shouting, "God is dead . . . And we have killed him." His writings have provoked two reactions, moral indignation or discipleship, but rarely indifference.

Compare Nietzsche's style with the following statement by Hitler:

> Was there any form of filth or profligacy, particularly in cultural life, without at least one Jew involved in it?
> If you cut even cautiously into such an abscess, you found, like a maggot in a rotting body, often dazzled by the sudden light—a kike!

Hitler's style, like Nietzsche's, is essentially hyperbolic. Nietzsche's objectives were philosophical, to make us question "truths" and to do it an unforgettable way. Hitler's objectives were political, to create a "fighting movement" and establish "a Thousand Year Reich." I will argue, using the Nazi example, that hyperbole is the idiom of political violence and an essential vehicle for preparing a nation for war. Human beings are called to war. The violence and cruelty so characteristic of our species is rooted in the hyperbolic resources of language.

Hitler seems to have turned his "maggot" aphorism into a strategy to achieve his political objectives. He turned the Jews into racial "monsters," and, in fighting Jews, he became "monstrous." But how is this possible? What is the "abyss" Nietzsche refers to? The abyss is the "bottomless pit" of "interpretations." The description of some group as "monsters" is an interpretation of their character. Nietzsche's aphorism suggests that we should look within for the sources of this interpretation. We should remember that he was a philologist and poet as well as a philosopher. The "abyss" is in the poetic possibilities of language. The homicidal violence of war is a way of talking to the enemy. The carnage in Eastern Europe and the Soviet Union was, to a very large extent, a function of the hyperbolic character of Nazi discourse: The Jews and Slavs were described as the murderers of everything the German masses identified as good, true, and beautiful. The Nazis talked themselves and then the German people into a war of revenge against "murderous" enemies, a war to determine who would govern Europe for the next thousand years. Hitler conceived the goals of the Nationalist Socialist movement in millennial terms.

This article describes the rhetorical tactics leaders employ to construct social problems and talk people into organizing, preparing, and executing a war. Hitler's speech practices particularly as they were enunciated in *Mein Kampf,* are a paradigm of fighting words—a rhetoric of war motives. Hitler enunciated his strategy while "dictating" the initial drafts of his Nazi "Bible" to his associates. The early drafts were repeatedly edited and revised (Maser, 1970). *Mein Kampf* can be viewed as a social production and Hitler's name as a shorthand device to designate "Hitler and his editors." I propose to see this text as a paradigm, a "how to do it," "nuts and bolts" manual of how to convince people to hate enemies.

My analysis of how discourse functions is derived from Kenneth Burke (1941, pp. 191–220; 1968b, Chap. 1) and Michel Foucault (1978, pp. 92–102; 1980, pp. 78–108) and the work of those who have elaborated on Burke's notion of "the victimage ritual" (Duncan, 1962, Chap. IX; Ivie, 1980, 1986; Gusfield, 1981, Chap. 4). Speaking and writing, listening and reading are cultural practices with observable social effects. My analysis of how this works is guided by the notion of the tactical polyvalence of discourses. I am not concerned with the analysis of the ideological dimension of discourse, its truth or falsity. I am concerned with the tactical efficacy of discourse "as a material force" in a field of forces (Reich, 1970, pp. 3–33). Political leaders like Hitler "deploy" words much as they do troops in an effort to achieve strategic objectives. They know that the masses must be incited to fight wars. I do not mean to suggest that talk is the only "force" at work in warmaking. But I do think that it is a decisive part of the practices that constitute the war system. Recent research has shown how the "grim determination" of the German soldier and worker to persevere to the bitter end, even beyond Hitler's suicide, was created and sustained by Nazi wartime propaganda (see Herzstein, 1987). Dawidowicz (1975, Chaps. 5 & 6) has argued persuasively that the Nazi war against the Jews was part and parcel of the World War.

In Gusfield's (1981) study the drinking driving problem is a less extreme but nonetheless cogent example of "the victimage ritual" at work in the rhetoric of social problems. In this instance Gusfield shows us how the rhetorical invention of the "killer-drunk" in the automobile accident literature structures the cognitive order and policy implications of an important public problem. The drinking driver is constructed as antisocial, willfully responsible for his irresponsible behavior, and a dangerous deviant who is morally and factually responsible for automobile accidents that kill the innocent. Derived from Burke's studies, Gusfield shows us how the political incitement to engage in "wars" against drunken-drivers constitute a moral drama implicating the norms and values at work in American culture. The logic of Gusfield's application of Burke's approach to social problems follows the logologic of the guilt/redemption symbol system that forms "the incunabula of our culture": "If Order, then guilt; if guilt, then need for redemption; but any such payment is victimage" (Burke, 1965, pp.

274–295; 1968a). The metaphorical logic structuring the many variants of this discursive formation, I will argue, is the cycle of murder and revenge.

Hitler, as Burke shows, "concocted" his discourse from available cultural resources (e.g., the Volkish tradition, "scientific racism," war, anti-Semitism). The European and Germanic tradition provided Hitler with a treasure horde of discursive elements (see Katz, 1980). Elements of discourse can be articulated and re-articulated in various ways according to the strategic objectives of the speaker or writer. We must imagine, Foucault has stated, "a multiplicity of discursive elements that can come into play in various strategies" (1976, p. 100). My analysis is guided by this rule of the tactical polyvalence of discourses. A medical term such as "disease," for example, can be deployed metaphorically in a political discourse (Sontag, 1978; Perry, 1983). The specific distribution of elements in a discourse is related to the cultural and political context of who is speaking to whom, and with what objectives.

My main objective is to identify the rhetorical strategy at work in the making of "enemies," and when effective, revolutions and wars, as a case study in the social construction of social problems. First, I discuss Hitler's "knowledge" of the magic power of the spoken word. Second, I describe the two-part system of Hitler's discourse, and explicate it as a prototype of all war discourse. I show how he employed the resources of language to construct the Jew and Aryan as hyperbolic characters. The effect of this discourse, I argue, is to constitute a dramatism of patriots locked in mortal combat with enemies. Third, I discuss the cultural background of national socialist discourse and why it worked its ways on the Germans. Finally, I sum up what we can learn from Hitler's rhetoric about the social construction of social problems and why people fight wars.

THE MAGIC POWER OF THE SPOKEN WORD

Wars, Quincy Wright wrote, are a form of social conflict in which political leaders attempt to intensify loyalty of the masses to the symbols of the political group. "Military conflict, " Wright argues, "is an incident in the continuous conflict of propagandas. . . " (1965, p. 1232). In the modern period this conflict has been carried on in the name of power, sovereignty, the nation, and life. War depends "upon an elaborate ideological construction maintained through education in a system of language, law, symbols, and ideals" (1965, p. 1291). Political leaders must gain the support of a loyal following, mobilize resources, and convince a nation's masses that they should fight. Or, as Hitler put it, the masses must be "schooled."

Wright's conception resembles Hitler's. The "war of words" is a pretext to the "war of tanks and bombers." Hitler's approach to war was calculated. His objectives were to create a fighting movement "consumed with fanatical patriotism" and committed to the creation of a "Thousand Year Reich." In *Mein Kampf* (1925) he asserts that "In general the art of all truly great national leaders at all times consists among other things primarily in not dividing the attention of a people, but in concentrating it upon a single foe" (1971, p. 118). The people must be focused on one objective—the annihilation of the one true enemy. He drives the point home with a critical discussion of the tactical failure of the religious anti-Semitism of Austria's Christian Social Party. The religious argument was ineffective. The "enemy" could not be redeemed through "a splash of baptismal water. " A truly effective argument would have to be based on "racial knowledge. " If the difference was biological, the enemy was beyond redemption. Annihilation could be the only solution.

Hitler's strategy was based on what he termed his "knowledge" of social movements. He asserts that " . . . the power which has always started the greatest religious and political avalanches in history rolling has from time immemorial been the magic power of the spoken word, and that alone" (Hitler, 1971, p. 106–107). He criticized the academic inclination to attribute more power to the written than spoken word, and cites several examples to prove his point.

> Let no one believe that the French Revolution would ever have come about through philosophical theories if it had not found an army of agitators led by demagogues in the grand style, who whipped up the terrible passions of the people tormented to begin with, until at last there occurred that terrible volcanic eruption which held all Europe rigid with fear.

The same can be said of the influence of Marxist-Leninist literature on the Bolshevik revolution. It was nothing in comparison to "the glittering heaven which thousands of agitators, themselves, to be sure, all in the service of an idea, talked into people" (Hitler, 1971, p. 475).

Hitler's approach to reading was tactical. Books are a resource to be mined for the right words, the most effective expressions.

> I know people who read enormously . . . yet whom I would not describe as "well-read." True, they possess a mass of "knowledge," but their brain is unable to organize and register the material they have taken in. They lack the art of sifting what is valuable for them in a book from that which is without value . . . For reading is no end in itself, but a means to an end. It should provide the tools and building materials which the individual needs for his life's work . . .; Secondly, it should transmit a general world view. In both cases, however, it is essential that the content of what one reads . . . like the stone of a mosaic should fit into the general world picture in its proper place, and thus help to form this picture in the mind of the reader. (Hitler, 1971, p. 35)

Books provide agitators with the discursive elements which they can bring into play in a political strategy. They are arsenals which contain the weapons—words, phrases, pictures, forms of discourse—the leader can muster up to fight the propaganda war. The leader of a movement must sift through the available books for the most effective elements of discourse.

Hitler did this effectively. Ralph Manheim, translator of *Mein Kampf,* describes him as "a self-educated modern South German with a gift for oratory." He was, Manheim argues, a "voracious" reader of the Austrian Press. He read numerous popular pamphlets on history, psychology, racist biology, and political subjects. "But the main source of his pet phrases," Manheim insists, "was the theater and the opera.

He is full of popular quotations from Goethe and Schiller, and largely unintelligible flights of Wagnerian terminology" (1971, p. xi). Werner Maser (1970, p. 67–72) is more specific about the sources of Hitler's "knowledge." He identifies Wilhelm Bölsche's (1921) *Vom Bazillus zum Affenmenshen* (From Bacillus to the Apeman) as the source of Hitler's metaphor of the Jews as "bacillus" or "parasite." The main sources of Hitler's approach to propaganda were Le Bon's (1903) *The Crowd—A Study of the Popular Mind* and McDougall's (1920) *The Group Mind*. Hitler had the capacity, Maser concludes, to translate popular pseudoscientific theories, widely discussed in late nineteenth-century Germany and Austria, into picturesque language and put them to effective political use. During World War I, he had been much impressed in this regard with the British approach to propaganda.

Hitler needed a scene within which he could deploy his words. He selected the "beer halls" for political "meetings" and "public squares" for "mass rallies." Munich, with its right wing tradition, would be the geopolitical center of the movement. The scene of action is crucial. Hitler cites the "theater," "movies," and the "Catholic churches" to make his points. The "hall" has a definite effect, "a performance of *Parsifal* in Bayreuth will always have a different effect than anywhere else in the world" (1971, p. 474). The time of day is also an important consideration. The masses are more suggestive late in the day. The orchestration of the meeting can also heighten the effectiveness of the speaker.

In chapter XII, Volume One, and VI, Volume Two, of *Mein Kampf* Hitler describes how he experimented with different discursive practices. His early speeches concentrated on "War Guilt" and "Peace Treaties," two enormously popular themes. His objective was to gain "mass effect and mass influence." He describes how he came to anticipate the questions that would be raised by his "foes." He developed the tactic of disarming their questions by raising them and answering them at the beginning of his speeches. He argues that "pictorial presentation" is always more effective than an article of any length. A speaker can perfect his oratorical practice by noting his audience's reaction. He could "read" it off their "facial expressions" and "roars of approval" (1971, pp. 470–471). If there is a failure of understanding, then be "primitive and clear"; if the audience can not follow the speech, then construct ideas "cautiously and slowly"; if they remain unconvinced, then repeat the argument "over and over in constantly new examples." Only the orator, claims Hitler, can overcome emotional resistance to an argument. It is in the immediate encounter of the speaker with an audience that revolutionary movements and wars are made.

Hitler was "calculating" in his approach to propaganda. The success of the National Socialist movement was in large part due to the way in which Hitler's blend of discursive elements functioned in the context of German society. In the early years of the movement, his audiences were largely composed of two elements: one was rural, racist, anti-industrial and populist; the other was urban, socialistic, and revolutionary (Schoenbaum, 1966, pp. 43–73). Later, after he gained access to the German state in 1933, Hitler would remain tactical in his discursive strategy. His goal was to fashion a unified "national organism"—a goal that appealed to many Germans after seeing Germany split into divisive classes during industrialization. The new community was to be a *Volksgemeinschaft* (national community) composed of Aryan "workers," "farmers," "soldiers," and "professionals" unified by blood and soil in opposition to the international Jewish enemy. Hitler argued that the Jewish doctrine of socialism had created artificial divisions within German society. He appropriated the vocabulary of socialism and gave it a novel sense. The National Socialist movement was not a class struggle, but a racial and nationalist one. Hitler later employed the same tactics to goad his soldiers into fighting a war of annihilation against his enemy. On June 21, 1941, on the eve of the German invasion of the Soviet Union, Hitler delivered a long speech to his *Wehrmacht* officers from the new Reich chancellory in Berlin. His objective was *to prepare* his generals and their troops for a war of annihilation. Like an army drill instructor who harangues a trainee into action, Hitler had to rev up his "military machine" to do "battle."

Hitler's discourse on words suggests that he defined himself as a political actor addressing a mass audience, and that he treated culture as a resource. This is confirmed by his discussion of the theater, opera, and the church. Hitler applied the doctrine enunciated by Le Bon. He who wished to be a *Führer* must impose himself on the masses through personal qualities. Those personal qualities must include a firm belief in one idea and an imperious will (Maser, 1970, p. 76). He "concocted" an insider discourse from cultural resources familiar to his German audience. The Jews were represented as the ultimate outsider—the one "true enemy." This enemy had caused the German defeat in World War I, and Germany's subsequent financial collapse. The national socialist movement would be the means to defeat the "enemy."

There is an implicit "system" to Hitler's discourse. A two-part system is suggested by the two volume organization of *Mein Kampf*(McGuire, 1977). The titles of the two volumes are translated as "A Reckoning" and "The Nationalist Socialist Movement." He dedicated the first volume to the "dead heroes"of November 9, 1923, who "fell, with loyal faith in the resurrection of their people" in the unsuccessful *putsch* which had landed him in prison. Describing it as his "vindication," volume one presents his "reckoning" or racial analysis of nationalism, and the need to settle accounts with the real enemies of the "Fatherland." The second volume is programmatic. It enunciates a political strategy, and the domestic and international policies to be followed by the national socialist movement and the state which would result. The text seems to have been organized around a metaphor of a medical diagnosis and cure, a religious rite of guilt and redemption, and a drama of murder/revenge. It closes by reinvoking "those heroes who sacrificed themselves for us all" in 1923.

A RHETORIC OF WAR MOTIVES

If people can be motivated to fight and kill in wars through the magic of words as Hitler believed, then what are those powers? Can we generalize Hitler's "knowledge" by turning it into a paradigm of a rhetoric of "enemies?" I believe that the magic powers Hitler refers to are the formal and poetic possibilities of linguistic symbolism. "One of the central properties of symbols . . . is their capacity for extensive elaboration" (Cuzzort and King, 1980, p. 331). Drawing upon the resources of symbolism, political leaders are able to elaborate a rhetoric of motives to recruit, intensify commitment, mobilize, and incite their followers to engage in violent action. They accomplish these effects by drawing on the hyperbolic resources of linguistic symbolism to constitute their followers as "patriots" at war with "enemies. " Subjects are recruited from the available individuals by "calling them to attention." They are transformed into patriots by gaining, sustaining, and intensifying their identification with a rhetoric of war motives. Hitler's discourse constituted his loyal supporters as "Teutonic Knights" caught up in a crusade against "Jewish" enemies. The victors would be the "lords of this world" for the next thousand years. Each of these terms is loaded with cultural associations and demands for certain lines of action. Social change is translated into an "identity crisis" of the social agents. The contending camps (e.g., Marxist and National Socialist) attempt through the articulation/disarticulation of discourses, to concoct a "system of narration" to disarticulate the discourse of the adversary (Laclau, 1977, pp. 100–111). The narrative involves a melodramatic employment of the scene of world history (see Wagner-Pacifici, 1986, pp. 272–294). Moral norms emerge that limit what can be said; a commitment to the one enemy is proscribed.

The efficacy of a discourse resides in its tactical use of victims to constitute villainous enemies. This involves the elaboration of a detailed knowledge of a system of power—of "cunning" Jews violating "innocent" German victims. The key is to gain the imaginative identification of the audience with these violator/victim subjectivities. In turn, this "knowledge" becomes the basis of a counter movement against the enemy—the struggle of heroic subjectivities against the villainous powers.

A war discourse dramatizes the current scene of world history. It does so by generating a sense of imminent danger, crisis, or catastrophe (for critique of rhetoric of crisis, see Megill, 1985, p. 347). It must suggest that, "It is almost too late!" The "international Jewish conspiracy" to destroy everything good, true, and beautiful, is upon us. The political leader must incite his forces to engage in battle. Typically, there is one catalytic event which ignites a war, a "Pearl Harbor," an assassination, attack or invasion.

Language is treated as a resource, a means to an end, a tactic, weapon, or force to mobilize and deploy to achieve an objective. It is used to lie, cheat, tell the truth, exaggerate, and make up convincing "facts" to persuade, organize, and activate a following. In the course of a political conflict, leaders perfect in practice, a rhetorically effective "vocabulary of motives." This vocabulary, composed of stock slogans, arguments, and speeches, is used to convince people of the rightness of the political objectives (e.g., "The Jew is to blame."). Hitler took his slogans from the traditional stock of anti-Semitic catchphrases, expressions long familiar to his *Volkish* audience (Maser, 1974, p. 212). This vocabulary functions rhetorically to create and intensify commitment to the crusade.

War motives take the form of a drama of murder and revenge or attack and retaliation—a rhetoric of social hierarchy or victimage ritual. There are two moments of identification in this narrative. First, the leader gains the audience's identification with the violator's murder of some appropriate victim. In the second moment the leader goads his audience into action through gaining their identification with the triumph over the enemy. The function of these identifications is to constitute dramatic characters or maximal types—patriotic heroes, who symbolize the great goods, fighting and sacrificing, in mortal combat with villainous "enemies" who represent the great bads (Alloway, 1971, p. 12).

In the first moment of the drama some agent, for example, the Jew, is represented as victimizing a cherished category. The victims, namely the Aryans, must be tailored to the audience to be addressed.The audience's sense of "moral outrage" is aroused by gaining its identification with a violation . Political orators such as Hitler accumulate clear and rhetorically effective examples of "enemy" violations of good, true, beautiful victims, which their audiences can identify with in sympathy and moral outrage. The victimizers and their institutions are "perfected" in their roles as villainous enemies—the causes of the destruction of some cherished practice, institution, or values. The act of violation constitutes the victims, which, in turn, constitutes the roles of "enemy" and patriots. The desire for revenge is "talked into" the masses.

The second moment in the drama is generated through a rhetoric of "militant" struggle against "bad" violators to purify the world of the danger. This discourse functions to constitute war roles by gaining the audience's imaginative identification with the victorious defeat of the enemy. The "moral outrage" aroused by the identification with the past and potential victims is transformed through an ethic of "action" directed toward removing the "causes" of the threat. Violators are represented as the murderers; patriots are struggling against villains in the name of victims. The transformation of the villain into the "enemy" has hierarchical implications. The "enemy" is described in inferior terms. This shift in discourse corresponds to a proposed shift in power relations. The enemy is torn down; the heroes built up. The victims of the villain's violation now rise up in a victorious struggle to defeat the enemy. This pattern is prototypical of the way in which war motives are constituted in discourse.

Michel Foucault's notion of power/knowledge can be used to explicate the model. The leader must elaborate a knowledge of the enemies' power and practices. Hitler, for example, elaborates extensively on the Jewish enemy. He constructs a racial, anti-semitic analysis that blamed "the Jew" for all the problems of German society, the defeat in World War I, the revolution, the economic collapse, the moral degeneracy, and political impotency of the Weimar Republic. This power/knowledge is negative in a double sense: it is a counter-knowledge to the claims of his opponents and it describes Jews as destroyers of the "culture creating" Aryan race.

The second form of power/knowledge is positive. It refers to the arsenal of practical techniques, discursive and non-discursive, developed by Hitler to build a "fighting movement" and unify Germany along new lines. Hitler elaborated a discourse on Aryan racial superiority and its "culture creating" powers. He mobilized the existing resources and got his followers moving in a crusade to establish a "Thousand Year Reich." The sense of "movement" is decisive. It suggests a change in position and, in a military context, a change in the location of troops, ships, or aircraft for tactical or strategic purposes, a maneuver. The notion of "a movement" is an element in military discourse. It is a part of a cluster of terms composed of campaign, crusade, mobilization, the march, and strategy, tactics, and objectives. National Socialism from the very beginning, was a rhetoric of war motives.

Burke (1941) argues that Hitler's use of dramatic form represented a political perversion of the religious notion of the struggle of good against evil. Of course, there is a difference. The Church had grounded natural law, the social order composed of nobles and serfs, in the Will of God. Hitler grounds his new order in the racial superiority of "Aryan blood." The Aryan race is "culture creating." Aryans are naturally heroic and sacrificing. They have an innate inclination toward military discipline and unity. The Jews, on the other hand, are egoistic and diabolical. Aryan personality and the Folkish state are pitted against Jewish-Marxist "cunning" and "arrogance."

Hugh D. Duncan (1962, pp. 225–249), following Burke's lead, argues that Hitler used rhetoric as a means to achieve social integration of the German masses. The Nazis applied religious forms of social interaction to the staging of mass appeals. The mass rallies at Nuremburg represented a perversion of religious modes of expression to create political community. Duncan argues that Hitler dramatized social relations by putting them in the form of a series of identifications. Hitler's presentations were allegorical. He would "*mount*" from topical identifications with his audience's everyday problems, to identifications "with angels locked in ethereal battle before the ramparts of heaven" (Duncan, 1962, p. 242). The *denouement* of Hitler's drama is the moment when the hero triumphs over the enemy.

HYPERBOLIC CHARACTERS

Hitler's discourse clearly shows us how a leader can exercise the magic power of dramatic form. I now show how he employed the hyperbolic resources of linguistic symbolism to accomplish the creation of enemies and patriots.

The notion of stereotyping guides most discussions of the dynamics of prejudice and political conflict. A stereotype, according to Gordon Allport (1954), is an *exaggerated* image associated with a category which functions to justify good and bad conduct toward that category. I want to modify this approach in a couple of ways. First, I want to stress that stereotyping is a practical accomplishment. Stereotypes are made of hyperboles, and hyperboles are made of metaphors. Figurative language is constitutive of subjects and objects, and structures discourse and action through a logic of entailments (Perry, 1983; Lakoff, 1987, pp. 377–415; Smith, 1985). Patriots and enemies are hyperbolic characters who are made of metaphors. Second, I want to give more emphasis than Allport and his followers have to the magical powers of discourse. Political leaders make and use hyperboles to constitute enemies and patriots, and use them to incite their followers to kill and die in wars. The act of killing is a logical entailment of a hyperbolic rhetoric of war motives.

The norm governing the production of an "enemy" involves accentuating the negative and minimizing the positive. Allport described how it is done:

1. Generalization: one experience with a category is used as a basis for characterizing all members of the category;
2. Selective memory: only positive or negative details are recalled;
3. Sharpening: positive or negative details are made precise and clear.

These devices are relatively familiar. What is not so familiar is the way in which political leaders use metaphors to make hyperbolic descriptions of enemies and patriotic heroes. Hyperbole is an exaggerated or extravagant figure of speech (e.g., The Jew is a disease, a devil, a murderer! Or, the Aryan is a Promethean hero, a Teutonic Knight!). The term derives from the Greek *hyperbole,* " a throwing beyond" or excess, which derives from the Indo-European root, *gwel*—one sense of which means to throw or reach.

Hyperbole is accomplished through simile and metaphor. Hitler's discourse is suffused with hyperbolic characterizations of Jews and Aryans. The "abscess" example cited at the beginning of the article is a simile: Jews are "like a maggot in a rotting body. " The Aryans, on the other hand are "culture creating" Prometheans, Teutonic knights of the Holy Grail, who possess a racial tendency to *Pflichterfullung* (fulfillment of duty). "The self-sacrificing will to give one's personal labor and if necessary one's own life for others is most strongly developed in the Aryan" (1971, p. 297).

Hitler's discourse is structured around a metaphor of murder and revenge. The Jews are transformed into murderers, both literally (they crucified Christ; they caused the murder of German soldiers in World War I) and metaphorically (they "killed" Germany in the Revolution of 1919; they are the destroyers of Aryan health, pure blood, morality, and culture). The notion of blood contamination is a central motif in Hitler's discourse. Since the Aryan/Non-Aryan differentiation is a racial one, blood is a loaded term. It condenses racial, biological, medical, religious, moral, and murderous chains of association. In Hitler's discussion of "The Causes of the Collapse," he issues this aphorism:

> Blood sin and desecration of the race are the original sin in this world and the end
> of a humanity which surrenders to it.

The theme of blood runs through Hitler's discourse. Jews are "bloodthirsty." They engage in ritual murder. Egoism is their strongest racial trait. And if they were not united in defense against some common "danger" or to gain some "common booty," they would turn into a "a horde of rats, fighting bloodily among themselves." The Jew is "bloodsucking," a "bacillus" that contaminates the life-blood of the nation.

The pure blooded "Aryans" are willing to sacrifice their blood for the community. They are heroic. The key to the preservation of the Aryan race as a superior race, is "blood purity" and "blood sacrifice." Hitler's racial analysis divides the world into three types: the culture-creating Aryan race (the *Übermensch),* the inferior, culture-bearing races (the *Untermensch),* and the monstrous Jew, the only real "counterpart" to the Aryan. The Jews are cultural "parasites" that feed off other races. All living things have "a natural instinct of self-preservation," manifesting itself in different forms in the various "races." Jewish "self-preservation" is manifested in a monstrous "Egotism." Aryan "self-preservation" is manifested in "service to the community." Hence the cunning and arrogant Jew has concocted Marxism, Communist Bolshevism, and Social Democracy as devices for achieving world domination. These instincts are in the blood, Therefore, the only way to counter this demonic force is through annihilation. Racial struggle is the dynamic of history, not class struggle. The notion of class struggle is "ideological," a deception, a lie, a trick to disguise the Jews' attempt to dominate the world, and divisive of Aryan racial unity.

Hitler describes Germany as "a living organism" composed of individual cells of "flesh and blood." In turn he argues that the health of the German national organism was in danger of being destroyed by the infectious disease of Jewish, Marxist, and Bolshevik influences. The goodness and purity of the Aryans was in danger of being destroyed by the bacillus of Jewish influence.

"SPIRITS OF VENGEANCE"

Now we can apply this analysis to Hitler's use of discourse to incite the desire for revenge. Hitler and his movement were political actors on a historical scene. Hitler and his party editors perfected the script in *Mein Kampf.* With the Nazi party, he built a formidable propaganda machine. Taking ideas from churches and the German theater, he had huge outdoor theaters built that featured the swastika, burning alters, and memorials to German soldiers who had died in World War I. These theaters became the stages for mounting gigantic mass rallies and popular, nationalistic dramas. The rallies were filmed and circulated to theaters around Germany and the world. His speeches were broadcast on national radio and reported in the newspapers. Nazi themes were echoed from 1933 to 1945 in films (Kracauer, 1947; Herzstein, 1987, Pt. III), pamphlets, posters, and newspapers (Mendelsohn, 1982), radio (Kris, 1944), and particularly the "German Weekley Newsreel" (Herzstein, 1987, Chpt. 6). The supe- riority of the German was amplified in all of these media, and celebrated in the fine and civic arts (Muller-Mehlis, 1976). A whole panoply of uniforms, symbols, rituals, terminology, and political liturgy was generated to celebrate and embody the new order (Sontag, 1975; Mosse, 1975).

The Jew, according to Hitler, is by nature a "cunning" and "arrogant" monster. This is how he is able to explain two apparently contradictory sets of facts. If all Jews are evil Communists out to destroy capitalism, then how can they also be evil "international Jew stock exchange capitalists"? If all Jews are evil capitalists and Communists, then how come there are poor Jewish workers? When questioned about this, Hitler responded that this was just further proof of Jewish cunning. It is just a part of the plot to confuse people and take over the world. But what about "Aryan" capitalists who exploit "Aryan workers?" Or, what about "Aryan" communists? This happens, Hitler insisted, because the Aryans are seduced by the cunning Jew. He employs the same twist of logic to explain the simultaneous involvement of Jews in the Bolshevik movement and international financial capitalism. It is all due to the "cunning" and "arrogance" of the Jewish seducers.

> Never yet has a state been founded by peaceful economic means, but always and exclusively by the instincts of preservation of the species regardless whether these are found in the province of heroic virtue or of cunning craftiness; the one results in Aryan states based on work and culture, the other in Jewish colonies of parasites.
> (Hitler, 1971, p. 153)

Sexual symbolism is woven into Hitler's discourse. The masses are "feminine" and desire to be led by a dominating male. The villainous Jew seduces the feminine masses. And Hitler does not just mean this metaphorically; he means it literally. Jews are poisoning the blood of the Aryan masses by intermarriage, polluting the nation's blood. He associates Jews with prostitution, incest, and syphilis. The Jews are responsible for infecting the gullible feminine masses with democratic ideas. "The people in their overwhelming majority are so feminine by nature and attitude that sober reasoning determines their thoughts and actions far less than emotion and feeling" (Hitler, 1971, p. 183).

By this means Hitler perfected a hyperbole of the "cunning" and "arrogant" Jew. This "Jewish Devil" was the cause of Germany's problems. The Jews were made into "scapegoats" in the full religious sense of the term. It was the Jewish "Marxists" who had stabbed Germany in the back and caused Germany's defeat in World War I. It was Jewish capitalists who had caused Germany's economic collapse. The function of this rhetorical tactic is obvious. It was not the German Aryans that were defeated in World War I. It was not the capitalist system that had caused the economic crisis. It was the Jewish press and Marxists who had caused the defeat; it was Jewish financiers who had caused the collapse.

Hitler argued the following: the "true" cause of Germany's ills is the Jew. The 'Aryan' is basically "constructive." The Jew is, as a matter of race, "destructive." In order for the constructive Aryans to go forward, they must *destroy* the Jewish *destructiveness*. The social democratic "Jews" agitated for World War I. The defeat was caused by the "Jews."

> And so it had all been in vain. In vain all the sacrifices and privations; in vain the hunger and thirst of months which were often endless; in vain the hours in which, with mortal fear clutching at our hearts, we nevertheless did our duty; and in vain the death of two millions who died. Would not the graves of all the hundreds of thousands open, the graves of those who with faith in the fatherland had marched forth never to return? Would they not open and send the silent mud-and-blood-covered heroes back as *spirits of vengeance* to the homeland which had cheated them with such mockery of the highest sacrifice which a man can make to his people in this world? Had they died for this, the soldiers of August and September, 1914? Was it for this that in the autumn of the same year the volunteer regiments marched after their comrades? Was it for this that these boys of seventeen sank into the earth of Flanders? Was this the meaning of the sacrifice which the German mother made to the fatherland when with sore heart she let her best-loved boys march off, never to see them again? Did all this happen only so that a gang of wretched criminals could lay hands on the father land?
>
> Was it for this that the German soldier had stood fast in the sun's heat and in snowstorms, hungry, thirsty, and freezing, weary from sleepless nights and endless marches? Was it for this that he had lain in the hell of the drumfire and in the fever of gas attacks without wavering, always thoughtful of his one duty to preserve the fatherland from the enemy peril?
>
> Verily these heroes deserved a headstone: 'Thou Wanderer who comest to Germany, tell those at home that we lie here, true to the fatherland and obedient to duty.' (Hitler, 1971, pp. 204–205).

The economic collapse of Germany is explained by the same "true" cause. It was "divine retribution, a consequence of moral poisoning ... which had already begun to undermine the foundation of the people." In turn, this moral decay had been caused by "a sin against the blood and the degradation of the race" by the Jews.

The hyperbolic characters constituted in Hitler's discourse can be summarized in two equations:

$$\text{Aryan} = \text{"service to the community," "sacrificing," and "heroic."} \qquad (1)$$

$$\text{Jew} = \text{"egotism," "cunning," and "arrogant" monsters.} \qquad (2)$$

HITLER'S GERMAN AUDIENCE

We have seen how Hitler identified himself as a political actor on a historical stage before the German masses. I will now discuss the cultural background of Hitler's German audience and the question of why they were willing to identify with his discourse?

The first interpretation builds on the notion of "cultural resources" advanced at the beginning of the paper. Hitler's discourse articulated discursive elements long familiar to a German audience. The theme of a German *Volkish* state was not original to the Nazis. The notion of a German folk tradition was a direct product of the romantic movement in nineteenth-century Europe that had been clearly enunciated by nineteenth-century German writers, Wilhelm Heinrich Riehl, Paul de Lagarde, and Julius Langbehn (Mosse, 1964; Stern, 1961) Volkish discourse was elaborated against "modernity," against the Bourgeoisie, Enlightenment rationality, and the movement for social equality, and above all against the Jew. These notions were elaborated in a trinitarian mystique of the individual personality, the Volk, and transcendent reality, the cosmos and life force, blood, soil. The German peasant landscape was viewed as infusing the individual personality with a racial character, hence the superiority of the Nordic, Aryan race. These notions were symbolized in the imagery of the tree and the serpent, and in the figures of the German peasant and the Jew:

> Thus the Jew's role in society, however exaggerated and distorted, identified him as the enemy of the peasant, and therefore also as the cause of the German people's misfortune. The Volkish cure was vividly presented: if the snake could be removed from the root of the tree, it would flourish and the strength of the Volk would cease to be sapped. (Mosse, 1964, p. 28).

The metaphorical logic at work in this imagery explains the particular effectiveness of Hitler's appeal to the Volk. The survival of the German Volk, the "rootedness" of German blood and soil, depended on a war to "remove" and "eliminate" the Jewish-Devil. The notion that the Jew was an incarnation of evil was amplified in periodic revivals of the accusation that Jews practiced "ritual murder" as part of their religious rites. Later toward the end of the nineteenth century, this discourse was rearticulated, incorporating 'racist' elements derived from "Social Darwinism" and Houston Stewart

Chamberlain's "scientific racism," and institutionalized in the schools, the Youth Movement, and the universities. Albrech Durer's famous engraving, "Knight, Death and Devil" (1513), was invoked by Volkish professors and students to enunciate the increasingly "activist" implications of Volkish discourse.

Thus Hitler called upon a system of discourse which was familiar to his German audience. *Mein Kampf* only summarized the already prevalent stereotype of the ghetto Jew as it had been elaborated in Volkish literature. It was World War I that transformed this discourse into a politically effective rhetorical weapon (Mosse, 1964, p. 237; 1970). Mosse concludes his fascinating account of the origins of National Socialist thought with an important point, one which should be stressed. It concerns the emphasis Hitler placed on "discipline and organization." In *Mein Kampf* we can see how a "rational" orientation to action has been rearticulated in the context of an explicitly anti-rational Volkish argument. Traditional Volkish discourse had rejected the social radicalism of the French Revolution and the notion of a mass movement. Hitler's strategy, perhaps suggested by the World War experience, involved "the Nationalization of the Masses" (Mosse, 1974).

Richard Wagner's "political operas" had long been familiar to Hitler's German audience (Perris, 1985, Chap. 3; Joll, 1985). Hitler once said that "Whoever wants to understand National Socialist Germany must know Wagner." He claimed that Wagner's political compositions were his favorite reading material, and *Mein Kampf* was written while he listened to Wagner's music. Wagner's music was played at the mass rallies and as background music to propaganda films. Hitler turned Wagner's "opera of redemption" into a dramatic form of discourse. Wagner, like Bismarck and Hitler, believed that the masses, like a woman, could be seduced with art and music. Nietzsche's critique of Wagner's theater could be applied to Hitler's use of Wagner. "It merely requires *virtue*—merely training, automatism, 'self-denial' . . . Teutons! Definition of the Teuton: obedience and long legs." Nietzsche's prescience on this matter is remarkable. Wagner's theater "coincides in time with the arrival of the 'Reich'" (1967, p. 180). He goes on to write that posterity would judge the coincidence of these two events to be the beginning of "the classical age of war." Subsequently, both Kaiser Wilhelm II and Adolf Hitler would have portraits made of themselves dressed in the shining armor of Lohengrin: "Each regarded himself as the holy knight destined to rescue the noble Elsa (Germany) from the diabolical Ortrud (the alien forces of evil)" (Perris, 1985, p. 52).

Another set of interpretations suggests that different groups identified with different parts of Hitler's discourse (see Burke, 1941). The middle and upper classes supported Hitler for purely opportunistic reasons. Hitler, it is argued, played on middle class resentment toward a prospering minority. Some of this resentment had its roots in the unpopular function of Jews as "pariah capitalists" (Chirot, 1986, p. 114). Hitler was able to shift responsibility for Germany's economic problems to the Jews. In addition, there was an historical association of Jews with money. When the inflationary collapse took place in Germany, the Jews were blamed for the collapse.

Right-wing veterans groups were receptive to Hitler's anti-Semitic explanation for Germany's defeat in World War I. It was not the heroic and sacrificing German soldier that lost the war. It was the Jews and Social Democrats who had betrayed

Germany in her time of need, "stabbing the Fatherland in the back!" This "wound" to German national pride accounts for the effectiveness of the slogan, "Jews not admitted" and "War victims free," which appeared on all circulars announcing Nazi meetings in the early 1920's.

Hitler's Aryan Germans were receptive to his anti-Semitic appeal on racial grounds. There had been a long tradition of prejudice in Europe directed against the Jews (Katz, 1980; Stern, 1961). German racists believed that they were the "blood" descendants of the ancient Teutonic tribes. Faucault has described the political background of this "symbolics of blood and race," and its return in the Nazi "combination of fantasies of blood and paroxysms of a disciplinary power" (1978, p. 149). According to the myth, the Teutonic tribes were the original Aryans. Hitler considered Luther, Frederick the Great, and Bismarck to be lineal descendants of this Aryan race. He thought that Bismarck had been a great German leader who had tried to maintain and recapture the Teutonic ideal. German racists thought Bismarck was a true example of the superior Aryan racial type. Bismarck embodied the heroic tradition of the Teutonic knight engaged in a crusade to revive German national consciousness.

One clue about the origin of Nazi hatred for the Jews is that the average Nazi voter in the early 1930's was a Lutheran who lived in northern and central Germany (Deak, 1983). This correlation suggests that religion played a role in the selection of Jews as Nazi scapegoats. Joshua Trachtenberg's (1943) study of *The Devil and the Jews* reinforces this interpretation as do Norman Cohn's (1975; 1967) studies of genocide in the European tradition. The accusation that Jews were killing Christian children and drinking their blood surfaced again in the thirties (Mendelsohn, 1982). George Steiner (1971), following a lead suggested by Nietzsche argues that the genocide of the Jews was culturally determined by a deep-seated *ressentiment* against the Jews for inventing monotheism. The suffocating guilt generated by monotheism accounts for the poisonous hatred of the Jew. The "death camps" were a materialization of the late medieval images of hell. Christians have been taught that it was the Jews who condemned the innocent Christ to death. Since that time the missionaries of Christianity had said in effect to the Jews: "You may not live amongst us as Jews." The secular rulers who followed them after the Middle Ages then decided: "You may not live among us " and the Nazis finally decreed: "You may not live." The Final Solution was a result of a series of minute but logical steps. The bureaucrats simply invented an "efficient" method to carry out Hitler's orders (Hilberg, 1985). The "good family man " concerned with "paying the bills," drove the trains.

A final interpretation derives from the psychoanalytic tradition of political psychology (Freud, 1921; Reich, 1970; Fromm, 1941; Erickson, 1950). Nationalism is the family writ large upon the screen. The German masses were receptive to Hitler's charismatic appeal as a result of the authoritarian structure of the German family. The Jew was a paranoid projection of forbidden sexual and violent impulses. Koenigsberg (1975) has elaborated this thesis through a content analysis of Hitler's statements: His "ideology" articulated an unconscious fantasy that was widely shared by German males at the time and represented a projection of the child's view of the mother's participation in sexual intercourse as "degrading" and wishes to "rescue" the mother from it. Hitler unconsciously equated Germany with his dying mother. The disease that killed his mother is killing the German nation (Koenigsberg, 1975, p. 55). Hitler refers to the "mother country" in his discourse describing "her" health and purity as threatened by the diabolical Jewish "him." Nazi "ideology" had an allegorical relation to this unconscious infantile fantasy.

CONCLUSIONS

What can we learn from Hitler's rhetoric of motives? His "success" shows us the power of the endless repetition of slogans in the media of mass communication. Modern advertising techniques can be adapted to the political campaign. Just as people can be talked into buying things they do not need, so the political leader can talk the desire for revenge into people. National Socialist themes were continuously reiterated in pamphlets, newspapers, radio programs, cinema, the arts and theater, and in the schools, military, daily discourse, and the law. This repetition served to amplify their effects.

The rhetoric of enemies is a potent means of gaining and sustaining social integration in modern society. The main feature of the rite of war is human sacrifice. Killing and dying in war is a way to accomplish the identification of masses with the political authority of the national state. In times of change, the politician can always claim that someone is to blame. Social change can be described in life and death metaphors which suggests the notion murder. "Who is causing the death of our way of life? They are!" When change is personified in this way it can lead to vengeance against those held responsible.

Leaders can influence people by giving them a "world view"—an enemy and a goal. Leaders like Hitler can use the scapegoat device to personify social change by creating enemies and patriots. He gave his people an enemy to fight and a patriotic goal—an ugly means to a beautiful end. He concocted hyperboles to incite his people by mixing up a brew of violent metaphors. He was able to motivate his followers to participate in the murder of millions of human beings in a "holy" crusade against "evil." Human violence is not a fall into a latent animality, but rather an extreme expression of our symbol-mindedness. It is in the hyperbolic possibilities of linguistic symbolism that we should seek an answer to the question of why human beings fight wars.

The culture of war motives can be traced to the tradition of the Greek tragic drama of murder and revenge, and the Christian elaboration of this in the drama of guilt and redemption through human sacrifice. The central actor in these dramas is the noble hero. Political leaders use the murder/revenge form to dramatize the evil of the enemy. The Christian theme of redemption through sacrifice is the key to the altruistic suicide of the noble military hero (see Durkheim, 1951, pp. 217–240). He must be brave, courageous, and noble in the face of the enemy's violence. If you ask a soldier why he fights, he will answer, "The price of freedom is always blood." It is in the cultivation of this willingness to give one's life for the nation that we should seek a solution to the problem of war motives.

Nazi hatred demonstrates that "violence breeds violence." The strategy of retaliation is contradictory; by killing the killer we legitimate killing (Archer and Gartner, 1984). World War I traumatized Germany, creating a legacy of violent death that haunted the Germans. The Nazis were the "spirits of vengeance." As Nietzsche put it, "Whoever fights monsters should see to it that in the process he does not become a monster."

The interpretation advanced in this article has implications for social problems theory and a sociology of emotion. Hitler's construction of the Jew as Germany's ultimate problem entailed the final solution, the holocaust and the World War. Gusfield's research suggests a logologic of victimage ritual is at work in less extreme form in a variety of campaigns to solve social problems. These campaigns are incited by a rhetoric of motives that features victims and villains, and heroes and enemies. The victim/villain hierarchy is necessary to the production of political incitement. This aspect of a rhetoric of war or social problems rhetoric has implications for a sociology of emotion. George Lakoff (1987; also see Blain, 1976) argues that emotions like anger and moral outrage have a complex conceptual structure composed of a system of metonymies and metaphors (e.g., Anger is heat, and when blood boils it rises!). The agitator seeking to constitute a social problem must make his audience's blood boil. This is the function of the villain/victim rhetoric.

Future inquiry should concentrate on how the tradition of "rationalized" military training produces the sacrificial victims of war. Michel Foucault's (1978) studies of discipline, the docility of the body, and its "basic" training are the background practices against which a rhetoric of war motives functions. The development of modern "scientific" psychology and sociology has had a dangerous complicitly with militarism. Stern (1985) has suggested that psychological testing might have had more to do with the efficiency of the Nazi war machine than did Hitler's racist discourse. We should see these two clusters of cultural practices working in tandem—"rationalized" training and a political drama of national survival.

Future research should focus on the relation between gender and the rhetoric of war. Hitler talked at length about the importance of masculine virility in his descriptions of his role as leader and the role of the soldier. Drill instructors employ a rhetoric of "cunt" and "pussy" to transform "mother's boys" into "a few good men" (Daly, 1978, p. 358). The language of war is saturated with gender metaphors. The enemy is feminized. A military campaign is described as "penetrating enemy territory." War, according to Daly, is a form of male bonding, a mode of male social integration in opposition to females (see Theweleit, 1987).

Sociological knowledge of how Hitler cast the Jews in the enemy role should be used to immunize people with knowledge. There is a growing literature on the rhetoric of danger crisis and the enemy as a means of achieving social integration. (Falk, 1982; Dower, 1986; Keen, 1986; Kwitny, 1984; Ivie, 1980, 1986). This has ominous implications in a nuclear armed world, with the superpowers mirroring each other in a tragicomic drama of "Communist" and "Imperialist" enemies. Alan Wolfe's (1984, pp. 133–134) analysis of the domestic uses of the "Soviet Threat" in the United States could probably apply with due regard for local circumstances to the USSR as well. He shows how the "threat" rises and falls as a function of the specific play of political party, presidential, military-bureaucratic, foreign policy, and corporate forces. We need to use this research to concoct a knowledge of the function of enemies and circulate it. This knowledge should be used to disarticulate the use of the rhetoric of enemies.

Robert Ivie's (1980) analysis of victimage rhetoric in American presidential justifications of war show us how the American ideal of "peace" and the Just War tradition require that advocates of war must construct the enemy's responsibility through a rhetoric of the enemy's savagery. The rhetoric of American war motives features two contrasting images, a rhetoric of hierarchy: on the one side is a savage, irrational aggressor who wishes to subjugate others by force, and on the other, a reluctant but noble freedom- and peace-loving America called to arms to defend civilization against the savage enemies. The analysis presented here confirms Ivie's analysis but goes beyond it in the specification of the devices rhetors deploy in the social construction of the savagery of the villain. The violation of order in war rhetoric "literalizes" the villain's status as murderer. The cycle of guilt and redemption identified by Burke and Ivie always corresponds in war motives to the cycle of murder and revenge, attack and retaliation. Nationalisms are consecrated in the memorials erected to the heroic victims of revolutions and war.

Sociologists must take their knowledge of how war discourse functions to the people. In the nuclear era, we cannot afford to risk war on the basis of hyperbolic descriptions of our enemies. Sociologists argue that human beings are self-interpreting beings. As self-interpreting beings, we act and continue to act in specific ways according to how we interpret the world. Sociologists should take leading roles in the movement to counter war talk whenever it rears its ridiculous head. We should counter the dangerous simplifications employed by the Hitlers of the world through sustained comic ridicule. Laughter is the only answer to those who "seriously" argue that massive displays of human sacrifice are God's will or in the national interest.

> But war's a game which were subjects wise,
> Kings could not play at.
>
> (William Cowper 1784)

REFERENCES

Alloway, L. 1971. *Violent America: The Movies 1946–1964*. New York: The Museum of Modern Art.

Allport, G. 1954. *The Nature of Prejudice*. Cambridge, MA: Addison-Wesley.

Archer, D. and R. Gartner. 1984 "Violent Acts and Violent Times: The Effect of Wars on Postwar Homicide Rates." Pp. 63–97 in *Violence and Crime in Cross-National Perspective*. New Haven: Yale University Press.

Blain, M. 1976. "The Role of Death in Political Conflict." *Psychoanalytic Review* 63: 249–266.

Bölsche, W. 1921 *Vom Bazilluszum Affenmenschen*. Jema: Eugen Diederichs Verlag.

Burke, K. 1941. "The Rhetoric of Hitler's Battle." Pp. 191–220 in *The Philosophy of Literary Form*. Baton Rouge: Louisiana State University Press.

———. 1965 [1954]. "On Human Behavior Considered 'Dramatistically.'" Pp. 275–295 in *Permanence and Change: An Anatomy of Purpose*. New York: Bobbs-Merrill Company.

————. 1968a. "Dramatism." Pp. 445–452 in D.I. Sills, (ed.) *International Encyclopedia of the Social Sciences,* V. 7. New York: Macmillan & The Free Press.

————. 1968b. *Language as Symbolic Action.* Berkeley: University of California Press.

Chirot, D. 1986. *Social Change in the Modern Era.* New York: Harcourt, Brace, Jovanovich.

Cohn, N. 1967. *Warrant For Genocide: The Myth of the Jewish World Conspiracy and The Protocols of the Elders of Zion.* New York: Harper and Row.

————. 1975. *Europe's Inner Demons: An Inquiry Inspired by the Great Witch-Hunts.* New York: Basic Books, Inc.

Cuzzort, R.P. and E.W. King. 1980. "Communication, Art, and Victims" Pp. 327–348 in *20th Century Social Thought, Third Edition.* New York: Holt, Rinehart and Winston.

Daly, M. 1978. *Gyn/Ecology: The Metaethics of Radical Feminism.* Boston, MA: Beacon Press.

Dawidowicz, L.S. 1975. *The War Against the Jews 1933–1945.* New York: Bantam Books.

Deak, I. 1983. "What Was Fascism?" *New York Review of Books* (March 3): 13–16.

Dower, J.W. 1986. *War Without Mercy: Race and Power in the Pacific War.* New York: Pantheon Books.

Duncan, H.D. 1962. *Communication and Social Order.* New York: Oxford University Press.

————. 1968. *Symbols and Society.* New York: Oxford University Press.

Durkheim, E. 1951. *Suicide: A Study in Sociology.* Tr. J. Spaulding and G. Simpson. New York: The Free Press.

Erickson, E. 1950. "The Legend of Hitler's Childhood." Pp. 326–358 in *Childhood and Society, 2nd Ed.* New York: W.W. Norton & Co.

Falk, R. 1982. "The Soviet Factor: A Useful Enemy." Pp. 159–170 in J. Harris and E. Markusen (eds.) *Nuclear Weapons and the Threat of War.* New York: Harcourt, Brace, Jovanovich.

Foucault, M. 1977 [1975]. *Discipline and Punish: The Birth of the Prison,* Tr. R. Sheridan. New York: Pantheon Books.

————. 1978 [1976]. *The History of Sexuality. V. 1: An Introduction,* Tr. R. Hurley. New York: Vintage Books.

————. 1980. *Power/knowledge. Selected Interviews and Other Writings, 1972–1977,* in C. Gordon (ed.), C. Gordon, L. Marshall, J. Mephan, K. Soper (Tr). New York: Pantheon Books.

Freud, S. 1960 [1921]. *Group Psychology and the Analysis of the Ego.* Tr. J. Strachey. New York: Bantam Books.

Fromm, E. 1941. *Escape from Freedom.* New York: The Avon Library.

Gusfield, J. 1981. *The Culture of Public Problems: Drinking-Driving and the Symbolic Order.* Chicago, IL: University of Chicago Press.

Herstein, R.D. 1987 [1978]. *The War that Hitler Won: Goebbels and the Nazi Media Campaign.* New York: Paragon House Publishers.

Hilberg, R. 1985. *The Destruction of the European Jews, Revised and Definitive Edition.* New York: Holmes and Meier.

Hitler, A. 1971. *Mein Kampf,* Tr. by Ralph Manheim. Boston, MA: Houghton Mifflin.

Ivie, R.L. 1980. "Images of Savagery in American Justifications of War." *Communication Monographs* 47: 279–294.

————. 1986. "Literalizing the Metaphor of Soviet Savagery: President Truman's Plain Style." *Southern Speech Communication Journal* 51: 91–105.

Joll, J. 1985. "Klingor's Apprentices." *New York Review of Books* (January 31): 9–11.

Keen, S. 1986. *Faces of the Enemy: Reflections of the Hostile Imagination.* San Francisco, CA: Harper & Row.

Katz, J. 1980. *From Prejudice to Destruction: Anti-Semitism, 1700–1933.* Cambridge, MA: Harvard University Press.

Koenisberg, R.A. 1975. *Hitler's Ideology: A Study in Psychoanalytic Sociology.* New York: The Library of Social Science.

Kracauer, S. 1947. *From Caligari to Hitler. A Psychological Analysis of the German Film.* New Jersey: Princeton University Press.

Kris, E. 1944. *German Radio Propaganda.* New York: Oxford University Press.

Kwitny, J. 1984. *Endless Enemies: The Making of an Unfriendly World.* New York: Congdon & Weed.

Laclau, E. 1977. "Fascism and Ideology," Pp. 81–141 in *Politics and Ideology in Marxist Theory.* London: New Left Review.

Lakoff, G. 1987. "Anger." Pp. 380–415 in *Women, Fire, and Dangerous Things: What Categories Reveal about the Mind.* Chicago, IL: University of Chicago Press.

Le Bon, G. 1987. *The Crowd: A Study of the Popular Mind.* London: T. Fisher Unwin.

Maser, W. 1970. *Hitler's Mein Kampf: An Analysis,* Tr. by R. H. Barry. London: Faber and Faber.

McDougall, W. 1920. *The Group Mind: A Sketch of the Principles of Collective Psychology.* New York: Cambridge University Press.

———. 1974. *Hitler's Letters and Notes,* Tr. by A. Pomerans. New York: Bantam Books.

McGuire, M. 1977. "Mythic Rhetoric in *Mein Kampf:* A Structuralist Critique. " *Quarterly Journal of Speech* 63 (1): 1–13.

Megill, A. 1985. *Prophets of Extremity: Nietzche, Heidegger, Foucault, Derrida.* Berkeley. CA: University of California Press.

Mendelsohn, J. (ed.) 1982. *The Holocaust: 4. Propaganda and Aryanization, 1938–1944.* New York: Garland Publishing.

Mosse, G. 1964. *The Crisis of German Ideology: Intellectual Origins of the Third Reich.* New York: Grosset & Dunlap.

———. 1970. *Germans and Jews: the Right, the Left, and the Search for a "Third Force" in Pre-Nazi Germany.* New York: Howard Fertig.

———. 1975. *The Nationalization of the Masses: Political Symbolism and Mass Movements in Germany from the Napoleonic Wars Through the Third Reich.* New York: Howard Fertig.

Muller-Mehlis, R. 1976. *Die Kunst Im Dritten Reich.* München: Wilhelm Heyne Verlag.

Nehamas, A. 1985. *Nietzsche: Life as Literature.* Cambridge, MA: Harvard University Press.

Nietzsche, F. 1967. *The Birth of Tragedy and The Case of Wagner,* Tr. W. Kaufmann. New York: Vintage Books.

Perris, A. 1985. *Music as Propaganda: Art to Persuade, Art to Control.* Westport, CT: Greenwood Press.

Perry, Steven. 1983. "Rhetorical Functions of the Infestation Metaphor in Hitler's Rhetoric." *Central States Speech Journal* 34: 229–235.

Reich, W. 1970 (1946). *The Mass Psychology of Fascism,* Tr. V. R. Carfagno. New York: Farrar, Straus & Giroux.

Schoenbaum, D. 1966. *Hitler's Social Revolution: Class and Status in Nazi Germany 1933–1939.* New York: Doubleday Anchor.

Smith, M.B. 1985. "The Metaphorical Basis of Selfhood." Pp. 56–88 in A.J. Marsella, G. DeVos, and F.L.K. Hsu (eds.) *Culture and Self: Asian and Western Perspectives.* New York: Tavistock Publications.

Sontag, S. 1975. "Fascinating Fascism." *New York Review of Books* (Feb. 6): 23–30.

———. 1978. "Disease As Political Metaphor." *New York Review of Books* (Feb. 9): 29–33.

Stern, F. 1961. *The Politics of Cultural Despair: A Study in the Rise of the Germanic Ideology.* New York: Doubleday & Co.

————. 1985. "Fink Shrinks," A Review of Die Professionalisierung der deutschen Psychologie im Nationalsozialismus. *The New York Review of Books* 32(20): 48–53.

Steiner, G. 1971. *In Bluebeard's Castle: Some Notes Towards the Redefinition of Culture.* New Haven: Yale University Press.

Theweleit, K. 1987 [1977]. *Male fantasies, V. 1: Women, Floods, Bodies, History,* Tr. S. Conway. Minneapolis, MN: University of Minnesota Press.

Trachtenberg, J. 1943. *The Devil and the Jews.* New Haven, CT: Yale University Press.

Wagner-Pacifici, R.E. 1986. *The Moro Morality Play: Terrorism as Social Drama.* Chicago, IL: University of Chicago Press.

Wolfe, A. 1984. *The Rise and Fall of the Soviet Threat: Domestic Sources of the Cold War Consensus.* Boston, MA: South End Press.

Wright, Q. 1965. *A Study of War: Second Edition, with a Commentary on War since 1942.* Chicago, IL: University of Chicago Press.

Victory Celebrations as Theater: A Dramaturgical Approach to Crowd Behavior

David A. Snow
Louis A. Zurcher
The University of Texas, Austin

Robert Peters
The University of Michigan, Ann Arbor

Drawing on data derived from a field study of victory celebrations, this paper suggests a dramaturgical approach to crowd behavior. Existing theories of crowd behavior are either contradicted by the field data or do not adequately account for the heterogeneity of activity observed, for the interaction between the various categories of participants, or for the shifts in the behavior of the participants and the resultant change in the character of the celebrations. Subsequent analysis indicates that the victory crowds are best understood from a dramaturgical standpoint. Several theoretical, conceptual, and research implications of a dramaturgical approach to crowd behavior are suggested and discussed. The paper concludes with an expanded conception of crowd behavior, one which emphasizes its spatial and temporal as well as interactional dimensions.

Even though conceptual discussions of crowd behavior typically include some reference to social interaction or personal interstimulation (Blumer, 1951; Brown, 1965: 728; Brown and Goldin, 1973: 178; Lang and Lang, 1968: 556; Milgram and Toch, 1969: 507; Perry and Pugh, 1978: 3) not enough is known about the structure and processes of interaction within collective encounters. Over two decades ago Blumer

Reprinted from Symbolic Interaction, 4(1):21–42.

(1957: 135) observed that "the retarded state of our knowledge in this area seems to be caused in part by the paucity of study of natural instances of collective behavior." In their recent review of the field, Marx and Wood (1975: 372) similarly noted that "systematic empirical research during instances of crowd behavior has been significantly lacking."[1]

Inasmuch as research is guided by theory, it is not surprising that crowd-specific interaction has received so little empirical attention. With the exception of the emergent norm approach (Turner, 1964a, 1964b; Turner and Killian, 1972), theories of crowd behavior tend to focus not on what goes on within collective episodes, but on the dispositions (Allport, 1924; Feuer, 1969; Johnson and Feinberg, 1977; Miller and Dollard, 1941) or cognitive states of the participants (Berk, 1974a, 1974b; Blumer, 1951; Freud, 1922; LeBon, 1903).[2] While such foci inform us about crowd participants and their states-of-mind, the nature of crowd-specific interaction and its relation to the development of crowd behavior remain problematic.

The purpose of this paper is twofold: (1) to contribute empirical data on crowd behavior by describing and analyzing a series of college football victory celebrations; and (2) to apply a dramaturgical analysis to crowd behavior, focusing on interaction rather than on the cognitive or demographic characteristics of the participants. The intent is not to displace existing approaches to the study of the crowd. Rather, it is to complement them, particularly the emergent norm thesis and the gaming or rational calculus perspective.[3]

DATA AND PROCEDURES

On five consecutive Saturday evenings from October 8, 1977 to November 5, 1977, students from The University of Texas and other Austin residents converged on the main street bordering the University and transformed it into an arena for celebrating the victories of the University football team. Data about the celebrations were derived from three sources. Following a team approach to fieldwork, we first observed the celebration *in situ*. One of the authors, who lived within earshot of the celebrations, assumed the role of a participant observer for each of the episodes. Another author, although attending some of the celebrations, functioned mainly as a detached observer. The participant observer roamed through the different spatial sectors of the celebrations, occasionally hitching a ride on a parading vehicle, and talked with representatives of the different segments of the crowd. He was able to record hundreds of behaviors and gestures and to interview informally several of the participants. The detached observer, functioning primarily as a cross-examiner, critically appraised the fieldnotes and interviewed the participant observer. Each Monday following a celebration the participant observer and the detached observer would meet in a debriefing session and establish a research agenda in the event of another celebration.

As a check on our own observations and fieldnotes, 15 university students, each of whom had participated in the victory crowds, were interviewed in the weeks following the celebrations. We were less interested in the representativeness of the student respondents than we were in how well their recollections corresponded with our own observations.

The third data source consisted of press accounts in the campus and city newspapers. These accounts, including letters to the editors regarding the celebrations, were examined for information about community reaction and for evidence confirming or disconfirming our observations. Although the three data sources yielded no major inconsistencies, it might appear that the data base was thin. We would argue, however, that the data we collected are far better than none, especially in a substantive area rife with theoretical speculation about phenomena that have too infrequently been directly studied.

THE VICTORY CELEBRATIONS

On October 8, 1977, The University of Texas football team unexpectedly defeated its arch-rival, the University of Oklahoma, for the first time in seven years. Immediately following the game's conclusion (4:30 p.m.), many students and other local fans began driving along "the Drag," the section of Guadalupe Street bounding the western edge of the University campus (see Figure 1). Even though the game had not been played at "home," by 8:00 p.m. approximately 3,000 people had gathered on the Drag. There was bumper-to-bumper traffic between Nineteenth and Twenty-Sixth Streets (which constitute the northern and southern boundaries of the University campus). The street resounded with the din of honking horns and shouts of "we're No. 1 !" The celebration, which was likened to "a big New Year's party" by one participant, lasted until early Sunday morning.

Throughout the evening six types of participants and corresponding behaviors were clearly discernible (see Figure 1). The first type consisted of the vehicular paraders or occupants of the motor vehicles who, as the focus of attention, constituted the main performers. A few of the cars had roof-mounted loudspeakers blaring "we're No. 1." All of the vehicles were filled with celebrants who, hanging out the car windows or sitting on the car roofs, guzzled beer, yelled, flashed the "Hook-em-Horns" sign,[4] and slapped hands with other paraders and spectators who lined the street.

The second group of participants consisted of relatively passive spectators who sat on the cement wall that separates the University campus from the public sidewalk. Periodically a few of these spectators would yell and flash the "Hook-em" sign, but their main activity was viewing.

The third type were the more animated spectators. Congregated mainly on the west side of the Drag immediately north of Twenty-Second Street, these participants actively supported the vehicular paraders by shaking their hands and cheering them on. Immediately behind these spectators was the fourth set of participants. This group consisted of a small number of people who were dancing to the rock music blaring out of a record store.

The fifth type was represented by males who stood across from the Student Union just south of Twenty-Third Street. Whenever a car or pickup approached, they would slap the side and top of the vehicle and attempt to "grope" the female occupants.

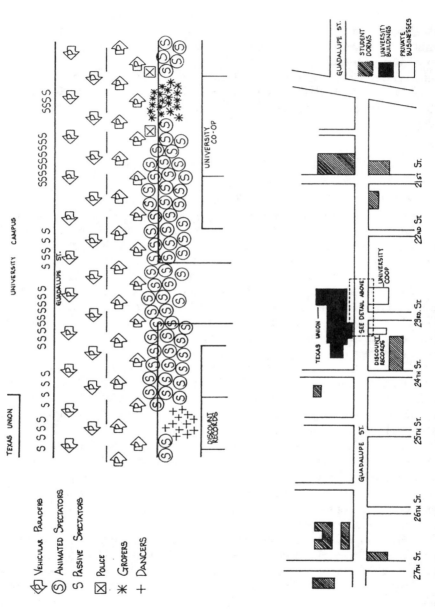

Figure 1. Diagram of "The Drag" and Location of the Six Types of Participants, 1st Celebraton, October 8, 1977.

196

The sixth group of participants was comprised of the police scattered along the Drag. Decidedly friendly, the police appeared to function more as supportive viewers than as control agents. Except for keeping the autos within their appropriate lanes and occasionally asking some of the more animated spectators to move back, the police maintained a low and cordial profile. This was reflected in part by the fact that none of the participants at this first celebration were arrested, even though many of them were in fact breaking the law.

The following Saturday (October 15), Texas' football team came from behind in the final quarter to defeat the University of Arkansas. Moments after the game, fans again converged on the Drag. They began celebrating in a manner similar to the previous week, but with three discernible differences. First, there was a greater number of vehicular paraders. Not only was the traffic backed-up further than the previous week, but there were more celebrants sitting in and on the cars and pickups. Second, females were not being molested by male spectators. Third, not only had the number of spectators increased, but they had become more animated. As before, the police did little to dampen the jovial mood or to stop the celebration, which could still be heard from a mile away at 4:30 Sunday morning.

While Texas was defeating Southern Methodist University on Saturday, October 22, No. 1 ranked University of Michigan was losing to the University of Minnesota. This upset, coupled with Texas' win, meant that Texas would probably become the No. 1 ranked team in the nation. Partly because of this unanticipated turn of events, the ensuing celebration was the largest and most vociferous to date. Honking horns rhythmically pounded out "we're No. 1" while riders waved Texas state flags, shook hands with spectators and tossed cans of beer to those weaving in and out of the bumper-to-bumper traffic which extended 15 blocks in either direction. But most of this activity was not evident until the vehicular paraders entered the area of Guadalupe that had been transformed into an arena for celebration. As paraders entered the "stage," their level of animation increased and the noise became almost deafening. The crowd activity reached its peak in the vicinity of Twenty-Third Street and the student Union (see Figure 1), where the number of spectators was most dense. Again, the police were unobtrusive. Most of the time they stood watching the celebrants, occasionally shaking hands with some of them and flashing the "Hook-em" sign.

Following Texas' defeat of Texas Tech University on Saturday, October 29, fans again converged on the Drag. With bumper-to-bumper traffic extending for 34 blocks by early evening, it appeared as if the celebration would be the wildest to date. The fact that this was the first celebration to follow a home game also suggested a likely increase in intensity. However, the celebration was subdued and constrained in comparison to those previous. There was less physical contact between paraders and spectators. There were fewer celebrants per vehicle. There was less hand-slapping and little rhythmical horn-blowing. The overall volume of noise had decreased.

These changes in the behavior of the celebrants seemed largely due to a shift in police strategy and demeanor. The number of officers had increased from the previous week's level of approximately 5 per block to a new level of 8 to 10 per block. In addition, the majority of the policemen were now suited in high leather boots and riot helmets. Now, rather than shaking hands and flashing the "Hook-em" sign, the police were concentrating on directing traffic, keeping celebrants off the tops and hoods of cars, and keeping spectators out of the street. In contrast to the earlier celebrations, the police were occasionally arresting lawbreaking celebrants.

Since these changes in police behavior interfered with the celebrating, some of the celebrants later in the evening (11 p.m.) shifted their activity further down the Drag where there were fewer police. Whereas the segment of the Drag directly across from the Student Union had functioned as "center stage," a substitute area was appropriated and redefined for celebration by some of the spectators. Until police reinforcements arrived at the new site, celebrants were once again sitting on car hoods and hanging out the windows, honking the car horns, walking back and forth between cars, shaking hands, and screaming "we're No. 1."

Texas' defeat of the University of Houston on Saturday, November 5, provided the impetus for another celebration. However, this post-game celebration was even more muted than the previous one. The major categories of actors returned, but their behavior had changed dramatically, as if the script had been rewritten. Though there were at least 1,000 celebrators on the Drag, there was little yelling. There were only scattered horn blowing and few overfilled cars and pickups. The mood was one of caution; the watchword was "Ssshhh." The apparent reason for the change was a significant increase in the number of police assigned to the Drag. Officers were standing every 30 to 40 feet on the center dividing line and on each side of the street. Police were stationed north of Twenty-Sixth Street for the first time since the celebrations had begun. The officers had been instructed (for reasons that will be discussed later) to reduce the overall level of noise. Whenever a horn was blown, the officer who spotted the violator would stop the vehicle or shine his flashlight on the side of the auto and the next policeman would stop the car. As a result of this tactic, the noise was greatly reduced.

Nonetheless, some vehicular paraders, coaxed by the spectators, continued to drive up and down the Drag. Whenever a car horn sounded, spectators in the immediate area would applaud and cheer. If a parader received a citation, the police were booed. Though the encouragement did not lead to an increase in the actual amount of horn blowing, it did help produce an atmosphere conducive to taunting the police. Many paraders would shout "honk, honk" as they passed police; others mockingly would put a finger to their lips in the "Ssshhh" position. In response, one officer commented, "I'd almost rather they did honk. At least there would be something to do." As the evening progressed, it became evident that the interaction between the police and the vehicular paraders had now become the focus of attention.

The following Saturday, November 12, when Texas defeated Texas Christian University, the only actors to appear on the Drag in full force were the police. There was little celebration; traffic was near normal. There were several reasons for the apparent disinterest in celebration. First, although Texas won, the victory was anticipated. Second, the Saturday morning edition of the city newspaper indicated that the police would attempt "to put a damper on any celebration." As on the previous Saturday, there were approximately 10 police per block. Moreover, they were giving a traffic citation to anyone who blew a car horn. This show of force and "crack-down" strategy seemed to intimidate potential celebrants. Only three "honks" were heard and recorded within a 15 minute period between 8 p.m. and 9 p.m. A third countervailing factor was the rumor that "a sniper would be on the Drag" on Saturday evening. Both Friday's edition of the campus newspaper and the Saturday morning edition of the city newspaper reported that the Austin police had received an anonymous letter warning that the writer would "shoot up the Drag Saturday night" in the event of another celebration. Although the police were "pretty satisfied it (was) just a crank," such a threat could not be fully discounted, especially since it stimulated memories of a sniper who in 1967 had terrorized the University of Texas campus. A fourth countervailing factor was the annual sausage festival (Wurstfest) south of Austin. The festival provided an entertainment alternative to the Drag, thereby siphoning many potential celebrants. Finally, it is reasonable to assume that for many of the participants the celebrations were becoming routine and predictable; the novelty had worn off.

After five weeks, the series of victory celebrations had run its course. In the weeks that followed, Texas won its final two regularly scheduled games. Neither were followed by a victory celebration of the kind that had occurred earlier.

ANALYSIS AND DISCUSSION

Students of collective behavior have long debated its proper conceptualization (Brissett, 1968; Couch, 1968, 1970; Currie and Skolnick, 1970; Marx, 1970; Smelser, 1970; Turner, 1964a, 1964b; Weller and Quarantelli, 1973). However, most scholars would agree that the victory celebrations on the Drag constituted a series of crowd episodes. On each occasion there was a large number of people in close physical contact within a limited spatial area. There was a common focus of attention. Though some "assembling instructions" (McPhail and Miller, 1973) such as shouts of "to the Drag" were heard after the first celebration, the assemblage and ensuing behaviors were relatively spontaneous and unplanned. The celebrations were neither on the community or university calendars nor were they the product of prior formal organization. This is not to suggest that the celebrations were devoid of organization or patterned behavior. To the contrary, it appeared as if the actions of the different segments of the crowd fit together, as if they were aligned in a complementary fashion. How can that coordination be best explained? How did the lines of action exhibited by the different categories of participants fit together and contribute to the development of the celebrations? Additionally, what accounts for the shift in the behavior of some of the participants and for the change in the character of the celebrations?

The dominant theories of collective behavior do not fully enough address these questions. In fact, they are contradicted by much of what we observed and heard.

Convergence Theory

Convergence theory views the action of crowd participants as parallel or homogeneous, and attributes this presumed uniformity of action to hypothetically shared backgrounds or dispositions among the participants (Allport, 1924; Feuer 1969; Gurr, 1970; Klapp, 1969; Miller and Dollard, 1941; Toch, 1965). The key to understanding crowd behavior is seen as residing within the characteristics of the participants rather than within what transpires once they become part of the collectivity. This view was of little use for understanding the victory celebrations. The crowds were characterized by differential participation, and the crowd members were not of one mind or background. The majority of participants appeared to be U. T. students, but "students" hardly constitute a homogeneous lot in background, orientation and allegiance to the university football team. This is especially true at a large state university.[5] Moreover, we observed considerable variation in the age, sex, ethnicity and style of dress of the participants. The convergence assumption that crowd participants are similarly motivated is also inconsistent with our data. Some participants indicated they were in the crowd because of "curiosity," some because they were diehard Longhorn fans, some because they thought it would be "fun," some because they had "nothing better to do," some because they were coaxed by friends, and some, such as the police, because it was their duty.

Contagion Theory

Contagion theory seems equally unhelpful when applied to the celebrations. It also views the crowd as a monolithic entity characterized by uniformity of behavior. Rather than explaining the presumed homogeneity of action in terms of shared characteristics that precede the formation of the crowd, contagion theorists (Blumer, 1951; Freud, 1922; LeBon, 1903) attribute it to a breakdown of participants' cognitive abilities. The reduction in rational faculty, coupled with the anonymity supposedly provided by the crowd, renders the participant susceptible to the uncritical acceptance and mechanical production of whatever suggestion is encountered. Hence, everyone behaves alike.

Our observations do not support that view. As already emphasized, the victory crowds did not involve uniformity of action. Instead, the celebrations were the work of several categories of participants engaging in rather disparate behaviors. Additionally, most of the participants could not be classified as social isolates or anonymous individuals lost in the crowd. Friends and acquaintances rode together in parading vehicles. Many of the spectators were in the company of familiar others. The police officers were at least acquainted with each other.[6]

The hypothetical link between crowd behavior and crippled cognition (LeBon, 1903) or non-interpretive interaction (Blumer, 1951) is also at odds with much of what transpired. When the police first began to make a concerted effort to halt the horn-blowing, for example, most people who blew their car horns almost simultaneously waved to the spectators. Since this action increased the possibility of being stopped by the police, it might appear to have been mindless or nonreflective behavior. But the police at that time were only warning violators rather than giving them citations. Hence, the violators had little, if anything, to lose. Moreover, the risk of being admonished by a police officer is likely to have been offset by the receipt of recognition from the cheering spectators. What may have seemed to have been indicative of "irrational" behavior appears to have been the obverse. That is, the behavior of some of the participants appears to have been based at least in part on consideration of potential rewards and costs. This interpretation is also suggested by the response of the vehicular paraders when the police increased their ranks and became more intent on reducing the overall level of noise. Rather than continuing to celebrate as before, the vehicular paraders as well as many of the spectators became more cautious, modifying their activities so as to decrease the prospect of being arrested. They still celebrated, but in a more subdued way.

Rational Calculus or Gaming Theory

Since the adjustment of one's actions in response to changes in the behavior of another is indicative of interpretive interaction rather than circular reaction, our observations are consistent with the rational calculus or gaming approach to crowd behavior (Berk, 1974a, 1974b; Brown, 1965). This perspective argues that crowd participants "exercise a substantial degree of rational decision-making and" are therefore no "less rational than in other contexts" (Berk, 1974a: 356) Crowd behavior is thus thought to be contingent on "enough crowd members" reaching "parallel assessments which make action for all a good bet" (Berk 1974a: 368). In other words, collective action in a particular direction is attributed to an aggregation of individual decisions defining actions as more rewarding or less costly than inaction. By empha- sizing the rational element in crowd behavior, we think that the gaming perspective provides a necessary and empirically sound corrective to the one-sided image of crowd participants suggested by the convergence and contagion approaches. But the individ- ual remains the primary unit of analysis and cognitive processes, albeit rational in character, the focus of attention. Consequently, the gaming model is not directly helpful to understanding how the actions of different segments of the crowd fit together and contribute to its flow and direction.

Risky-Shift Theory

The risky-shift variant of the rational calculus approach suggests that the direction of collective action is determined by a natural selection process (Johnson 1974; Johnson, et al., 1977; Johnson and Feinberg, 1977). It hypothesizes that the course of action taken—from a number of possibilities suggested by leaders or keynoters—is the one which is congruent with the dominant mood or opinion within the crowd. A shift in the direction of high risk, for instance, is regarded as most likely when the dispositions of crowd members are skewed in the direction of risk-taking. Those people who are not disposed to shift are likely to withdraw from the crowd, thereby moving the crowd towards greater consensus and uniformity of action. Accordingly, whether a particular keynoter's or leader's exhortations function to move the crowd in one direction or another is dependent on the distribution of dispositions throughout the crowd.

This line of explanation may be especially pertinent in those situations where there are identifiable leaders calling for different lines of action. However, it is often unclear in many crowd situations whether there are in fact any leaders. Throughout the victory celebrations there were innovators who might be construed as keynoters, but certainly not as leaders in the traditional sense. Moreover, the innovators tended to be groups of people acting in concert rather than single individuals. The argument that the direction of collective action is primarily a function of the congruence between leaders' exhortations and dispositions within the crowd thus seems to pertain to crowds with clearly defined leaders and followers rather than to crowds comprised of several categories of actors.[7] As a consequence, interaction between various segments of the crowd is ignored by risky-shift theory.[8]

Emergent Norm Theory

The approach that appears best to explain the victory celebrations is the emergent norm thesis developed by Turner and Killian (1957, 1972; Turner, 1964a,b). Crowd behavior is taken to be regulated by a definition of the situation. The definition emerges from a process of crowd-specific interaction and hypothetically functions in a normative manner by encouraging behavior in accordance with the definition. While one could reasonably argue that the actions of the various groups of victory celebrants were normatively regulated, it is questionable whether there was a single dominant norm which all the participants supported. To the contrary, it appeared that whatever the emergent normative constraints, they were *specific to the various categories of actors* rather than to the collectivity as a whole. Additionally, the alteration in the patterns of activity we observed do not seem to be fully explained by the emergent norm thesis. Each week there were changes in behavioral patterns, with some being modified, some being added, and some deleted. During the initial celebration, for example, there was no distinctive pattern of horn-blowing. In the following week the honking of horns to the rhythm of "we're No. 1" emerged as a dominant pattern, and then faded during the final celebrations. It might be argued that the shifts were due to the emergence of new norms; but such an answer strikes us as tautological. Moreover, it leaves unanswered the question of what accounts for the emergence of one particular pattern of behavior rather than another, and the question of how norms specific to different components of the crowd fit together in an interactive pattern.

Summary of the Dominant Theories

The existing approaches to crowd behavior do not adequately account for the victory celebrations that developed on the Drag. Those approaches either ignore or gloss over the existence of various categories of actors, the ongoing interaction between them, and the role the interaction plays in determining the direction and character of crowd behavior. There are three reasons for the oversights. First, the approaches fall prey to the perceptual trap of taking the behavior of the most conspicuous element of the crowd as typifying the whole crowd, thereby giving rise to the "illusion of unanimity" (Turner and Killian, 1972: 22). Attention is directed away from the less dramatic segment of the crowd and their contributions to the collective episode. As a consequence, the range of interactions that occur within collective encounters are ignored. Turner and Killian (1972), who originally criticized the convergence and contagion approaches on these grounds, fall prey to this perceptual trap by emphasizing the emergence of a dominant norm that applies to all participants. Second, for all but emergent norm theory, individual participants and their states-of-mind (i.e., frustration, hostility, rationality) are the focus of research and analysis. Attention is thereby deflected away from crowd-specific interaction. Third, the bulk of the data on which much theoretical speculation is based has been derived from either laboratory experiments or post-facto interviews with participants. The importance of interaction between various segments of participants in relation to the development and direction of crowd behavior has been given insufficient attention.

A Dramaturgical Approach

Dramaturgy, as a mode of analysis, articulates the patterns of behavior occurring whenever two or more persons come into each other's presence.[9] Attention is focused on social interaction rather than on the individual and his or her background characteristics and cognitive states. Drawing on the imagery of the theater, interactants are viewed as conducting themselves *as if* they were theoretical performers, spectators, or alternating between the two.[10] Whenever one's behaviors or gestures are the object of another's attention, he or she is seen metaphorically speaking, as being "on stage" (performing). When one is engaged in the business of monitoring others, he or she is defined as audience or spectator. The nature of the audience's behavior is a consequence of members' "impressions" about the performance. The performer's subsequent behavior is in turn influenced by his or her reading of the audience. The character of much social action is regarded as a consequence of the adjustments interactants make to "the impressions" they formulate about each other.

We suggest that the character and direction of the victory crowds we observed can be best understood in terms of the interaction among the participants who either functioned as performers and spectators, or alternated between the two categories. We will first consider the performers, and then examine the "proximal spectators" and their relative influence. Since the police functioned as both spectators and performers, their behavior and influence are considered in relation to another audience, the bystanders or "distal spectators."

Task Performers

During the course of the celebrations a variety of activities were readily observable. Wright (1978), who similarly reported considerable behavioral heterogeneity during his first-hand examination of collective encounters, has suggested that these behaviors may be differentiated according to whether they are "task" or "crowd" activities. Crowd activities refer to redundant behaviors seemingly universal to all collective encounters, such as assemblage and milling. Task activities include those behaviors that are particular to and necessary for the attainment of a specific goal or resolution of a specific problem. From a dramaturgical standpoint we would add that task activities constitute the primary objects of attention, and that those crowd participants engaging in such activities constitute the task performers.

Throughout the celebrations several task performers were clearly observable, such as the vehicular paraders, the "gropers," the dancers, and the police. There was even a group of religious fundamentalists that appeared one evening in an effort to promote their cause and recruit members. What distinguished the various task performers from the spectators is that rather than visually attending to the business of others, they engaged in activities specific to the tasks of celebrating, dancing, molesting women, or promoting Jesus. It was these performances that provided the spectators with something to view.

However, not all of the task performances were equally attended to by the spectators. Indeed it appeared as if all but the vehicular paraders, and later the police, were ignored. Consequently, it is useful to classify task activities according to the amount of attention they receive, and according to their salience to the character of the collective encounter. Those behaviors which are the major focus of attention and which give meaning to the occasion can be regarded as the *main task activity*. Those task performances subordinate to the main task activity constitute side or *subordinate task activities*. Put metaphorically, the major task activity is the main performance. It is on center stage. In contrast, the remaining task activities are side shows, subordinate and often parasitic to the main event. In the victory crowds the vehicular paraders functioned as the main task performers, at least until the fifth celebration when the police and their interaction with the paraders became the focus of attention.

Since the activities of the vehicular paraders were more in keeping with the spirit of the occasion, it is understandable why they, rather than the other task performances, were the focus of attention. But why did the paraders keep performing? Why was the performance confined to a specific spatial area? What defined "the stage?" What accounted not only for alteration in the behavior of the vehicular paraders, but also for the shift in orientation of the police? To answer these questions we must consider the spectators in detail.

Proximal Spectators

By proximal spectators we mean those physically co-present participants who function primarily as viewers. Whether voluntary or involuntary, animated or passive,[11] their major activity consisted of watching the paraders celebrate.

Turner and Killian (1972: 93–94) have noted that spectators constitute an important element of the crowd because they swell its ranks and thereby create the impression of solidarity. Our observations suggest that spectators function not only in this supportive manner, but they also define the character of the activity they observe. In some instances, spectators offered verbal or gestural support for a new line of activity exhibited by innovative paraders. In other instances spectators called for specific lines of action. Those "calls" included thrusting out an open palm in order "to get five" from the passing paraders, yelling for the performers to ignore the police, and urging the performers to get on with "the show." When the police began to curtail the noise, for example, groups of spectators would call for the paraders to honk their horns. Rather than only responding to the main task performance and accepting the activity as given, the more animated spectators attempted to influence the character of the celebration.

The presence of spectators also functioned to determine the level of animation and noise produced by the vehicular paraders. Whenever spectators were absent, the paraders were relatively quiet and motionless. The only apparent activity occurred when a car approached from the opposite direction and blew its horn. However, as the vehicles approached an area where spectators were present, the paraders would "go into play"; that is, they would begin to yell, blow their horns, hang out the window, and flash the "Hook-em-Horns" sign. This interactional pattern was so dominant that paraders would cease to celebrate once out of view of the spectators. Then, after turning their cars around and getting back on the Drag, the paraders would "turn on" or "come into play" once again.

The influence of the presence of spectators was demonstrated even more dramatically during the fourth celebration when many of the spectators moved north of the Drag, redefining the portion of Guadalupe between Twenty-Ninth and Thirty-First Street as the "new stage." The vehicular paraders driving into that area went into "play," performing as they had earlier when the Drag was defined as the arena for celebration.

These observations indicate that the audience more than the main task performers defined the stage or area in which the celebrations were conducted. It is thus reasonable to suggest that in this particular series of crowd episodes the audience, rather than being merely supportive or facilitative, was structurally essential. Simply put: no audience, no victory celebrations.[12]

Social Control Agents and Distal Spectators

Another group of actors which comprised part of the crowd and influenced the course and character of the celebrations were the police. We emphasized earlier that the character of the fourth celebration was strikingly different from those previous. Not only was there a discernible change in the behavior of the vehicular paraders, who had become more constrained, but there was a corresponding shift in the orientation of the police. Our observations suggest that the alteration in the activity of the main task performers was largely due to the change in the demeanor of the police.

Initially the police viewed the celebrations as good clean fun. They maintained a low profile, alternating between being supportive spectators and subordinate task performers. As one of the commanding officers commented after the first celebration:

This crowd was in a partying mood . . . not a trouble-making mood. They were not intent on tearing up anything. Far be it from us to interfere with a good party.

In the midst of the third celebration another officer, who stood on the sidewalk watching the "party," similarly commented that "there's not much else we can do. They're just having fun." There were other lines of action that might have been pursued, but the police had adopted a policy of nonintervention. In the middle of the week prior to the fourth celebration a public information officer confessed that the police had been "rather lenient the last three weeks," adding that "we have not put some people in jail that we could have." However, shortly after the fourth celebration began it was clear that the police had redefined the crowd activity as something other than "fun." Twice as many officers were assigned to the Drag, and they were wearing riot helmets and high boots. They were also less congenial and more task oriented. Instead of standing on the sidelines and flashing the "Hook-em-Horns" sign, they were now stopping the paraders. They directed people to remain in their cars and to refrain from blowing their car horns. They issued warnings and citations. Finally, and most significantly, by the end of the evening the police had arrested several celebrants.

In attempting to control the proceedings, the police had become a focus of attention for both the vehicular paraders and the proximal spectators. They were competing with the vehicular paraders for control of "center stage," while simultaneously neutralizing the influence of the animated spectators. What was previously an occasion condoned or tolerated by the police had been redefined as an occasion that needed to be controlled and diffused. What transpired between the third and fourth celebrations to account for the change?

The answer to this question requires consideration of another audience that Turner and Killian (1972: 238–240) have termed a "bystander public." The concept denotes a diffuse collectivity that emerges when prolonged crowd behavior is perceived as a threat to personal routines and public order. According to Turner and Killian (1972: 238), bystanders have no particular stake in the demonstration, celebration, or conflict that constitutes an object of attention. Rather, they are concerned with the "restoration of order and the elimination of danger and inconvenience," whether real or anticipated. Since our observations indicate that each celebration prompted the emergence of bystander spectators, and that their responses were not all unfavorable, we find it necessary to broaden the conceptualization. Accordingly, we define a bystander public or audience as a diffuse collectivity of distal spectators who indirectly monitor an instance of crowd behavior and respond to it, either favorably or unfavorably, by registering their respective views with the media, the press, and/or with community officials.[13] Although not directly involved in the crowd attended to, distal spectators can effect its career and outcome by indirectly influencing one or more groups of participants.

Our research indicates that the emergence of distal spectators did indeed influence the behavior of the police in particular and the character of the celebrations in general. This observation is suggested by the data derived from a content analysis of all celebration-related articles, editorials, and letters-to-the-editors appearing in the *Austin American Statesman* and the University *Daily Texan* from the day after the first celebration to seven days following the last regularly scheduled game.[14] As indicated in Figure 2, which summarizes the findings, it was not until the week following the third celebration that distal spectators began to clamor for the control and dissolution of the celebrations. Since the change in police demeanor and strategy occurred during the following (fourth) celebration, we argue that the shift was largely attributable to the emergence of distal spectators who viewed the celebrations negatively, publicly calling for the restoration of order.

Prior to the third celebration, distal spectators, including the press, responded favorably to the victory crowds. Following the first celebration, for example, the city

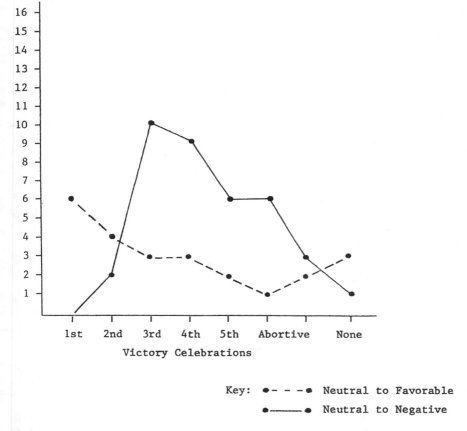

Figure 2. Number of Articles and Editorials Responding Favorably or Negatively to the Celebrations.

newspaper referred to the celebration as "Happy Days;" and a letter to the editor encouraged celebrants to "Keep (their) Horns High." The following week such terms as "ecstasy" and "joy" were still being used to describe the celebrations. However, by the end of the week following the third celebration it was clear that either there had been a change in attitude among distal spectators or that a less congenial group of distal spectators had emerged. Whatever the case, not only had the celebrations become more of a community issue, as evidenced by the increase in the number of newspaper accounts devoted to them (see Figure 2), but the celebrations were now being described as "unruly," "childish," "drunken sprees," "expensive," and "public disturbances." In response to the negative public reaction, local officials urged the celebrants to "cool it." On the Thursday following the third celebration, the city mayor issued a press release in which she called on the police to "clamp down" on the celebrants whose actions "would harm any citizen, damage property or abuse any individual's rights." In a letter appearing in the campus newspaper on the same day, a university official called on "students to exercise. . . maturity and good judgment," and warned that continued celebration would make "large numbers of students subject to traffic citations, arrests, and prosecution."

In light of the distal spectators redefinition of the celebrations as "disturbances," and their demand for celebrant restraint and police vigilance, the change in police behavior is understandable. Although this change altered the character of the fourth celebration, distal spectators continued to pressure public officials to control the "fanatics" and put an end to the "curse." The police thus maintained their "show-of-force" and "crack-down" strategy. As a result, the fifth celebration was the most subdued to date. In the weeks that followed, the police were the only group of actors to appear in significant presence. By the time the last regularly scheduled game was completed, it was clear that the police had become the main task performers. The Drag was once again a street rather than an arena for celebration. As one supportive distal spectator commented, "the spectacle wasn't loyal Texas fans waving their horns, but the 80 or so cops who lined the Drag."

In summary, our observations suggest that just as the activity of the vehicular paraders was influenced by the proximal spectators, including the police, so the police activity, and ultimately the character of the celebrations, was influenced by the emergence of distal spectators calling for the restoration of order.

CONCLUSIONS AND IMPLICATIONS

This paper has described and analyzed a series of victory celebrations that were observed as they evolved. Post hoc analysis revealed that existing theories of crowd behavior were either contradicted by our observations or did not adequately account for the heterogeneity of activity observed. Nor did they account for the interaction among the various categories of participants, or for the shifts in behavior of the participants and the resultant change in the character of the celebrations. Subsequent analysis indicated that the celebrations could best be understood from a dramaturgical standpoint. Dramaturgy views social action as the consequence of the adjustments interactants make to the impressions they formulate about each other in specific situations. Behavior is seen as situationally-constructed action. As such it cannot be accounted for by reference to predispositions, whether they be demographic or cognitive. When applied to crowd behavior, dramaturgy shifts emphasis from concern with the backgrounds and dispositions of the participants to the emergent and ephemeral roles (Zurcher, 1979) they construct. Such an approach provides little insight into socio-historical conditions that give rise to crowd behavior. Nor does dramaturgy account for why some individuals rather than others participate in specific crowd episodes. But dramaturgy does focus attention on what has generally been regarded as a key defining characteristic of crowd behavior but which has seldom been the object of empirical investigation—crowd-specific interaction. Therein lies the analytic strength and utility of a dramaturgical approach to crowd behavior.

Several theoretical, conceptual, and research implications for understanding crowd behavior emerge from our observations and from our application of dramaturgy.

First, a dramaturgical approach to crowd behavior neither contradicts nor displaces the gaming or emergent norm perspectives. Instead, it complements them and provides a perspective into which both can be integrated. Since interaction, from a dramaturgical standpoint, is contingent upon the role-taking and role-making processes (Brissett and Edgley, 1975), a dramaturgical approach to crowds assumes what the gaming or rational calculus perspective emphasizes—rationality on behalf of crowd participants.

A dramaturgical approach to crowd behavior also acknowledges the salience of emergent norms, but with two qualifications. First, there is seldom, if ever, one overarching norm that influences the behavior of all participants. Rather, there are different norms that are specific to different categories of actors. Second, a dramaturgical view suggests that emergent normative understandings are largely the function of verbal and non-verbal interactions and negotiation between main task performers and spectators.

Second, the observation that the character and direction of the celebrations were largely the result of interaction among several categories of performers and spectators suggests that spectators are structurally essential for the emergence of some, and perhaps all, forms of crowd behavior. Although several scholars have suggested that spectators contribute to the overall context of collective encounters, they are generally regarded as being a relatively passive and nonessential element in the crowd process (Turner and Killian, 1972; Wright, 1978). Certainly collective task performers could carry out their tasks independently of spectators (Wright, 1978: 71). But would they? Our findings suggest that both proximal and distal spectators not only help to define the arena in which crowd behavior occurs, but that they also influence the pattern of activity they observe. We thus argue, from a dramaturgical standpoint, that the relationship between spectators and task performers is reciprocal and frequently interdependent. The extent to which this interdependence obtains is an empirical question. But until the relationship between performers and spectators is better understood for different types of crowd behavior, analyses which fail to examine the influence of spectators are likely to be one-sided and incomplete.

Third, our findings raise additional questions about "sequenced" approaches to crowd behavior. For example, it would have been impossible to describe the pattern and evolution of the victory celebrations according to Smelser's (1962) stages of collective behavior.[15] The *ad hoc* nature of the interactions among different types of participants, and the shifting of those situational interactions defies categorizing by a fixed and limited set of stages. Heirich's (1971) work on the "spiraling" nature of crowd behavior, though not specific enough about interactive phenomenon, seems more useful and consistent with our observation and analysis.

A fourth implication pertains to the relation between crowd behavior and everyday behavior. Crowds have generally been viewed as explicable only in terms of concepts specific to collective behavior itself. With the exception of a few scholars (Berk, 1974a;

Brissett, 1968; Brown and Goldin, 1973; Couch, 1968, 1970; Johnson, 1974, 1977; McPhail and Miller, 1973; Turner and Killian, 1972; Weller and Quarantelli, 1973), discussions of crowd behavior have eschewed concepts relevant to everyday, institutional life. This tradition has emphasized the difference between collective and everyday behavior. Moreover, it has undermined integration of theories of social behavior.

In contrast, the dramaturgical approach applies to both crowd and everyday behavior. The interactive mechanisms that characterize social interaction in everyday life are assumed to be operative in crowd behavior. The differences are largely spatial and temporal in character. Everyday behavior is usually scheduled and acted in spatial areas or structures designed and traditionally used for such behaviors. Crowd behavior, on the other hand, is more likely to be unscheduled and staged in spatial areas and structures that were designed and are currently used for purposes other than crowds— that is, for so-called institutional or everyday behavior.[16]

Implicit within the foregoing distinction between everyday and crowd behavior is an expanded conception of crowd behavior. It is behavior that is not only guided by emergent norms (Turner, 1964a, 1964b; Turner and Killian, 1972) or characterized by emergent social relationships (Weller and Quarantelli, 1973). It is also characterized by the appropriation and use of a spatial area (street, park, mall) or physical structure (building) for purposes other than those for which it was intended at a particular time. It may well be that the collective appropriation of space for purposes other than intended constitutes, from a phenomenological standpoint, a key factor in defining crowd behavior as something special. It is the unanticipated appropriation that alerts us that something out-of-the-ordinary is occurring. Football fans charging onto the playing field with 30 seconds remaining in the game is thus viewed as an instance of crowd behavior; fans charging onto the field 30 seconds after the game is completed is seen as ordinary fan behavior. Viewed from a dramaturgical standpoint, crowd behavior may thus be regarded as a social production constructed during the course of interaction in a spatial area or structure that has been appropriated and redefined for purposes other than designed or intended at a particular point in time. Crowd behavior, therefore, along with everyday behavior, is not only an interactional phenomenon, but has a spatial and temporal dimension as well. The relative weight of each of these components in the generation of crowds, and the manner in which the components interact in the processes of crowd behavior, are fertile areas for further research.

ACKNOWLEDGMENTS

The authors wish to thank the anonymous reviewers and Peter M. Hall of SYMBOLIC INTERACTION for their helpful comments.

NOTES

1. There has, of course, been a proliferation of research on crowds since the early 1960s. However, aside from a few studies (Berk, 1974a; Fisher, 1972; Heirich, 1971; McPhail, 1969;

Seidler et al., 1976; Wright, 1978), the data have typically been "gathered before or after the crowd behavior occurs" (Marx and Wood, 1975: 372). Hence, most of the research reveals little about patterns of interaction within collective encounters.

2. In suggesting that most of these works share a common focus of attention, we do not imply that their respective images of crowds or crowd participants are similar. In fact, many of the works focusing on either dispositions or cognitive states differ considerably in terms of their respective views of crowd participants. Some of these differences will be discussed later in the paper.

3. Because of the nature of the crowd behavior we observed, our analysis and generalizations pertain primarily to the compact crowd, and not to diffuse crowd phenomena or collective behavior in general. For a discussion of the distinction between compact and diffuse crowds, see Turner and Killian (1972: 111).

4. The "Hook-em-Horns" sign is formed by extending the index and little fingers while at the same time curling the thumb and remaining two fingers. The hand thus forms a representation of the head of a "Longhorn" steer, the athletic mascot of The University of Texas. The hand, formed into the "Hook-em-Horns" sign, is thrust upward, above the head, in an exuberant manner.

5. The University of Texas at Austin had over 40,000 students in attendance in 1977.

6. These findings are similar to those reported by Aveni (1977) following a study of individuals participating in a victory celebration in Columbus, Ohio in 1974. Aveni found that 74 percent of the 204 persons interviewed were with one or more friends. In contrast to the "anonymity" assumption, such findings indicate that crowds include not only isolated individuals, but also persons in groups or who are socially linked with each other.

7. We would argue that a crowd composed of several categories of actors is more common than the leader-follower type. This is, of course, an empirical question. But our recollections of the student protests and urban disorders of the 1960s suggest that the leader-follower type of crowd is probably an empirical rarity that might therefore be best conceptualized as an ideal type of crowd.

8. It would also seem reasonable to argue that the risky-shift thesis may be more directly applicable to those situations involving considerable risk, a condition which did not appear to be the case with the celebrations. But just how "risky" a situation or particular line of action is or appears from the vantage point of the participants is difficult to ascertain. Certainly the degree of risk cannot be assumed a priori. Nor can the absence of risk or minimal risk be inferred from action in a particular direction. To do so strikes us as tautological.

9. The best known dramaturgical analysis within sociology is provided by Goffman (1959). For a fuller discussion of dramaturgy as a mode of analysis, see Brissett and Edgley (1975), Burke (1962, 1965), and Messinger, et al. (1975). A dramaturgical approach to crowd behavior is implicit in the work of Brissett (1968) and Brown and Goldin (1973).

10. We are not inferring anything about the actor's consciousness. That is, we are not assuming or arguing that interactants are consciously or intentionally engaged in impression management. Instead, the theatrical model is invoked "as a device, a tool . . . to focus attention on the consequences of those perceptions or "impressions" for subsequent action (Messinger, et al., 1975: 37).

11. The distinction between animated and passive spectators has already been noted. Voluntary spectators refer to those individuals who have chosen to observe the main task performers. Involuntary spectators refer to those individuals who have no interest in the proceedings, but who find themselves functioning as spectators because they live or work in the immediate area in which the crowd episode is occurring, or because they are passing through

it. Their presence at the scene of the collective encounter is therefore largely coincidental. For further discussion of different types of spectators, see Wright (1978).

12.   The importance of the audience in relation to crowd activity was indicated again two months later when The University of Texas unexpectedly upset the nationally third ranked University of Arkansas in basketball. All the elements for a post-game celebration were seemingly present: an unanticipated event; a lack of conflicting student commitments (it was Saturday night); assembling instructions were voiced (several fans yelled "to the Drag" and "Let's go to the Drag"); several "horn honking" autos were on the Drag. But there was no crowd celebration. A main ingredient was missing. There were no spectators to define the stage and to provide encouragement and support. With the exception of a few "horn honking" autos, the post-game traffic moved quietly and quickly along the Drag, stopping only for traffic signals. No police were present.

13.   It may appear that we have merely rediscovered public opinion. It is important to emphasize that we do not see distal spectators or public opinion as being conceptually interchangeable or empirically identical. What is frequently construed as public opinion typically represents the solicited responses of a sample of individuals. In contrast, the responses of distal spectators are unsolicited. Distal spectators make a concerted effort to air their views in hopes of stimulating or retarding the crowd behavior in question. Moreover, the opinion of distal spectators may not be in accord with so-called public opinion.

14.   Sixty-one celebration-related accounts appeared in the 2 newspapers during the 8 week period in question. The newspaper accounts were categorized according to whether they were (1) negative in tone or control-oriented; or (2) favorable towards or supportive of the celebrations. Thirty-five of the newspaper accounts were classified as control-oriented or negative in tone; twenty-six fell into the supportive or favorable category. The 61 newspaper accounts were coded independently by two of the authors. There were no major coding disagreements or discrepancies.

15.   For other critiques of Smelser's value-added approach to collective behavior, see Brown and Goldin, 1973; Currie and Skolnick, 1970; Milgram and Toch, 1969; Oberschall, 1973; Quarantelli and Hundley, 1969.

16.   It is important again to emphasize that we are referring to collectivities that can best be described as compact crowds. Diffuse crowds, such as fads, fashion, and forms of mass hysteria, are seldom limited to or played-out in spatial areas or physical structures intended for everyday behavior.

REFERENCES

Allport, F.H. 1924. *Social Psychology*. Boston: Houghton.

Aveni, A.F. 1977. "The Not-so-lonely Crowd: Friendship Groups in Collective Behavior." *Sociometry* 40: 96–99.

Berk, R.A. 1974a. "A Gaming Approach to Crowd Behavior." *American Sociological Review* 39: 355–373.

———. 1974b. *Collective Behavior.* Dubuque, Iowa: Wm. C. Brown.

Blumer, H. 1951. "Collective Behavior." Pp. 167–222 in A.M. Lee (ed.) *Principles of Sociology*. New York: Barnes and Noble.

———. 1957. "Collective Behavior." Pp. 127–58 in J.B. Gittler (ed.) *Review of Sociology Analysis of a Decade*. New York: Wiley.

Brissett, D. 1968. "Collective Behavior: The Sense of a Rubric." *American Journal of Sociology* 74: 70–78.

Brissett, D. and C. Edgley (eds.) 1975. *Life as Theater: A Dramaturgical Sourcebook.* Chicago: Aldine Publishing Company.

Brown, M. and A. Goldin. 1973. *Collective Behavior.* Pacific Palisades, CA.: Goodyear.

Brown, R. 1965. *Social Psychology.* New York: Free Press.

Burke, K. 1962. *A Grammar of Motives and A Rhetoric of Motives.* New York: The World Publishing Co.

————. 1965. *Permanence and Change.* Chicago: Bobbs-Merrill.

Couch, C.J. 1968. "Collective Behavior: An Examination of Some Stereotypes." *Social Problems* 15: 310–322.

————. 1970. "Dimensions of Association in Collective Behavior Episodes." *Sociometry* 33: 475–71.

Currie, E. and J. Skolnick. 1970. "A Critical Note on Conceptions of Collective Behavior." *Annals of the American Academy of Political and Social Sciences* 391: 34–45.

Feuer, L.L. 1969. *The Conflict of Generations.* New York: Basic Books.

Fisher, C.S. 1972. "Observing a Crowd." Pp. 187–221 in J.D. Douglas (ed.) *Research on Deviance.* New York: Random House.

Freud, S. 1922. *Group Psychology and the Analysis of the Ego.* London: The Hogarth Press.

Goffman, E. 1959. *The Presentation of Self in Everyday Life.* Garden City, New York: Doubleday.

Gurr, T.R. 1970. *Why Men Rebel.* Princeton, N.J.: Princeton University Press.

Heirich, M. 1971. *The Spiral of Conflict: Berkeley, 1964.* New York: Columbia University Press.

Johnson, N.R. 1974. "Collective Behavior as Group Induced Shift." *Sociological Inquiry* 44: 105–110.

Johnson, N.R. and W.E. Feinberg. 1977. "A Computer Simulation of the Emergence of Consensus in Crowds." *American Sociological Review* 42: 505–521.

Johnson, N.R., J.G. Stemler, and D. Hunter. 1977. "Crowd Behavior as Risky-shift: A Laboratory Experiment." *Sociometry* 40: 183–187.

Klapp, O.E. 1969. *Collective Search for Identity.* New York: Holt, Rinehart and Winston.

————. 1972. *Currents of Unrest: An Introduction to Collective Behavior.* New York: Holt, Rinehart and Winston.

Lang, K. and G. Lang. 1968. "Collective Behavior." Pp. 556–565 in D.L. Sills (ed.) *International Encyclopedia of the Social Sciences.* New York: MacMillan and Free Press.

LeBon, G. 1903. *The Crowd.* London: Unwin.

Marx, G.T. 1970. "Issueless Riots." *Annals of the American Academy of Political and Social Sciences* 391: 21–33.

Marx, G.T. and J.L. Wood. 1975. "Strands of Theory and Research in Collective Behavior." Pp. 363–428 in A. Inkeles, J. Coleman and N. Smelser (eds.) *Annual Review of Sociology, Vol. 1.* Palo Alto, CA.: Annual Reviews, Inc.

McPhail, C. 1969. "Student Walkout: A Fortuitous Examination of Elementary Collective Behavior." *Social Problems* 16: 441–455.

McPhail, C. and D. Miller. 1973. "The Assembling Process: A Theoretical and Empirical Examination." *American Sociological Review* 38: 721–735.

Messinger, S.E., H. Sampson, and R.D. Towne. 1975. "Life as Theater: Some Notes on the Dramaturgic Approach to Social Reality." Pp. 32–42 in D. Brissett and C. Edgley (eds.) *Life as Theater.* Chicago: Aldine.

Milgram, S. and H. Toch. 1969. "Collective Behavior: Crowds and Social Movements." Pp. 507–610 in G. Lindzey and E. Aronson (eds.) *The Handbook of Social Psychology, Vol. 4.* Reading, Mass.: Addison-Wesley.

Miller, N.E. and J. Dollard. 1941. *Social Learning and Imitation.* New Haven: Yale University Press.

Oberschall, A. 1973. *Social Conflict and Social Movements.* Englewood Cliffs, N.J.: Prentice-Hall.

Perry, J.B. and M.D. Pugh. 1978. *Collective Behavior: Response to Social Stress.* New York: West Publishing Co.

Quarantelli, E.L. and J.R. Hundley, Jr. 1960. "A Test of Some Propositions about Crowd Formation and Behavior." Pp. 538–54 in R.R. Evans (ed.) *Readings in Collective Behavior.* Chicago: Rand McNally.

Seidler, J., K. Meyer and L. MacGillivray. 1976. "Collecting Data on Crowds and Rallies: A New Method of Stationary Sampling." *Social Forces* 55: 507–519.

Smelser, N.J. 1962. *Theory of Collective Behavior.* New York: Free Press.

———. 1970. "Two Critics in Search of a Bias: A Response to Currie and Skolnick." *Annals of the American Academy of Political and Social Sciences* 391: 46–55.

Toch, H. 1965. *The Social Psychology of Social Movements.* Indianapolis: Bobbs–Merrill.

Turner, R.H. 1964a. "Collective Behavior." Pp. 382–455 in R.E.L. Faris (ed.) *Handbook of Modern Sociology.* Chicago: Rand McNally.

———. 1964b. "New Theoretical Frameworks." *Sociological Quarterly* 5: 122–132.

Turner, R.H. and L.M. Killian. 1957. *Collective Behavior.* Englewood Cliffs. N.J.: Prentice-Hall.

———. 1972. *Collective Behavior,* 2nd Ed. Englewood Cliffs, N.J.: Prentice-Hall.

Turner, R.H. and S.J. Surace. 1956. "Zoot-suiters and Mexican Symbols in Crowd Behavior." *American Journal of Sociology* 62: 14–20.

Weller, J.M. and E.L. Quarantelli. 1971. "Neglected Characteristics of Collective Behavior." *American Journal of Sociology* 79: 665–685.

Wright, S. 1978. *Crowds and Riots: A Study in Social Organization.* Beverly Hills, CA.: Sage Publications.

Zurcher, L. 1979. "Role Selection: The Influence of Internalized Vocabularies of Motive." *Symbolic Interaction* 2: 16–30.

Deviance, Rule-Breaking and Male Dominance in Conversation

James D. Orcutt
Lynn Kenneth Harvey
Florida State University

Previous research on dyadic interaction indicates that cross-sex conversations (male-female) are characterized by more frequent interruptions than same-sex conversations. More specifically, males consistently tend to interrupt their female co-conversationalists. Survey data from three student samples suggest that normative definitions reflected in perceptions of interruption are inconsistent with the empirical distribution of rule-breaking observed by conversational researchers. These results provide some strategic insights into the problematic distinction between deviance and rule-breaking that has been central to labeling theory.

For a body of theory and research that lays claim to the title "interactionist perspective on deviance," the labeling tradition has paid remarkably little attention to actual interactional processes. Conversation is treated mainly as a symbolic medium through which labels are applied or encounters are negotiated between agents of social control and putative deviants. This paper explores a different, more patently "interactionist" approach to issues raised by the labeling tradition. Here, the *form*, rather than the *content*, of interaction will be analyzed as a resource for the study of deviance. Specifically, we will be concerned with the distribution and social definition of a common rule-breaking act—conversational interruption. This is hardly the sort of transgression that inspires official commissions of inquiry or moves the public to lock its doors at night. Yet, as we will show, this form of conversational deviance is an

Reprinted from Symbolic Interaction, 8(1):15–32.
ISBN: 1-55938-551-0

unusually promising site for research on how relations of power fundamentally structure the patterning and perception of social order.

We will begin by articulating this unconventional analytical problem with some familiar issues in deviance theory. Next, we will examine previous research on the objective contours of this rule-breaking act, which documents its high incidence among males in cross-sex conversations. We then present a contrasting view of this phenomenon based on perceptual data gathered from three student samples. These data reveal some marked discrepancies between normative definitions of conversational deviance and the empirical distribution of the act of interruption. In the concluding section of the paper, we reflect on some reasons for incongruity between the objective patterning and social definition of conversational rule-breaking, and discuss implications of this misperception for sociological theorizing on deviance.

THE REGULATION OF SOCIAL INTERACTION

How is orderly social interaction possible? This diminutive phrasing of the Hobbesian question is the central concern of interactionist social psychology. If the assumption of integrated and consensually based functional order flies in the face of structural and cultural cleavages in modern industrial societies, the accomplishment of coordinated interaction is an undeniable fact of everyday social experience. Those instances where orderly interaction becomes problematic or impossible serve not only as striking reminders of our routine dependence upon it but also as vital resources for its investigation. Constituent features of the ordinary social world can often be seen more clearly in the brilliant reflection of deviance and disorder. However, there are numerous occasions where potentially disruptive events or marked deviations from the normal course of interaction appear to escape the attention of participants. These instances of "normalization"—and, particularly, their patterning—are likewise revealing to the student of interactional order. The phenomenon of conversational interruption is a research site offering both kinds of opportunities for sociological insights into the regulation and preservation of orderly interaction.

Research from such diverse fields as psychiatry, experimental social psychology, communications, family sociology and ethnomethodology has nourished a hefty body of scientific knowledge on conversational interruption. We will examine some of this literature later. For present purposes, it is sufficient to note two conceptual themes that run through much of this research: (1) interruptions constitute *violations* of conversational rules that (2) can be interpreted in most contexts as expressions of *power* or interpersonal dominance. The rule-violating property of interruption is highlighted especially in sociological works based on the turn-taking model of conversational organization proposed by Sacks et al. (1974; also see Zimmerman and West, 1975). Briefly, Sacks et al. specify a simple set of rules that can be observed to regulate the transition of speaking turns among participants in a conversational sequence. These rules allow that only one party speak at a time and that speaker change recurs. A current speaker has the *right* to complete his or her utterance (termed a "unit-type"). At the conclusion of the current speaker's turn *but not before,* this right can be transferred to another participant. By the technical criteria of these conversational rules, then, an interruption constitutes rule-breaking behavior, a violation of the interactional order of turn-taking.

Characterizations of interruptions as manifestations of power or dominance in interaction have been based partly on conceptual considerations, partly on empirical grounds. Conceptualized according to the turn-taking model, an interruption usurps another's right to speech. Whether the victim resists, ignores, or accedes to this infringement is another question; but, the *attempt* to exercise power or to dominate talk is implied by the impositional nature of the interruptive act itself. In empirical work, researchers have focused on *relational* aspects of power as revealed in patterns of persistent and asymmetrically distributed interruptions over the course of a conversation (e.g., Zimmerman and West, 1975; Hadley and Jacob, 1976; Manderscheid et al., 1982). This paper will be especially concerned with generalizations about males' relational dominance of females through the use of interruptions in cross-sex conversations.

It should be clear at this point that the phenomenon of interruption shares some conceptual qualities with other forms of interpersonal behavior more commonly thought of as suitable topics for the sociology of deviance. Just as a theft of property or ideas is a violation of rules that govern the market economy of capitalism, the unrightful taking of another's claim to speech violates the turn-taking economy of conversation (cf. Sacks et al., 1974: 696). Referring to the relational pattern of interruptions that will be of specific interest here, West (1979: 81) has suggested that "[m]ale dominance in conversation might be likened to our cultural (and sometimes legal) conceptions of rape." To be sure, these other infractions are wholly set apart from interruptions by moral and political definitions—a socially constructed distinction that is well-worthy of relativistic analysis. However, we contend that the sociology of deviance should take its warrant for inquiry into this or other phenomena from theoretical rather than moral or political bases. In the following section, we will attempt to show how the study of conversational interruption can potentially inform some crucial conceptual and theoretical issues in the interactionist tradition.

RULE-BREAKING AND DEVIANCE RECONSIDERED

So, conversational interruption violates interactional rules of turn-taking; but, is it "really" deviance? A distinction between "rule-breaking" and "deviance" has been central to many theoretical and empirical developments in the sociology of deviance over the past two decades. Building on Lemert's (1951) seminal work on societal reactions to primary deviation, labeling theorists, in particular, have treated the relationship between objective instances of rule-violation and social attributions of deviance as analytically and empirically problematic (e.g., Becker, 1963; Erikson, 1962; Scheff, 1966). This distinction was an important tool in the labeling theorists' efforts during the 1960s to set apart their relativistic perspective on collective definitions of deviance from the earlier normative perspective on the etiology and distribution of deviant behavior. In their critical writings these theorists discounted the sociological utility of the normative focus on rule-breaking. For instance, Becker (1963) and Scheff (1966) stressed the sheer volume and ubiquity of unlabeled "secret deviance" and "residual rule-breaking" in everyday life, and argued that the objective rule-breaking act was only one of a host of contingencies that enters into the selective social control processes through which certain persons are singled out and defined as deviant. Other, more radically relativistic critics like Kitsuse (1962, 1972) went even further to question whether such abstractions as "rules" or "norms" have any significant bearing on the study of deviance as an interpretive accomplishment. In this view, the moral meanings that are attached to behavior or actors are inherently contextual and variable across situations (also see Douglas, 1971; Katz, 1972; Rains, 1975).

In deemphasizing the analytical utility of rules and the objective characteristics of behavior, labeling theorists were able to highlight the intimate, constitutive relationship between the definitional phenomenon of deviance and processes of social control. Unfortunately, the conceptual link between deviance and conformity, already tenuous in the works of normative theorists, was virtually broken when relativistic analysts redrew the boundaries of the sociology of deviance. It is indeed curious, given its strong roots in symbolic interactionism, that labeling theory employs imagery of moral differentiation, disruption, exploitation and coercion at the expense of anything more than passing concern with coordinated joint action (cf. Blumer, 1969). In contrast, the notion of rule-breaking, whatever its other deficiencies, at least potentially invokes the complementary activity of socially regulated behavior. Although they certainly did not give equal attention to both sides of this conceptual coin, classic theorists in the normative perspective such as Merton (1957) and Sutherland (1947) did explicitly incorporate the phenomenon of conformity into their analyses of deviant behavior. This prospect for an integrated analysis of conformity and rule-breaking is most fully realized, perhaps, in Hirschi's (1969) social bonding theory of delinquency, which expressly takes conformity as problematic. As Hirschi (1969: 4) sees it, "the problem of conformity and the problem of deviance are the same problem."

The problem with this problem, as we see it, is that neither Hirschi nor other deviance theorists come to grips with conformity as a *social process* in quite the same way that they treat rule-breaking or social control as processual phenomena. Rather than dealing with rule-*following* or social coordination as ongoing activity, normative and relativistic theorists typically leave conformity in conceptual limbo as a more or less passive and unproblematic state of being. Even Hirschi tells us more about how social bonds prevent deviant behavior than about how conformers move about within those social constraints. Most often, theorists simply handle conformity as a residual category, as the *absence* of rule-breaking or as the *failure* to define acts or actors as deviant. Their unequal treatment of the problem of conformity casts the field of deviance adrift from the rest of sociology.

Several aspects of the problem of conversational interruption suggest its heuristic potential for a reconsideration of issues raised by the rule-breaking/deviance distinction. A particularly relevant feature of the turn-taking model is that it anchors a form of rule-breaking and a regulated interactional process within a common conceptual framework. Turn-taking rules describing orderly interaction also specify departures from that order. In a very real sense, then, the problem of conformity (rule-following) and the problem of deviance (rule-breaking) are joined together in the same analytical model of regulated interaction.

Equally important, as sociologically constructed and empirically observable descriptions of interaction, the rules of turn-taking are not necessarily grounded in or constituted by normative definitions used by social actors. The fact that interactants *do* follow these rules *may or may not depend* on conventional understandings between them that these rules *should* be followed. To approach it differently, the sociological question of whether rule-breaking occurs in a given interaction can be answered without any reference to normative criteria actually or potentially applied by members of society. Sociological observations of conversational rule-breaking and members' perceptions of interruptions as norm-violations are conceptually independent. In fact, as we shall see later, the correspondence between these distinctive phenomena—the relationship between rule-breaking and norm-violation—is a theoretically strategic problem for empirical investigation.

Pending our analysis of empirical evidence on interruption, we can at least provide a tentative answer to a refined version of the question raised earlier: is this form of rule-breaking really seen by conversationalists as a norm-violating act? Yes, in some instances. Virtually anyone (especially parents) can offer examples of prescriptive statements ("Wait 'til I'm finished talking!") or proscriptive admonitions ("Don't interrupt!") that disclose normative conventions about turn-taking and its disruption. However, interruptions appear to be subject only rarely to this sort of normative notice. In an analysis of transcripts from 31 dyadic conversations, Zimmerman and West (1975: 123–124) noted 55 interruptions, but only one instance where one party objected to the other's intrusion upon his turn. There is clearly a huge volume of unnoticed and/or unsanctioned rule-breaking (n.b., we carefully avoid Becker's [1963] term "secret deviance") in everyday conversation.

Even rarer are those occasions where participants go beyond the point of perceiving interruption as a mere violation of norms to define it as a morally or legally objectionable form of deviant behavior. Examples of such definitional reactions can be found in the ritualized turn-taking of courtroom proceedings. Attorneys or plaintiffs who interrupt each other's turns to talk may be "ruleed out of order" and "held in contempt" by the judge. However, judges undoubtedly hold *their* greatest "contempt" and the most severe penalties for those who interrupt *them*. Another occasion for the use of legal definitions that more closely parallels everyday conversation is suggested by Piliavin and Briar's (1964) observation of police encounters with juveniles. Given officers' readiness to arrest youths who fail to exhibit deference and respect during interrogation, one can easily imagine their reaction to the "insubordinate" behavior of a juvenile who interrupts repeatedly in the course of their questioning.

These possibilities, as remote as they may seem, point to an important theoretical implication: the visibility and definition of conversational deviance may be fundamentally contingent on relations of power in interactional settings. Consider, for instance, how much more remote are the possibilities that interruptions initiated by the dominant figures in these situations—judges interrupting attorneys or police stopping juveniles in midsentence—would even be "seen" as norm-violating, much less defined as morally problematic. While the technical rules of turn-taking are "blind" to the relative status of parties to a conversation, actors' perceptions and definitions of norm-violating behavior are filtered selectively through the relational context of interaction. An interruption will become visible as an act of insubordination only when it is initiated by a subordinate.

The study of conversational interruption, then, provides an opportunity to examine power and other contingencies that affect normative perceptions of rule-breaking acts. This problem has gone virtually unexplored in the labeling tradition. Like the normative researchers before them, labeling researchers have tended to focus on forms of behavior that are widely recognized as potentially deviant in American society (e.g., theft, illicit drug use). In practice, the distinction between rule-breaking and deviance has been operationalized as a distinction between norm-violating behavior and deviance. Here we deal instead with an act whose normative meaning is situationally problematic. After reviewing evidence on the relational and situational distribution of conversational interruption, we will compare these objective variations with normative perceptions of this act among student audiences. Through this comparative strategy, we will attempt to shed light on several aspects of the relation between rule-breaking and definitional processes that have escaped notice in the labeling tradition as well as in everyday life.

THE SOCIAL DISTRIBUTION
OF CONVERSATIONAL INTERRUPTION

The study of social and ecological variations in rates of deviant behavior has been characterized as the classic sociological approach to deviance (Cohen, 1959). Beginning with the research of Durkheim and the Chicago School, sociologists in the normative perspective have relied on epidemiological description to locate structural and environmental contexts in which social regulation of behavior is relatively weak or ineffective.[1] In a very similar way, this section analyzes variations in the social regulation of interaction by exploring the micro-epidemiology of conversational rule-breaking. We will be concerned with two general issues: (1) the *micro-ecology* of rule breaking—In what kinds of interactional settings are interruptions most likely to occur? (e.g., cross-sex vs. same-sex conversations)- (2) *the micro-structure of rule-breaking*—How are interruptions distributed within interactional settings? (e.g., equal vs. unequal distribution among participants). In reviewing literature that bears on these questions, we will also touch on several methodological issues that must be considered in assessing empirical research on conversational interruption.

The most widely cited research on conversational interruption has been conducted by Zimmerman and West (1975; West and Zimmerman, 1977). Their study of dyadic conversations in natural settings provides a useful benchmark for our exploration of the micro-ecology and the micro-structure of interactional rule-breaking. Using the Sacks et al. (1974) turn-taking model as a guide, they analyzed instances of simultaneous speech occurring in 20 same-sex conversations (10 male-male and 10 female-female) and 11 cross-sex conversations recorded covertly in public places and private residences around a university community. Zimmerman and West were careful to distinguish interruptions from two other, less intrusive types of simultaneous speech.

First, active listeners often insert "minimal responses"—e.g., "uh huh," "um hmm," "yeah"—that reinforce or support the current speaker and "display continuing interest and coparticipation in topic development" (Zimmerman and West, 1975: 108). Second, a listener may sometimes misjudge an end point of a unit-type (e.g., a complete sentence) and begin speaking before the current speaker's turn is finished. Such errors in timing are termed "overlaps" by Zimmerman and West, and are defined as "instances of simultaneous speech where a speaker other than the current speaker begins to speak at or very close to a possible transition place in a current speaker's utterance [i.e., within the boundaries of the last word]" (1975: 114). They offer the following exchange as an example of overlapping speech (1975: 114):[2]

```
A2:    Oh I did too:::it just doesn't sit well with them not being
       specialized enough [right] (?)
A1:                       [Or  ] empirically grounded enough ha (!)
```

In contrast, an "interruption" is defined by Zimmerman and West (1975: 114–115) as a violation of turn-taking rules that "penetrates the boundaries of a unit-type *prior*" to a possible point of transition. The following excerpt in West and Zimmerman (1977: 527–528) vividly (and repeatedly) illustrates this form of conversational rule-breaking:

```
Female:    How's your paper coming?=
Male:      Alright I guess (#) I haven't done much in the past two weeks
(1.8)
Female:    Yeah:::know how that [can ]
Male:                          [Hey] ya' got an extra cigarette?
Female:    Oh uh sure ((hands him the pack))
           like my [pa ]
Male:              [How] 'bout a match?
(1.2)
Female:    Ere ya go uh like my [pa ]
Male:                           [Thanks]
Female:    Sure (#) I was gonna tell you [my ]
Male:                                    [Hey] I'd really like
           ta' talk but I gotta run (#) see ya
(3.2)
Female:    Yeah
```

Applying these definitions to their 31 recorded conversations, Zimmerman and West were able to find a total of 86 instances where one speaker overlapped or interrupted the other. In the 20 same-sex conversations, they observed 22 overlaps and 7 interruptions (male-male and female-female conversations were combined in these analyses). Both forms of simultaneous speech were found to be *symmetrically* distributed between speakers, where the first person heard on the recording was arbitrarily designated as "Speaker 1" and the other as "Speaker 2." On the other hand, the 11 cross-sex conversations contained 9 overlaps and 48 interruptions. What is most striking however, is the *asymmetric* distribution of simultaneous speech in these mixed-sex dyads. Males initiated all 9 overlaps and 46 out of 48—*a full 96 percent*—of the interruptions in these male-female conversations.[3] Thus, Zimmerman and West's results suggest that interruptions are not only far more likely to occur in cross-sex as opposed to same-sex interactions, but that these violations of turn-taking rules are overwhelmingly perpetrated by males. At least in the natural settings where these conversations were recorded, males' interactional dominance is clearly in evidence.

In later work, West (1979, 1982; West and Zimmerman, 1978, 1983) focused on reaction between previously unacquainted college students in a more controlled laboratory setting. Recordings were made of twelve-minute conversations between five cross-sex dyads, five female-female dyads and five male-male dyads who were simply instructed to "relax and get to know one another." An initial unpublished report of this research by West and Zimmerman (1978: 5) presented data on the frequency of "deep interruptions"—simultaneous speech initiated "more than two syllables away from the terminal boundaries of a word, phrase, clause, or sentence"—in all three types of dyads. In this analysis where the duration and number of recorded conversations were standardized, interruptions were still somewhat more likely to occur in cross-sex dyads (n = 55) than in female-female (n = 44) or male-male (n = 46) dyads. Furthermore, the majority of interruptions in each of the cross-sex dyads was initiated by the male. Overall, West and Zimmerman reported that 73 percent of the "deep interruptions" in cross-sex conversations were male-initiated. However, they also found some evidence of asymmetry in several same-sex dyads when the more frequent interrupter was compared to the other participant.

Published reports of this research (West, 1979, 1982; West and Zimmerman, 1983) are apparently based on a more restrictive criterion for "deep interruptions" that includes "only those instances (of simultaneous speech) which appeared to disrupt a current speaker's turn at talk" (1979: 86).[4] While somewhat fewer interruptions were identified in cross-sex than in male-male dyads according to this stricter measure (28 versus 40), males continued to contribute 75 percent (21 out of 28) of the violations of turn-taking rules in conversations with females.

Other researchers have conducted analyses of dyadic interaction in laboratory settings that show patterns of conversational rule-breaking similar to those observed by West and Zimmerman. Octigan and Niederman (1979) counted instances of "dominant behavior"—a combination of overlaps and interruptions—in 20-minute conversations between 12 cross-sex undergraduate dyads, 9 male-male dyads and 9 female-female dyads. Whereas only 8 dominant behaviors were recorded in all the male-male dyads and 15 in the female-female dyads, a total of 133 overlaps and interruptions were found in the cross-sex conversations. Moreover, Octigan and Niederman (1979: 52) report that "(i)n each of the mixed-sex dyads, the male was responsible for from 56 percent to 100 percent of the dominant behavior—that is, the majority in each case." Although these authors indicate that 68 percent of the cross-sex interruptions and overlaps were initiated by males, a recalculation of the raw frequencies given in their article yields a higher figure of 82 percent male-initiated "dominant behaviors."[5] One additional feature of this study is particularly noteworthy in the present context. After the first 10 minutes of each conversation, an observer made the following comment to the participants (1979: 52):

> Excuse me for a moment. Did you know that research has shown that male speakers are more likely than female speakers to interrupt partners in conversation? Now, please continue with your discussion for a few more minutes.

Participants of both sexes responded to this implicitly normative revelation by decreasing their tendency to overlap and interrupt during the final 10 minutes of the conversation. Males' overlaps and interruptions decreased by 67 percent (from 88 to 29 instances). However, the frequency of "dominant behaviors" by females showed an even greater decline of 79 percent (from 34 to 7)—almost disappearing completely during the last 10 minutes. Ironically the observer's normative definition of male dominance had a more pronounced impact on the victims than on the perpetrators of conversational rule-breaking.

Whereas the studies above used transcribing techniques based on the Sacks et al. (1974) turn-taking model to identify overlaps and interruptions, many laboratory studies have used more mechanized but less discriminating measures of simultaneous speech in dyadic conversations. Natale et al. (1979) used an analogue-to-digital computer system (AVTA) that counted any instance of simultaneous speech (i.e., minimal responses, overlaps, interruptions) as an "interruption."[6] Their analysis of 30-minute conversations between 12 cross-sex, 12 male-male and 12 female-female dyads failed to find significant differences in rate of interruption across these three compositional types. Yet, one of the few significant findings in this complex multivariate investigation was that males interrupted more often than females.

Several laboratory studies of dyadic conversations between unacquainted persons have failed to find significant sex differences in simultaneous speech (Markel et al., 1976; Duncan and Fiske, 1977; Leffler et al., 1982). The most interesting of these is the recent experiment on status differentiation and "nonverbal behavior" by Leffler and her associates. One partner in cross-sex and same-sex undergraduate dyads was randomly assigned the role of "teacher" and the other partner the role of "student" in a task-training situation. In a second phase of the experiment, these roles were reversed, with the former "student" becoming the "teacher" in another training exercise. One of the nonverbal behaviors coded from videotapes of these teacher-student discussions was a standardized measure of attempted "interruptions"—total overlaps and interruptions divided by the interruptee's total speaking time. Although the diffuse status characteristic of gender was not a significant predictor of interruptions in these dyads, the task-specific status of teacher vs. student was. In both phases of the experiment, the partner who occupied the teacher role interrupted significantly more often than the student. This result then provides important experimental evidence that interruptions are employed as a mechanism of interactional dominance in asymmetric role-relationships.

Despite their negative findings on gender effects, Leffler et al. (1982) support West and Zimmerman's (1977) conclusion that interruptions represent "displays of dominance" in conversations between parties that are culturally defined as being of unequal status (also see Roger and Shumacher, 1983). This inference not only seems to follow from the cases of cross-sex interaction we have examined above, but from field observations of other asymmetric dyads as well. West and Zimmerman (1977) found that 86 percent of the interruptions in five parent-child interactions were initiated by the parent. More recently West (1984) analyzed 21 videotaped encounters between resident physicians and patients in examining rooms of a family practice clinic. Of a total of 188 interruptions in 17 encounters involving *male* physicians, two-thirds (67 percent) were initiated by the physician. In direct contrast, patients initiated 68 percent (40 of 59) of the interruptions in four encounters with *female* doctors. The bulk of the latter were contributed by two male patients who initiated 80 percent of the interruptions in their encounters with a "lady doctor." Such instances of status inconsistency raise interesting questions for further research; however, the interactional "treatment" that most patients received from their male physicians was in keeping with the basic asymmetry of the doctor-patient relationship.

In sum, the empirical literature on interruptions in dyadic conservations provides some relatively clear answers to the descriptive questions we posed at the beginning of this section.[7] First, with reference to the micro-ecology of conversational rule-breaking, interruptions appear to be most prevalent in dyadic contexts where the participants are of unequal status. In the specific case of gender relations, cross-sex conversations stand out dramatically in several studies as the primary locus of violations of turn-taking rules. Second, the research in this area shows that the distribution of interruptions within dyads is patterned along the lines of relational asymmetry between participants. Particularly, both field and laboratory studies provide abundant micro-structural evidence of male displays of dominance over females through interruption. Thus, gender and other sociocultural distinctions of status and power are exhibited and reproduced in interaction via the mechanism of conversational interruption.

These generalizations coupled with our earlier observations about the normative definition of conversational deviance lead us to an intriguing hypothesis: that *the distributions of the incidence and the perception of conversational rule-breaking will be inversely related.* We have suggested at different points that the normative recognition of violations of turn-taking rules and the empirical distribution of those violations are both contingent on the symmetry of relations between parties to an interaction. However, the relational circumstances that have been found to contribute the highest frequencies of conversational rule-breaking are precisely those in which such acts are *least likely* to be perceived as unseemly or inappropriate. In much the same way that the relational contexts of courtrooms or streetcorner interrogations grant normative immunity to rule-breaking by judges and police officers, males' "displays of dominance" may take on a conventional appearance in cultural settings where they are viewed as the "dominant sex." On the other hand, what if a member of the "weaker sex" interrupts a male? While she may escape a charge of insubordination (maybe "bitchy" or "pushy"), her "unladylike" display of dominance will not so easily escape notice. The net effect of these definitional processes should be a gross misperception of the empirical distribution of interruptions. We will present data bearing on this argument below.

We will also examine contingent effects of the symmetry of gender relations on perceptions of the micro-ecology of conversational rule-breaking. Are breaches of turn-taking rules more visible in same-sex as opposed to cross-sex interactions? We believe they are. Where parties to an interaction share the same status, as in male-male or female-female dyads, interruptions may stand out as unwarranted violations of relational norms of equality and "fair exchange." Where neither party is expected to dominate, a display of dominance is more readily perceived as unconventional or inappropriate. Males, of course, will witness such intrusions on their equal right to talk in conversations with other males, and females with other females. Thus, if our earlier reasoning is correct about the relative invisibility of male dominance in cross-sex conversations, both sexes should be more sensitive to the normative implications of rule-breaking by members of the same sex. Again, the net result should be a misperception of the micro-ecological distribution of rule-breaking as documented in research on conversational interruption.

SOME EMPIRICAL EVIDENCE ON PERCEPTIONS OF CONVERSATIONAL RULE-BREAKING

Methodology

The series of surveys that provide the perceptual data analyzed below are initiated as a classroom exercise in the senior author's sections of General Sociology at Florida State University. The surveys were administered at the beginning of a regularly scheduled lecture on "Gender Differentiation." In each of the three class samples examined here, students were given a brief questionnaire prefaced by the following statement:

> Today in lecture, I will be discussing a study by Candace West and Don Zimmerman on *conversational interruptions.* This research is based on recordings of conversations between pairs of individuals in various natural settings such as restaurants or student unions. Among other things, West and Zimmerman analyzed these taped recordings by counting the number of times one individual interrupted the other during the conversation. Some of these conversations were between individuals of the same sex, while other recorded conversations involved a male interacting with a female ("cross-sex" conversations). Please answer the following questions about this research as honestly as you can.

Because West and Zimmerman's (1977) study received widespread publicity when it appeared in *Social Problems,* an initial screening question asked if students were "familiar in any way" with the research described in the opening statement. Those few students who acknowledged familiarity with the study were eliminated from the present analyses.

Data on the perceived distribution of interruptions in cross-sex conversations were gathered in three mass sections: General Sociology at Florida State University, Fall 1981 and Spring 1983, and Introduction to Sociology: Principles at the University of Iowa, Spring 1982 (during the senior author's sabbatical leave). These data are based on the following question:

Based on how I've described the West and Zimmerman study, what would be your
best guess about the distribution of interruptions *in cross-sex conversations*?
1. Males would interrupt the females more than vice versa _____
2. Females would interrupt the males more than vice versa _____
3. Interruptions would be about equally distributed between males and
    females _____

In the two most recent classes (Florida State, Spring 1983, and Iowa, Spring 1982),
normative perceptions of the micro-ecology of interruptions were obtained by an
additional question:

Overall, in which of the following types of conversations would you expect
interruptions to occur most frequently?
1. Cross-sex conversations between males and females _____
2. Same-sex conversations between males _____
3. Same-sex conversations between females _____

Responses to these questions by sex of respondent were tabulated during class by a
research assistant and were presented to each class near the end of the lecture, just
before the actual findings of Zimmerman and West's (1975) first investigation were
described. The results presented below are based, of course, on more careful tabula-
tions carried out subsequent to the class meetings.

As shown in Table 1 below, these three student samples are similar in size
(approximately 100 students) and sex composition (two-thirds female). All three
sections were largely comprised of freshmen and sophomores taking the course to
fulfill undergraduate liberal studies requirements.

Results

Table 1 shows how respondents of each sex perceive the distribution of interruptions in cross-sex conversations. Although a substantial plurality of respondents of
both sexes in all three samples do perceive that males tend to interrupt females, in no
case is male dominance recognized by a majority of students. Particularly in the two
Florida State samples, substantial proportions of both males and females instead define
females as more prone to interrupt in cross-sex conversations. Most notably, nearly
half of the 1983 Florida State males identify females as the main initiators of
interruptions. In contrast, Iowa students of both sexes are as likely to see interruptions
as equally distributed in cross-sex dyads as they are to perceive males' "displays of
dominance" over females. While a majority of students at both schools misperceive
the micro-structure of rule-breaking, they misperceive it differently. Although we have
no additional evidence which might shed more light on this interesting regional
variation, it may reflect differences in sex-role expectations or in patterns of conversation between southern and midwestern students. Finally, we should note that,
somewhat surprisingly, no significant differences in perceptions of cross-sex conversation were found in any of the samples by respondents' sex.

However, some marked sex differences did emerge when two samples were asked

Table 1. Qualitative Estimate of Distribution of Interruptions in Cross-Sex Conversations by Sample and by Respondent's Sex

Sample and Sex		Males Interrupt Females	Females Interruipt Males	Sexes Interrupt Equally	Total
Florida State University (1981)*					
Male	% =	47.2	30.6	22.2	100.0
	N =	(17)	(11)	(8)	(36)
Female	%=	43.5	32.2	24.2	100.0
	N =	(27)	(20)	(15)	(62)
Florida State University (1983)*					
Male	% =	37.8	48.6	13.5	100.0
	N =	(14)	(18)	(5)	(37)
Female	% =	40.0	38.6	21.4	100.0
	N =	(28)	(27)	(15)	(70)
University of Iowa (1982)*					
Male	% =	44.1	14.7	41.2	100.0
	N =	(15)	(5)	(14)	(34)
Female	% =	36.2	23.2	40.6	100.0
	N =	(25)	(16)	(28)	(69)

Note: *Chi-square for sex differences nonsignificant

to describe the micro-ecology of conversational interruption. In both the 1983 Florida State sample and the 1982 Iowa sample as shown in Table 2, females overwhelmingly selected same-sex/female dyads as the site where interruptions occur most frequently. In comparison males were more likely to expect the most frequent interruptions in same-sex/male dyads. While Iowa males were somewhat more likely than Florida State males to perceive cross-sex interruptions as most frequent, only relatively small

Table 2. Perceived Context of Most Frequent Interruptions by Sample and by Respondent's Sex

Sample and Sex		Cross-Sex	Same-Sex/Males	Same-Sex/Females	Total
Florida State University (1983)					
Male	% =	10.8	51.4	37.8	100.0
	N =	(4)	(19)	(24)	(37)
Female	% =	18.6	12.9	68.6	100.0
	N =	(13)	(9)	(48)	(70)
		$\chi^2 = 18.58$, 2 df., p < .001			
University of Iowa (1982)					
Male	% =	29.4	35.3	35.3	100.0
	N =	(10)	(12)	(12)	(34)
Female	% =	20.9	11.9	67.2	100.0
	N =	(14)	(8)	(45)	(67)
		$\chi^2 = 10.96$, df., p < .01			

proportions of students selected cross-sex dyads over same-sex dyads in responding to this question. The differential patterning of micro-ecological perceptions by respondents' sex, which is generally consistent with our expectations, is highly significant statistically in both samples.

DISCUSSION AND CONCLUSION

These survey results provide at least a preliminary indication of substantial inconsistency between patterns of rule-breaking and normative conceptions of the act of interruption. We have no reason to suspect that the actual distribution of interruptions in these particular student populations are any different from those observed by Zimmerman and West (1975) and other researchers. Neither, of course, do we have any firm evidence that their findings would generalize to conversations among the undergraduates we surveyed. Clearly, further research is needed to establish a more direct link between the interactional events and definitional processes at issue here.[8] However, the weight of observational evidence from previous studies gives us good grounds for concluding that a major share of our respondents selectively misperceive the structure and situational contexts of conversational rule-breaking.

Taken at face value, then, our results point to a fundamental irony of social regulation and social control of interaction. The very parties and relations that have been found to adhere most closely to the rules of turn-taking are disproportionately singled out as exemplars of norm-violation by respondents. Considering how infrequently females appear to initiate interruptions with males or with each other in natural and laboratory settings, they indeed loom large in the normative typifications made by the student samples. While females may not exactly be (in Becker's [1963] words) "falsely accused," the social reaction to their rule-breaking does appear to have (in Lemert's [1951: 55] words) "a spurious quality out of proportion to the deviation which engendered it." The same can be said, moreover, for males in same-sex conversations, where their interruptions appear to be less frequent but more visible than in cross-sex interactions. This particular case makes it clear that reactions to conversational deviance depend less on the sex of the perpetrator than on the relational context of rule-breaking.

Specifically, the misperception of rule-breaking manifested in our data seems to hinge on the relational property of power. Although the contingent effects of power in definitional processes have been emphasized in the theoretical literature on deviance (e.g., Scheff, 1966; Thio, 1973), empirical evidence for the efficacy of this contingency has been less than satisfactory (see Gove, 1980). There is no question that powerful members of society are less subject to official labeling and social control than are those who are structurally subordinate to them. However, it has been difficult in most areas of deviance research to rule out the possibility that this differential in social control is directly tied to differentials in deviant behavior; that is, the powerful are at less risk of labeling simply because they are less prone to break rules. We believe, of course, that this possibility has been ruled out in the present instance by research showing that powerful parties in asymmetric relations are, in fact, much more likely to break turn-taking rules through interactional displays of their dominance. Yet, these disruptions of the interactional order seem relatively unlikely to be recorded as norm-violating acts in the definitional accounts maintained by our respondents.

Thus, the study of male dominance in conversation has truly strategic implications for deviance theory. As an objectively identifiable variety of rule-breaking behavior, this phenomenon and other patterns of interruptions generically related to it offer a new source of insights into the old problem of explaining variations in the conditions and consequences of social regulation. Our review of conversational research suggests the utility of a micro-epidemiological approach for inquiry into the relational and situational determinants of conformity and deviant behavior. The very fact that interruptions are not commonly defined as deviant—that breaches of turn-taking rules are typically "normalized"—creates empirical and analytical opportunities that are precluded in studies of acts and actors that are more conventionally subject to labeling. Generally, our analysis points to power as a crucial contingency in both the social distribution and the social definition of conversational deviance.

Finally, we must acknowledge the late Erving Goffman's (1983: 11) parting words of caution to micro-sociologists that features of the interactional order such as "preferential interruption rights in talk . . . (may) . . . have only loosely coupled relations to anything by way of social structures that might be associated with them." Research on conversational rule-breaking may, indeed, have little to contribute to a field that has been preoccupied with broad structural variations in deviance and social control by class, race, age, and, even, gender. However, we believe that the interactional and definitional processes revealed in conversational displays of dominance are more than "loosely coupled" to these larger theoretical concerns of the sociology of deviance. This, of course, is ultimately an empirical question. We recommend that students of deviance take a closer look at this intriguing phenomenon which is, in a manner of speaking, right in front of their noses.

ACKNOWLEDGMENTS

This is a revised version of a paper presented at the 1983 Annual Meeting of the Midwest Sociological Society, Kansas City. We wish to thank Al Imershein, Malcolm Spector, Maxi Szinovacz and the anonymous reviewers for *Symbolic Interaction* for their thoughtful comments on earlier drafts.

NOTES

1. Many of these early efforts to link social regulation to variations in deviant behavior were, of course, plagued by circular reasoning and moralistic conceptions of social organization (see Clinard and Meier 1979: 61–67). The turn-taking model provides a more acceptable sociological conception of regulation.

2. We have adopted the transcribing convention employed by West and Zimmerman (1977) in later reports by enclosing segments of simultaneous speech in brackets. See Zimmer-

man and West (1975) or West and Zimmerman (1977) for descriptions of other notation appearing in these excerpts.

3.   Zimmerman and West (1975) call attention to the disruptive effects of interruptions by analyzing frequent instances of silence among females following the intrusions by males. Note four periods of silence (in parentheses) subsequent to the male's interruptions in the excerpt immediately above.

4.   Unfortunately, the specific changes in criteria that restricted the coding of interruptions are never made explicit in the published reports of this laboratory study. As in their unpublished paper, West and Zimmerman (1983:104) consistently refer to "incursions initiated more than two syllables away from the initial or terminal boundary of a unit-type" in later articles (also see West, 1979: 82; 1982: 15). In their unpublished paper, West and Zimmerman (1978: 5, emphasis added) additionally state that they "mean to specify only such interruptions which *tend* to disrupt a turn," whereas this qualification is slightly modified to refer "to those deep incursions that have the *potential* to disrupt a speaker's turn" in their most recent report (1983:104, emphasis added, also see West, 1982: 11). The most restrictive phrasing of this second, judgmental criterion—the reference we have cited above to "instances which *appear* to disrupt"—was used in the first published report of this research (West, 1979: 86, emphasis added). For some additional commentary on the implications of different criteria for coding interruptions, see West and Zimmerman, 1983, note 4.

5.   Octigan and Niederman (1979) appear to have based their calculation on a summation of *percentages* across dyads rather than raw frequencies. The latter information can be reconstructed from same-sex and cross-sex frequencies reported in their article.

6.   While Natale et al. (1979: 867) did conduct a separate coding and analysis of back-channel responses, it appears that these brief utterances were also included in other measures of simultaneous speech derived from the AVTA system.

7.   Note the restriction of our generalizations to *dyadic* interaction. As Sacks et al. (1974: 712–714) suggest the dynamics of turn-taking may be altered in larger groups where competitive pressures for speaker selection and the possibility of multiple conversations exist. Accordingly, evidence on the patterning of interruptions in meetings and other multi-party conversations has less consistently shown the status distributions observed in dyadic conversation. On the one hand, Eakins and Eakins (1976) found that interruptions in seven tape-recorded faculty meetings in one academic department were asymmetrically distributed both by sex and by faculty rank. Not only were the four female faculty members interrupted more often than six male members, but, within sex groups, lower ranking members were interrupted more frequently than higher ranking members. On the other hand, males were not more likely to interrupt females in seminars and work groups at a midwestern university (Kennedy and Camden, 1981) and in tutorial groups at a British university (Beattie, 1981). Furthermore, students in the latter study were significantly more likely to interrupt their tutor than vice versa—one of the few instances in the literature where the typical status differential is reversed. Finally, Edelsky (1981), working with audio recordings of faculty committee meetings, developed a distinction between two types of "floor" (F1 and F2) that seemed to characterize different segments of these conversations. In contrast to the more prevalent F1 episodes, which involved orderly "one-at-a-time" speech—with males taking longer turns than females—F2's were marked by episodes of simultaneous, mutually elaborated speech, in which males and females participated equally. Given the complexity of turn-taking in multi-party conversations and the mixed findings on the distribution of interruptions in larger groups, we have limited the focus of our arguments and of the questions employed in our study to dyadic contexts.

8.   Aside from the unlikely prospect that the student "speech communities" at Florida State University and University of Iowa are in fact characterized by substantially different conversa-

tional practices than the student samples observed by conversational researchers, other questions can be raised about our inference that respondents systematically misperceive conversational dominance. For instance, our measure of "best guesses" about the distribution of interruptions in cross-sex conversations might tap cultural stereotypes about female (or male) discourse that bear little or no relationship to students' personal conversational experiences or perceptions. The inconsistency that we interpret as misperception could, alternatively, be seen as independence between two unrelated and differentially distributed phenomenal domains. These and other questions might be resolved in an experimental design that evokes perceptual and normative definitions in direct response to concrete instances of conversational dominance. Subjects in different conditions could be asked to listen to and provide ratings of carefully scripted recordings of dyadic conversations in which the proportion of interruptions is standardized but the sex (or other status characteristics) of the initiator and target of interruptions is systematically manipulated. If our line of reasoning is correct, interruptions initiated by female actors in cross-sex dyads would be more visible and more subject to normative judgment than would a corresponding proportion of rule-breaking by a male actor. For a closely related example of this experimental strategy, see Stang (1973).

REFERENCES

Beattie, G.W. 1981. "Interruption in Conversational Interaction, and its Relation to the Sex and Status of Interactants." *Linguistics* 19: 15–35.

Becker, H.S. 1963. *Outsiders: Studies in the Sociology of Deviance.* New York: Free Press.

Blumer, H. 1969. *Symbolic Interactionism: Perspective and Method.* Englewood Cliffs, N.J.: Prentice-Hall.

Clinard, M.B. and R.F. Meier. 1979. *Sociology of Deviant Behavior.* 5th Ed. New York: Holt, Rinehart & Winston.

Cohen, A.K. 1959. "The Study of Social Disorganization and Deviant Behavior." Pp. 461–484 in R.K. Merton, L. Broom and L.S. Cottrell, Jr. (eds.) *Sociology Today: Problems and Prospects.* New York: Basic Books.

Douglas, J.D. 1971. *American Social Order: Social Rules in a Pluralistic Society.* New York: Free Press.

Duncan, S., Jr. and D.W. Fiske. 1977. *Face-to-Face Interaction: Research, Methods, and Theory.* Hillsdale, N.J.: Erlbaum.

Eakins, B. and G. Eakins. 1976. "Verbal Turn-taking and Exchanges in Faculty Dialogue." Pp. 53–62 in B.L. Dubois and I. Crouch (eds.) *The Sociology of the Languages of American Women.* San Antonio: Trinity University Press.

Edelsky, C. 1981. "Who's Got the Floor?" *Language in Society* 10: 383–421.

Erikson, K.T. 1962. "Notes on the Sociology of Deviance." *Social Problems* 9: 307–314.

Goffman, E. 1983. "The Interaction Order: American Sociological Association, 1982 Presidential Address." *American Sociological Review* 48: 1–17.

Gove, W.R. 1980. *The Labelling of Deviance: Evaluating a Perspective.* 2nd Ed. Beverly Hills: Sage.

Hadley, T.R. and T. Jacob. 1976. "The Measurement of Family Power: A Methodological Study." *Sociometry* 39: 384–395.

Hirschi, T. 1969. *Causes of Delinquency.* Berkeley: University of California Press.

Katz, J. 1972. "Deviance, Charisma, and Rule-defined Behavior." *Social Problems* 20: 186–202.

Kennedy, C.W. and C.T. Camden. 1981. "Gender Differences in Interruptions Behavior: A Dominance Perspective." *International Journal of Women's Studies* 4: 135–142.

Kitsuse, J.I. 1962. "Societal Reaction to Deviant Behavior: Problems of Theory and Method." *Social Problems* 9: 247–256.

———. 1972. "Deviance, Deviant Behavior, and Deviants: Some Conceptual Problems." Pp. 233–243 in W.J. Filstead (ed.) *An Introduction to Deviance: Readings in the Process of Making Deviants.* Chicago: Markham.

Leffler, A., D.L. Gillespie, and J.C. Conaty. 1982. "The Effects of Status Differentiation on Nonverbal Behavior." *Social Psychology Quarterly* 45: 153–161.

Lemert, E.M. *Social Pathology.* New York: McGraw-Hill.

Mandershied, R.W., D.S. Rae, A.K. McCarrick, and S. Silbergeld. 1982. "A Stochastic Model of Relational Control in Dyadic Interaction." *American Sociological Review* 47: 62–75.

Markel, N.M., J.F. Long, and T.J. Saine. 1976. "Sex Effects in Conversational Interaction: Another Look at Male Dominance." *Human Communication Research* 2: 356–364.

Merton, R.K. 1957. *Social Theory and Social Structure.* Rev. Ed. New York: Free Press.

Natale, M., E. Entin, and J. Jafee. 1979. "Vocal Interruptions in Dyadic Communication as a Function of Speech and Social Anxiety." *Journal of Personality and Social Psychology* 37: 865–878.

Octigan, M. and S. Niederman. 1979. "Male Dominance in Conversations." *Frontiers* 4: 50–54.

Piliavin, I. and S. Briar. 1964. "Police Encounters with Juveniles." *American Journal of Sociology* 63: 381–389.

Rains, P. 1975. "Imputations of Deviance: A Retrospective Essay on the Labeling Perspective." *Social Problems* 23: 1–11.

Roger, D.B. and A. Schumacher. 1983. "Effects of Individual Differences on Dyadic Conversational Strategies." *Journal of Personality and Social Psychology* 45: 700–705.

Sacks, H., E. Schegloff, and G. Jefferson. 1974. "A Simplest Systematics for the Organization of Turn-taking for Conversation." *Language* 50: 696–735.

Scheff, T.J. 1966. *Being Mentally Ill: A Sociological Theory.* Chicago: Aldine.

Stang, D.J. 1973. "Effect of Interaction Rate on Ratings of Leadership and Liking." *Journal of Personality and Social Psychology* 27: 405–408.

Sutherland, E.H. 1947. *Principles of Criminology.* 4th Ed. Philadelphia: Lippincott.

Thio, A. 1973. "Class Bias in the Sociology of Deviance." *The American Sociologist* 8: 1–12.

West, C. 1979. "Against Our Will: Male Interruptions of Females in Cross-sex Conversation." *Annals of the New York Academy of Sciences* 327: 81–97.

———. 1982. "Why Can't a Woman Be More Like a Man? An Interactional Note on Organizational Game-Playing for Managerial Women." *Work and Occupations* 9: 5–29.

———. 1984. "When the Doctor is a 'Lady': Power, Status and Gender in Physician-Patient Encounters." *Symbolic Interaction* 7: 87–105.

West, C. and D.H. Zimmerman. 1977. "Women's Place in Everyday Talk: Reflections on Parent-Child Interaction." *Social Problems* 24: 521–529.

———. 1978. "Strangers When They Met: A Study of Same-Sex and Cross-Sex Conversations between Unacquainted Persons." Paper presented at the Annual Meeting of the American Sociological Association, San Francisco.

———. 1983. "Small Insults: A Study of Interruptions in Cross-Sex Conversations between Unacquainted Persons." Pp. 102–117 in B. Thorne, C. Kramarae, and N. Henley (eds.) *Language, Gender, and Society.* Rowley, Mass.: Newbury House.

Zimmerman, D.H. and C. West. 1975. "Sex Roles, Interruptions and Silences in Conversation." Pp. 105–129 in B. Thorne and N. Henley (eds.) *Language and Sex: Difference and Dominance.* Rowley, Mass.: Newbury House.

Patriarchal Women:
A Case Study of Newly
Orthodox Jewish Women

Debra Renee Kaufman
Northeastern University

Although it seems obvious why men might turn to a community steeped in patriarchal tradition, it is much more difficult to explain women's attraction. To explain their attraction the author conducted in-depth interviews with 75 newly orthodox Jewish women. Although many of these women began their journeys toward Jewish Orthodoxy partly as a backlash against feminism or any liberation movement they perceived as placing individual freedom above social responsibility, the data also suggest that almost all of them selectively incorporate and adapt some protofeminist values about the family and about men. This article explores the ways in which these women seem to make "feminist" sense out of patriarchal religion and social structure.

This study explores the attitudes, values and experiences and concerns of newly orthodox Jewish women (called *baalot teshuva* in Hebrew) who have voluntarily entered a world many regard as patriarchal and oppressive to women. There is ample evidence attesting to women's second class status within Jewish orthodoxy. Feminists have emphasized the most blatant, and at times the not so obvious, areas of discrimination and oppression. They have asked for changes in divorce law (in orthodoxy only a man can initiate and obtain a divorce), inclusion in the secular leadership of Jewish communal agencies and for concrete changes in the structure of the community (from day care centers to the acceptance of single mothers and homosexuals within the Jewish community). The inviolability of the Jewish code of laws in orthodoxy prevents

Reprinted from Symbolic Interaction, 12(2):299–314.

the possibility of women challenging a legal system created and continuously defined and redefined by males (Baskin, 1985). Moreover, if women are not encouraged or given the opportunities to study the very texts from which the interpretations of those laws derive, they cannot challenge those laws in a manner that will be perceived by the community as authentic or legitimate; or to develop female leadership.

Rachel Adler, a leading feminist and critic of Orthodox Judaism, describes the orthodox woman's ritual responsibilities in the follow way:

> A woman keeps kosher because both she and her family must have kosher foods. She lights the *Shabbat* (Sabbath) candles so that there will be light, and, hence, peace, in the household. She goes to the *mikvah* (ritual bath) so that her husband can have intercourse with her and she bears children so that, through her, he can fulfill the exclusively male *mitzvah* (commandment) of increasing and multiplying (1983, p. 13).

Theology's role in transforming women within Judaism is paramount to feminist Suzannah Heschel:

> Questions of role and identity cannot be raised outside the larger context of the images which give rise to them and the theological positions which legitimate them. . . . Clearly, there is a need for theological reinterpretations to transform women in Judaism from object to subject (1983, p. xxxii).

However, the ways in which the *baalot teshuva* describe their experiences within patriarchal living suggest a range of feeling and experience many feminists might not expect. The data suggest that these women selectively adopt and even incorporate protofeminist attitudes and values into their familial lives. Most puzzling is the finding that although many *baalot teshuva* began their journeys toward Jewish Orthodoxy partly as a backlash against feminism and any "liberation" movement they perceived as placing individual freedom above social responsibility (see Tipton, 1982 for similar findings among young Americans in movements in the seventies), they also maintain a gender identity deeply informed by and consonant with many values associated with some contemporary feminists, specifically those who celebrate the female, her life cycle experiences and feminine attributes (For a fuller discussion of second wave feminism and the *baalot teshuva* see Kaufman, 1985a; 1985b, 1987).[1]

To understand these seeming paradoxes, it is important to understand the significance of Jewish orthodoxy from these newly orthodox women's perspectives and experiences. Beginning with the assumption that these women share in the construction of social reality and that their experiences are central to the construction of that reality, the focus of this study revolved around the following questions: How do these women react to the world of Jewish orthodoxy; reflect upon the meanings of phenomena in that world; wield symbols and communicate about those symbols? What do they incorporate, discard, and choose to ignore as they practice orthodoxy? The answers to these questions help us address the paradox of how these women seem to make "feminist" sense out of patriarchal religion and social structure and how they seem simultaneously to accommodate and resist patriarchy.[2]

SAMPLE

The data consist of in-depth interviews conducted with 75 newly orthodox Jewish women in the early 1980's[3] in five major urban areas across the United States.[4] Most women were between 16 and 34 years of age at the time of their orthodox conversions and all had identified in some way with countercultural youth. One-third claim they had once identified with the women's movement.

Several methods were used to locate respondents. Interviews with leading rabbis, lay community leaders, and known *baalot teshuva* in each community helped to locate respondents according to three identifiable frameworks in Jewish orthodoxy— modern, centrist, and ultraorthodox (hasidic). Once within these settings, the referral method or snowball technique of sampling was employed, thereby identifying smaller interactive groups of *baalot teshuva* in each community.[5]

Of the seventy-five women reported here, all are married, forty-five are hasidic, twelve are centrist, and eighteen are modern. Of those married, almost all married men who were also *baalei teshuva* (plural of newly orthodox Jews). The husbands were often as uneducated about Jewish orthodoxy as their wives. In fact, the demographics suggest that if there were any differences in Judaic background between husbands and wives, the wives more often than the husbands were better educated (knew more Hebrew and/or had a better Jewish education). Almost all these women had become *baalot teshuva* before they were married and before they met their husbands.

METHODOLOGY

Focused and structured interviews were not useful in mapping the world of these newly orthodox Jews. The interviews began not with specific questions and probes, but with the women themselves, their concerns, their perspectives.[6] They spoke not as those nurtured, secluded and structurally dependent upon orthodox communities or institutions all of their lives (and therefore easily marked as a byproduct of that particular environment), but as those who had at some time in their young adult lives made a choice to embrace the structural and theological conditions of traditional living. None had any familiarity with Orthodox Judaism: Of the seventy-five women, only twenty had ever attended Sunday school and five had gone to a late afternoon Hebrew school program three times a week.

A number of predefined topics were covered in each interview. Such topics focused on the history of these women's embracing of orthodoxy, their beliefs, practices, knowledge and feelings about orthodoxy, their current familial and communal life-style, and their views about gender-roles and feminism. The interviews lasted from two-and-one-half to five-and-one-half hours with an average of slightly over three hours each. A ten page demographic questionnaire was left with each respondent along with a stamped envelope for its return.

To understand these women's links and ties to one another, families, community and to the theology they embraced, I spent many weeks in each community. While not an ethnographic nor participant observation study, I used many of these techniques. I attended lectures, sabbath services, classes, informal afternoon gatherings, sisterhood meetings, and coffee get togethers. I also found myself changing diapers, walking in parks, celebrating Jewish holidays, accompanying one woman to the hospital on the birth of her first baby, sharing La Leche and LaMaze notes from the days when my own children were that young. I visited wig shops (orthodox Jewish women are required to cover their hair when in public), went to *mikva* (ritual bath-house), sat behind a *mechitza* (partition between men and women in the synagogue), ate meals in strictly kosher restaurants, to put into a concrete context the experiences these women described (see Roberts, 1981 for a detailed discussion of feminist methodology).

Refiguring Patriarchal Meaning: Celebrating the Feminine

As predominately middle-class, educated and somewhat liberal youths, these women stuck out in many directions in their late teens and early adult years. Like countercultural youth (Wuthnow, 1976; Glock and Bellah, 1976; Tipton, 1982; Breines, 1982) who protested the Vietnam War, the amoral use of technology, the racial, ethnic and gender injustices and those who moved in other religious directions these women found the quality and focus of contemporary living deeply troubling.

Of the women studied, including those who came into their young adult years during the waning days of the counterculture, one out of three had had some experience with oriental/mystic traditions (especially Zen, transcendental meditation, and yoga) and/or one of the personal growth movements such as est or scientology. Twenty-five women claimed to have identified with and/or participated in the women's movement. Ten had been actively involved in feminist consciousness raising groups. Moreover, twelve women admitted to active involvement in the proabortion campaigns of the early seventies. All describe themselves during their searching years as pro-choice and claim that certainly in appearance they were "liberated" women.

In part, because many had personally experienced or feared the familial and economic instabilities of our times, these newly orthodox women reject all secular liberation movements and quasi-religious communities, which, they feel, compromise responsibility to the family and community and promote individual autonomy and self-fulfillment (see Z. Eisenstein (1981) for a fine analysis of the links between individualism and the limitations of liberal feminism). For instance, many who had joined human growth potential movements found them to be a trap. One woman referred to her early seventies experiences with transcendental meditation as if it were "a great big organized be-in". "Something was missing," she continued, "I didn't want to be, I wanted to do. I wanted to feel I could make decisions that would lead to right actions." "Feeling good" and "actualizing oneself" through many of the human growth potential movements or oriental/mystical traditions did not seem to provide for community and "right living on a here and now, day to day basis," as one woman phrased it.

All women expressed some concern about the loss of clear rules and expectations in marital, familial, and sexual relationships. Discussing their relationships prior to orthodoxy, some emphasized their relationships with men who were unwilling or unable to make lasting commitments. One woman put it this way:

> There I was 25 years of age. I had had my fill of casual sexual relationships, drugs, communal living. I looked at myself and said: What will I be like at 40 years of age? An aging hippie with no roots and maybe just a history of bad relationships? I wanted something true and lasting.

For many the "dark side" of individualism had become a real, not merely abstract or theoretical, problem. Freedom at the expense of commitment was a theme prevalent in many of the interviews. Secular versions of liberal feminism were not satisfactory either. Several women compared their feminist experiences to the ways in which Jewish Orthodoxy spoke to them as women.

> You know, before I became *frum* (orthodox) I was in a feminist consciousness raising group. We talked a good deal about our problems . . . about being women, students, lovers, and working women . . . we talked about whatever it was that was going on in our lives at that time, but we never really were able to formulate anything beyond or larger than ourselves. . . . We were good at defining the negatives. I needed something that spoke to me directly about being a woman.

Still another woman put it this way.

> In Judaism there is a positive assertion of who we are as women . . . the older I get the more I realize how good that is . . . I have found meaning in all this ritual . . . meaning I have never really had at any other time in my life. Torah [Five Books of Moses] has so much to say to me as a woman . . . My feelings about myself as a sexual person . . . the family purity laws[7] are so in line with me as a woman. . . . it is commanded that I not be sexually taken for granted that I have two weeks each month for myself. . . . It is mind boggling to me to think that this wonderful Torah knows who I am as a woman for centuries.

The specialness of woman and the importance of her sphere of activity was stressed throughout the interviews and often juxtaposed to a rather rigid conception of what was described as feminism. For these women, feminism represents the liberal tradition equated with the "early" Betty Friedan and the National Organization of Women. That is, feminism for most of these women (who were not familiar with some of the more recent changes in feminist thinking or Betty Friedan's *Second Stage*), is defined as the women's liberation movement primarily focused on dismissing differences between men and women and on the world of work, where equal pay is the most important issue.[8]

By idealizing the feminine and emphasizing gender differences already present in this sex-aggregated community, these women develop powerful images of themselves and their activities. Excerpts from conversations with three women illustrate their celebration of gender differences and how they make positive use of symbols and rituals within Jewish Orthodoxy.

Miriam, a thirty-six year old biologist with five children living in an ultraorthodox community, emphasizes the moral discipline women provide for the orthodox community:

> The world needs more of what we do as women naturally. We must teach and guide men. You know in orthodoxy women are not required to do any of the time-bound *mitzvot* [commandments].[9] Men need the discipline we don't. We are closer to God—we are the *Shekhina* [in-dwelling of God]. We provide understanding—knowledge to alone means nothing. We have a natural understanding of things. We don't need to go to *shule* [synagogue] three times a day or study regularly to fulfill our bond with God. Our discipline is in the everyday actions of our lives, in our intuitive understanding of what is right.

In response to my probing what she meant by "intuitive" and "natural" understanding, Miriam responded with the following:

> Look, I don't mean that we should not take advantage of education and other opportunities. Chaim [husband] agrees with me when I say that Dvorah [daughter] should be afforded every opportunity to go to medical school. She is very good in science, like I was. This, of course, after she has had a good religious education and has her values straight. You know, there are orthodox women doctors. There is nothing in orthodoxy that prevents women from receiving advanced training or education. In that sense we can do everything a man can do . . . but we have a different understanding, you know, a different way of going about it.

The following excerpts are from a recently married childless twenty-four year old law student named Aliza. While she is not ultraorthodox, but self-identified as centrist, she has just told me of her fondness for hasidut, the philosophy associated with Hasidism.

> There is no doubt that what I love about it is the way in which women are understood. The intensity of women's relationship to God is overwhelming. I think women are the collective unconscious way of safeguarding prayer in Judaism. Women in the Bible are known for their prayers—Sarah, Rachel, and Chana. They have such an intense relationship to God . . . it reminds men that what goes on in *shule* [synagogue] is not important but that the relationship to God is. We are the holders of the key for the most important aspect of inner life. The experience of being a woman in Judaism I would say is like Jungian "anima"—a profound introspection and inner intensity.

> I like the fact that the men and the women are expected to reach holiness through different means. I think it suits our personalities. Before I was married I tried davaning [praying] in an all woman's *minyan* (prayer quorum), but I always felt something was missing. I like being with men and being separated. It makes two statements simultaneously—that we are separate, different, yet together.

The following excerpts are from Debra, a thirty year old modern orthodox mother of three and a journalist.

I know this is going to sound strange to you but I feel like a spiritual feminist. Often when I awaken in the morning and I am saying my prayers I feel this profound spirituality, it's actually liberating. I go to this wonderful workshop once a week. It is offered by a *frum* [orthodox] woman who is a psychologist. There is music, meditation, group exercise, and, since most of us are vegetarians, some veggie snacks. We study the role of the feminine in Jewish thought. I feel so in touch with myself and the rhythms of my body. We've learned a lot about Jewish mystical thought, too. In the past I have taken a lot of courses—mostly having to do with ethics . . . but this workshop for women is the most important one. The others just make me know what good sense the Torah makes for personal living and mental hygiene, but my course on feminine spirituality relates the most to me as a woman. You know, I don't just feel good but I feel connected to a past and to a future.

I think in a world that isn't *frum* most women are male-identified. I think before I became orthodox I was like that. You know, what's male is better. Not in Judaism. If anything it is a bit reversed. Difference doesn't mean inferiority. In fact, only in Judaism have I found out who I really am. I am different, not just because I am Jewish, but, also because I am a women. I have taken part in anti-nuclear demonstrations because I truly believe that women, more than men, understand those things which are life threatening. Those insights are all there in the Torah. I like being with other women a good part of the time, I like studying about myself and other women with other women, I like being separate with other women. It is a real sense of strength for me.

These women celebrate the feminine and the domain most associated with the female in religious orthodoxy—the family. Marriage and family are key components in the structure of Orthodox Jewish women's everyday religious lives. One woman suggests that marriage is at once a personal and a sacred act. Through her familial practices as wife and mother she is able, she claims, to make a "dwelling place for God below." Another woman stated that marriage is the symbol of the highest relationship possible: "The day God gave the Jewish people the Torah is called the day of his wedding." These *baalot teshuva* assert an unambiguous "pro-family" stance based on strong assertions that the family, like the spiritual, is essentially their realm. They take from orthodoxy the religious values consonant with the "light" and nurturance they, and the tradition, define as essentially female.

The *baalot teshuva* focus on the most powerful and sacred images of themselves and their functions in this religious tradition. These women reclaim and emphasize classical theological sources to describe their roles as orthodox Jewish women. Moreover, they make explicit the strong family-centered values that orthodoxy prescribes for both men and women. For instance, the family, "their" domain is described as "the sanctuary on earth. " They often refer to the *Shabbat* (Sabbath) as "feminine" or as "a taste of the world to come." Among many of the hasidic women there is an implicit belief that they "will prepare the world for the coming of the Messiah." Still others associate the female with the "indwelling" of God. These powerful images evoke for these women a sacred community of which they are a principal part, in direct contrast to the male, secular culture most have consciously rejected.

Practicing Jewish Orthodoxy: Making "Feminist"
Sense of Patriarchal Social Structure

Perhaps, however, these *baalot teshuva's* discussion of the family purity laws are the most instructive of how these women seem to make "feminist" sense out of patriarchal religion and social structure. The laws of "nidda" and "mikva" as part of the family purity laws (one of the three most important social practices pertaining to orthodox Jewish women) demand that there be a sexual and physical separation between husband and wife during her menstrual cycle. According to Talmudic law, separation between husband and wife should be maintained for at least twelve days, five for the actual period of flow and seven additional days during which no bleeding is visible (called clean or white days). On the evening of her seventh clean day, or any day thereafter upon her choosing, a woman goes to the *mikva* (a ritual bath).

"During nidda", explained one particularly articulate woman, "the woman falls between categories of life and death". She noted that when she teaches seminars, she often introduces non-legal, but traditional, sources of explanation to frame discussions of "nidda" and "mikva".

She explains:

> For instance, when it is questioned why women and not men are still subject to impurity rituals I look to traditional explanations . . . you can find one that suggests that women are closer to God because of their ability to create life and that they are, therefore, subject to purity rituals . . . still another views the woman's body as the second temple. I like to think of a woman's cycle as part of all the sacred time rhythms in Judaism—the *Shabbat*, holidays . . .

All the women rejected the term "unclean" as an uninformed and mistaken translation of "nidda". Many explained that impure is a better translation for its places the meaning of "nidda" and "mikva" in the sacred context in which it belongs. "Blood", argues one woman, "is the symbol of both birth and death. This is recognized in the balance between "nidda" and "mikva"; the first is the mourning of our temporarily lost capacity to give life, the other a celebration of our capacity to give life." Not one woman doubted the importance of the "mikva" to the community. As one woman put it: "There is no doubt about it . . . if a choice has to be made a community has to build a "mikva" before it can build a "shule" or even acquire a "Sefer Torah" (Five Books of Moses):" While not directly challenging the sacred status of the Torah in orthodoxy, these women use the legal tradition to their own advantage. While these women may be making a virtue of their impurity (and in so doing accommodating themselves to patriarchal interpretation), they are simultaneously claiming strong traditional sources for normative and institutional support for women's sacred status within Judaism as well.

This same process is apparent in their discussion of the function of family purity laws. Almost all women noted the positive functions of such laws. Although newly married women were more likely to complain about the length of sexual separation, those married over longer periods of time and with more children emphasized the positive effects of those laws over the adult life-cycle. On woman notes: "When we were first married, I found it hard to consider sexual separation as a positive thing. In fact, during my menstrual cycle I felt I wanted to be held and loved more than at other times of the month. But I must admit over the years it truly serves as a renewal . . . it is really like being a bride again . . . well almost". Even among the newly married, many claimed that forced separation heightened desire. Referring to the sexual separation from her husband during "nidda", one woman noted: "The separation restores our passion and places the control of it in my hands".

Many feminists have pointed to the way in which menstrual taboos have been a way to control and demean women and the insidious way such beliefs continue in our contemporary culture (see Douglas, 1966; Culpepper, 1974). Yet the *baalot teshuvas'* acclaim for the laws of "nidda" and "mikva" suggest a range of experience and meaning not anticipated by some feminists. Because these women have to attend intimately to their bodies to engage in sexual activity according to "halacha" (religious law), many speak of an increased awareness and harmony with their bodies they had never known before. Comparing their sexual lives prior to and after their embracing of Orthodoxy, these women claim a control not known before and a newfound respect for their bodies and their sexuality. They repeatedly reminded me that they cannot be "taken for granted."

In answering questions about abortion and contraception, these women were consistent in their belief that orthodoxy gave them latitude in making reproductive decisions. None doubted that in Judaism the mother's health (mental and physical) takes precedence in matters concerning childbearing and rearing. Except for hasidic women, most women readily distinguished between continual childbearing and the need for quality family relationships and a healthy family environment. Most of the "centrist" and "modern" orthodox women, and even some among the "ultraorthodox" women currently use or have used contraception at some point in their marital life cycle.[10] As one woman put it: "Family planning does not necessarily mean small families."

Specific data on the frequency of sexual intercourse and sexual satisfaction and experimentation were not forthcoming. Modesty rules inhibit truly open discourse about such details. Therefore, the data on sexual practices are limited. However, it is quite clear that these women believe that the laws of "nidda" and "mikva" function positively for women within marriage.

Yet despite their profamily stance and their emphasis on gender differences, these women are not restricted to practices traditionally associated with familial roles. Three-quarters of them currently work, and almost all intend to participate in the paid labor force at some time.[11] All but three of the women with children under the age of six who worked, held either part-time jobs or jobs with flexible hours. The flexibility needed to maintain dietary laws, the many holidays, and the Sabbath encourages both men and women either to take part-time jobs or positions allowing great personal autonomy and decision making. Almost all of the women who did not have advanced degrees intend to retrain and or obtain more education before returning to the labor force.

Whether they work or not, all of those women with children living at home use some form of child care or day care services regularly. Irrespective of their wives' work status, all husbands have some responsibility for the care of children. All husbands were responsible for some regular domestic activity as well—the most usual activity was weekly grocery and meat shopping. In addition to their husbands' help, one half of those women who work full-time have someone living in the household to help with the childcare responsibilities and/or housekeeping. Many of the live-in help are young women who are in the process of "converting" to orthodox Judaism. Of the remaining women, almost all have at least weekly help with housekeeping.[12]

Several reasons account for husbands' participation in household labor and their clear presence in the home. Men's religious obligation to pray three times a day and to study necessitates flexibility in their work patterns. This flexibility often allows them either to work at home or to be home during the day. Their presence in the home and the strict observance of holidays and the Sabbath as family-centered events, structures frequent interaction among husbands, wives, and children. Moreover, men's frequent and consistent presence in the home fosters a strong family-centered orientation for them.

Finally, the data suggest that although most of these women do not focus on male privilege and authority in Jewish Orthodoxy, some maintain a strong belief that those areas that clearly mark women as second class citizens will eventually change. For instance, fifteen women knew of and ten were actively involved in GET, an organization of orthodox women designed to change the divorce laws which currently allow only men to initiate and obtain a divorce. It is interesting to note that such blatant inequalities in Orthodoxy were attributed to "poor" interpretation of "halacha" (Jewish code of law considered inviolable) not to orthodox theology. Interestingly, when asked about what they might want to see changed in Orthodoxy, a few women talked of changes in the synagogue and yeshiva. "In time," said one woman, "women will be able to read from the Torah and study the gemara. It will take maybe another 300 years, but it will happen. I'm in no hurry." While one or two women could see the opening of men's roles to women, none wished dramatically to alter the practices associated with women in Jewish Orthodoxy.

DISCUSSION

Feminist sociology begins with the premise that women and their experiences are central to the construction of social reality. Loosely structured interviews allowed me to uncover the issues, concerns, and kinds of things that were of significance to these newly orthodox women, rather than the frequency of predetermined events, or those events and issues that male leaders of the community might consider important to these "converts". What are the issues and concerns of newly orthodox Jewish women? How do they react to the world of Jewish Orthodoxy and reflect upon the meanings of phenomena, wield symbols and communicate about them?

These women claim that much of what attracts and holds them in this traditional life style is the nature and description of the feminine and the female in orthodoxy. Both Hasidic and non-Hasidic women evoke classical Jewish sources to express their positive identification and participation in orthodoxy and, consequently, in the world at large. The selected bits and pieces of tradition and theology they choose to relate, strongly suggest that they consciously reformulate that orthodoxy in their own image.

Ironically, it is through their "return" to a patriarchal tradition that many of these women claim they are in touch with their own bodies, and the so-called feminine virtues of nurturance, mutuality, family and motherhood. It is in the sex-segregated world of Jewish Orthodoxy that many of these women claim they have found their identities as women. They describe the orthodox community as normatively organized around feminine principles and values, and correlate that which is associated with the female in orthodoxy with the sacred and spiritual meaning of life.

Recognizing that social movements and/or ideologies which promise self-fulfillment and personal autonomy over familial and communal values almost always leave women at a distinct disadvantage (Ehrenreich, 1983), these *baalot teshuva* negotiate their familial and personal status within Jewish Orthodoxy through the positive and sacred use of the symbols and structure associated with the female and the feminine. In so doing, they claim they hold men and the community account-able to them. For many, the formal world of patriarchy in Jewish Orthodoxy is preferable to the informal secular patriarchal one they have rejected. Concrete rules and expectations, especially about their lives as women in a community of believers, are an improvement, they claim, over the theoretical ideologies the political and social liberalism of the sixties and seventies advocated. They view themselves not merely as passive reflections of male imagery, but rather as moral agents for positive action. They not only believe in gender difference, they celebrate it.

Because they feel that many values and qualities associated with women, such as, mothering and the capacity for connectedness, are undervalued in society at large, these *baalot teshuva* link the feminine and the female with the sacred and spiritual meaning of life within the orthodox community. By so doing, they take the feminine (regarded in the secular world as low status and lacking authority) and turn it into a high status aspect of orthodoxy—the sacred. In the religious world, claim these women, femininity and that which is associated with it, is seen as a positive source of value, not only for the self but for the community as well. These *baalot teshuva* focus on "feminine" values which the community as a whole celebrates for both men and women. In this way, the *baalot teshuva* claim feminine qualities as normative for the community at large (see Handelman, 1984). For instance, in Jewish Orthodoxy, passivity is equated with infinite capacity to receive divine understanding in the religious world. Both men and women are held to the practice of *tzniut* (modesty). That is, neither men or women are to present themselves in an aggressive or self-important manner.

Although many *baalot teshuva* began their journeys toward Jewish Orthodoxy partly in reaction against feminism or any "liberation" movement they perceived as placing individual freedom above social responsibility, the data also suggest that almost all of them selectively incorporate and adapt approaches to the family and to men consonant with a woman-centered approach characteristic of some contemporary feminists. Therefore, while most of these women openly reject feminism or what they perceive feminism ultimately to represent and advocate, they also maintain a gender identity deeply informed by many protofeminist (although depoliticized) attitudes and practices. Like some second wave feminists (Miller, 1976; Rich, 1976), the *baalot tashuva* celebrate the feminine not only by contrasting it with the masculine ethic of success, individualism and aggressive stances, but as a source of power and strength for themselves as well. They negotiate their familial and marital roles in ways, they claim, that help them maintain control over their bodies and their sexuality. They also claim strong family-centered values for the community at large and hold men accountable to them and family life on those grounds. They symbolically reconstruct the sex/gender system not only to enhance female status but also bring men's aspirations and value systems more in line with women's. In this sense, they are protofeminist.

However, although they have little doubt that they are theologically equal to men, they do not directly challenge the social structural sources of gender inequality. They do not challenge male hegemony in the public, legal community that is identified as Jewish Orthodoxy (the world of synagogue and study). They ignore the very premise of orthodoxy which places men at the center of the religious community as rabbis, leaders and as those who study and interpret the heart of orthodoxy—religious law. They do not explicitly acknowledge that the feminine virtues they celebrate also help to maintain a gendered religious division of labor. That division of labor helps to maintain their secondary status to men—in public religious ceremony and in religious law. In this sense, they are depoliticized.

Feminist anthropologists have contributed to a burgeoning literature on the ways in which women have actively negotiated their own social and physical space within patriarchal societies (Rosaldo, 1974). Feminist historians have pointed to the ways in which the defense of the domestic sphere and "femininity" have served feminist as well as antifeminist purposes (see *Feminist Studies,* Spring 1980). Even more recently, some feminist sociologists have pointed to the ways in which "evangelical theology and institutions may be flexible resources for renegotiating gender and family relationships, and not exclusively in reactionary or masculinist directions" (Stacey and Gerard, 1988, p. 2; see also Pohli, 1983; Brusco, 1986; Ammerman, 1987).

Indeed, in the orthodox Jewish community the shared belief system for both men and women is steeped in patriarchy. Feminists are not incorrect in their recognition that this serves as a powerful social control mechanism in maintaining male-dominance and in keeping women in their secondary place within the community of synagogue and study. Yet there is another set of belief systems that affect the everyday actions of men and women as separate groups. In this specific sense, women's shared meanings of the religious community with one another are simultaneously accommodation and resistance to patriarchy; they simultaneously ignore those institutions important to men and to what maintains male-dominance, while creating and/or maintaining their own more relevant systems of meaning. In turn, these systems help them negotiate their familial and marital roles.

CONCLUSION

Interpretive models of sociology encourage us, as Weber claimed, to give "an interpretive understanding of social action insofar as the acting individual attaches a subjective meaning to it" (1964, p. 88). Or as Blumer suggests to "get inside their worlds of meanings" (1969, p. 51). The epistemological and methodological basis of the majority of feminist and interpretive sociology call for analytic categories as complex as the lives people actually live (see Cook, 1983; Stacey and Thorne, 1985; Farganis, 1986; Kasper, 1986; Cook and Fonow, 1986; Grant, Ward, and Rong, 1987; Stacey, 1988). Feminist models focus on women's value systems through their own self-understandings. A feminist framework does not begin with the assumption that what goes on in the public world of men's relations is the most important focus in an analysis of female relationships or of community relations in general. Interactionist models highlight consciousness, language and agency. Together the two provide an analytic model capable of capturing the complexities and tensions that make up everyday behavior of any gendered subgroup. As "minded" social actors, women are capable of constructing their own systems of meaning and of negotiating their social reality; they are not simply or necessarily "robots," "victims," or "fools" (Stacey, 1983).

However, a feminist model forces us to move beyond the value-neutral description of the actor's point of view to the consequences of action, behavior and belief in light of the larger social and historical relations in which they are embedded. These women selectively adopt and even incorporate protofeminist attitudes and values into their familial lives. However, their female consciousness (Kaplan, 1982) is limited to Orthodox, heterosexual, Jewish women. Since the most important roles for these women surround their functions as wives and mothers, unmarried, divorced, widowed, separated, and childless women face clear problems within such communities. Moreover, although the *haalot teshuva* may reclaim or retrieve values attached to the women's community, those values are limited almost exclusively to the roles of motherhood and wifehood (within the family). Furthermore, while they may claim positive values associated with the feminine, they do so without the mechanisms or legitimacy to reject what is still oppressive to them and others. Or, as Lipman-Blumen notes in her discussion of women who have used moral authority in the past, most "fail to extend moral authority so that it becomes part of social institutions beyond the family" (1984, p. 32).

The feminine principles, of which the *baalot teshuva* speak, are abstract qualities, giving, perhaps, an ideological cast to the community, but without the mechanisms to change or claim such practices for the community as a whole. In this sense the social practices from which the feminine are born still emanate from the world of women, not from the community of men and women. These women do not directly challenge a system of law defined and continually refined by men. At best, then, these women adopt short term tactics which may provide a certain amount of psychic autonomy and space from men but are not capable, in the long run, of directly addressing and changing the politics of religious patriarchy or the division of labor that helps to maintain it.

ACKNOWLEDGMENTS

This article is a revised version of a paper given at "New Directions", Qualitative Research Conference, McMaster University, Hamilton, Ontario, Canada, May 1987. I am most indebted to Gary Alan Fine, Sherryl Kleinman and anonymous reviewers for their constructive comments and insights and to Dorothy Oliver for her fine research assistance.

NOTES

1. Some contemporary feminists believe that the female experience ought to be the source for dominant values for the culture as a whole (Miller, 1976; Rich, 1976), others argue that women are not only different from men but superior to them (Rich, 1976; Daily, 1978). Among both *baalot teshuva* and some contemporary feminists, there is a celebration of the feminine and the female, especially in light of her seemingly greater relational capacities.

2. In most social science studies the orthodox Jewish community is generally explored and then analyzed through the perspectives and experiences of men, especially through the male-oriented activities associated with synagogue and study. Even the two most recent books published on Jewish orthodoxy, despite their rich detail and keen insights, fail to give us any compelling sociological explanation of orthdoxy's potential appeal to women. In his book *From Suburb to Shtetl* (1979), Egon Myer cannot gain access, in that highly sex-segregated community, to the institutions relevant to orthodox women's lives nor can he explore women's experiences within them. In *The World of the Yeshiva* (1982), William Helmreich confines his study to the all-male world of the yeshiva. Neither focus exclusively on *baalei teshuva* (Hebrew plural for newly orthodox Jews). Moreover, while the only full length book on *baalei teshuva*, *Return to Judaism: Religious Renewal in Israel* (1983), written by Janet Aviad, contributes much to defining some of the characteristics and properties of newly orthodox Jews, it is limited to only those within yeshivot (schools of higher education) in Israel.

3. These data reflect one half of a larger sample of women (150) and are the basis for my forthcoming book about feminism and the religious right (Kaufman, 1990).

4. The five cities are: Boston, Cleveland, New York City and the Crown Heights section of Brooklyn, Los Angeles, and San Francisco. All five cities have among the largest recorded orthodox Jewish populations in the country (from 5% to 13% claiming orthodox affiliation).

5. There are no demographic portraits of *baalei teshuva* after they have committed themselves to marriage, family, and community. No claims are made that the *baalei teshuva* under study were randomly drawn as a sample of a defined universe, nor can the interviewed be considered statistically representative of those who return to orthodoxy nor of orthodoxy itself.

6. Since my interest was in the orthodox world according to the women who had embraced patriarchal living, I did not interview men of the community. I did spend time talking with husbands and lay leaders in each of the communities.

7. The family purity laws require a two week separation between husband and wife during menstruation.

8. As newly orthodox women, only three remained active in any political feminist causes. Three had signed a petition for the Equal Rights Amendment.

9. In Orthodox Judaism women are exempt from commandments which are related to time and place. For example, men must pray at specific times during the day, women need not.

10. The custom, as opposed to legal tradition, in Orthodox communities, is to bear as many children as possible. Yet, despite this tradition, the average number of children for this population of women was 3.4.

11. Only forty percent (30) of these women had earned less than a bachelor's degree. Of these women, five worked. Of the forty-five who had earned more than a bachelor's degree, 20 had earned at least a master's degree and 11 of these had professional degrees (four lawyers, two doctors, and five Ph.D.s). Of those who work, only those with advanced degrees work in what might be classified as male-dominated professions (e.g., law, university teaching, medicine, or executive positions). Except for several computer analysts, the remainder are in female-dominated semi-professional occupations (teachers, librarians, social workers, nurses). The higher her educational degree, the more likely the woman was to work full time. Similarly, the average number of children for those working was less (3.2) than for those who were not working (3.6).

12. These *baalot teshuva* are squarely within a middle-class socioeconomic category. The combined average income for this group was $37,000 a year.

REFERENCES

Adler, R. 1983. "The Jew Who Wasn't There: Halakhah and the Jewish Woman." Pp. 12–18 in S. Heschel (ed.) *On Being a Jewish Feminist*. New York: Schocken Books.

Ammerman, N. 1987. *Bible Believers*. New Brunswick, NJ: Rutgers University Press.

Aviad, J. 1983. *Return to Judaism: Religious Renewal in Israel*. Chicago, IL: University of Chicago Press.

Baskin, J. 1985. "The Separation of Women in Rabbinic Judaism." Pp. 3–18 in Y.Y. Haddad and E.B. Findly (eds.) *Women, Religion and Social Change*. Albany, NY: SUNY Press.

Blumer, H. 1969. *Symbolic Interactionism: Perspective and Method*. Englewood Cliffs, NJ: Prentice-Hall.

Breines, W. 1982. *Community and Organization in the New Left: 1962–1968*. New York: Praeger Publishers.

Brusco, E. 1986. "Columbian Evangelicalism as a Strategic Form of Women's Collective Action." *Feminist Issues* 2: 3–13.

Cook, J. 1983. "An Interdisciplinary Look at Feminist Methodology: Ideas and Practice in Sociology, History and Anthropology." *Humbolt Journal of Social Relations* 10:127–152.

Cook, J. and M. Fonow. 1986. "Knowledge and Women's Interest: Issues of Epistemology and Methodology in Feminist Sociological Research." *Sociological Inquiry* 56: 2–29.

Culpepper, E. 1974. "Menstruation Mantra: Red, Crimson, Sienna, Scarlett." Dissertation, Harvard University.

Daly, M. 1978. *GYN/ECOLOGY: The Metaethics of Radical Feminism*. Boston, MA: Beacon Press.

Douglas, M. 1966. *Purity and Danger*. London: Routledge and Keegan Paul.

Ehrenreich, B. 1983. *The Hearts of Men: American Dreams and the Flight from Commitment*. New York: Anchor Press.

Eisenstein, Z. 1981. *The Radical Future of Liberal Feminism*. Boston: Northeastern University Press.

Farganis, S. 1986. "Social Theory and Feminist Theory: The Need for Dialogue." *Sociological Inquiry* 56: 49–68.

Glock, C. and R. Bellah. 1976 *The New Religious Consciousness*. Berkeley and Los Angeles, CA: University of California Press.

Grant, L., K. Ward and X.L. Rong. 1987. "Gender and Methods in Sociological Research."
    American Sociological Reviews 52: 856–862.
Handelman, S. 1984. "The Crown of Her Husband: The Image of the Feminine in Chassidic
    Philosophy." Unpublished paper available from the Department of English, University of
    Maryland, College Park, Maryland.
Helmreich, W. 1982. *The World of the Yeshiva.* New York: The Free Press.
Heschel, S. 1983. On *Being a Jewish Feminist.* New York: Schocken Books.
Kaplan, T. 1982. "Female Consciousness and Collective Action: The Case of Barcelona
    1910–1918." *Signs* 7: 545–566.
Kasper, A. 1986. "Consciousness Re-evaluated: Interpretive Theory and Feminist Scholarship."
    Sociological Inquiry 56: 29–49.
Kaufman, D. 1985(a). "Women Who Return to Orthodox Judaism: A Feminist Analysis."
    Journal of Marriage and the Family 47: 543–555.
———. 1985(b). "Feminism Reconstructed: Feminist Theories and Women Who Return to
    Orthodox Judaism." *Midwest Sociologists for Women in Society* 5: 45–55.
———. 1987. "Coming Home to Jewish Orthodoxy: Reactionary of Radical Women?" *Tikkun*
    2: 60 63 July–August.
———. 1990, forthcoming. *Coming Home.* New Brunswick, NJ: Rutgers University Press.
Lipman-Blumen, J. 1984. *Gender Roles and Power.* Englewood Cliffs, NJ: Prentice-Hall.
Meyer, E. 1979. *From Suburb to Shtetl.* Philadelphia: Temple University Press.
Miller, J. 1976. *Toward a New Psychology of Women.* Boston: Beacon Press.
Pohli, C. 1983. "Church Closets and Back Doors: A Feminist View of Moral Majority Women."
    Feminist Studies 3: 529–558.
Rich, A. 1976. *Of Women Born.* New York: W. W. Norton.
Roberts, H. 1981. *Doing Feminist Research.* London: Routledge and Kegan Paul.
Rosaldo, M. 1974. "Women, Culture and Society: A Theoretical Overview." Pp. 17–42 in M.
    Rosaldo and L. Lamphere (eds.) *Women, Culture and Society.*
Stacey, J. 1983. "The New Conservative Feminism." *Feminist Studies* 10, 4(Fall): 559–583.
Stacey, J. and B. Thorne. 1985. "The Missing Feminist Revolution in Sociology." *Social
    Problems* 32: 301–316.
Stacey, J. and S. Gerard. 1988. "We Are Not Doormats: Post-Feminist Evangelicalism in the
    U.S." Unpublished Paper, Sociology Department, University of California, Davis, Cali-
    fornia.
Tipton, S. 1982. *Getting Saved From the Sixties.* Berkeley: University of California Press.
Weber, M. 1964. *The Theory of Social and Economic Organization.* Trans. A.M. Henderson
    and Talcott Parsons. New York: Free Press.
Wuthnow, R. 1976. *The Consciousness Reformation.* Berkeley, Los Angeles, CA: University
    of California Press.

Producing Family Problems: Organization and Uses of the Family Perspective and Rhetoric in Family Therapy

Gale Miller
Marquette University

This article applies and extends literature on the micropolitics of trouble and family rhetoric perspectives by analyzing how therapists in a family therapy agency practicing the brief model used family rhetoric in defining and responding to client problems. Family rhetoric is the use of images of family (the family perspective) to (1) persuade others to one's preferred orientation to issues of mutual concern and (2) attribute identities to one's self and others. The article focuses on how the therapists rhetorically enacted and applied the family perspective in interactions with colleagues and clients to define and remedy client troubles. In general, troubles were defined and remedied by treating them as products of clients' family systems, defined as enduring roles, relationships, and perspectives. The therapists sought to remedy client troubles by initiating changes assessed as appropriate for their troubles and family systems. The article concludes by considering some of the implications of the findings and analysis for the sociological study of human service work.

This article is intended to apply and extend recent literature on the social organization of human troubles and family rhetoric. In part, it is based on Emerson and Messinger's (1977) micropolitics of trouble perspective, which treats human service work as a dialectical process centered on human service professionals' efforts to define and remedy client problems. They analyze the process as contingent and variable based on professionals' and clients' ongoing assessments of the appropriateness and effectiveness of past definitions and remedies. The analysis is also based on recent literature

Reprinted from Symbolic Interaction, 10(2):245–265.

concerned with the organization and use of family rhetoric in human service organizations (Gubrium and Buckholdt, 1982; Gubrium and Lynott, 1985; Gubrium, 1987). This literature focuses on the ways in which practical orientations to family order are produced and expressed by human service professionals and others concerned with the amelioration of clients' troubles. In so doing, they produce client troubles as family problems calling for remedies that take account of the putative organization of clients' families.

The orientation to rhetoric taken here is generally consistent with Burke's (1950) analysis of the concept. He analyzes rhetoric as communication that (1) is intended to persuade others to adopt and act on one's preferred understanding of social reality and (2) produces identity. Although different, both aspects of rhetoric have micropolitical implications. The first involves the ways in which communication is organized and expressed to influence one or more audiences. The second involves the ways in which it is used to classify aspects of social reality to produce similarities and differences between otherwise discrete aspects of everyday life. Similarities and differences so produced may be used to justify preferred, joint actions.

The perspective on troubles and family is applied and extended by analyzing social interactions occurring in a family therapy agency. The analysis differs from other interactional studies of psychotherapy focusing on negotiations between psychotherapists holding differing professional ideologies and the conversational structure of therapeutic interviews (Labov and Fanshel, 1977; Pittenger, Hockett, and Danehy, 1960; Scheflen, 1973; Strauss, Schatzman, Bucher, Ehrlich, and Sabsin, 1964). This study considers the social organization and rhetorical use of the family perspective in a family therapy agency practicing the brief model. It focuses on how the therapists enacted and applied the family perspective to formulate and express orientations to clients' reported problems by classifying them as family problems and identifying and justifying responses intended to remedy the problems. The family perspective was enacted and applied to produce a variety of types of client families, family problems, and related responses.

SETTING AND ORGANIZATION OF THE STUDY

The family therapy agency was studied over a 12-month period beginning in the summer of 1984. I observed sessions conducted by therapists affiliated with the agency and observation of a 9-month training course given to a group of human service professionals as a part of their certification as family therapists. The training course involved a weekly seminar at which the philosophy and general techniques of family therapy were discussed and supervised therapy sessions conducted by trainees with agency clients. The size of the agency staff shifted over time depending on whether training sessions were being conducted. The full-time therapeutic staff consisted of four persons, but several other therapists were involved with the agency on a part-time basis. The others included three persons who helped supervise trainees and several others who were associated with local educational and human service agencies. They used the agency's offices to conduct their private practices. Finally, the 10 trainees also conducted therapy sessions during their training period. The findings reported here are based on observations of all such therapy sessions.

Overall, approximately 300 therapy sessions were observed involving clients reporting a wide range of problems, including interpersonal disputes at work, eating disorders, sexual impotency, children's performance in school, alcohol and drug abuse, adultery, child neglect, and adapting to the termination of relationships. The sessions were observed from observation rooms that were linked to interviewing rooms (where therapists and clients met) by one-way mirrors and speaker systems allowing others (most notably, other therapists) to see and hear the interviews. I observed the interviews from the observation rooms where I also observed interactions occurring in the observation rooms. My role was limited to that of an observer. At no point did I participate in interviewing clients or deliberations about how to respond to client problems.

I next consider how family may be analyzed as a perspective and rhetoric. It is followed by discussions of the therapists' professional philosophy and how they rhetorically enacted and applied the family perspective in their work. The analysis concludes with a discussion of some of the implications of the study for sociological analysis of human service work.

FAMILY AS RHETORIC

Viewed as an orientation that persons sometimes use to organize aspects of everyday life, family is a perspective that may be applied to cast persons in distinctive social roles and statuses involving distinctive relationships, obligations, and expectations. The family perspective is also used as a background or context for assessing persons' actions. In part, their actions are assessed in relation to those of others taken to be members of their families. The family perspective may also be enacted and applied as an idealized image of family roles, statuses and relationships. In these ways, otherwise discrete actions of everyday life are linked and given distinctive meaning.

Although the family perspective may be enacted and applied in a number of ways, it is frequently expressed as rhetoric. As such, images of family are used to explain and justify persons' preferred orientations to issues of concern to themselves and others. It is also used to categorize persons and their actions, thereby attributing social identities to them. Of special interest is the use of family rhetoric in human service work that is primarily focused on the definition and remedying of client problems (Emerson and Messinger, 1977). Through their use of family rhetoric, human service professionals and clients produce images of families as ordered social units characterized by observable and recurring roles, relationships, and activities (Gubrium and Lynott, 1985).

Thus, in applying the recent literature on family rhetoric in human service institutions to the family therapy agency studied, I will focus on the ways in which situated images of enduring family order and conduct were produced by therapists to explain and justify preferred definitions of and responses to client troubles. A beginning for the analysis of family rhetoric in therapeutic practice is Emerson's (1969) analysis of the uses of the family perspective in a juvenile court. He states that court officials produced images of family as signs and causes of juveniles' past, present, and future behavior. They also used images of family to explain and justify actions intended to counter the predelinquent tendencies attributed to juveniles coming from families assessed as "bad." In this way, the family perspective was enacted and applied as a rhetoric legitimizing court intervention.

The following analysis builds on Emerson's study by considering the ways in which family therapists produce clients' troubles as family problems by enacting and applying the family perspective. In so doing, they treat family as a context of client troubles and justify preferred responses to them. There is, however, at least one major difference between the juvenile court officials' and therapists' use of family rhetoric. For practical and philosophical reasons, the therapists were unable and unwilling to impose remedies on clients in the manner of a court. Rather, they sought to identify and justify responses that clients would find sensible and appropriate for their lives. One implication of the therapists' orientation was that much of their family rhetoric was intended to persuade clients who were portrayed as frequently acting from ineffective orientations to their problems and families. The therapists portrayed themselves as attempting to "reframe" clients' understandings and orientations to their problems and families in order to produce a cooperative therapist-client relationship as well as effective remedies to client problems.

Also, the family perspective was one of several perspectives used by the therapists in fulfilling their professional responsibilities. Two alternate perspectives and rhetorics involved treating client troubles as work and legal problems. The therapists used such formulations of client problems to explain and justify alternate orientations to the "real" clients and issues at stake in the therapeutic relationship. For example, the therapists used "work rhetoric" to explain and justify the exclusion of some family members (notably, children and sometimes spouses) from therapy sessions. The formulation of client troubles as legal problems was used to cast the central issue at stake in the therapeutic relationship as, "How do we get the court off your back?"

SOCIAL ORGANIZATION OF BRIEF THERAPY

The therapists stated that the "brief approach" to therapy that they practiced as evolved over the last 30 years and, in recent years, has been elaborated and applied in several different ways.[1] Central to all forms of brief therapy, however, is an emphasis on finding solutions to clients' problems. The therapists stated that this emphasis distinguished them from most psychotherapists who focus on the underlying and intrapsychic causes of problems. The latter therapists assume that underlying causes and proper solutions to client problems are necessarily related, whereas brief therapists do not make such an assumption.

This is not to say that brief therapists never speak of cause; rather, portrayals of cause are expressed in therapist-therapist interactions as working orientations to the issues at stake in therapeutic relationships and in therapist-client interactions as preferred understandings of clients' problems. Further, such causes are not produced as assessments of clients' lives based on extended analysis of childhood experiences and unconscious processes, but based on limited information provided by clients during one or a few interviews and assessments of their demeanor and appearances during the interviews. It was in these ways that the therapists treated family as a cause of their clients' problems.

The therapists stated that most client problems can be solved by using a few, simple psychotherapeutic techniques. One such technique was the typical "first-session task" given to new clients. It involved asking them to think about aspects of their lives that pleased them and that they wished to leave unchanged. Clients were asked to report on their thoughts at the next session. The therapists stated that in dealing with the question, clients often develop new and "positive" understandings of their lives and orientations to their problems. They stated that the new understandings and orientations could be used by therapists to help clients solve their problems. As one therapist stated to a group of trainees,

> Research shows that a good proportion of [the agency's] clients find a satisfactory change between the first and second sessions. That's the solution [to their problems], right there. Just build on it. You don't need all this other crap. That's the solution. What we do in the following sessions . . . is building on it.

A related distinguishing feature of brief therapy is its emphasis on reducing the amount of time that clients are in therapy. Brief therapists contrast their orientation to that of other psychotherapists who keep clients in therapy for months, if not years. The therapists explained and justified their emphasis by portraying long-term clients as therapy dependent. They stated that such clients had come to believe that they could not manage their lives without therapeutic help and that such a condition was an unacceptable outcome of therapeutic intervention. They sought to help clients find ways to take greater control over their lives, making it possible for them to solve present and future problems on their own.

Looked at one way, the brief therapy philosophy is the source for a cynical professional culture, because the therapists were willing to consider a variety of working definitions of the causes and solutions to client problems, including some that outsiders might consider bizarre or unresponsive to the clients' "real" problems. Further, in their deliberations about how to respond to clients, the therapists frequently spoke of clients and their problems in a flip manner, suggesting a lack of concern for them. Looked at another way, however, the therapists' actions were part of their pragmatic orientation to clients' problems, not a reflection of their lack of concern for clients.

They did not agonize over the intrapsychic causes to clients' problems because, from their standpoint, such causes were unrelated to solving client problems. Further, they stated that there were many ways of solving clients' problems and, if an intervention strategy was unacceptable to clients or was assessed as having not worked, they sought other ways of solving them. The therapists stated that, like agonizing over the intrapsychic causes of client problems, extended analyses of the reasons why an intervention had not worked was a waste of time. In general, they sought to solve clients' problems in the quickest and simplest manner possible.

The therapists implemented the brief model by use of the therapeutic team. Clients met with a therapist (interviewer) in an interviewing room and one or more therapists observed from an adjoining observation room (the team). Team members could and occasionally did communicate with the interviewer by means of an in-house telephone system. Typically, their communications involved requests for further information from clients or a recommendation that the interviewer utilize a different interviewing strategy.

Therapy sessions were organized around three major activities. Most of the session was taken up with a therapeutic interview that involved approximately two-thirds of a typical 50- to 60-minute session. During the first interview the therapists focused on the clients' reasons for seeking therapy and the establishment of goals toward which they would strive. Later interviews focused on the degree to which clients were successfully dealing with their problems and achieving their goals. The second major activity of the sessions was the team meeting, which was held in the observation room and involved both the interviewers and team members. Much of the team meeting involved using information provided by clients in the interview to formulate and express professional understandings of clients' lives and troubles and to justify responses intended to create a change in clients' lives. The meeting ended with the development of the intervention message that typically included a request that clients complete an assigned activity (therapeutic task) prior to the next session and/or the "reframing" of aspects of clients' lives by recasting them in a "positive" light. Finally, the sessions ended with the presentation of the intervention message to clients.

THE FAMILY PERSPECTIVE AND BRIEF THERAPY

The therapists formulated family as a context for understanding and responding to clients' problems. They portrayed family as a system organized around members' recurring behaviors and typical perspectives and motives. The therapists stated that healthy and satisfying families might be organized in a variety of ways; including single-parent families, gay and lesbian families, and heterosexual families organized around unconventional roles and relationships. However they are organized, the therapists stated that "normal" family life is an ongoing process of managing conflicts and other troubles associated with the members' differing behaviors and perspectives. According to the therapists, the management of everyday life is a skill centered on persons' abilities to adapt to the changing conditions of everyday life. They stated that, on occasion, persons and families "get stuck" and are unable to satisfactorily manage aspects of family life. Consider the following statement made by a therapist to a group of trainees:

> I think therapists talk too much about families not having problem-solving skills. What they mean by that a lot of times is that they don't agree with what the family is doing. They [families] do have problem-solving skills. Just think about what it takes to have a baby and raise it to, say, six months. That takes a lot of problem-

solving skills to just get to that point. So, they do have problem-solving skills and we shouldn't minimize that, but it's just that they don't [always] use the right method [for solving their problems].

In so portraying the general process by which family troubles develop, the therapists explained and justified their concern for producing change in clients' family systems. They stated that brief therapists seek to create limited changes in clients' family systems. In so doing, therapists initiate a larger process of change. They stated that other changes follow from the initial change because all aspects of the family system are related and, once clients learn how to manage one set of problems, they will use the same insights and skills to manage others. Thus, the therapists explained that in seeking the simplest and quickest solution to client troubles, they were producing social conditions that could have far-reaching implications for clients and their families.

Two such solutions involved the first-session task intended to alter clients' exclusive focus on their lives as troubled by emphasizing positively valued aspects of their lives and reframing intended to recast aspects of clients' lives portrayed by clients as problems as having positive consequences for their lives. The therapists portrayed both intervention strategies as methods for disrupting family systems that had become stuck. They further stated that, in disrupting clients' family systems, they would set in motion processes through which clients could more reasonably and effectively evaluate their lives and change aspects assessed as unsatisfactory.

The primary source of information used by the therapists in seeking to solve client problems was the therapeutic interview. They stated that although other sources of information were sometimes helpful in understanding and responding to client problems, they were not necessary in doing effective family therapy and should not be used in place of information obtained through therapeutic interviews. The therapists portrayed the interview as a source of information about both the unique characteristics and concerns of family members and organization of their family systems. Indeed, they stated that effective family therapy may be done with only one family member by asking questions that require the client to report on other family members' behavior, perspectives, and motives. Through the therapeutic interview, the therapists sought to produce information that was both necessary and sufficient for understanding the contexts of clients' problems and solving them.

The therapists interest in the interview was pragmatic. They used it to define clients' problems and assess their family contexts. They stated that the assessments were necessary because, although many responses might be used to remedy client problems, each client and family system is different. Consequently, all remedies will not be equally effective in helping them solve their problems. The therapists explained and justified their concern as a matter of finding responses that "fit" with the perspectives and motives held by clients and other members of their family systems. They added that identifying remedies that fit with clients and their family systems was important because they were the simplest and quickest solutions to client problems.

The process of determining which of the available responses to client problems fit was complex, involving consideration of both information reported on by clients during interviews and therapists' assessments of the therapeutic meaning of their statements, demeanor, and appearances in interviews. The therapists used client reports and their assessments to define and contextualize clients' problems, thereby organizing the issues at stake in therapeutic relationships. The family perspective was a major way in which the therapists contextualized client problems. In general, it involved locating problems in a system of interrelated family roles and statuses (husband-wife, daughter-son, etc.) organized around recurring behaviors and enduring perspectives. In so organizing and assessing client reports and actions in interviews, the therapists were able to categorize the family in question and attribute identities to family members. Such categorizations and attributions were rhetorically expressed in therapists' efforts to persuade others.

FAMILY RHETORIC AND THE THERAPEUTIC PROCESS

The family perspective was rhetorically enacted and expressed through therapists' accounts of client problems and family systems. Through their accounts, the therapists linked problem and context and made them congruent. Congruency was produced by casting client problems and family systems as elements of a background-foreground relationship in which each was defined in relation to the other. In this way, client problems were portrayed as aspects of larger family systems that were treated as signs and causes of problems emergent within them. Further, therapists' portrayals of both client problems and family systems were formulated based on information expressed by clients during the interview and therapists' assessments of client demeanor and appearance. Through their portrayals of client problems and family systems, the therapists explained and justified preferred orientations to the interviews as well as to the solution of client problems.

The therapists' rhetorical enactment and application of the family perspective involved the use of many different images of clients' problems and family systems. They did not advocate a single model of proper family life. Rather, they sought to assess how client problems were related to aspects of clients' everyday lives as members of family systems. The assessments focused on identifying aspects of clients' everyday lives in which they were stuck and that could be changed through the use of the techniques of brief therapy. Clients who would not specify at least one problem which the therapists assessed as solvable through brief therapy were told that the agency could do nothing to help them (until they had a problem) or that their problem was, unbeknownst to them, already solved and they no longer needed therapy. In telling clients that the agency could do nothing for them, the therapist usually indicated how they might think about aspects of their lives as problematic and in need of change.

Consider the following interactions involving clients assessed as inappropriate for brief therapy. The first is an intervention message read to a client who states that she is in therapy because the court has taken her children out of the home and will not return them until she has completed family therapy. She states during the interview that she has no problems and would like the therapist to write a letter to the court indicating that she should have her children returned. The second exchange involves a couple who express a number of complaints about their marriage, but resist specifying concrete aspects of their lives that they would like to change.

Therapist:	I'm impressed that you didn't try to bullshit me, many people would make up a problem to please the therapist and the court. I'm glad you didn't do that, even though it may be troublesome for you [it will take longer to get her children back]. It seems to us and the court that there is some problem here between you and your kids. We don't know if you have the problem or the kids do. Maybe that's confusing you too? But there seems to be some problem here, otherwise [the court] wouldn't have sent you. You don't have to agree that there's a problem. All you have to do is what you need to do to get your kids back, but nobody knows what that is. We do need to have a problem to work on and, if there's no problem, I can't see you. But then you have a different problem, because the court says you have to come [to therapy].
Team Member 1:	I don't think there's a problem here.
Team Member 2:	Maybe you're right. There's a whole string of complaints, but no problem. We can't deal with them if they don't have a problem. [He proposes giving the couple a standard "first-session" response which asks them to pay "attention to the good things in their lives,"] and when they come back next time we'll tell 'em they don't have any more problems. You know we're not gonna get anywhere trying to find the problem, so let's just solve the Goddamned problem.

Thus, the images of clients' family systems used by the therapists were situationally contingent. They were inextricably tied to client reports and actions during the interview and the therapists' overriding interest in identifying problems that could be solved through brief therapy. The therapists' rhetorical portrayal of clients' family systems was also related to the audiences with whom they worked. One such audience was made up of other therapists who participated in team meetings intended to assess interviews and identify appropriate responses to client problems. The second audience was made up of clients for whom the therapists rhetorically enacted and applied the family perspective in delivering intervention messages.

Family Rhetoric and the Therapeutic Team

Family rhetoric expressed in social interactions between team members focused on identifying therapeutically meaningful and useful understandings of and responses to client problems. The responses were formulated, explained, and justified by linking them to aspects of clients' family systems cast as relevant to their problems. Portrayals of client problems and family systems expressed in such interactions were treated as professional understandings of and orientations to the issues at stake in the therapeutic relationship.

Consider the following responses given to trainees asking team members to explain their portrayals of clients as a "fog" and "boring." In explaining and justifying their portrayals, the therapists cast their clients and their family systems into types and express orientations toward the interviews as revealing unexpressed aspects of their problems and family systems. They also link their portrayals of clients to their interest in solving the clients' problems.

Team Member: A fog is when both parties of a couple don't know what's happening. Everything is unclear, fuzzy, a fog. It's not that rare either. There's a subtype of it that's called the piano. . . . That's when they think they know what's going on, but they don't. They have the mistaken notion that they know what's happening to each other, but they really don't know what the other [person] is thinking. We have to get through that before we can do anything with 'em.

Team Member 1: Well, boring is how clients present their problems, their problems aren't boring. Like with this guy, he doesn't show any energy or involvement in his problems. He just sits there and talks along in a monotone and he's kinda distant from it all.

Team Member 2: Yeah, and his boringness here reflects what he does at home. It's symptomatic of his inability to handle relationships. His wife is bored with him too and she's trying to get him going, but she can't.

Initially, at least, such understandings and orientations were treated as matters that should not be discussed with clients who were portrayed as often bringing a different set of interests and concerns to the therapeutic relationship. The therapists stated that a basic feature of effective therapy involves satisfying clients while also initiating changes intended to alter other aspects of clients' lives; specifically, those aspects defined as problems by the therapists. Thus, the therapists' use of family rhetoric in their interactions with each other was expressed as professionally appropriate orientations to the issues at hand and as rationales intended to persuade other therapists to express support for the orientation. One aspect of such rhetoric was the explanation and justification of recommended responses as appropriate for achieving the therapists' interests in the therapeutic relationship while satisfying clients. When the therapists portrayed their interests as different from those of clients, such interactions also involved efforts to persuade others that the recommended response could be cast as consistent with the concerns and interests of clients.

Consider the following exchange occurring in a team meeting about a couple who complain of their son-in-law. They state that they are worried about the future of their daughter and grandchild and are considering several ways of breaking up the marriage, including legal action intended to remove the grandchild from the home. While observing the session, the team members expressed disbelief of the clients' portrayal of the son-in-law as "rotten" and portray them as "litigious family." They state the "real" problem involves how to get the couple to leave the daughter and son-in-law alone, including how to get them to reject the idea of attempting to gain legal custody of their grandchild.

Team Member 1:   They're [the clients] hurting the grandchild.
Team Member 2:   Oh yeah, but we can't say that [to them]. We can't say that.

[Discussion turns to the clients' talkativeness, redundancy and the interviewer's difficulty in paying attention to their lengthy list of complaints about the son-in-law.]

Team Member 2:   . . . [W]e tell this couple how they are helping this rotten son-in-law by being, by doing what they are doing, because, obviously, there is a marriage problem here. He, the son-in-law, . . . is so intent on blaming the grandparents, blaming the [daughter's] parents, that he gets off scot free. Plus, the problem is the marriage. So, they are doing, continuing to do what they are doing because they assume that they are helping their daughter get out of the marriage and are [really] helping the son-in-law, this rotten son-in-law, 'cause he looks good. The more that he fights with them, the better he looks to the daughter. That's what we are going to do.

Family Rhetoric and the Intervention Message

The therapists' major interests in constructing intervention messages involved establishing client trust and producing quick and simple changes in clients' family systems. In part, they sought these goals through "positive" portrayals of clients and their families. The portrayals were intended to persuade clients that the therapists were not making negative judgments about them and that their exclusive focus on their lives as filled with problems was inaccurate. The therapists stated that clients could not begin to deal with the "real" problems in their lives so long as they held negative perspectives casting themselves as powerless to change their lives. A major way in which the therapists sought to achieve these interests was through the expression of compliments which began the intervention message.

The compliments emphasized the ways in which clients and other family members made positive contributions to their families. Through the compliments, the therapists sought to cast clients as belonging to loving and committed family units and to persuade them to reinterpret the meaning of their own and others' actions. The therapists sometimes built on the compliments by stating that, although they were not certain why family members portrayed as problems acted as they did, the therapists suspected that they were acting "for the good of the family." The therapists concluded such messages by asking clients to consider further how family members taken to be problems might be making positive contributions to the family and to report on their thoughts at the next session. In this way, the therapists sought to reframe aspects of clients' everyday lives, attribute new identities to family members, and initiate changes in perspective intended to have far-reaching implications for clients' family systems.

The second way in which the therapists used the intervention message to pursue their interests in the therapeutic relationship was through the contextualization of clients' problems and their recommended responses to them. Such contexts were produced in team meetings by reviewing clients' statements made during the interviews, seeking words or phrases that might be used to explain and justify the therapists' recommendations. In using clients' words and phrases, the therapists sought to achieve fit between clients' family systems and their recommendations. The therapists stated that achieving such a condition increased the probability that clients would act in preferred ways. For example, when clients spoke of their families as having unique or distinctive qualities, the therapists attempted to elaborate on client portrayals and categorizations by emphasizing the ways in which their recommended responses took account of clients' distinctive family qualities. They also contextualized client problems and recommended responses by elaborating on clients' statements of affection and concern for other family members.

Consider the following intervention message given to a couple who are seeking help in curbing their arguments about the husband's problems at work. In part, the message casts the couple as a "loving family."

> [To the husband,] So, uh, it also struck us, you know, how thinking and talking about how much you care for each other and how good it is that you are aware that a career is one thing, but a relationship is hard to come by, it struck us that [the wife] loves you so much . . . that she actually wants to take all your hurts away, you know, her questioning [him about his workday] is her way of . . . wanting you not to hurt and trying to alleviate anything bothering you. And, it struck us that you, that you love her so much that you want to spare her some of your frustrations and not upset her. . . . Uh, now we have a task for you, . . . What we'd like you to do . . . , you sound like a really creative person, so we'd like you to figure out some creative signal for [the wife] to know when you want to talk about work and when you don't. [To the wife,] And we want you to guess what those signals are. [To the husband,] We'd like you to . . . predict for yourself beforehand whether she'll guess them or not.

Through such rhetorical procedures, the therapists sought to both satisfy clients and initiate professionally appropriate changes in clients' family systems. The therapists' rhetorical use of the family perspective may be further analyzed as a process involving the (1) initial formulation of clients' problems and family systems, and (2) reassessment of prior formulations in light of subsequent client reports and therapist assessments of their perspectives and motives.

FORMULATING CLIENT PROBLEMS AND FAMILY SYSTEMS

The therapists' efforts to establish congruence between portrayals of client problems and their family systems were organized as a testing process in which client reports on their problems and family systems were first evaluated in light of the therapists' assessments of their actions and appearances in interviews. Later, the assessments were evaluated in light of the reports. Through such evaluations, the therapists produced and differentiated between "accurate" and "inaccurate" client reports and "appropriate" and "inappropriate" professional assessments. The evaluations were also central to the therapists' efforts to identify and justify responses to client problems that fit with their family systems. The testing process was organized around two questions involving the therapists' interest in solving client problems as well as their assumptions about the relationship between client problems and family systems. The questions are: "Do clients act as if they have the problem or problems about which they complain?" and "Are clients' expressed attitudes toward the issues at hand consistent with those of most other persons having such problems?"

Acting Like a Troubled Family

Client reports were partly assessed against a background made up of the therapists' assumptions about how persons and families having such problems should act, including the issues about which they should be concerned. In expressing such assumptions, the therapists categorized clients' problems and family systems and attributed identities to them. When clients' reports were assessed as congruent with their demeanor and appearances, the therapists treated the reports as accurate and sought to formulate responses intended to remedy the reported troubles.

Consider the following exchange occurring between team members observing a client who reports that her husband unexpectedly announced that he was leaving her after many years of marriage. Through their assessments of her statements, the team members cast the client as typical of a spouse so treated. They also used the statements to explain and justify a therapeutically appropriate response intended to confirm the legitimacy of the client's expressed attitude toward her problem.

[The client states several times during the interview that she does not want the children to blame her for the break-up of the marriage.]

Therapist 1:   It just keeps coming up, over and over again. She doesn't want to be blamed? Do you think she's [feeling] guilty?

Therapist 2:   I think she's just pissed.

Therapist 3:   Yeah, she's pissed. He moves out while she was [out of town]. . . . She has a right to be pissed, you'd be pissed too.

Therapist 1:   I'd clobber him. Well, we have to tell her that she has been dumped on and has a right to be angry. You know, validate her anger.

When clients' demeanor and appearances were assessed as incongruent with their reported problems, the therapists treated the reports as inaccurate and expressed alternative understandings and categorizations of clients' problems and their family contexts. In this way, they sought to establish congruency by recontextualizing clients' reported problems. Consider the following assessment expressed by a team member in explaining and justifying his rejection of a couple's report that they "cannot get along" and are "on the verge of divorce." In so doing, he redefines and recontextualizes the clients' problem as a matter of boredom and seeks to persuade other team members to his preferred orientation to the issues at stake in the therapeutic relationship. He also elaborates on the rewards of fighting for bored couples, thereby making sense of their complaints.

> You know, I don't buy this picture [of the couple being unable to get along.] [Pointing to the couple chatting and laughing in the interview room,] I buy this picture. I think they're bored with each other and their life, so they spice things up by doing things to upset the other person. It makes their marriage interesting. . . . They just don't act like a couple on the verge of divorce.

In so producing congruence between clients' problems and family systems, the therapists formulated and expressed preferred orientations toward the issues at stake in the therapeutic relationship, including the relationship between their interests and those of clients. The therapists also produced congruency between client's problems and family systems by assessing the typicalness of clients' expressed attitudes toward the questions at hand in the interview.

Expressing a Typical Attitude

The therapists treated clients' expressed attitudes toward issues emergent in the interview as reflections of their underlying and enduring perspectives on social reality. The perspectives were also treated as aspects of clients' family systems having implications for how they understand and respond to many aspects of everyday life. Further, the therapists stated that members of clients' family systems take account of each other's perspectives; thereby, producing complex family systems within which the issues at hand were grounded. Thus, in assessing the typicalness of clients' expressed attitudes toward the issues at hand, the therapists expressed professional understandings of the contexts of clients' problems. Understandings so produced could also be used to predict client responses to therapists' preferred solutions to their problems. In this way, assessments of client attitudes were used to evaluate the fit between therapists' preferred responses to their problems and their family systems.

Consider the following exchange occurring in a team meeting concerned with a couple portrayed by the therapists as typical of family systems in which the husband acts like a child and the wife acts like his mother. They stated that one aspect of the wife's maternal attitude toward her husband was her desire to control the marriage.

> [A team member suggests that the intervention be organized as a game in which the husband gives signs to his wife of his desires and needs.]

Team Member 1:   Yeah, he'd like that. He's at about age 3, so he should love it.

	[Others laugh] Well, he must be hard to live with. He's such a child.
Team Member 2:	We've got to give her a game back though.
Team Member 1:	Well, mothers let their children play games, don't you think? A good mother goes along with it and we have to let her still be the good mother as long as he can feel more in control, because I don't think she's gonna give up her control. Do you?
Team Member 2:	No, but we have to do something with her response though. Um. Maybe, just have it that he can't tell her what the code is, that she has to figure it out. That might be enough.
Team Member 1:	OK. Yeah.

Therapist portrayals of clients as atypical were also efforts to make sense of aspects of client statements and actions in the interview. The portrayals were used to cast such clients as unique and requiring a different therapeutic orientation than that taken toward most clients. Client uniqueness so produced was then used as a background for assessing clients' family systems and their problems. The assessments involved attending to aspects of clients' actions in the interview as signs of the uniqueness of their perspectives and the social relations making up their family systems.

Consider the following exchange occurring as team members observe an interview with a couple who complain of inability to get along. Of special significance is the way in which the husband's actions in the interview were assessed by the therapists. They initially cast him as retarded and later as holding a unique perspective on life. The portrayals were elaborated to account for aspects of the wife's actions and, more generally, to produce a context for understanding the relationship and problems. Specifically, the casting of the husband as atypical, but rational was central to the therapists' rejection of the initial formulation of their problem as centered on the husband's retardation and the wife's efforts to protect him.

[At the outset of the interview, the wife expressed concern about being observed by the team. Team members stated that her concern was a sign that "she is self-conscious." The exchange begins with a team member stating that the husband is "strange" because his responses to the interviewer's questions are "off track."]

Team Member 1:	Well, maybe it's the way his mind works. He goes off on things. He almost sounds retarded.
Team Member 2:	Yeah, he does, but she [the wife] doesn't seem to think he is.
Team Member 3:	Yeah, you know she was real concerned with the mirror [being observed by the team]. Maybe its because of him, ya know, she's protecting him.
Team Member 4:	Yeah, I know, but she doesn't say he's dense; she doesn't seem to see it.

[A team member raises the possibility that the client is a drug user. The portrayal is evaluated as an alternative to his being retarded.]

Team Member 2:   Maybe he's just thinking in a new way that he hasn't thought before?
Team Member 1:   Yeah, he's talking too abstract to be retarded.
Team Member 2:   He's a poet, maybe he's a poet. He's offering us different meta-phors [of his life and troubles]. He's offered us two M*A*S*H [references to the television show] and one Republican Party one.

[Others express agreement. Discussion turns to the meaning of the metaphors for under-standing the client's world view and the difficulties of living with a poet.]

REASSESSING CLIENTS' PROBLEMS AND FAMILY SYSTEMS

The therapists' major interest in subsequent interviews was in identifying signs of change in clients problems and family systems. The therapists' assessment of change began with clients' entry into the interview room. They treated clients' dress, groom-ing, and demeanor as signs of their state of mind and success in remedying their problems. The assessment continued as interviewers asked clients to report on their activities since the previous session and their efforts to change aspects of their family systems. As with the therapists' initial formulations, such client reports were assessed in light of clients' appearances and demeanor in the session. Further, clients were asked to substantiate their claims that their problems were getting better, had not changed, or had gotten worse by providing detailed response on how their lives had improved, stayed the same or gotten worse. The therapists used the reported details as tests of clients' expressed conclusions about the state of their lives and problems.

Assessments of the state of clients' problems and family systems were related to therapists' evaluations of the appropriateness and accuracy of previous understandings and remedies. The therapists' concern for evaluating previous understandings and remedies was partly expressed through their response to clients reporting that no positive change had occurred in their lives. Initially, the therapists' treated the reports as inaccurate and sought signs of change in clients' reports. When signs of change were identified by the therapists, they were used to formulate and express alternative conclusions emphasizing the ways in which clients' lives were getting "a little better." The conclusions were often rhetorically expressed to clients as efforts to persuade clients that their problems and lives had improved. When signs of change were not identified, their absence was used to explain and justify new understandings and responses to client problems and their contexts.

Based on their evaluations of clients' problems and family systems, the therapists expressed three conclusions about previous remedies. They may be summarized in the following way: (1) "The problem is solved," (2) "We're on the right track," and (3) "It's not working." The first two conclusions were most frequently expressed by the therapists, particularly the "we're on the right track" conclusion. They were part of the therapists recommendations that the therapeutic relationship be terminated or that existing courses of action be continued until such time as the relationship can be properly" terminated. The conclusions were explained and justified by elaborating on previous portrayals of aspects of clients' problems and family systems. Although expressed less frequently than the first two conclusions, the therapists sometimes stated, "It's not working." The conclusion was a part of therapists' recommendations that existing courses of action be ceased and new assessments and responses to clients' problems and family systems be made.

Elaborating on Client Problems and Family Systems

Therapist portrayals of previous responses as working were associated with accounts of why and how they were successful. In general, the accounts were expressed as confirmations of the usefulness of the brief therapy model for producing change in clients' lives. More specifically, they involved using signs of change identified in interviews as confirming the accuracy of previous understandings of and responses to clients' problems and family systems. The elaborations were part of discussions about the selection of responses to client problems. In the discussions, aspects of previous interviews were assessed as significant indicators of the "real" state of clients' problems and family systems.

Consider the following exchange concerning a couple who originally reported that the husband was depressed and felt left out of the family. One part of the therapists' response was the recommendation that the husband assume more home maintenance tasks.

[The husband reports that he is no longer feeling so depressed.]

Team Member 1:	Of course he feels better, she isn't doing everything, she's not carrying the whole load. She was doing everything and he was feeling useless, uh, unneeded. . . .
Team Member 2:	Was it during the last session that you got the idea that his problem was that she was doing everything?
Team Member 1:	Uh, no, I think at the end of the first session. It was what she said, you know, she kept the kids away from him and does everything so that he could be depressed. What else was he going to do? It was her whole demeanor and her anger, she got angry at some point in that session. . . . I'll bet her behavior changed [taking over the running of the household] six years ago [when he was seriously ill], I'll bet it's been going on a long time.

Of special interest to the therapists were occasions when clients reported faster or more extensive changes in their lives than had been anticipated. Although often depicted as miracles, such client reports were treated by the therapists as extraordinary confirmations of the brief approach to therapy and signs of the clients' willingness and abilities to apply the approach to their lives. Thus, one aspect of intervention messages given to such clients was the expression of compliments intended to attribute all of the reported change to the clients' actions; thereby, encouraging them to continue to act in new ways. Such cases were also occasions for the expression of therapists accounts about why the unanticipated improvement occurred. The accounts focused on how clients might have intentionally or unintentionally changed their behavior to alter their family systems and solve their problems.

Consider the following therapist's account of a couple who had complained of their uncontrollable son. The therapists previously recommended altering the usual ways in which the parents dealt with their son's behavior, including that the father no longer debate with his son about his behavior, and, when such debates did occur, for the mother not to intervene to mollify the father and son.

Therapist 1:   What did we call this case [after the first session]?
Therapist 2:   The Hopeless Brat.
Therapist 1:   That's right. Well, he [the son] may be [a hopeless brat], but they
                    [the parents] aren't. This is the kind of case that gives you the
                    delusion that your theory works. I was really worried last time
                    that. . . [the father] wouldn't cooperate with us. [Notes several
                    reasons for his skepticism] He liked to debate with the kid. He
                    either isn't doing it anymore or the woman [mother] isn't inter-
                    fering [in the debates]. Whatever, something's happening that's
                    different.

Reformulating Client Problems and Family Systems

The "It's not working" conclusion was explained and justified by assessing clients as showing no signs of change. In expressing such a conclusion, the therapists called into question previous efforts to establish congruence between portrayals of client problems and family systems. The conclusion was part of therapists' recommendations that existing courses of action be ceased and new assessments of and responses to clients' family systems and problems be developed. The recommendation was ex- plained and justified by reformulating aspects of clients' reports, appearances and demeanor as incongruent.

The therapists responded to such a recasting of their previously expressed under- standings and responses by reconsidering questions and issues raised at previous sessions. Specifically, they asked: (1) What kind of family is this? (2) What is their problem? and (3) What can we do about it? In considering the questions, the therapists produced and expressed new understandings of the accuracy of client reports, meaning of client appearance and demeanor in the therapy session, and the familial context of their expressed problems. The new understandings were used to explain and justify new responses to client problems that were portrayed as congruent with their family systems, professionally appropriate, and satisfactory to new clients.

Consider the following exchange occurring in a team meeting and concerning a couple who, previous to the session, were portrayed by the therapists as frustrating because they had been in therapy for a long time and shown no signs of change. One way in which the therapists responded to clients so portrayed was to formulate previous responses as based on their own misunderstanding of clients' problems and family systems. Further, the therapists assessed proposed responses intended to remedy the newly defined problem and context by reinterpreting the clients' motives and concerns in seeking therapy, responses to previously tried remedies, and the range of remedies available to the therapists in dealing with the clients. Finally, the proposed response is justified as a possible source of change in the clients' family systems.

Team Member 1:	I think we've misunderstood this couple all along. What I'm wondering about here is if they're really suffering from this [problem] or not. They don't seem to really be suffering here, they seem to be getting along. Are they really suffering as much as they say, you know, I wonder? They say that they want to change, but I don't think they do.
Team Member 2:	Yeah, I agree. Maybe what we have here is a couple that fits the stereotype of the Irish couple, you know, they just love to fight. They don't want to split up or to murder each other, they just fight. They must love to fight.
Team Member 1:	Do you suppose they have any good times together? You know, do you think they have any good times when they aren't fighting?
Team Member 2:	Oh yeah. I'll bet they have lots of good times together, between fights. Just look at how they get along here (points to the couple who are quietly chatting in the interviewing room while the team is meeting), that's not a couple that never has any fun together. . . . Is there an Irish saying or custom that would fit here? You know, some Irish tradition that we could use to give them the message?
Team Member 1:	Well, I don't know, why don't we just say that the team has decided in their case the Irish stereotype is correct and that they just love to fight. You know, that the team has decided that they are both committed to the marriage and that they love to fight and that they're just Irish and that's the way it is and that we can't do anything for them. Wouldn't it be okay to just tell them that and then tell them that they're just going to have to accept this as part of their marriage? Then we can tell them that the team doesn't think that we can do anything more for them and thank them for coming.
Team Member 2:	It won't work. They take their fights seriously . . . They're not going to like that message because they're serious about their fighting. They're concerned that it is a problem.
Team Member 1:	What if you blame it on the unconscious? You know, that unconsciously they don't believe that they can have a peaceful relationship.
Team Member 2:	[We've] done that. It didn't work.
Team Member 1:	It didn't work? Well, how about if we say that it [the marriage] won't work, that there's no way to work it out?
Team Member 2:	That's the only way. We don't have any other choice.
Team Member 1:	No, what if we say that it won't change, but they are welcome to come and uh, . . . bitch at each other and get things off their

	chests every once in a while. You know, they're welcome to keep coming [to therapy]. . . . What else are we gonna do? They don't wanna split up. They don't wanna do anything about this.
Team Member 1:	They don't do tasks; that's right. So, let's just do that. What do you think?
Team Member 2:	'course if we tell them that there's no hope for change, then they may change.

[Discussion turns to a similar case in which a couple responded to the claim that they would not change by changing.]

Through the procedures analyzed here, the therapists rhetorically enacted and applied the family perspective to aspects of their clients' lives. In so doing, they cast clients' problems as family matters, attributed familial identities to clients, and sought to persuade each other and clients to act in preferred ways.

DISCUSSION AND CONCLUSION

The purpose of this article has been to apply and extend recent literature on human troubles and family rhetoric. The literature has been applied to a family therapy setting within which the family perspective was used to organize reports given by clients and formulate therapist assessments of the contexts of clients' problems. The perspective was rhetorically expressed through therapists' efforts to persuade other therapists and clients to act in preferred ways. The literature has been extended through analysis of the procedures used by the therapists in rhetorically enacting and applying the family perspective to achieve therapeutic fit and remedy client problems.

The findings may be further developed in, at least, two major ways: through the study of (1) human service work as rhetoric and (2) the family perspective as an interpretive framework for contextualizing and defining social problems.

Human Service Work as Rhetoric

Basic to this analysis is the treatment of family therapy and other forms of human service work as political and rhetorical activity involving the application of perspectives to matters of practical concern. Perspectives are enacted and applied to organize the issues at hand, attribute identities to concerned parties, and persuade others to one's preferred understanding and response to the issues. One way in which the approach may be elaborated is by linking it to other political orientations to human service institutions that treat institutional perspectives as ideologies. Viewed this way, human service professionals' rhetoric is an aspect of their ongoing ideological work intended to link preferred, abstract images of reality to the practical conditions of everyday life (Berger, 1981). The ideologies and rhetorics may be further analyzed as conservative or radical, depending on human service professionals' orientations to client problems as properly remedied through conventional, institutional procedures or through alternative means.

A related issue involves the relationship between human service professionals' rhetoric and their ability and willingness to use institutional resources to impose their perspectives on others. The therapists studied sought to develop "cooperative" relations with clients. They sought responses to client problems that were mutually acceptable to themselves and clients. Thus, much of their rhetoric was directed toward clients whom they sought to persuade to act in preferred ways. In other settings, however, human service professionals are more willing and able to impose preferred perspectives on clients. For example, Miller's (1983) study of a Work Incentive Program (WIN) shows how staff initially dealt with clients defined as troublemakers by attempting to persuade them to cooperate. Clients who objected to the staff's portrayals, however, were told that they must cooperate with the staff or lose all or a significant portion of their welfare grants. Thus, in WIN and related institutions, rhetoric may be analyzed as partly ceremonial because it is used to explain and justify institutional responses to client problems that are beyond the control of clients (Emerson, 1969). In sum, one way in which the findings can be developed is by analyzing ceremonial and nonceremonial uses of family rhetoric in human service institutions.

Human Service Work and the Family Perspective

In the therapy agency studied, the family perspective was expressed and applied as a clinical understanding of the contexts of clients' problems. They formulated family as a system and, in their teaching of trainees, elaborated on the perspective by analyzing family systems as made up of distinctive structures and processes. But the family perspective can be expressed and applied in other ways. In addition to being a clinical perspective, it is also a lay theory of human organization and problems.

Although beyond the scope of this analysis, lay uses of the family perspective were observed in the clients' portrayals of their problems. Clients used images of "proper" and "normal" family life to explain and justify their portrayal of persons and/or events as problems and portrayed aspects of family relations as causes and signs of their problems. Thus, one way in which this study may be developed is by considering the ways in which the family perspective is used as a lay theory for organizing persons' troubles and identifying third parties to whom they may appropriately turn for help. Both aspects of lay constructions of problems and solutions may involve family rhetoric directed toward others in their social worlds.

A related approach to the development of the findings involves human service professionals' application and elaboration of the family perspective by linking it to other perspectives, such as perspectives on racial and social class groups. For example, Strong (1979) analyzes how pediatricians attribute identities and moral character to parents based, in part, on assessments of their social class standing. The physicians assumed that different social classes involved different types of "normal" family life calling for different attitudes to and relations with clients assessed as middle- and lower-class. Dingwall, Eekelaar, and Murray (1983) report similar uses of the social class and family perspectives by health care visitors and social workers in assessing whether children were abused or neglected. Such studies suggest that the family perspective may be applied and enacted in many different ways by combining it with other perspectives and rhetorics. In so doing, human service professionals attribute a variety of identities to clients and justify diverse definitions of and responses to their problems.

However it is elaborated, a promising area of social research and analysis involves consideration of how human service professionals and others enact and apply the family perspective in formulating and expressing orientations to aspects of everyday life. This article is intended as a contribution to the development of such literature.

ACKNOWLEDGMENT

This is a revised version of a paper presented at the annual meetings of the Western Social Science Association, El Paso, April 1987.

NOTE

1.   Although the therapists stated that the brief approach may be used to deal with a wide variety of human troubles, it is typically classified as a kind of family therapy. Family therapy is generally distinguished from other forms of therapy by its systemic emphasis. The emphasis involves defining and treating problems reported by clients as embedded in family roles and relationships. Brief therapy is classified as family therapy because it is based on such an assumption. The therapists studied stated that the brief approach departed from other forms of family therapy in its emphasis on identifying quick and simple solutions to client problems. Persons interested in the relationship between family therapy and other therapeutic orientations may consult Corsini (1979) who gives an overview of contemporary approaches to psychotherapy. Persons interested in the assumptions and approaches making up contemporary family therapy should consult Hansen and L'Abate (1982), Hoffman (1981), and Kolevzon and Green (1985). Finally, persons interested in the approach discussed here should consult de Shazer (1982,1985), the major source used by the therapists in explaining and justifying their orientation to psychotherapy and clients' problems.

REFERENCES

Berger, B. 1981. *The Survival of a Counterculture.* Berkeley: University of California Press.
Burke, K. 1950. *A Rhetoric of Motives.* Englewood Cliffs, NJ: Prentice-Hall.
Corsini, R.J. (ed.) 1979. *Current Psychotherapies.* 2d ed. Itasca, IL: F.E. Peacock.
de Shazer, S. 1982. *Patterns of Brief Family Therapy.* New York: Guilford Press.
———. 1985. *Keys to Solution in Brief Therapy.* New York: W.W. Norton.
Dingwall, R., J. Eekelaar, and T. Murray. 1983. *The Protection of Children.* Oxford: Blackwell.
Emerson, R.M. 1969. *Judging Delinquents.* Chicago: Aldine.
Emerson, R.M. and S.L. Messinger. 1977. "The Micro-Politics of Trouble." *Social Problems* 25: 121–135.

Gubrium, J.F. 1987. "Organizational Embeddedness and Family Life." Pp. 23–41 in T. Brubaker (ed.) *Older Families and Long-Term Care*. Beverly Hills: Sage.

Gubrium, J.F. and D.R. Buckholdt. 1982. "Fictive Family." *American Anthropologist* 84: 878–885.

Gubrium, J.F. and R.J. Lynott. 1985. "Family Rhetoric as Social Order." *Journal of Family Issues* 6: 129–152.

Hansen, J.C. and L. L'Abate. 1982. *Approaches to Family Therapy.* New York: Macmillan.

Hoffman, L. 1981. *Foundations of Family Therapy.* New York: Basic Books.

Kolevzon, M.S. and R.G. Green. 1985. *Family Therapy Models.* New York: Springer.

Labov, W. and D. Fanshel. 1977. *Therapeutic Discourse.* New York: Academic Press.

Miller, G. 1983. "Holding Clients Accountable." *Social Problems* 31: 139–150.

Pittenger, R.E., C.F. Hockett, and J.J. Danehy. 1960. *The First Five Minutes.* Ithaca: Paul Martineu.

Scheflen, A.E. 1973. *Communicational Structure.* Bloomington: Indiana University Press.

Strauss, A., L. Schatzman, R. Bucher, D. Ehrlich, and M. Sabshin. 1964. *Psychiatric Ideologies and Institutions.* New York: The Free Press of Glencoe.

Strong, P.M. 1979. *The Ceremonial Order of the Clinic.* London: Routledge and Kegan Paul.

Children's Negotiation of Meaning

Nancy Mandell
York University

Focusing on the interaction of children with other children in day care centers, this paper examines the various ways in which children take the role of the other toward oneself. Using a sample of sixty-two children aged two to four, data was provided from a field work study involving intensive participant observation. Within a Meadian perspective, a model of negotiating meaning emerged with four characteristic stances of children's involvement in the process of taking children into account. Each stance is outlined using field work examples. The overall result is the provision of a continuum of interaction which documents the basic ways in which individuals move from the realm of private understandings to public or shared objects of attention.

Research on childhood socialization stresses the emergence of role-taking as essential to the ontogenesis of self. Role-taking refers to taking the attitude of others, becoming aware of other's thoughts and feelings and putting oneself in their place (Mead, 1934;[1] Cooley, 1922; Piaget, 1962; Vygotsky, [1927] 1962). It is an imaginative construction of the role of another while maintaining the separation of personal identities in order to gain an insight into the other person's probable behavior (Coutu, 1951; Turner, 1956; Kohlberg, 1969). Despite its centrality, the concept remains understudied. I will begin by considering how the term has been used in studies of children.[2] Then I will be in a position to outline my construction of role-taking among young children (aged two to four years) in day care centers as a gradualistic process of involvement in negotiating meaning.

Reprinted from Symbolic Interaction, 7(3):191–211.

USES OF THE TERM ROLE-TAKING

Research and theory has typically been divided according to whether the strictly mental or cognitive (Piaget and Inhelder, 1969; Flavell, 1968; Feffer and Gourevitch, 1960; DeVries, 1970; Lickona, 1976; Weininger, 1979; Rubin, Maioni, and Hornung, 1976; Parten, 1932; Smilansky, 1968), empathic or affective (Kohlberg, 1969; Cottrell and Dymond, 1949; Gough, 1948; Burns and Cavey, 1957; Bridges, 1931; Murphy, 1937; Turiel, 1975; Lickona, 1976), or social-interactional (Feffer and Gourevitch, 1960; Selman, 1971; Selman and Byrne, 1974; Hoffman, 1976; Goldman and Ross, 1978). While psychologists discuss all three of these components, sociologists generally confine themselves to the last two.

Following Cooley and Mead, sociologists (Coutu, 1951; Turner, 1956, 1961; Couch, 1970; Denzin, 1972) have analyzed qualitatively distinct modes of role-taking as products of situated activity. This work reveals the elaborate forms of role and self-assignments (Couch, 1970); the shifting levels and degrees of reflexivity in any action sequence (Turner, 1956, 1961); the critical import of interactional willingness, awareness and ability in children's situated behavior (Denzin, 1977); and following this approach, analysis of children's competency in negotiating the social life of a preschool through the use of techniques of exclusivity, territoriality and behavior control (Joffe, 1973). Research to date suggests that the following four directives deserve inclusion in considerations of how children join in acts with other children.

In the first place, substantial evidence now exists to suggest that role-taking is a situated product (Hoffman, 1976; Selman and Byrne, 1974; Turner, 1961; Denzin, 1977). Both anecdotal records (Hoffman, 1976; Flavell, 1968) and qualitative research (Stern, 1977; Bower, 1977; Schaffer, 1977; Denzin, 1977; Stone and Farberman, 1981) demonstrate that in familiar, close attachment and natural settings, certain forms of role-taking are common. Where there is common experience (Markey, 1928), children are capable of being aware of another's inner states distinct from their own.[3]

Secondly, in any action sequence, there are shifting levels and degrees of reflexivity (Turner, 1956; Couch, 1970). As a social process, the self represents not only a cognitive process, but all the activities of the individual that call out responses in him that are similar to those being called out in another individual (Denzin, 1972). These multiple levels of reflexivity are observed through a child's dress, public announcements, alignments of action, acknowledgments of others and negotiation of social objects (Stone and Farberman, 1981; Denzin, 1972; Fine, 1979). Acquiring reflexivity is not as decisively linear or sequential as stage development approaches to the emergence of self insist.[4]

The third directive concerns the centrality of the act-object relationship in understanding divergent degrees of role-taking. By testing isolated role-taking abilities, by breaking up and not considering the whole situation and the whole person's range of interactional competency, researchers overlook the notion of situational context and underlying elements of familiarity, objects and others that Mead (1934, 1938) would have us consider.

The final assumption is that researchers should shift attention away from role or attitude and concentrate on the line of action taken by others (Denzin, 1980). Even if young children cannot take the role of the other as holistically as the generalized other concept demands, they can witness the public actions of others, visually and auditorily track others and act on these public actions. In this way children manage to get inside on-going public actions.

Role-taking is then not a unitary concept. It holds a variety of meanings depending on the relationship of self-other to social objects. The more inclusive concept of negotiating meaning incorporates the varied ways in which children take account of themselves and others.

THE STUDY

This study describes the processes by which children engage in what I call negotiating meaning with other children in their daily interactions in school settings. The essential Meadian question becomes one of documenting how little children move from private, hidden meanings to publicly shared understandings of involvement objects.[5]

My focus is on the process by which children take the line of action of the other. What is critical in this process is the basic self-other-object relationship which encompasses all forms of interaction.[6] Do the children understand other's situational use of objects? Can the children act on this understanding behaviourally (which is thus observable to a field worker) by picking up the other's act and working that line of conduct into one's on-going activity? How do the children recognize, articulate, build upon and negotiate these social objects in regulated ways? It is not role-taking per se which is at issue, but rather interactional awareness, and the ability and willingness to act on the actions of others.

How the children accomplish these interactional competencies provides four qualitatively distinct types of involvement.[7] Visualized as a continuum, these stances vary along two dimensions: the extent to which the act and its meaning are private or public, and the extent to which the interacting unit shares an understanding of the meaning of the act in which they are involved. There is no underlying hierarchy or progression of logic as one moves through these involvements. Rather these stances represent multiple levels of reflexivity and shifting degrees of interactional aware-ness. Knowledge of the act-object relationship is crucial for grasping the flow of the interaction. Each stance represents a situational and relational production in that it assumes varying levels of familiarity and understanding of the child with the acts of others.[8] Each social construction contains elements of time, duration, intensity, mood[9] and complexity which bear on its enactment. Regularities in production and presenta-tion emerge then as characteristic stances of engrossment.

THE SETTING AND METHODS

This continuum of involvement is derived from participant observation research conducted over a two year period on children aged two to four years. The sample consists of sixty-two children from two different day care centers observed for a total of 106 hours. The study is not concerned with day care in any exhaustive sense. Day care centers represent convenient locations within which to find regularly assembled groups of children. Both centers observed serviced children aged two to four. However, in most other physical and sociostructural characteristics, the two centers differed.

The American center, named Eastern, was located in a large, metropolitan city in the Northeast. It was physically located in an old home, situated on a well equipped, fenced-in yard. As a parent cooperative, the relationship between the parents and teachers took on an adversary, rather than a complimentary nature. Three teachers cared for the 17 children in the "toddler" section. In all, Eastern serviced 55 children in both its day care and after school program. A full-time director was employed to look after the administrative and funding operations.

In contrast, the Canadian center, named Northern, was located in a medium-sized city in South Central Ontario. The center was physically located in a one-story building belonging to the public agency with which it was affiliated. As a public, non-profit organization, the center maintained an open, responsive relationship with its users while daily decision-making remained in the hands of the one supervisor and the two to three other teachers. The director of the agency ultimately oversaw the financial operation, the hiring and firing of staff and maintenance of the facility—all the tasks which the parents of Eastern controlled. Northern serviced 37 children using 4 teachers.

In terms of the content of the scheduled activities, Northern varied from Eastern in only one important respect. The Northern teachers organized their weekly art and circle activities thematically. Parents were informed of the weekly theme (weather, snow, Christmas) by a sign on the door of the main activity room. In spite of this difference in planning activities, the qualitative distinctions of child-teacher interaction differed minimally between the two centers.

I gained entree to Eastern in the late spring of 1977. I presented the director and teachers of the "toddler" section with a field work proposal stating that I wished to observe two to four year olds with the goal of gaining as complete an overview of their daily activities as possible. I explained that this entailed trying to see the center through the eyes of the children with a view to understanding how the center works on a day-to-day basis. I included a copy of Joffe (1973) and Denzin's (1973) work on children as examples of the kind of participant observation work which I intended to follow. A similar proposal and approach was used at Northern in 1978 with an equally positive and quick response.

My role as "participant-as-observer" (Gold, 1969) included closely following the children, interviewing the teachers and the directors, both formally and informally, attending the parent meetings and "helping" the teachers with routine tasks when they were overloaded.[10] By following the children's ways, by doing what they did, and by becoming involved with them on a daily basis, I was able to gain an understanding of their thoughts and actions. Specifically I focused on small (2–3) groups of children and literally followed them around their play space. If they sat in the sandbox making cakes, so did I. If they scrambled up the climbers, crawled under the porch or chased each other around the yard as "Supermen," I followed. While I did not "become a child," I nonetheless became as "minimally adult" as possible. This required that I neither judge nor evaluate their actions, nor act as a nurturing nor authoritative teacher.

I was a person who visited regularly and who was there to play with the children. When the children asked me who I was, I replied that I wasn't a teacher, just a visitor. While the children initially attempted to engage me in a teacher's role, with consistent refusal their demands subsided. They taught me their openers, rules for entry, procedure and exit from interaction and I, in turn, demonstrated who I was to be to them. Naturally the latter involved considerable testing of my neutrality, confidentiality and physical dexterity. However in time they either forgot I was there or engaged me fully in their activities.

The data accumulated comes from two different centers in two different countries. I analyzed the data separately and then, finding few negative cases (Geer, 1967), collapsed them into one analytic model. What emerged is a depiction of role-taking as a processural and gradualistic ability displayed within a child's particular interaction with others.

STANCE ONE: SELF-INVOLVEMENT

The first stance, labeled self-involvement, includes self-reflective activity. Following Mead's triadic theory of meaning, the children are self-absorbed, completely engrossed with themselves and the object of their involvement to the exclusion of all others. This field work example captures the essence of self-reflective activity.

> Norm was sitting at one of the small tables. He had taken out the Fisher-Price toy phone, picking up one receiver and was talking into the phone and at the same time, moving the dials of the Fisher-Price clock. He kept repeating "Hello clock, hello clock, are you moving?"

The children are busy exploring and manipulating objects and taking themselves and their relationship with objects into account. Private meanings prevail and the extent to which the child's self-other interaction with an object is meaningful for the child is indicated by the child's total absorption with his own activity.

Children absorb themselves in this stance with varying degrees of gusto and for varying lengths of time. They may be physically removed from a group of children or sitting side by side with others. They may be engaged in any degree of physical activity from sitting rather still, to walking around with a toy, to racing up and down the gym or yard with their bikes. They may be shouting, laughing, crying, or silent as they engage themselves. They may alter physical locale and cross several time-activity changes in the day care center and still be self-involved. Changing space and time, use of physical or verbal motion, being separated or beside others—none of these superficial identifying characteristics are central to self-involvement. The essential element of this stance is the private self-other-object involvement within which the child becomes so engrossed that he is oblivious to other activity around him.[11]

Self-involvement can be subdivided into two categories including the private self-object exchange with self-chosen activities, or, the children's involvement in teacher directed activities. In each of these categories the children are still making their own objects, all of which have essentially a private meaning for the child. Yet the structure within which they manipulate objects and the actual physical material they use may have been provided by a teacher. Each way is equally as engrossing and shares the same elements as the other category. In fact, the lack of difference between these two ways indicates that the sociostructural organization of a day care setting is quite unlikely to prohibit this stance of involvement.

While I conceptually see no qualitative difference between these two forms of self-involvement, the teachers often do. A child who is self-absorbed with objects of his own choosing is often seen as egocentric. However, a child self-absorbed, involved with objects of a teacher's choosing is often labelled an active, cooperative child. Consider the two following examples.

> This whole time (meeting time) Roy is sitting on the floor outside the door of the toddler's meeting room playing with a spinning top, twirling it over and over again. He is not interested in listening to the others.

Now, compare this example with a second one from my data in which a child is self-involved using teacher designated objects.

> I sat down at the paint table; Adam, Tricia and Josh were painting. They were all concentrating on their painting judging by the lack of noise or conversation and their disinterest in my arrival and each other. Their motions were very slow and deliberate and they all seemed to be painting very slowly and with great caution. Their faces were all serious and involved in their work. They were not talking so I didn't talk either.

From an adult viewpoint, the latter group is seen as being more productive and constructive. They are doing something with their time. In the first example, the child is seen as being engaged in a relatively meaningless action.

There is a tendency in the literature (Smilansky, 1968) on children's play (Parten, 1932; Weininger, 1979) to differentiate between what is usually called solitary play (my first example) from what is called parallel play (my last example) on the basis of the extent to which the engaged child is in the actual presence of other children, and the extent to which the child is absorbed in some sort of meaningful play from an adult point of view. These categories fail to appreciate that from the child's point of view, active involvement with others is not being sought. Whether beside others or alone, the self-involved child is engaged in reflective activity. To assign a valuational assessment on this type of behavior overlooks the amount of absorption, creativity and problem solving which engages the self-involved child.

Regardless of chronological age, becoming engrossed with ourselves in an activity seems characteristic of how we, as social role takers, develop. Acts become engaging for the children, repeated and also approached in different ways. Denzin (1977: 130–131) has described this type of activity as "playing at a self" in which there occur dramatic encounters with the self that reside in the covert features of the act. The person converses with his alter while he is casting himself in a variety of different stances. The phrase "playing at a self" conveys the message that there are many different selves children try on as they take account of themselves, others and their experiences through self-reflective activity.

A characteristic feature of self-involvement, especially as it increases in absorption, is the amount of repetition involved. In fact, the amount of repetition in this stance is so pervasive that it becomes one of the most trying features of observation. Repetition provides a framework for continued interaction (Garvey, 1977). When the involvement is no longer absorbing, the children move on and create new situations for themselves.

As the children become involved with themselves during the act, their verbal manipulation of their involvement objects becomes indicative of their absorption. The children adapt their speech to the objects which they are addressing. Denzin (1972: 292) has made the same point stating that it is consistent with an interactionist tradition to view language as a situated production which varies according to the definitions which people give objects, selves, others, time, place and the social relationship between speakers. Psychologists (Fein and Clarke-Stewart, 1973) have noted that children learn to use linguistic forms that are appropriate to particular occasions and settings. The children learn how to formulate diverse and subtle repertoires of information and intentions. They develop a theory of speaking and listening that deals with the appropriateness of language to their place and setting. Hence, I have examples of the children gooing like babies, hissing like bionic men and reading out loud like teachers.

The children also display long attention spans indicative of their engrossment in the act. In the following example, Abby spent longer than the twelve minutes I actually measured her acting, since she initially got my attention by being quietly absorbed for so long.

> Abby spent twelve minutes trying to place eight small wooden people upright on a school bus. She would knock them down with her arm as she set them up and start all over again. She would finish, run the bus, the people would fall over and she would start all over again.

In the process of their self-reflective involvement, the children quite literally and mentally make objects. In some ways, the process of taking account of other children becomes the object. The children are involved in a more general sense, in the process of learning to take account of others and themselves within this particular setting. Making objects and manipulating these objects becomes a vehicle for sustaining this involvement. By recognizing the seriousness of this engagement for the children, the observer is better able to understand this stance of reflection as merely one among other qualitative types in which the child is engaged.

STANCE TWO: INTERPRETIVE OBSERVATION AND DISPLAY

In contrast to a stance of self-involvement, interpretive observation and display is best conceptualized as children's attempts to learn the ropes. Through various techniques, the children make it evident that they are trying to monitor and follow the ways of others. However, I have called this interpretive observation or involvement "from afar" since it represents only a peripheral commitment from the observing child. The observer is, in fact, a bystander, a marginal man who hovers on the sideline of involvement eager to take in as much information as he can about children's behavior and yet not willing to participate with another child.[12]

Marginal involvement often takes place beside other children. How else to learn their ways if you do not follow closely? Interpretive involvement is not a developmental stage in the production of self nor does it characterize only newcomer behavior. Children move in and out of this involvement stance constantly and use it most fruitfully as a well defined period of quiet observation and reflection. As Mead pointed out in stage one of the act, reflective thinking is only necessary when the act is inhibited or halted. The identifying of objects is a continual problem for children since in the flow of action, new objects constantly arise leading to the reconstruction of past events. Since acts require this continual redefinition and reflection on the emergence of new objects, periods of time required to assess these emergents is continually sought and used by individuals.[13] Marginal involvement is not representative of an underdeveloped self but is an involvement stance central to the continual reassessment which permits the innovation and novelty of human life (Strauss, 1959: 26).

Most characteristic of this stance is that of *staring*.[14] Examples abound of children standing around staring at one child or groups of other children involved in activities. Newcomers are most often seen spending what initially appears as excessively long amounts of time sitting, standing or following the actions of others.

> Jesse wandered in and out of the two (play) rooms watching everyone. Then, he stood in the doorway connecting the two rooms. He spent approximately the next fifteen to twenty minutes doing this. He generally scanned the rooms and then focused on certain children for periods of time, often focusing on wherever the greatest noise was coming from.

By strategically placing himself in the doorway, this child was able to scan and observe all the activities that were going on in the two rooms. Clearly, staring is an initial and necessary way of learning what other children are all about.

While staring is the most extreme form of interpretive observation, there are other characteristic stances by which the children begin to make initial indications of their presence to others. Of these, public *announcements* are common.

> Kevin is running back and forth across the gym floor witn a hockey stick saying "Watch me score."

> Jeremy comes running by, picks up a board and yells "Superman."

In all of these examples, an indication is being made to others that their action is a public display. Their action is to be acknowledged by others by staring, commenting on or joining in with. More often than not, the observing children merely watch and resume their own acts. The essential differentiating quality of this stance is its public nature in the form of an announcement or overture. Others are requested to take account.

Similar to these public announcements are *direct invitations* to join in an action. While, in the first case, the overture is decidedly open-ended, in the latter a specific demand is placed on another child. Typically the physical presence of the child is too close to be ignored.

> Norm comes into the lunch room singing "tea" to himself repeatedly He goes over to the box of felt sticks in the corner, takes one out and brings it over to me saying "lemon, lemon" and thrusts it in my face.

Or the invitation to join is phrased in the character of a question or an overt demand which is, again, difficult to ignore.

> Kevin approaches me on his bike in the gym and says "Chase me."

> Lila looks over and calls out, "Warren, do you want to be my baby?"

Repeatedly then, the children make obvious their willingness to be joined in action by others. Yet, by virtue of their delivery, these statements and actions are attempts to get others to merely take account of them, recognize their presence and actions. Whether or not the other joins in is superfluous, otherwise more tried and successful joining in tactics would be used. Yet an attempt has been made to become part of the taking account process.

The inner (private) and the outer (public) sides of interaction are not as clearly differentiated in observed action as the concepts suggest. Inner thought expressed outwardly through observable action or language is what Vygotsky (1962) and Markey (1928) and Flavell (1968) called sociocentric declarations of intent. The child is treating other children, or any other child who happens to be present, as an audience for their actions. They are not taking the perspective of the other child, but literally acting at them (Denzin, 1980: 256). The children display this in the form of public monologues, public announcements and making initial overtures to others. These children's acts are transitional between the hidden covert self-reflection of stance one and the more public other-reflective engagement of stance three. By looking outside his own behavior and casting others in the stance of audience, the child creates a non-participating, socially distant forum for his acts. While audience members always have the option of commenting directly (Goffman, 1959), the child has the option of not attending to this corrective feedback. Children understand the interactional rule of their mutual obligation to attend to other's views in reciprocal involvements. Children are also notorious rule breakers in that these rules are constantly negotiated. However, the transitional interactional stance of interpretive observation and display allows the child to attend to others to an extent that he alone controls.

In the next type of interaction, which I call *making initial overtures,* the children typically physically join a group without greetings, announcements or any overt displays and, simply, get on with the action.

> Susan arrives in the room that morning, goes over to the mats where some girls
> are laughing, sits down beside them and starts moving the blocks around, as the
> others are.

Throughout this kind of episode, the joining child typically remains interaction-ally aloof, content to be physically present, watching and listening, and yet not directly involved with the others in the creation of an ongoing, meaningful act. There is enough shared understanding in their acceptance into the group and also their knowledge of how to remain anonymous in that situation. By neither disrupting the act nor contrib-uting to its flow, the interested bystander stance is maintained.

A qualitatively distinct yet theoretically similar type of action is found in the form I call *crowding*. Defined as "invasion of interactional space," it remains analytically distinct from common instances of invasion of property such as grabbing valued possessions. While usually not deliberate, crowding is a frequent form of involvement from afar. There are frequent instances of crowding in which children attempt to join other children who are self-absorbed, an involvement stance in which others are rarely welcome.

Joffe (1973: 107) has observed in her analysis of a pre-school setting how the children engage in territoriality, a tendency to stake out geographical spaces, objects and people as one's own. Territoriality arises over struggles for limited supplies and demands for privacy.

> Angie sat down in the car seat she found lying in the yard. Margo walks over and
> tries to also sit down beside her. Angie yells "Get off. Mine." Angie shoves her on
> the ground. Margo starts howling.

In this example and others, the child's privacy is being invaded and attempts by others to break into their space are strongly resisted.

In addition to literally crowding a child's interactional turf, often attempts are made to take the trappings of the action. For example,

> Brad arrives at the table and grabs Cindy's playdough. Cindy screams, "That's my
> birthday."

It is not the object *per se* which is desirable to the child but rather the action enveloping the object which makes the object become a desirable thing. The crowder correctly takes account of the other child's involvement and wants to join in. What he has yet to learn is that self-involved children rarely want others to join them.

All of these interpretive observations and displays entail a peripheral or marginal involvement with others. Meanings are usually not understood or at best, are shared only minimally with others. In brief, these various stances represent the most initial phases of the taking account process.

STANCE THREE: CO-INVOLVEMENT

The third stance, called co-involvement, is characterized by the attempts of the children to track the public actions of other children and to fit or join their actions with the others. In these involvements, the children have moved into the realm of public interaction. In presenting varied lines of action, the children are attempting to create a situated or focused interaction based on a mutual understanding of social objects. For sustained interaction, there must be sufficient understanding among the children on the common involvement objects in order to continue joint acts. In fact, we rarely do comprehend all aspects of interaction. There simply has to be enough meaning, perhaps roughly understood, for an act to continue. When the children are engaged with others in an attempt to join their lines of action, they are often unsuccessful. A great deal of guess work goes on as the child tentatively puts forth an idea, an action, a physical object, a nonverbal glance or gesture. If these cues are picked up by another child and interpreted accurately, then an initial joint encounter is created. For this exchange to continue, the simultaneous sharing and sending of cues must proceed. However, the characteristic element of this involvement stance is the inability of interaction to proceed in this turn-taking manner.

Problematic activity[15] forces the children to search for alternative lines on which joint acts can be built. Building joint acts is attempted but not accomplished. Enough meaning is not shared. Reciprocal social role taking thus fails. This stance is differentiated from the fourth stance of public action by the child's inability to accurately take into account the feelings, attitudes and interpretation of the other and articulate, negotiate and build on these.

There are many tactics which the children use to find these common grounds. When problems halt the flow, if the children are committed to working out tentative agreements to overcome the momentary impasse, they will prod one another, propose alternatives and doggedly pursue new activities.[16] In short, by continually digging at one another's meaning, the children are engaged in a trial and error process of reaching common understanding.

The degree to which a child is committed (Becker, 1970b) to join an act appears to determine the extent to which the prodding goes on. The key to this concept appears to be that the child sees his searching for alternative lines of mutually agreeable action as consistent with his overall commitment to the involvement object and others. Children spend extended periods of time attempting to adjust their lines of action to the other, sometimes to no avail. The search takes on a protracted negotiated character as the action shifts from one object to another. Co-involved interactive sequences thus strike the observer as disjointed, bumpy, random and rather chaotic occasions. They no doubt strike the children the same way. The children encounter frustration and the fatigue of continual attempts to get another person to understand what they are trying to articulate or perform. For example,

Lorna says to Jackie, "You be the baby." Jackie replies, "You be the baby, okay Lorna? Lorna then says, "No lets cook." Jackie shakes her head and walks off to the water table. Lorna lies down on the floor beside the piano saying, "Then I'll be the baby if Jackie won't play. "

In this case, the children never did agree on their involvement objects and the continual switching of themes suggests the dissatisfaction felt.

While these above examples have indicated the verbal element of digging, the search for common ground also goes on non-verbally. In the following example, gestures prevail. After a period of fighting over a train,

> Michael takes Norm's hand and they walk over to the shelf and Michael takes down a train for Norm. Michael then takes his train and runs it along the floor making train noises. Norm starts to tentatively move his train along. When I looked back a minute later, Norm was following Michael around the room as Michael moved his train around. Michael looked up and said, "Are you walking with me?" Norm nods his head. Michael replies, "You walk with me and the trains, okay Norm?" Norm smiles and gets down on the floor and starts to push the back of the train with Michael.

Given an openness to joining and being joined, if the children persist, try new lines of action and jointly dig for common ground, they can usually work out a satisfactory agreement. Accomplishing working agreements is a trial and error process in which two or more children continually search for common lines of agreement. The manipulative stage in which something is actually done to the common objects of involvement is rarely smooth. Interpretive problems continually threaten to halt the action unless new areas of understanding are reached.

STANCE FOUR: RECIPROCAL INVOLVEMENT

The final involvement stance is characterized by a smooth, running process in which action is jointly created on shared definitions of the situation.[17] The children stand firmly on the same grounds. While overt digging takes place, it is not the central element in this process. More characteristic is the active, understood, ongoing flow of involvement. It represents a rather finished product of the whole taking account process in which the joint action is not circumvented by the problem of perception, definition or evaluation. The children are adept at reading the cues put forth by their partners and adjusting their responses. They are, as Becker (1970c) has coined the phrase, capable of situational adjustment.[18]

The children can be mutually involved with one another through a complex series of gestures. In fact, studies of infants in cribs done by, among others, Spiro (1965) and Provence et al. (1977) attest to this quality of non-verbal shared understanding.

As verbal competency increases, the children combine their gestural skills with their verbal skills in advancing reciprocal involvement. In this example, talking becomes a focus for their involvement.

> Amanda gets out a book and starts to ad-lib the story, holding the book open to the rest of the children as the teachers do and turning the pages as she tells the story. (There is no story line.) Jason, John and Clare sit absolutely quiet as she reads. When Amanda gets silly by turning to a page and saying, "wee, wee, wee, gee, gee, gee," the children laugh for four pages of this and then start fidgeting and looking away. Amanda picks up on this cue and starts to read again.

Perhaps of all the incidents of shared involvement, to both the observer and, judging by their engrossment and repetition, also to the children, the most fascinating are those in which the flow of shared understanding runs on and on, shifting themes and physical locations.[19] I have numerous examples of, among others, children "watching" Sesame Street on broken televisions, rushing friends in and out of "hospitals," dashing about putting out "fires," gassing and repairing broken trucks and cars, attacking as, and fending themselves from "monsters," cooking, eating, drinking sand food and, "painting" porches. Throughout all of these positions of shared involvement, the central thrust is one of moving the action along, sorting out minor problems and getting on with the business of being finely attuned to the others. Sometimes what the children are doing, like riding buses or making muffins, provides an opportunity for focused interaction and the "bus riding" is an ancillary activity (Denzin, 1977: 152).

While the most interesting and complex of these examples would take a page to quote, short excerpts will perhaps provide the flavour of this process. The action can include the familiar themes of "playing house."

> Lorna is in the doll bed lying down as the baby. Jackie is the mother. Lorna cries like a baby saying, "wa, wa, wa," Jackie laughs and sticks a small toy in her mouth and says, "Stop crying baby. Here's your bottle." Lorna smiles and drinks; Jackie laughs again. Lorna says, "Pat me." Jackie leans over and pats her. Lorna says, "I'm hungry." Jackie walks over to the doll center, pretends to take something out of an empty doll cup, returns and says, "Here baby, here's your food."

In all of the cases, I was struck by the relative speed and ease of the exchange. The children are tuned into each other in the sense that they seem to understand and be able to follow and anticipate changes in the other's line of action. Denzin (1977: 167–168) has commented on the concept of interactional age. As situational awareness increases and incorporates an expanding range of interactional others, the social exchanges of children become more complex. Obviously, what has come before for a child will have some force in the present, as the ". . . presents slip continually one into another" (Mead, 1932: 9). Yet, without a very detailed and lengthy focused observation, it is quite impossible to do more than hypothesize that newcomers to the taking the role of the other toward self process would not initially be participating in these sometimes lengthy and complex exchanges.

CONCLUSION

As this involvement continuum suggests, negotiating social meanings is a complex process ranging from private self-reflective activity to publicly shared agreements. The first two stances include the private, covert side of interaction. Self-reflective activity or self-involvement is conceptually similar to what James (1890) called the phenomenological stream of interaction or stream of consciousness. This is the hidden, stance in which the child is thinking, planning and wrestling with objects.

Acts characteristic of the second stance, interpretive observation of and display to others, are again essentially private in that distinct others are not invited to join in an activity. However, the involvement is peripheral or marginal to that of others, since it is these others' lines of action which constitute the focus for the observing child. Being essentially private interpretations of others' activities, the extent to which self-object understanding is shared is indicated by both the child's absorption in the activities associated with this stance and by his ability to involve himself in observation of others without shattering the flow. The child as field-worker is tracking the ways of others. By visually and auditorily monitoring others, he is attempting to grasp the complex cues and construction of fluid rules of interaction for entry into, procedure within and exit from a focused interaction. The child imaginatively and mentally is rehearsing how he would fit into other's lines of activity. If his assessment of their ways is accurate, the child can maintain his marginal stance neither publicly contributing to, nor disrupting the actions of others.

The third and fourth stances involve public attempts to fit lines of action together. The third involvement stance, labeled co-involvement, is characterized by its essential failure to accomplish this mutual joining of activity. Children in this stance are constantly negotiating with and prodding at one another's public actions to reach an understanding about shared social activities. However, despite their wrestling with these stubborn and troublesome objects and despite the often tremendous guesswork which takes place, the children are unable to sustain mutual interaction based on sufficient understanding. Meadian problems halt the flow of activity.

Mistakes at work (Hughes, 1958) or failure of interaction (Goffman, 1959) provide us with a taste of the essential negotiative elements of the children's work. Strauss (1959: 61) has noted that it is unusual for anyone to note all aspects of interaction. In many situations, a great many aspects of interaction are taken for granted. By tentatively putting forth public lines of action, the children are engaged in a continual trial and error process Which provides them with corrective feedback. Given their limited interactional experience, many situations are not yet conventionalized. Each child enters a focused interaction with a fund of prior knowledge concerning the social production of situational definitions. This prior experience includes repetition with some familiar others and fewer, regular encounters with unfamiliar others. Hence this co-involvement stance of reaching working agreements with other children is characterized by the constant digging for mutual understanding by switching lines of action until a common object can he grasped. Negotiation (Strauss, 1978), as Meadian problem solving, is central to everyday life for the children in day care centers. The children can commit themselves to handling misunderstandings as they arise by situationally adjusting their public behavior and thus resolving disputes. However, whether for lack of commitment (Becker, 1970c) or lack of conventionalized methods of handling these problems, the joint attempts fail. Over time, observations of stable groups (Fine, 1979; Becker et al., 1961; Denzin, 1977) reveal that individual, corporate histories and traditional patterns of reaching working agreements (co-involvement) will become part of the group's perspective. What has gone before and perhaps become codified in rules, albeit situationally negotiable, will obviously affect that which is ongoing. But, as Mead's concept of novelty suggests, each emergent in new situations is itself unique and neither structurally nor historically determined. Simply spending time in creating mutual interactions with unfamiliar others no doubt provides the child with a wider range of experience with which to participate in the production of emergents. The children evolve a variety of negotiative tactics which they use to prod the other child into accepting their proposed definitions. Through this interplay of suggested lines of action, the children negotiate a situated product.

The fourth involvement stance,[20] called reciprocal (reciprocated) involvement is based on successful mutual alignment of joint activity. This stance is characterized by a smooth, running process of children creating publicly shared meanings of social objects. They share similar definitions of their mutual activity and hence stand firmly on the same grounds. While problems arise which threaten to disrupt their actions, these are easily manipulated. What differentiates this involvement from the previous stance is not so much their success at mutually sustaining the interaction but rather their active creation of shared meanings sufficiently agreed on to allow joint acts to continue. The result is reciprocated and often instantaneous understanding of others' public displays. This is the stance characteristic of what Strauss (1959: 55) calls a rhythmic ballet, and what Schaffer (1977: 61) calls a harmonious dialogue. In both cases, the participants are attuned to one another, share the same code of signals and send and receive these signals via several channels simultaneously (Schaffer, 1977: 61).

Sociological research into the world of children (Denzin, 1973; Corsaro, 1981; Glassner, 1976; Fine, 1979; Joffe, 1973) has begun to catalogue the range and complexity of situational behavior within naturalistic settings. Movement in this research direction has the effect of slowing the search for causal connections of appropriate child behavior. This is accomplished by emphasizing the gradualistic and relational emergence of role-taking and negotiative behaviors.

Documentation of children's interaction with other children and with themselves demonstrates that role-taking is not a unitary concept. It holds a variety of meanings depending on the relation of self-other to social objects. For this reason, the term involvement in negotiating meaning captures the variety of instances in which children engage.

The notion of various stances of interactional awareness contributes to the growing literature on interpretations, understandings and hermeneutics (Scheler, [1913] 1954; Schutz, 1962; Denzin, 1980). How we understand and interpret the other is essential to Mead's philosophy of the act. In this light, children can be viewed as hermeneutic interpreters of one another's actions in schooling settings. As such, this study suggests that the interpretive process in which the children are engaged is more complex than simply imaginatively projecting oneself into another's line of action or thought. Imaginative projection glosses over the actual process by which the children translate and piece together the meanings of and other's actions and place these actions within a meaningful totality. These units of action might include what adults call play, routines, rituals or encounters. But basic to each unit is the child's process of interpretation and comprehension of the acts and objects of others. Our task in childhood socialization studies is to analyze these social fields of experience as they are repeatedly generated in collective settings of young children.

Clearly there are a number of more specific questions left unanswered. Much more detail into the interactional careers of specific groups of children is needed to indicate the place of interactional age and histories of role-taking with unfamiliar others. We require more detail on degrees of reflexivity as these relate to the children's interactional position with others. Does the child adopt the standpoint of the other (Turner, 1961) as his own or as a depersonalized norm? Finally, we need to investigate the place of emotions (Denzin, 1980) in the child's adoption of varying interactional stances with other children.

NOTES

1.   Mead (1959: 49) originated this concept of "taking the role of the other toward oneself" in order to demonstrate the reflexive, interpretative nature of social interaction in which individuals define, redefine and negotiate meanings with others about objects by considering another's point of view toward that object or activity.

2.   See Ellis (1973), Denzin (1977) and Schwartzman (1976) for reviews of the concept play.

3.   Markey (1928: 151) goes further to assert that Piaget's assumption that there is no real interchange of thought is gratuitous. The only basis for saying that there is no interchange is that the child's thinking is drawn from a common social process but there is certainly interchange in this process.

4.   Lewis and Rosenblum (1975: 1) have argued that psychoanalytic and Piagetian theories of human development have so dominated research that they have led to a suppression of active study of children's early social behavior other than that directed toward the parents.

5.   Other studies of children's play, notably psychological accounts, rely almost exclusively on the child's physical actions as defined by an adult observer, and make no attempt to discern the child's definition of the act, object or situation.

6.   The children's objects I deal with belong essentially to stage two of Mead's act. Some of these objects are mentally manipulated and some are concrete and resistant, such as sand which is defined by the children in non-adult ways and used by the children as food. But generally, stage two objects resist in the sense that they may not permit continuing the act especially if others are involved. See Mead (1938: 59, 74) for a discussion of the resistance of objects, and Mead (1938: 32–33) for a discussion of differing objects in each stage of the act.

7.   Goffman (1963: 36) defined involvement close to its dictionary meaning. To "involve" means to occupy oneself absorbingly, to engross oneself fully. To be engaged in an occasional activity means to sustain some kind of cognitive and affective engrossment in it, some mobilization of one's psychological resources, in short, it means to be involved in the activity.

8. Interactional age is a dynamic and relatively unexplored concept in studies of children. In order to fully examine this concept, one would need to follow the careers of children.

9. See Denzin (1980), Hochschild (1975), Scheler ([1913] 1954), and Schutz (1962) for discussion of the emotional content of interactional analysis.

10. The particular problems I encountered in this role with the teachers are dealt with in another article (Mandell, 1983).

11. Self-involvement is conceptually distinct from Goffman's (1963: 69) "being away." This will be discussed in Stance Two, Interpretive Observation and Display.

12. See Geer et al. (1968: 209–213) for a discussion of "learning the ropes."

13. See Mead (1959: 9–12) for his discussion of reflection and emergence.

14. In the psychological literature (Weininger, 1979: 34) what I encompass under one technique of interpretive observation namely staring, psychologists have labelled onlooker play.

15. For Mead, a problem was always an event or an idea in philosophy or science which did not make sense. My idea of "Meadian problem solving" relates more narrowly to Mead's stages of the act in which misunderstandings halt the flow of the act. My use of problem solving does not appear as such in *The Philosophy of the Act*. See Mead's (1938: 79) discussion of problems.

16. While negotiation goes on throughout many of these involvement stances, it is not defined here as a distinct perspective. It seems that the initial use of the concept negotiation (Strauss, 1963) as a separate category in various socialization studies was in part a way to remind the reader of the interactional nature of the study. Here, I moved beyond that point and suggest that the interaction socialization perspective always assumes a negotiative character.

17. As Polanyi and Prosch (1975: 44) state, our capacity for making sense of, for understanding another person's action emerges by entering into his situation and by judging his actions from within his own point of view.

18. Becker (1970c: 279) defines situational adjustment as the individual's capacity as he moves in and out of a variety of social situations, to learn the requirements of continuing in each situation and achieving success in it.

19. Much has been written about the role of fantasy in children's play usually with a view to exploiting its functional significance. See Markey (1928), Ellis (1973), and Herron and Sutton-Smith (1971).

20. According to Mead (1938: 77), the relationship between act and object and these two considered as one can be called a situation. Each involvement stance thus represents varying situations.

REFERENCES

Bateson, M.C. 1975. "Mother-infant Exchanges: The Epigenesis of Conversational Interaction." Pp. 101–113 in D. Aaronson and R.W. Rieber (eds.) *Developmental Psycholinguistics and Communication Disorders*. New York: New York Academy of Science.

Baumrind, D. 1980. "New Directions in Socialization Research." *American Psychologist* 35(7): 639–652.

Becker, Howard S.L. 1960–1961. "Notes on the Concept of Commitment." *American Journal of Sociology* 66: 32–40.

———. 1970a. "Field Work Evidence." Pp. 39–62 in *Sociological Work*. New Brunswick, N.J.: Transaction Books.

———. 1970b. "Problems of Inference and Proof in Participant Observation." Pp. 25–38 in *Sociological Work*. New Brunswick, N.J.: Transaction Books.

————. 1970c. "Personal Chance in Adult Life." Pp. 275–288 in *Sociological Work.* New Brunswick, N.J.: Transaction Books.

Becker, H.S.L., B. Geer, E.C. Hughes, and A.L. Strauss. 1961. *Boys in White: Student Culture in Medical School.* Chicago: University of Chicago Press.

Bem, D.J. and D.C. Funder. 1978. "Predicting More of the People More of the Time: Assessing the Personality of Situations." *Psychological Review* 85: 485–501.

Blumer, H. 1969. *Symbolic Interactionism.* Englewood Cliffs, N.J.: Prentice-Hall.

Bower, T.G.R. 1977. *The Perceptual World of the Child.* Cambridge; Harvard University Press.

Bowers, K. 1973. "Situations in Psychology: An Analysis and a Critique." *Psychological Review* 80(5): 307–336.

Brainerd, C. 1977. "Cognitive Development and Concept Learning: An Interpretive Review." *Psychological Bulletin* 84: 919–939.

Bridges, K.M.B. 1931. *Social and Emotional Development of the Preschool Child.* London: Routledge.

Burns, N. and L. Cavey. 1957. "Age Differences in Empathic Ability among Children." *Canadian Journal of Psychology* 11: 227–230.

Cooley, C. 1922. *Human Nature and the Social Order.* New York: Charles Scribner's Sons.

Corsaro, W. 1981. "Entering the Child's World: Research Strategies for Field Entry and Data Collection in a Preschool Setting." in J. Green and C. Wallat (eds.) *Ethnography and Language in Educational Settings.* Norwood, N.J.: Ablex.

Cottrell, L. and R. Dymond. 1949. "The Empathic Responses: A Neglected Field for Research." *Psychiatry* 13: 355–359.

Couch, C. 1970. "Dimensions of Association in Collective Behavior Episodes." *Sociometry* 33(4): 457–471.

Coutu, W. 1951. "Role-playing vs. Role-taking: An Appeal for Clarification." *American Sociological Review* 16: 180–187.

Denzin, N. 1970. *The Research Act.* Chicago: Aldine.

————. 1972. "The Genesis of Self in Early Childhood." *The Sociological Quarterly* 13(Summer): 291–314.

————. 1973. *Children and Their Caretakers.* New Brunswick, N.J.: Transaction Books.

————. 1975. "Play, Games and Interaction: The Contexts of Childhood Socialization." *The Sociological Quarterly* 16: 458–478.

————. 1977. *Childhood Socialization.* San Francisco: Jossey-Bass.

————. 1980. "A Phenomenology of Emotion and Deviance." *Zeitschrift für Soziologie* 9(3): 251–261.

DeVries, R. 1970. "The Development of Role-taking as Reflected by the Behavior of Bright Average and Retarded Children in a Social Guessing Game." *Child Development* 41(September): 759–770.

Ellis, M.J. 1973. *Why People Play.* Englewood Cliffs, N.J.: Prentice-Hall.

Feffer, M.H. and V. Gourevitch. 1960. "Cognitive Aspects of Role-taking in Children." *Journal of Personality* 28: 383–396.

Fein, G.G. and A. Clarke-Stewart. 1973. *Day Care in Context.* New York: Wiley.

Feldman, D.H. 1980. *Beyond Universals in Cognitive Development.* Norwood, N.J.: Ablex.

Fine, G.A. 1979. "Small Groups and the Creation of Culture: Determinants of the Development of Idio Culture." *American Sociological Review* 44(October): 733–745.

Fine, G.A. and B. Glassner. 1979. "Participant Observation with Children." *Urban Life* 8(2): 153–174.

Flavell, J.H. 1968. *The Development of Role-Taking and Communication Skills in Children.* New York: Wiley.

Fletcher, R. 1971. *The Making of Sociology: A Study of Sociological Theory, Vol. 2: Developments*. London: Michael Joseph.

Garvey, C. 1977. *Play*. Cambridge: Harvard University Press.

Geer, B. 1967. "First Days in the Field." Pp. 372–398 in P. Hammond (ed.) *Sociologists At Work*. New York: Basic.

Geer, B., J. Haas, C. ViVona, S.J. Miller, C. Woods, and H.S. Becker. 1968. "Learning the Ropes: Situational Learning in Four Occupational Training Programs." Pp. 209–213 in I. Deutscher and E. Thompson (eds.) *Among the People: Encounters with the Poor*. New York: Basic.

Glassner, B. 1976. "Kid Society." *Urban Education* 11(1): 5–21.

Goffman, E. 1959. *Presentation of Self in Everyday Life*. New York: Doubleday.

———. 1963. *Behavior in Public Places*. New York: Free Press.

Gold, R. 1969. "Roles in Sociological Field Observation." Pp. 30–38 in G. McCall and J.L. Simmons (eds.) *Issues in Participant Observation*. Reading, Mass.: Addison-Wesley.

Goldman, B.D. and H.S. Ross. 1978. "Social Skills in Action: An Analysis of Early Peer Games." Pp. 177–212 in J. Glick and K.A. Clarke-Stewart (eds.) *The Development of Social Understanding*. New York: Gardner.

Gough, H.G. 1948. "A Sociological Theory of Psychopathy." *American Journal of Sociology* (March): 359–366.

Herron, R.E. and B. Sutton-Smith (eds.) 1971. *Child's Play*. New York: Wiley.

Hochschild, A. 1975. "The Sociology of Feeling and Emotion: Selected Possibilities." Pp. 280–307 in M.M. and R.M. Kanter (eds.) *Another Voice*. Garden City, N.Y.: Doubleday.

Hoffman, M. 1976. "Empathy, Role-taking, Guilt and Development of Altruistic Motives." in T. Lickona (ed.) *Moral Development and Behavior*. New York: Holt, Rinehart and Winston.

Hughes, E. 1958. *Men and Their Work*. Glencoe: Free Press.

———. 1960. *Introduction in Field Work by Buford Junker*. Chicago: University of Chicago Press.

Isaacs, S. 1952. *Social Development in Young Children*. London: Routledge and Kegan Paul.

James, W. 1890. *The Principles of Psychology in Two Volumes*. New York. Holt.

Joffe, C. 1973. "Taking Young Children Seriously." Pp. 101–116 in N. Denzin (ed.) *Children and Their Caretakers*. New Brunswick, N.J.: Transaction.

Kagan, J., R. Kearshley, and P. Zelazo. 1978. *Infancy: Its Place in Human Development*. Cambridge: Harvard University Press.

Kohlberg, L. 1969. "Stage and Sequence: The Cognitive Developmental Approach to Socialization." Pp. 347–480 in D.A. Goslin (ed.) *Handbook of Socialization Theory and Research*. Chicago: Rand.

Lewis, M. and L.A. Rosenblum. 1975. *Friendship and Peer Relations*. New York: Wiley.

Lickona, T. (ed.) 1976. *Moral Development and Behavior*. New York: Holt, Rinehart and Winston.

Lovell, K.A. 1959. "A Follow Up of Some Aspects of the Work of Piaget and Inhelder on the Child's Conception of Space." *British Journal of Educational Psychology* 29: 107–117.

Mandell, N. 1983. "Studying Children: The Field Worker's Challenge." Unpublished manuscript, Department of Sociology, York University, Toronto.

Manis, J.G. and B.N. Meltzer. 1978. *Symbolic Interaction: A Reader in Social Psychology*. Boston: Allyn and Bacon.

Markey, F. 1976. *Imaginative Behavior of Preschool Children*. New York: Arno.

Markey, J. 1928. *The Symbolic Process and Its Integration with Children*. New York: Harcourt, Brace.

Martin, W. 1976. *The Negotiated Character of the School*. Toronto: MacMillan.

Mead, G.H. 1932. *The Philosophy of the Present*. Charles Morris (ed.). La Salle: Open Court.

————. 1934. *Mind, Self and Society.* C. Morris (ed.). Chicago: University of Chicago Press.

————. 1938. *The Philosophy of the Act.* C. Morris (ed.). Chicago: University of Chicago Press.

————. 1964. *Selected Writings.* A. Reck (ed.). Indianapolis: Bobbs-Merrill.

McDermott, J. (ed.) 1973. *The Philosophy of John Dewey, Vol. 2: The Lived Experience.* New York: Putman.

Murphy, L.B. 1937. *Social Behavior and Child Personality.* New York: Columbia University Press.

Overton, W.F. and H.N. Reese. 1973. "Models of Development: Methodological Implications." in J.R. Nesselroadt and H.W. Reese (eds.) *Life-Span Developmental Psychology: Methodological Issues.* New York: Academic Press.

Parten, M.B. 1932. "Social Participation among Preschool Children." *Journal of Abnormal and Social Psychology* 27: 243–269.

Piaget, J. 1962. *Play, Dreams and Imitation in Childhood.* New York: Norton.

Piaget, J. and B. Inhelder. 1969. *The Psychology of the Child.* Trans. Helen Weaver. New York: Basic.

Polanyi, M. and H. Prosch. 1975. *Meaning.* Chicago: University of Chicago Press.

Provence, S., A. Naylor, and J. Patterson. 1977. *The Challenge of Day Care.* New Haven, Conn.: Yale University Press.

Reck, A. 1963. *Recent Philosophy: Studies of Ten Representative Thinkers.* New York: Pantheon.

Rosen, C. 1974. "The Effects of Sociodramatic Play on Problem-solving Behavior among Culturally Disadvantaged Preschool Children." *Child Development* 45: 920–927.

Rubin, K.H., T.L. Maioni, and M. Hornung. 1976. "Free Play Behaviors in Middle and Lower Class Preschoolers: Parten and Piaget Revisited." *Child Development* 47: 414–419.

Sampson E.E. 1978. "Scientific Paradigms and Social Values: Wanted: A Scientific Revolution." *Journal of Personality and Social Psychology* 36: 1332–1343.

Schaffer, R. 1977. *Mothering.* Cambridge: Harvard University Press.

Scheler, M. 1954 [1913]. *The Nature of Sympathy.* Trans. Peter Heath. W. Stark (Introduction). Hamden, Conn.: Archon Books.

Schutz, A. 1962. "The Problem of Social Reality." In M. Natanson (ed.) *Collected Papers, Vol. 1.* The Hague: Martinus Nijhoff.

Schwartzman, H. 1976. "The Anthropological Study of Children's Play." *Annual Review of Anthropology* 5: 289–328.

Selman, R. 1971. "Taking Another's Perspective: Role-taking Development in Early Childhood." *Child Development* 42: 1721–1734.

Selman, R. and D. Byrne. 1974. "A Structural-developmental Analysis of Levels of Role-taking in Middle Childhood." *Child Development* 45: 803–806.

Smilansky, S. 1968. *The Effects of Sociodramatic Play on Disadvantaged Children.* New York: Wiley.

Speier, M. 1976. "The Adult Ideological Viewpoint in Studies of Childhood." Pp. 168–186 in A. Skolnick (ed.) *Rethinking Childhood.* Boston: Little, Brown.

Spiro, M. 1965. *Children of the Kibbutz.* New York: Schocken.

Stern, D. 1977. *The First Relationship.* Cambridge: Harvard University Press.

Stone, G. 1970. "The Play of Little Children." Pp. 545–553 in G. Stone and H. Farberman (eds.) *Social Psychology Through Symbolic Interaction.* Waltham, Mass.: Ginn.

Stone, G. and H. Farberman. 1981. *Social Psychology Through Symbolic Interaction.* 2nd ed. New York: Wiley.

Strauss, A.L. 1959. *Mirrors and Masks.* Glencoe: Free Press.

————. 1963. "The Negotiated Order." Pp. 147–169 in E. Freidson (ed.) *The Hospital in Modern Society*. Glencoe: Free Press.

————. 1978. *Negotiations: Varieties, Contexts, Processes and Social Order*. San Francisco: Jossey-Bass.

Thomas, W.I. 1931. *The Unadjusted Girl*. Boston: Little, Brown.

Turiel, E. 1975. "The Development of Social Concepts." in D. DePalma and J. Foley (eds.). Hillsdale, N.J.: Lawrence Erlbaum.

Turner, R. 1956. "Role-taking, Role Standpoint and Reference Group Behavior." *American Journal of Sociology* (January): 316–328.

Vygotsky, L.S. 1962 [1927]. *Thought and Language*. Cambridge: MIT Press.

————. 1965. *Mind in Society*. Cambridge: MIT Press.

Weininger, O. 1979. *Play and Education*. Springfield, Ill.: Charles C. Thomas.

Restoring the Semblance of Order: Police Strategies in the Domestic Disturbance

Phillip W. Davis
Georgia State University

The study of third party intervention in private disorders has tended to emphasize the fateful and stigmatizing consequences of intervention for the person. Where private disorder exists and officials intervene, the interchange is usually viewed as rife with labeling potential and as a critical "turning point" or springboard for deviant careers (see, for example, Becker, 1963; Jackson, 1954; Spradley, 1970; Yarrow, 1955). Another view of the matter, however, is one which posits third party intervention as but one contingency among several which might transform the nature of social trouble. Intervention may or may not result in the application of particular deviant labels to the troublesome actor (Cavan, 1966; Daniels, 1970; Emerson and Messinger, 1977). From this perspective, agents of social control are often reluctant, for "reasons of their own," to initiate the processing of the rule-violator. It has been noted, for example, that psychiatrists may resist pressures to find disorder (Daniels, 1970), despite the common presumption of illness (Scheff, 1966). Similarly, parole agents may "bank" or store rather than report known violations (Irwin, 1970). The practicalities of enacting social control may dictate decisions of "inattention" even though the apparent needs of the client or merits of the case would seem to dictate official action.

This article is an examination of the interactive strategies employed by police who, as agents of social control, routinely deal with private disorder. For occupational reasons the police often seek to restore the "semblance" (Skolnick, 1966) of an order *status quo ante* in such encounters rather than extract, label, and process the troublesome person. The particular disorder which we will examine is commonly referred to as the domestic disturbance or family fight. The disturbance call is known to be distasteful for officers (Black, 1980; Lundman, 1974; Parnas, 1967; Rubenstein, 1973;

Reprinted from Symbolic Interaction, 6(2):261–278.

Wilson, 1968) but the strategies and tactics by which officers manage the assignment have been neglected. Black (1980) has analyzed police reactions in terms of broad control styles and Lundman (1974) notes an absence of conflict and violence in the encounter. But the sequential structure of the encounter has largely been ignored. The purpose of this paper is to examine: (1) the conceptual framework with which officers approach the encounter; (2) the control strategies used by officers to "contain" the call and take their leave; and (3) the implications of this analysis for an understanding of social disorder and official intervention. This paper will examine only those role strategies (see Lofland, 1976) which are pursued as an alternative to making an arrest. Following a discussion of methods, the paper will discuss the preconceptions of the assignment as an "opening gambit, " the several strategic axes pursued in managing the call, and the dynamics of leave-taking.

METHODS AND CONTEXT

The case materials for this study were gathered through six months of participant observation and depth interviews with the officers of a relatively small municipal police department. The municipality employed sixty-one sworn officers and was part of a large western metropolis. The community itself was primarily a middle class residential city with some light industry in the area. The chief granted access to his department after having made several statements in public about the need for "social science input" into police operations. A research role of observer-as-participant (Gold, 1958) was adopted in which most officers defined the researcher as a "criminology prof studying family fights." On one occasion the researcher was introduced by a sergeant to a lieutenant as ". . . our bleeding heart liberal," no doubt because of the "social work" tenor of the research topic.

Officers were interviewed across all shifts about their beliefs concerning domestic disturbance calls in general and about the details of particular calls they had recently been assigned. The log of radio calls and assignments was scanned daily for "318: Family" calls.[1] "318: Family" is a dispatchers' and officers' classification of a radio assignment covering domestic quarrels and disturbances. "318" (a pseudonumeral) is the section of the state penal code which covers disturbances of all sorts. Officers may be assigned, for example, a radio assignment coded "318: Party," "318: Barking Dog," or a "318: Loud Motorcycle." The initial coding of the call is a matter of dispatcher discretion and the call may later prove in reality to be another type of situation. Throughout the study, the "318: Family" was approached nominally, that is, according to the classifications of the police. Officers might note, for example, that even though they had been assigned a "318: Family" according to the log, the call was "not really a 318: Family." Perhaps it was a neighborhood dispute or "just a woman screaming at someone" instead. Conversely, officers would come forward with information about particular calls they had handled which were "really family fights" even though they had not been coded as such.

The actual "intervention" of officers in domestic disturbances was also observed directly. Observation of the encounter posed a few difficulties, especially when both disputants were present at the address. As will be discussed, a common tactic when both disputants are present is to talk to the disputants separately (two officers are usually assigned the call). I thus had to choose between the two small encounters, that is, whether at a given time to "listen in" on the exchange between the officer and the husband, or the other officer and the wife. I did not move back and forth between the parties in order to avoid creating a sense of coordination to the call and arousing suspicion by the citizens that something was "brewing." In doing so, of course, I did not have immediate access to both sets of negotiations and had to obtain a more complete picture after the call.

Data were thus derived from three sources; interviews, observations, and the department's log and records. In the final analysis, the officer's definition and classification of an assignment as a "family fight" was the one accepted for research purposes. A problem in accepting the officer's interpretation is that they probably tend to rule out "common-law" relationships as "real families." Furthermore, officers continually recap their assignments to one another and there is a danger in taking the officer's recap at face value. Rookie officers, especially, are wary of being observed and quizzed about their actions. Questions about "what happened" and what was said in the encounter were sometimes met with a description plus the officer's own evaluations (e.g., "We handled it very well!"). Despite these difficulties, it is believed that these three sources provide a more valid representation of police experiences, attitudes, and strategies in domestic disturbances than any one source taken alone.[2]

The sample of episodes upon which this analysis is based is not representative of all forms of police intervention in domestic disturbances. The selective concern was for those encounters which did not eventuate in arrest. Black (1980) notes that in his sample, one-fifth of the disputes were handled in a "penal" fashion and, of these, twenty-three percent led to arrest. Arrest is not too common an occurrence in disputes. For a discussion of the conditions which lead to arrest in domestic disturbances, the reader is referred to Black (1980) and Parnas (1967).

PREFERRED OUTCOMES AND OPENING GAMBITS

The routine intervention of municipal police in domestic disturbances has its own social organization and structure.[3] Officers carry with them a set of preconceptions about the types of actors and settings they are likely to encounter as well as the arrangements they would prefer to have established by the time of their departure. While there does not appear to be a "natural history" to the encounter, there are different temporally ordered concerns that the police have. From the officer's perspective, the encounter begins when they are assigned the call and approach the setting with preconceptions about what they will find. These preconceptions and the officers' mode of entering the home constitute what Cavan (1966) and Corzine and Kirby (1979) have called "opening gambits."

Officers harbor a preference for nonarrest in domestic disputes which shapes their initial stance or alignment towards the call. It is part of a conceptual package (Scheff, 1966) with which control agents approach and initially manage cases (see Davis, 1981;

Emerson and Pollner, 1978; Sudnow, 1966). The preference for nonarrest reflects the police officers' internalization of administrative priorities and their conceptions of what constitutes "real" police work. Nonarrest constitutes what Scheff (1963) has termed a preferred outcome. Preferred outcomes are those arrangements, circumstances, and decisions which agency workers value and pursue, given a particular type of assignment. They represent an overarching conception of the preferable mode of managing a case which is part of a larger "task sphere" (Hughes, 1971). The outcome preferred by police in domestic encounters might be termed "containment." Containment is a working policy of nonarrest and "order restoration."

There are several reasons behind this nonarrest policy. First, as Parnas (1961) has noted, in training officers are told to arrange an "adjustment" or "settlement" of the dispute, although it is rarely made clear just what that adjustment should be. Second, the widespread understanding among control agents is that the citizen's sense of his or her own victimization is one which will quickly dissipate. The aggravation or grievance which lies behind a complainant's possible demands for arrest are likely to be viewed as inappropriate and organizationally unrealistic. Officers believe that disputants' stories are likely to be contrived and self-serving. Perhaps prompted by the wish for vengeance in a fight which they may have originally started, disputants who demand the arrest are thought to be subject to sudden changes of mind. In short, it is thought that because of the family's emotional and economic ties grievance will quickly evaporate. The citizen's anger is thought to have been quickly gained and it will be quickly lost, resulting in wasted report and filing time if an arrest has been made (see Davis, 1981).

A third reason behind the containment policy has to do with the assumption that the family fight is an inevitable result of the condition of intimacy. The phenomenon is thought to be so common that to make many arrests, even though technically justified, would pose a burden upon department-court relations and would suggest that the individual officer has become overly concerned with trivial affairs. The conflict and its violence are thus normalized by family members (Gelles, 1974) and by intervening third parties. While the couple is thought to have a marital problem which transcends the call, officers are concerned with the demand condition (Bittner, 1967) that something be done. Fourth, the family disturbance is typically viewed as a situation of double jeopardy for the officer. They have only a tentative sense of what to expect and they believe family calls are "hard to do right." The meaning of handling the call "right" is never clear for the uniformed patrol officer. At the same time, officers define the domestic disturbance as dangerous (Black, 1980; Davis, 1981; Parnas, 1967). Officers believe that arresting a husband, for example, can prompt the wife to "turn" on the officer. Traditional academy training is likely to emphasize the dangerousness of the call (Parnas, 1967).

In a more literal sense, the opening gambit used by police is to approach the call in pairs and, if the conflict appears to have subsided, enter the home space of the disputants with cautious nonchalance.

> The officers approached the screen door from either side and knocked. Inside, a
> couple was seated on a couch and waved the officers in. The man was clad in a

white T-shirt and jockey shorts and the woman was in a bathrobe and slippers. One of the two officers said, 'I understand you've been having some problems .'

Caution may outweigh "cool" (see Lyman, and Scott, 1968), however, if there are signs of danger of pending violence.

> The mother called the police saying that her son was threatening her. Robedo drove up in front of the home where the teenage boy was standing in the driveway. The boy saw Robedo who reached into a trash heap and pulled out a slat of wood. Robedo groaned and said we had better wait. He radioed the assigned back-up officer and asked his location. When the back-up arrived the three of us approached the boy.

In low-income neighborhoods where disputants are more likely to have called the police themselves (Black, 1980), the citizen will usually initiate the exchange herself by telling her story. In an extensive analysis of the structural characteristics of disputes handled by police, Black (1980) notes that the complainant is alone when the police arrive in about one-third of all disputes. The complainant is absent in less than one-tenth of the cases. "True disputes," where both parties to the conflict are present and where the conflict is in progress, are to be found in one-half of the dispute assignments handled by police. The strategies and tactics pursued by police to "restore order" and containment will now be examined.

STRATEGIC AXES IN MANAGING THE 318: FAMILY

From the officers' perspective, the restoration of "order" consists of the manipulation of the setting, the actors, and the situation in a way which enables a justifiable exit. "Order" in a family dispute consists of a relationship between the disputants, their audience, and the residential environment in which volume is reduced, physical contact is obstructed, complainants are assuaged, and reintervention appears unnecessary. In this sense officers try to restore the semblance or signs of order to the police-citizen encounter and not to the domestic unit. They pursue a containment of the domestic crisis by addressing the disputant's definition of the events, the proximity of the disputants, the disputant's definition of police action, and the disputant's definition of remedy.[4]

Dissuasion: Managing Definitions of Crisis and Criminality

The reporting party in a domestic disturbance will often initially adhere to a criminal definition of the situation. This definition entails a description of some preceding "deed" (Goffman, 1971) committed by the opposing party in a "dispute." The preceding events may include issues in the family's distant and not so distant past, e.g., a history of beatings. These preceeding deeds are depicted in terms of their worst possible implications for the alleged offender. The actor's version of the disputatious deeds will usually be offered as an account for having invoked the police.

But the police are less concerned with the substance of the grievance than with the family member's demands upon them as officers. To this extent the officers' attitudes towards family disturbances reflects what Bittner (1967b) describes as an "attenuated regard for culpability."

When family members profer a criminal definition of the deeds, the officer is likely to pursue a strategy by which to discourage, or dissuade the citizen from demands for an arrest. Various lines of reasoning are employed as the officer points out the undesirability of making an arrest, pressing charges and filing a complaint. The bureaucratic and organizational base of that undesirability is rarely laid bare for the citizens. Officers more frequently fall back upon the ostensible inconvenience that formal procedures would present for the citizen.

> The wife sat at the dining room table sobbing and rubbing her bruised elbow from the beating she said she received from her husband as he grabbed the daughter and fled from the house. She said that her lawyer had told her to get a restraining order if her husband caused trouble as they planned on a divorce. She did not have the order yet, ' . . . I guess I should get one.' 'Yes,' the officer told her, ' . . . that would be the thing to do here.' The officers turned lo leave but the wife said, 'But he's got my little girl, and he's drunk. She could be hurt or killed. And he beat me up, and now you're telling me there's nothing you can do; now what are you going to do about this?' The officer told her that there was nothing they could do about the daughter since the husband was entitled to have her. The beating could be a criminal matter however; that was assault. A report could be taken and she could press criminal charges.
>
> The wife paused and said, 'Well, I guess there's nothing else I can do. I'll have to press charges on him.' One of the officers said, 'But if you do that mam, you'll have to go to court and testify on this. Are you sure that's what you want to do?' The other officer told her that often people change their minds on these things and later wish they hadn't filed charges: 'We can't take the report if you don't prosecute. Are you willing to do all that?'
>
> Outside, one of the officers said, 'Report! I'm sure we're going to take report on that!' (What do you make of all that?) 'That, that was all horse (. . .)! It was just nothing; they'll get over it or get divorced.'

The police expression that "nothing can be done" can be seen as an attempt to "beg off" (Schatzman and Strauss, 1973) the call and avoid the incriminating implications of the citizen's sense that "nothing has been done."

Officers may dissuade the citizen from pursuing a criminal interpretation of their plight by pointing to the essentially "civil" character of the problem. When police designate the citizen's grievance as civil in nature they are proffering the understanding that the disputant has contacted an inappropriate agency. By offering the citizen an alternative role (civil plaintiff as opposed to criminal complainant), officers shift the locus of administrative responsibility to the civil court machinery. They distance themselves from the helper role and inform the citizen that the police are not the appropriate benefactor (Wiseman, 1970) for the client beneficiary. In one case the police were told by a husband that he and his wife were getting a divorce and that his wife had taken furniture from their house.

Officer:	'Was anything stolen?'
Man:	'I don't know . . . and I don't want to be held responsible for it. I didn't take anything and it's gone.'
Officer:	'Now look, this is then a civil manner, that's civil, because the house and the furniture all belong to the both of you . . . and if no crime has been committed then it's a civil matter and there's absolutely nothing we can do about it!'

Officers may attempt to capitalize on existing legal arrangement to dissuade the complaining party from a criminal interpretation of the disturbance. Some disputants, for example, already have court-issued restraining orders which usually require the husband to stay away from the home. Wives will then ask the police to evict or arrest on the basis of the husband having apparently violated the terms of the order. A spouse may have returned to the home for property or to visit the children, and the disputant with the restraining order may invoke the order in complaining to the police. The police will then tend to view the family as already in a stage of active dissolution and the "returning" party is likely to be regarded by the police as an interloper. While they refute any claims upon their role to arrest on the basis of the order, they may allude or appeal to the terms of the order in getting the spouse to leave. Officers may tell the returning spouse that his "case" in the divorce will be weakened if he violates the order.

> The restraining order indicated that the husband was not to be in the house under any circumstances. Bernard told her that he could not enforce the order because that was the job of the Marshal's office. The husband claimed that he still had some of his things to pick up at the house and that the wife 'had let him in the door' when he knocked. The wife then claimed that he didn't have any more of his things there and that he was not supposed to be there because of the order. She wanted him 'out.' The husband listened as officer Bernard told him that he was in direct violation of the restraining order. While they could not arrest him, the Marshals could, and the mere fact that the police had to come out to the house would go badly against him in court with the judge.

The strategic axis of dissuasion often resembles the process of "cooling out the mark" (Goffman, 1952). Goffman suggests that the actor may lose a role in three basic ways. He may either be promoted out of it or may abdicate from the role in which he has failed. The third way is to " . . . be involuntarily deprived of his position or involvement and made in turn something that is considered a lesser thing to be" (1952: 454). Officers in the 318: Family provide alternatives to the victim/complainant role by suggesting that the case is civil in nature and that another agency is the appropriate recipient of their claim. In this sense, claimants to the role of criminal victim are often *encouraged to abdicate* that role by having their crisis redefined by the police as a civil rather than criminal issue. Officers extend a "second chance" to have the police deal with the predicament ("call us back") and also "stall" (Goffman, 1952) the party by directing them to another agency of redress. The civil rather than criminal definition provides an alternative whereby citizens might more easily accept their failure in seeking a criminal definition.

Severance: Enacting Separation and Eviction in Addressing Disputant Proximity

Given the objective of containing the call and avoiding an arrest, officers approach the domestic crisis with an apriori assumption that it is best to "separate" the disputants and talk to them individually. Under the presumption that it takes "two to tango," officers seek to dissociate the disputants from each other in restoring the semblance of order. As a strategic axis, severance takes essentially two directions in the domestic disturbance. Officers will separate the couple and distance them from each other in the home. They may also "evict" one of the disputants. In both cases the parties to the disturbance are spatially and symbolically separated from one another.

Severance as Managing Disputant Proximity

Whether or not the disputants still appear to be absorbed in conflict, the police will attempt to physically and symbolically separate the disputants by relocating them in the home. The disputants are taken from each other and escorted to different areas of the house. The front porch is frequently selected as one interview site because of its accessibility to the living room where the police-citizen encounter in the 318: Family usually begins. The porch most closely resembles the working province of the police, that is the "streets." It is somewhat visible to the public and not entirely a part of the "home." Front porches represent that space affixed to a house where persons are neither fully in nor completely out of the home place. Having been placed physically and symbolically closer to the street, persons might more easily be evicted, having already, in a sense, begun their journey. The officers remain within hailing distance of one another and usually are within view of one another as they take up these positions. The disputants' access to each other is significantly restricted and their control made easier by this spatial arrangement. In the more remote areas of the home might lie weapons, sleeping children, potential confederates, points of exit, telephones, and doors with locks.

Once on the porch an officer might make use of its public visibility to calm a distraught or shouting disputant. In the following case, the officer appealed to the interest of the wife in keeping the matter "quiet."

> One officer looked around and, stepping towards the front door, said to the wife, 'Come out here.' They stepped out onto the front porch. The officer asked the wife what she wanted them to do. She said that she wanted the husband arrested. He told her that it was as much his house as it was hers and that he 'seems OK now.' The woman began to sob and protest loudly. The officer told her to 'relax and get hold of yourself. You don't want the neighbors to see all this do you?'

Separating the parties for individual face-to-face encounters is not always problem free. Usually the couple will allow themselves to be dispersed to different locations within the home, but on occasion one disputant will try to get back into the discussion between the other officer and the other disputant. In the following interview excerpt the couple was well known to the officers because of their earlier disputes.

> Mickey is a painter going with this broad for seven years. He has a temper. Before, the other time, he had hit her and broke her ribs. He was arrested then. She wanted him out. We told him he might go to jail and he kept telling her that he would marry her soon. There were about six kids running around. One of the boys had called the police. This is all a recurring thing. When she had gone to the hospital before, the day after she got out Mickey had gone and kicked her door in and then tore the screen door off. Tonight he kept saying 'If I wanted to, I could go in there (the bedroom) right now and bust her ribs. I could bust her head open.' Mickey would flare up each time the woman would come out from the bedroom. I told her to stay in there. She kept saying over and over, 'I just want you out of here, Mickey.' I told Mickey, 'Look, you can be cool or you can get beat up and go to jail.' Mickey kept saying he didn't want to get beat up, and he said he didn't want to go to jail. He'd calm down and then blow up again. When the woman would come out, I had to tell her. 'Look, he blows up when you come out, now get back in there and stay.' He'd keep blowing up and with us in the middle.

The disputants first bound by a cohabitative relationship and secondly by their conflict, are symbolically and physically divided and addressed in isolation. Officers utilize existing architectural resources of the home space in enacting a strategy of severance.

Having separated the parties and having listened to their grievance to see "what they have," officers typically reconvene either in the living room or on the porch to confer. One officer will simply move over to the other to confer and it is at this point that a decision to enact what might be termed a "make-leave" policy is often made.

Severance as Outcasting

The domestic disturbance often leads to a working policy of eviction.[5] The co-presence of the disputants can be shattered more directly and more effectively if one of the partes is literally evicted from the home place. But just as the separation of disputants can pose practical problems, the nonlegal eviction of someone from their own home can involve considerable labor.

A successful exiling usually requires several things. The outcasting agent must designate the terms of exile (e.g., length of ban, place of relocation), portray himself as having the right or obligation to exile the designated party, and portray the outcast as able to meet the terms of exile. Eviction is often depicted as a lenient option available to the citizen in light of more legalistic alternatives. It is a nonlegal strategy in which citizens are told to take a walk around the block to "cool off" or leave the house for the night. Believing the conditions which led to their intervention to be fleeting in nature, officers may enforce a working policy of "make-leave" to allow the disputants time away from one another.

Which disputant is made to leave and the manner in which he or she is made to leave depend upon which party is placing demands upon the officers to take action, which party appears to remain the more potentially disruptive actor, and which party appears to be most susceptible to various reasoning techniques. It is when an officer enacts a make-leave policy that citizens come to believe that the officer has "taken sides." And yet "taking sides" in the 318: Family depends less on the respective moral and legal merits of each disputant's case, story, or position, and more upon the visibility of strategic alternatives most likely to produce a ready halt to the call. It appears as though a "side" were being taken but the interests of the officers are oriented to the most expeditious arrangement. Officers are guided by a greater orientation to situations than to individuals (Bittner, 1967a).

Enacting the make-leave working policy is neither so simple or expedient as it might seem. Officers try to allocate the outcast role by attaching the quality of reasonableness to the departure. The disputant may resist the allocation or may assume the outcast role under protest. Officers appeal to the understanding that the outcast role is of limited duration.

> The call was for a '318: Family, returning husband.' The officer in the living room with the wife said to the officer on the porch, 'He's going!' He told the husband to give him his keys and asked where he was living now. The husband told him that this was his house and that he had only been away for a short while. 'Whose house is it?' the officer asked. The husband said that it was his. 'Who pays the rent?' the officer asked. The husband replied, 'I do. I give her money, lots of money, to pay the rent.' The officer asked him if he had any money 'on him.' The husband touched his hip pocket and said that he had about twenty dollars. 'Well,' the officer said, 'that's enough to spend the night somewhere else,' he was told. 'Maybe tomorrow you can come back and talk it out, but tonight you stay away.'

When officers decide to enact the make-leave policy, they may first try to reason with the party in terms of their right to be present in the home. Failing these reasoning themes, the officer may more directly "order" the party from the home. By questioning the parties about property and ownership, officers appeal to the social meanings of private property and territorial priority in outcasting the actor.[6]

> Officers spoke with the woman and her husband on the street corner, finally understanding that the relationship was, as one officer put it, common law. One officer spoke with the "husband."

> Officer: Who's car is that? Is it hers?
> Man: No, she's going to buy it; it's not hers.
> Officer: Then it's yours?
> Man: No, it belongs to a friend of mine; she's going to buy it from him.
> Officer: So then it's going to be hers, it's sort of hers. Who owns the house? (Another officer nodded towards the woman) Then she owns the house, and the car is hers, so you really don't have any right to stay.

fficers may or may not try to *ensure* the departure of the disputant. Usually they will get exiled actor's keys to the home, quiz him as to an available place to go for the night, tell him not to return until morning, and stand by while the party leaves. They may threaten him with arrest if he returns. But the eviction is never as complete or final as it might seem. They oust the person from the immediate encounter, hoping that he will not return. But they will not follow up the outcasting by checking later. They realize that the person may return and that there is nothing short of arrest to prevent this. Officers are aware of their own "intervention effects," realizing that having come to the house in response to a disturbance call may further fuel the dispute. As one officer said after evicting the husband:

> I'd better stay here until he leaves. He'll just go back and he'd beat the (. . .) out of her after all that.

In this case "staying here" consisted of remaining on the sidewalk for a few minutes until the husband disappeared around the corner.

Allocating the outcast role in the 318: Family usually involves not only designating the time of egress but the tentative site which the emigrating disputant should seek. Officers elicit or construct alternative locations as they "disperse" disputants. They make use of the emergent availability of the houses and apartments of friends and relatives in order to point the outcast on his way. They will also send the outcast to hotels, motels, and boarding facilities such as the YMCA. If the 318: Family involves a "returning" spouse who already has an alternative residence then the choice of an ostensible site is made easier.

> In an interview the officer said that the couple in the 318: Family was already divorced but the wife had gone to the husband's place and was 'making threats.' The husband 'complained that the wife was always throwing tantrums. Tonight the husband had been sitting at home drinking and stacking the empty beer cans in a pyramid. The wife knocked over the stack of beer cans. He smacked her, and knocked her on to the floor. The wife was hysterical for some time and wouldn't listen to us. The husband had been drinking also but was more cool about it. We dispersed her back home and she got into her car.'

Severance refers to the physical separation of the disputants and the symbolic diffusion of the conflict. Eviction as a working police strategy stems from the officer's wish to avoid reintervention and symbolically designates one of the disputants as an outcast and offender.

Cooptation as Seduction and Client Conversion

In addition to dealing with disputant proximity, officers will also address the actor's definition of the police by pursuing a strategy of cooptation. They may try to exact promises, cajole cooperation, and seduce sentiments. Cooptation refers to police efforts to manage the actor's definition of the rightful presence of the officer.

While not dependent upon the citizen's sympathy and "understanding" of their work, police often seek to account for what might appear as "inaction." This effort is directed towards shaping the family member's views of the officer as harried, over-worked, or subject to a hierarchy of demands. An officer will try to convince disputants that their deeds, claims, and demands are of low priority from the police perspective. Officers thus socialize or train the actor in the ways of the police and the demands to which they are subject. In some ways this process resembles the "apostolic function" of physicians who may seek to convert the patient to the medical perspective (Balint, 1957).[7]

> The Chicana wife, the husband, and the officers met on the sidewalk near the home. Officer Biggins told the man, 'In the morning you two can talk it over. Maybe by then things'll be OK.' As the wife turned towards home she said 'He's no good; he's with women. I seen them.' The husband scowled saying, 'Bull! That's not true! She's jealous. She's not good for the kids.' As the wife walked off she said something in Spanish. Alone now with the husband, Biggins asked him what she had said. 'She said that I was going to go off and spend the night with another woman.' Biggins told him, 'So go off with another woman. Just don't come back here tonight since we'll have to come out here again. We'd have to come back out here and we're pretty busy tonight.'

In addition to citing the irrelevance of the call to "real" police work, officers may also attempt to convert the disputants to the police perspective by pleading with them or exacting "personal promises" from them. They may ask citizens to "promise" that they will or will not take certain courses of action once the police leave.

> The husband and wife had struggled at the gas pump of a filling station after having argued about how much money to spend on their evening out. The wife had grabbed the gas hose from the husband and doused him and their two children and then threatened to set fire to the husband. The officer separated the couple, putting the husband in the back seat of the back-up unit which soon arrived, and after listening to the wife tell how the husband had grabbed all of their money, tried to coax the husband into giving the wife back the money since it has been cashed from her pay check. The husband refused and the officer then suggested he give the wife back only half the money as this would 'be fair.' The wife was taken to a nearby hospital and the husband calmed down, saying that he was going to go straight to the hospital and see how his wife was. The officer then asked the husband to 'promise me' that you won't go to the hospital. The husband at first insisted on going and again the officer asked the husband to 'promise' him that he wouldn't go, fearing that the fracas would begin anew at the hospital.

Coaxing is perhaps the epitomy of what Lundman (1974) noted to be a polite or civil tone to most police-domestic encounters. The decrease in authority is regarded by police as acceptable in the quest for expeditious order.

Pawning Off

Officers may create the semblance of order, peace, and official action and yet still pursue the preferred outcome of containment by pawning off the call onto another help source. Continuing to work against the potential accusation of inaction, officers may advise the disputants to get help. The advice may appear gratuitous, but the police may claim it is "all that can be done."

The substance of pawning off takes several forms. Advice which might otherwise appear illogical, partial, or even illegal might be given in hopes of calming or appeasing the couple.

> The husband had called in fear that his wife had attempted suicide by taking several sedatives in the midst of one of their fights. She was still quite conscious. The couple was known to the officer. The officer said, 'She was complaining about her husband: 'I've had it with him! And I want the marriage annulled.' Annulled! They've been married twenty some years and she's talking about annulment! So I told her that I didn't want to keep coming out here, that we have a lot of calls to handle, and I told her to go ahead and start to have the marriage annulled.

The advice may also be especially judgmental, flip, cursory, or glib. Officers will give nonlegal commonsense advice which outside the encounter may resemble kibitzing.

Officers may also provide citizens with a sense of remediated future by invoking fourth parties. The fourth party is likely to be an agency or person which the officer portrays as available, capable, and appropriate. The officer in this way makes use of the resources of his own construction and enlists the witting or unwitting aid of others in handling the call and expediting an exit. There is little the officer has to lose in advising, recommending, or telling the disputants to "see" someone else.

The fourth party may be a volunteer who makes himself or herself available to the police and the disputants. Other family members, friends, relatives, and, on occasion, bystanders, may offer to supervise, watch over, or aid the disputants in handling the situation without further service from the police.

> The seventeen year old son had taken the car without the mother's permission. He got a flat tire and the mother, who was pissed off, drives up behind him and takes the keys away from him while reprimanding him. The boy had abandoned the car when we got there. Another son who was there said he would mediate between the mother and the boy.

Other family members are already in the home, and have access to the disputants. Their partiality is relatively inconsequential for the officers so long as they have not participated directly in the dispute. The working bias is that family disputes are characteristically between two persons and it is this wrangling dyad that concerns the officer. The superficial responsibility for a disputant may be "pawned off" onto another family member.

Actual referrals to other agencies are rare and, with the exceptions of "4250's" (mental cases) and "Title K's" (immigration cases), do not involve paper work.

Officers usually do not provide disputants with the specific names and phone numbers of referral agencies but may conversationally refer the disputants to any of several agencies or helping institutions in pawning off the call. Bittner (1967b) discovered that the police carry rather conventional and nontechnical understandings of insanity and mental illness. Police similarly view marital conflicts as best treated by conventional helping professions. One officer described a recent 318: Family he had helped handle.

> The husband was separated from the wife after having been married twenty years. They were always fighting and now there was a Casanova living next door. The husband and wife owned several adjacent houses, and the young buck had moved into one of them. The husband didn't like this. The young buck was out of work and the wife told him to paint a room and she would pay for it. The husband now accused the young buck of flirting with his wife. . . .When the police arrived the young buck was on the husband's back beating the (. . .) out of him. The wife came out for a few minutes after Cane had taken the husband aside. Gate advised her that maybe a neutral person, a psychiatrist, a counselor, could help if they could afford one.

By advising the disputants to seek help, officers appear to do their duty to "do something." The ostensible responsibility for improving the current situation is shifted from the shoulders of the police to some fourth party. Whether the fourth party is called, intervenes, or actually performs a service for the domestic unit tends to be of little concern to the individual patrol officer who is pawning off the call.

"GETTING OUT" AS LEAVE-TAKING

If the bulk of the labor involved in handling the call is aimed towards an expeditious exit, a final word must be said concerning the closing of the encounter and the techniques used to get out. If the police "manage the call" more than they "settle the dispute," how do officers "take their leave" and terminate the call?

Getting out of the home, getting away from the disputants, and "clearing" their unit with dispatch by radio are the actions which bring the call to a close. Officers will then view the *call* as over, however much the *disturbance,* dispute, and plight of the citizens remains. Believing that essentially unpredictable contingencies determine repeat visits, the police "clear" the call knowing that they may or may not return to face the disputants again.

Continuing their efforts to avoid the potential interpretation by the citizens that "nothing has been done," officers employ a variation of the leave-taking ritual (see Goffman, 1963: 110–111). They do not feel compelled to abide by the rituals of civility that might be found among equals in taking one's leave. They take their leave by further cooling out the disputant in a final display of ostensible concern. The most common tack here is to tell the complaining disputant that she should "call again" if the other disputant returns or causes further trouble. They convey the sense that they are willing to honor some future claim upon their services.

> A mother-in-law and her son were present at the address. She had called the police because the ex-wife of her son had parked her car outside their house and screamed at her. The ex-wife had a court order saying that the husband could not see the kids. The ex-wife had left by the time we arrived. I told the mother-in-law to call back if she returned.

Another part of the leave-taking ritual is when the officer asks in summary fashion whether "everything is going to be OK?" or if there's "anything more we can do for you?" Leave-taking civility might be severely truncated as higher priority radio calls arise. The officers will not be assigned another call until they have "cleared" with dispatch, formally indicating that they are now available for another assignment. But should "something good go down" nearby, they may informally take on a back-up role and go to the more important call.

> The handling of the 318: Family was interrupted by the portable radio of the officer talking to the wife on the porch. Another unit was being assigned a '211: just happened (robbery); possible shots fired.' The address was nearby and the officer called to his partner in the living room with the husband. 'We got a call.' Turning to the wife he asked, 'You going to be OK on this? We got an emergency call and have to leave right away. But if you have any more problems give us a call.' The officers ran from the porch.

Officers will likely clear the call with the phrase "All parties advised," or simply "Parties advised." This is the most common clearance category, regardless of the strategic axis which they have pursued in handling the call. Whether or not the officers have actually "advised" the disputants, they cite the phrase for the benefit of the record. Unless an arrest or crime report is filled out by the officer, this log entry becomes the only official record of the call, its handling, and its outcome. As the above discussion suggests, the formal designation of police activity bears little resemblance to the rather complex series of interactions between officers and disputants.

DISCUSSION

A normative or applied model of "family-crisis intervention" by police depicts the work of the officers as revolving around the ostensible "problem" of the family, i.e., the "crisis." We have examined, on the other hand, the ways in which officers in fact address "the call." The directive to render a "settlement" provides the officer with neither the working tactics nor the evaluative criteria by which to judge the effectiveness of those tactics. According to an applied model of "peace-keeping," situations are "diagnosed" and remedied (see Coffey, 1974). In practice, however, the management of the call consists of manipulating the social environment such that the *semblance* of order becomes apparent. Restoring or generating the semblance of order is important in that it is a demonstration for the citizens that the officers have "done something" and it reduces the likelihood that the officers will have to return.

Control agents routinely encounter persons and situations which symbolize danger. These "symbolic assailants" (Skolnick, 1966) are approached by agents with an unusual degree of caution. The signs which officers recognize as likely preludes to violence are part of their typical knowledge (Emerson and Pollner, 1978; Sudnow, 1965) about people, places, and situations. Officers associate domestic disturbances with violence, danger, and volatile complainants (Davis, 1981). While for Skolnick (1966) the concept of the symbolic assailant comprises a ". . . perceptual shorthand to identify certain kinds of people" (p. 45), the danger thought to lie within family fights is a quality of certain kinds of situations. Severance represents one strategy by which to neutralize the symbolic assailant.

When official third parties harbor conventional rather than esoteric theories of disorder, it seems likely that the encounter will proceed somewhat smoothly and devoid of violence and conflict. Lundmand (1974) notes that most domestic encounters with police proceed on this level. It also appears likely that such formulations would be slow to change, given their prevalence in the surrounding society as well as within the occupational subculture. It appears as though containment strategies tend to reaffirm control agent folk theories about disorder. As more labor is invested in pursuing nonarrest or containment, the view that such assignments do not and should not lead to further processing is reaffirmed.

The four strategic axes represent the officer's efforts to allocate non-legalistic roles to the citizen-alters; citizens will often thwart those efforts by insisting to some degree that they are indeed "victims." They may offer a range of evidence such as bruises, injuries, and restraining orders to attest having suffered an illegality or at least an injustice. Officers are more willing to subscribe to the injustice of the reporting party's plight than to acknowledge the illegality. This tack in containing disorder may have consequences for the label or definition applied to persons involved. Should the citizen pursue a referral to some other control agency (e.g., lawyer or psychiatrist) the problem may be defined in terms suitable to the new agency. If officers are effective in their dissuasive efforts, the trouble is more likely to remain free of criminal definitions and labels. Should citizens resort to a civil rather than criminal definition of the situation they might reframe the trouble in the form of restraining orders.

In many ways the conditions of successful exile in the domestic disturbance are similar to the conditions of a successful degradation or denunciation ceremony. Garfinkel (1956) and Emerson (1969) have examined the nature of these conditions. The conditions revolve around the ability of the degrading and denouncing parties to represent themselves as above reproach and as representing a larger and conventional constituency. Yet in the case of the outcast there does not appear to be the complete transformation of identity as in the case of the degraded person, nor the need to demonstrate the exhaustion of alternative dispositions as in the case of the denounced. This paper has examined the several tactics employed in the extralegal eviction of residents and nonresidents from private territory. Informal eviction of troublesome parties from commercial and public settings is a traditional form of social control. Tavern staff for example, have usually mastered the techniques of keeping close wraps on routine trouble by employing eviction (Cavan, 1966; Spradley and Mann, 1975). Eviction of troublesome patrons is pursued by staff in theaters, restaurants, and libraries. Department store staff evict more than they prosecute (Cameron, 1964). The invocation of third parties such as the police to effect eviction usually represents an escalation of the trouble's level of seriousness (Emerson and Messinger, 1977). The strategies and tactics utilized in informal and formal eviction of troublesome actors by inhouse and third party agents requires further attention and analysis.

The distinction between order and the semblance of order is an important one. As control agents with widespread "trouble-shooting" responsibilities (see Aubert, 1965), police officers seek to impose standardized symbols of order upon the actors and setting symbols which reflect bureaucratic rather than therapeutic requirements. Quietude, separation, and acquiescence become the cues which agents believe to indicate "order enough." Actors involved in the disorderly situation, however, are likely to view order in terms of future as well as present trouble. For the police, order consists of a situational arrangement which they can justifiably leave after having generated an impression that something has been done. For the actors involved, especially the complaining party, "real order" is more likely to extend beyond the present situation into a remediated future. This latter version of order is more likely to be generated by third party interveners with specific rather than general trouble-shooting responsibilities. Order which extends into a remediated future is more likely to comprise the labor of control agents with a therapeutic rather than enforcement ideology. The goal of containment places emphasis upon the semblance of order as opposed to order which extends beyond the encounter.

The fact that police officers often try to comply with citizen demands has not gone unnoticed (see, for example, Black, 1979, 1980). But the grievance of a complaining party (beatings, drunken husband, disobedient children, philandering spouse, etc.) is either irrelevant or secondary to the actor's demands or wishes. Officers are more reactive than proactive as control agents, and in disputes they react to the demands of citizens more than to the grievance or complaint *per se*. The grievance is viewed as the manageable part of the underlying domestic disorder which is unmanageable. Attending to the grievance would be doing something *for* the person (see Hughes, 1971). But the officer's concern for the citizen's demand reflects their interest in doing something *to* the situation. Officers define the trouble underlying the grievance as lying outside their occupational jurisdiction.

ACKNOWLEDGMENTS

The author thanks Robert M. Emerson and Ralph Turner for their help on this work in its earlier stages, and the anonymous reviewers of *Symbolic Interaction*.

NOTES

1. "318" is a pseudonumber to further assure some degree of anonymity for the state under study. Pseudonyms have also been used throughout the paper.

2. For extensive reviews of the use of field methods in the study of police see McCall (1978) and Van Maanen (1978).

3.   The police response to the family disturbance has been examined primarily in evaluative terms. In this tradition (see, for example, Bard, 1970; Bard and Zacker, 1971; Coffey, 1974), the police role is examined, criticized as part of an attempt to heighten the sensitivity and improve the communicative skills of individual officers. Accused of confounding the problem of family violence (and of running too great a risk of being armed themselves), the police are encouraged to devote more time and greater resources to their "crisis intervention" techniques. Police "intervention" is treated in normative terms and refers to the steps officers should take in the diagnosis and solution of family problems. Our concern here, however, is to examine the presuppositions held by police and to analyze the strategies by which they intervene as a *matter of course* rather than as part of a prescriptive package.

4.   Black distinguishes between penal, compensatory, therapeutic, and conciliatory styles of social control (Black, 1976). In nearly half of all "true disputes," Black (1980: 131) claims that the police use a combination of conciliatory and penal styles, that is, they ". . . make an effort to find a solution satisfactory to both partes, but at the same time they relate to the conflict partly in terms of who is to blame. . . " Black further distinguishes between modes of conciliation, believing conciliation to consist of passive reaction, mediation, arbitration, emotional support, and referral to a nonpolice agency. Mediation was the most frequent form of conciliation (45% of the cases), followed by arbitration (30%), and passive reaction (little or no positive action, 23%). One percent of the conciliation cases were referred to a nonpolice agency. The penal style of social control incorporates arrest, eviction, threat of arrest, and scolding.

5.   Black (1980: 133) uses the term "situational banishment," but does not discuss the interactive labor involved .

6.   Should an officer feel it inexpedient for the husband "to go." they will appeal to the *same* themes they utilize in eviction. They may tell the wife that the husband has an equal right to be in the house and that they do not have the power to "throw him out of his own house." Officers make use of the meanings of rightful territorial presence and their own authority to issue proclamations of right-of-presence. Wives might thus be dissuaded from insisting that the husband be ejected.

7.   Balint (1957) in an examination of the doctor-patient relationship found that decisions which are presumed to be the exclusive prerogative of the physician, such as diagnoses, are in fact an interactive product. Physicians were found to serve an "apostolic function" whereby they would attempt to convert the client to the particular view of the illness and its remedy. Physicians were found to be "apostolic" primarily in instances where their own practice was dependent upon the good will of the patient, i.e., private practice. Conversion efforts were not as likely in county hospitals and community clinics. While police are not directly dependent upon the good will of their clients, they nonetheless will seek to convert the citizen to their perspective and similarly perform an apostolic or proselytizing function.

REFERENCES

Aubert, V. 1965. *The Hidden Society.* Totowa, N.J.: Bedminster Press.

Balint, M. 1957. *The Doctor, His Patient, and the Illness.* New York: International Universities, Inc.

Bard, M. 1970. *Training Police as Specialists in Family Crisis Intervention.* Washington, D.C.: U.S. Government Printing Office.

Bard, M. and J. Zacker. 1971. "The Prevention of Family Violence: Dilemmas of Community Intervention." *Journal of Marriage and the Family* 33: 677–682.

Becker, H. 1963. *Outsiders: Studies in the Sociology of Deviance.* New York: Free Press.

Bittner, E. 1967a. "The Police on Skid Row: A Study of Peace-keeping." *American Sociological Review* 32: 699–715.

———. 1967b. "Police Discretion in Emergency Apprehension of Mentally Ill Persons." *Social Problems* 14: 278–292.

Black, D. 1970. "Production of Crime Rates." *American Sociological Review* 35(Aug.): 733–748.

———. 1976. *The Behavior of Law.* New York: Academic Press.

———. 1980. *The Manners and Customs of Police.* New York: Academic Press.

Cameron, M.O. 1964. *The Booster and the Snitch.* New York: Free Press.

Cavan, S. 1966. *Liquor License.* Chicago: Aldine.

Coffey, A.R. 1974. *Police Intervention into Family Crises.* Santa Cruz: Davis Publishing Company.

Corzine, J. and R. Kirby. "Cruising the Truckers: Sexual Encounters in a Highway Rest Area." Pp. 574–591 in D. Kelly (ed.) *Deviant Behavior.* New York: St. Martin's Press.

Cumming, E., I. Cumming, and L. Edel. 1965. "Policeman as Philosopher, Guide, and Friend." *Social Problems* 12(Winter): 276–286.

Daniels, A.K. 1970. "The Social Construction of Military Psychiatric Diagnoses." in H.P. Dreitzel (ed.) *Recent Sociology No. 2: Patterns of Communicative Behavior.* New York: Macmillan.

Davis, P.W. 1981. "Structured Rationales for Nonarrest: Police Stereotypes of the Domestic Disturbance." *Criminal Justice Review* 6(Fall): 8–15.

Emerson, R. 1969. *Judging Delinquents.* Chicago: Aldine.

Emerson, R. and S. Messinger. 1977. "The Micro-politics of Trouble." *Social Problems* 25(Dec.): 121–134.

Emerson, R. and M. Pollner. 1976. "Dirty Work Designations." *Social Problems* 23(Feb.): 243–254.

———. 1978. "Policy and Practices of Psychiatric Case Selection." *Sociology of Work and Occupations* 5(Feb.): 75–96.

Garfinkel, H. 1956. "Conditions of Successful Degradation Ceremonies." *The American Journal of Sociology* 61: 420–424.

Gelles, R.J. 1974. *The Violent Home.* Beverly Hills: Sage.

Goffman, E. 1952. "On Cooling the Mark Out: Some Adaptations to Failure." *Psychiatry* 15: 451–463.

———. 1963. *Behavior in Public Places.* New York: Free Press.

———. 1971. *Relations in Public.* New York: Harper and Row.

Gold, R. 1958. "Roles in Sociological Field Observations." *Social Forces* 36: 217–223.

Goldstein, J. 1960. "Police Discretion Not to Invoke the Criminal Process: Low-Visibility Decisions in the Administration of Justice." *Yale Law Journal* 69(March): 577–580.

Hughes, E.C. 1971. "The Sociological Eye. Chicago: Aldine.

Irwin, J. 1970. *The Felon.* Englewood Cliffs, N.J.: Prentice-Hall.

Jackson, J.K. 1954. "The Adjustment of the Family to the Crisis of Alcoholism." *Quarterly Journal of Studies on Alcohol* 15(Dec.): 562–586.

LaFave, W. 1965. *Arrest.* Boston: Little, Brown.

Lofland, J. 1976. *Doing Social Life.* New York: Wiley.

Lyman, S.M. and M.B. Scott. 1968. "Coolness in Everyday Life." Pp. 92–101 in M. Truzzi (ed.) *Sociology and Everyday Life.* Englewood Cliffs, N.J.: Prentice-Hall.

Lundman, R.J. 1974. "Domestic Police-Citizen Encounter." *Journal of Police Science Administration* 2(March): 22–27.

McCall, G. 1978. *Observing the Law: Field Methods in the Study of Crime and the Criminal Justice System.* New York: The Free Press.

National Institute of Law Enforcement and Criminal Justice. 1978. *Police Crisis Intervention: Selected Bibliography.* Washington, D.C.: U.S. Department of Justice.

Parnas, R. 1967. "The Police Response to the Domestic Disturbance." *Wisconsin Law Review* 4: 914–960.

Schatzman, L. and A. Strauss. 1973. *Field Research: Strategies for a Natural Sociology.* Englewood Cliffs, N.J.: Prentice-Hall.

Scheff, T. 1963. "Decision Rules, Types of Error, and their Consequences in Medical Diagnosis." *Behavior Sciences* 8: 97–107.

Skolnick, J. 1966. *Justice Without Trial: Law Enforcement in a Democratic Society.* New York: Wiley.

Spradley, J.P. 1970. *You Owe Yourself a Drunk: An Ethnography of Urban Nomads.* Boston: Little, Brown.

Spradley, J. and B. Mann. 1975. *The Cocktail Waitress: Woman's Work in a Man's World.* New York: Wiley.

Sudnow, D. 1965. "Normal Crimes." *Social Problems* 12: 255–276.

Van Maanen, J. 1978. "On Watching the Watchers." Pp. 309–349 in P. Manning and J.V. Maanen (eds.) *Policing: A View From the Streets.* Santa Monica. Cal.: Goodyear.

Wiseman, J. 1970. *Stations of the Lost.* Englewood Cliffs, N.J.: Prentice-Hall.

Yarrow, M.R., C. Schwartz, H. Murphy, and L. Deasy. 1955. "The Psychological Meaning of Mental Illness in the Family." *Journal of Social Issues* 11: 1–24.

Play Theory of Delinquency:
Toward a General Theory of "Action"

Ikuya Sato
Ibaraki University

This article presents an exploratory conceptual framework for the understanding and analysis of the "play" quality of delinquency by reviewing urban ethnographies treating the relationship between group delinquency and play. An examination of interpretations of the causal mechanism of "action" shows that situation-specific definitions of the situation or "frames" rather than self-sustaining and autonomous (sub)cultural imperatives regulate the active pursuits of youths. This article argues that playlike deviance arises when there is precarious balance between the playlike definitions of the situation and the definitions of the situation associated with the primary reality. Collective encouragement, intense involvement, and a challenge to reach the limit are mentioned as three elements of action that lead to fatal and irrevocable consequences.

INTRODUCTION

Thrasher's boys enjoyed themselves being chased by the police, shooting dice, skipping school, rolling drunks. It was fun. Miller's boys do have a little fun, with their excitement focal concern, but it seems so desperate somehow. Cohen's boys and Cloward and Ohlin's boys are driven by grim economic and psychic necessity into rebellion. It seems peculiar that modern analysts have stopped assuming that "evil" can be fun and see gang delinquency as arising only when boys are driven away from "good."   Bordua (1961, p. 136)

Reprinted from Symbolic Interaction, 11(2):191–212.

Bordua made the above comment at the conclusion of his perceptive review of sociological theories of gang delinquency. The image of delinquency in academic literature does not seem to have changed much over the last quarter of a century. Deviance, crime, and delinquency are explained by painful social conditions and/or related psychological strain. For many second-hand observers the delinquency is guided by conformity to deviant subcultural values or prodded by turbulent emotion (cf. Kornhauser, 1978); the delinquent does not seem to enjoy "evil" at all. Still, the words "play, " fun, thrills, kicks, excitement, and make-believe creep into the sociologist's vocabulary when the action-seeking lifestyles and deviant behavior of young people are encountered. While using such terms, however, many sociologists seem to be reluctant to allow the delinquent to enjoy evil from the bottom of his heart. They either regard enjoyment of deviant behavior as secondary to turbulent emotion or characterize "action"-type deviance as enactment of cultural imperatives such as "value," "norm," or "focal concerns." Consequently, play-like deviance is characterized as either playground chaos or as the behavior of cultural automatons.

A review of the literature of urban ethnography and the results of my own field research on Japanese motorcycle gangs (Sato, 1986), however, suggest that much of the "action"-type deviance can be meaningfully analyzed as a type of social play. In this article I present an exploratory framework by means of which "action" undertaken "just for the hell of it" can be more adequately understood and analyzed. The conceptual framework characterizes action as a manifestation of the young person's attempt to create his own definitions of the situation amid the sociocultural void in which he cannot have sense of meaning and purpose. I argue that an alternative definition of the situation makes it possible for the youngster to construct an alternative reality in which he has a high degree of involvement and a strengthened sense of self. Reviewing ethnographic descriptions of action-oriented people and examining premises of subcultural theories of delinquency, I show that alternative definitions of the situation are quite situation-specific and the "action-seekers" have the ability to manipulate different types of definitions of the situation; i.e., those belonging to the play world and those associated with the primary reality. I also mention several components of "action," which often override the action-seekers' ability to control the situation and lead to fatal and irrevocable consequences.

CRIME AND PLAY IN ETHNOGRAPHIC WORKS

The action-seeking lifestyles of street youths have attracted the attention of urban ethnographers who frequently observe such ways of life firsthand. Confronted with the active pursuits of young people, and impressed, fascinated, or bothered by such activities, ethnographers not only depict these active lifestyles but relate them to the broader social and cultural context. Three groups of literature can be identified among such ethnographic works from the 1920s to the present: (1) studies on delinquency by the Chicago School of Sociologists in the 1920s and 1930s; (2) urban ethnographies in the 1950s and 1960s; and (3) studies on delinquency and youth culture in the 1970s and 1980s. Although they differ in their interpretations of the causal mechanism of action-type behavior, there are striking similarities in their descriptions of such activities.

Chicago School of Sociologists

During the 1920s and 1930s, the "golden age" of ethnographic studies (see Faris, 1967; Suttles, 1976; Bulmer, 1984), the Chicago School of Sociologists investigated the lifestyles of "social types" that emerged with the rapid growth of American cities (Park, 1914/15; Angell, 1945). Among them were such students of crime and delinquency as Thrasher, Shaw and McKay, and Tannenbaum. This group of sociologists produced data that remains the backbone of many current conceptions of delinquency and gang life (Yablonsky, [1962] 1970, p. 157). Through intensive case studies and detailed field observation, they described the natural history and activities of spontaneously formed adolescent play groups. According to these studies, the play groups emerge in social milieus characterized by social conflict and disorganization, family weakness, and attenuated neighborhood controls. These play groups later grow into gangs in response to intergroup conflict and the youths' struggles against the restraints adults seek to impose (Bordua, 1961, pp. 120–121; see Thrasher, 1927; Shaw and McKay, 1931; Tannenbaum, 1938).

Shaw and McKay's theory of delinquency was based on intensive case studies of delinquents and extensive analysis of the social milieu of urban areas. They saw juvenile delinquency as normal activity, a product of "social training" in the slum neighborhood which was, in turn, the result of urban social disorganization. The first step in a delinquent career given this social training, according to Shaw and McKay, was a playful act or a kind of game:[1]

It may be assumed that Stanley's initial experience in delinquency was an aspect of the play activity of his gang and neighborhood (Shaw, 1930, p. 50).

The delinquent careers of the brothers had their origin in the delinquent practices of the play group. (Shaw, McKay, and McDonald, 1938, p. 354).

Thrasher's analysis and interpretation of adolescent gangs were based on his thoughtful observations of 1,313 youth groups in Chicago's gangland. He, like other Chicago school sociologists, found the ultimate source of delinquency in the process of urban disorganization and in the lack of social control accompanying the disorganization process (Thrasher, 1927, p. 490). He also regarded adolescence as a developmental stage contributing to delinquency (p. 80). In this stage of physical and social development, when the young person's need for expression is not satisfied in an effective way by conventional agencies, the gang functions as an "interstitial phenomenon" providing kinds of activities particularly appealing to the youth. In the following excerpt, Thrasher characterizes gang activity with respect to the adolescent's cravings for thrills, excitement, and new experience as both satisfying and instigating:

How to break the humdrum of routine existence—this is a problem for the boy. It is the problem of life generally and a great deal of human energy is expended in the flight from monotony and the pursuit of a thrill. . . .

The quest for new experience seems to be particularly insistent in the adolescent who finds in the gang the desired escape from, or compensation for, monotony (Thrasher, 1927, p. 82).

Among other works by Chicago school sociologists, Thomas' *The Unadjusted Girl* (1923) and Cressey's *The Taxi-Dance Hall* ([1932] 1969) provide important clues for discerning the relationship between deviance and play. These books describe the social and personal lives of young prostitutes and female dancers, respectively, who are moved by a "desire for new experience." The authors attribute the girls' quest for romantic and thrilling ways of life to the attenuation of social controls over women in modern society.

Thomas applied some of the general theoretical schemes formulated in his *The Polish Peasant in Europe and America* (Thomas and Znaniecki, [1919] 1927) to the analysis of the problem of prostitutes. Among these schemes, there was the theory of the "four wishes." This theory was formulated as an analytical framework for understanding human motivations, and was integrated into his theory of social change. Thomas argued that the expression of the four wishes (the desire for new experience, security, response, and recognition) could not be channeled adequately by the old mores in a changing modern society, and this failure of social control led to an increase in prostitutes. Of these four wishes, the desire for new experience was assigned an important role in the initiation into the career of a prostitute. Thomas (1923) writes:

The beginning of delinquency in girls is usually an impulse to get amusement, adventure, pretty clothes, favorite notice, distinction, freedom in the larger world which presents so many allurement and comparisons (p. 109).

Although Whyte was educated at Harvard, it was the University of Chicago who awarded him a Ph.D. for his *Street Corner Society* ([1943] 1955). This ethnography provides "an incredibly conscientious and sensitive 'time study' of the seldom interrupted leisure of the unemployed 'corner boys' (Riesman, 1964, p. 147), who were in their twenties and lived in a Boston slum. Whereas *Street Corner Society* does not deal directly with the deviant behavior of street corner boys, it shows that "leisure" activities are crucial to the life and self-esteem of the jobless lower-class "youths."

Urban Ethnographies in the 1950s and 1960s

During the late 1950s and 1960s, when poverty was "rediscovered" in the United States (Suttles, 1976, p. 8), a number of sociologists and anthropologists investigated the action-oriented lifestyles of adolescents and young adults who were from slum, lower class, or working-class neighborhoods. Some of these investigations dealt with various community groups of youths or young adults who were considered to exemplify subtypes of certain lifestyles. These subtypes include the "action-seeker" (Gans,

1962), the street corner boy (Sherif and Sherif, 1964; Downes, 1966; Suttles, 1968), and the "street corner man" (Hannerz, 1969). Other studies focused on specific social types, such as black drug users (Finestone, 1957), lower-class youths (Miller, 1958) and street corner gangs (Yablonsky, [1962] 1970; Short and Strodbeck, [1965] 1974). These ethnographic studies provided much detail descriptive of urban societies fostering those involved in action-seeking ways of life.

These researchers view "kicks," "fun," and the excitement of action as constituting the keynote for each lifestyle. Miller (1958) comments on "excitement" as one of the six "focal concerns" of lower class culture. Gans sees action-seeking as a major component of the activity of an adolescent peer group in a Boston slum. His description of the lifestyle of Italian youths resembles Miller's description of the way of life of lower class youths:

> In the adolescent peer group, manifesting the episodic search for action in an almost pure, ideal-typical form, life alternates between killing time and searching for action. Some of it takes place right within the group, in a dialectic of conformity and competitiveness through which the individual realizes himself. Most satisfying,. however is the search for action by the group as a whole. In this activity the adolescent achieves a kind of personal autonomy that he gets nowhere else. "Action" generates a state of quasi-hypnotic excitement which enables the individual to feel that he is in control both of his own drives and of the environment (Gans, 1962, p. 65).

Some studies use "play" and related concepts more explicitly in their analysis of crime and delinquency. For example, Finestone (1957) employs Huizinga's descriptive definition of play in describing generic features of the life of black heroin users in Chicago. The generic features include voluntariness, stepping out of reality, secludedness and limitedness, and aesthetic emphasis. Yablonsky ([1962] 1970) underlines the importance of "sounding" and fantasies regarding group size and turf to the self-esteem and the generation of "senseless violence" of violent gangs in New York. He also sees the strong influence of the mass media in the violent gangs' subterranean values about violence. Through his field research in two East London boroughs, Downes found that delinquency constitutes a crucial part in the leisure time of British working-class boys. Downes argues that although working-class boys have abundant time for pursuing "leisure goals," which are in part provided by commercial teenage culture, they lack legitimate means to fulfill such goals. There is, then, Mertonian anomie between culturally induced leisure goals and structurally distributed legitimate means. The boys, Downes maintains, find their means for satisfying leisure goals in the excitement of delinquent acts (Downes, 1966, pp. 134, 242–247). Hannerz (1969) regards that street corner myth-making centering on ghetto-specific masculinity provides an opportunity for sociability which is intrinsically rewarding. He also argues that the myths program as well as legitimize the active pursuits of black street corner men in Washington D.C.

Studies on Delinquency and Youth Culture in the 1970s and 1980s

More recently, several British scholars, as well as some American ones, have published ethnographic studies that deal with playlike deviance among youths who seek active lifestyles. Among such studies are those often referred to as the "Birmingham school" (e.g., Hall and Jefferson, 1976; Hebdige, 1979; Willis, 1977; Corrigan, 1979; Frith, 1981). In their works, special attention is paid to the significance of consumer goods and to the influence of the mass media in the leisure life of British adolescents. They mainly consider expressive styles and delinquency among British working-class youths. They depict the search for action as an attempt to create meaningful experience amid pervasive boredom or as an expression of resentment arising from life in deprived neighborhoods, and from class antagonism.

Among other British scholars who are not considered members of the Birmingham school, Cohen ([1972] 1980) discusses the Mods and Rockers, and Marsh, Rosser and Harré (1978) analyze the subcultural styles and behavior of football hooligans. Like scholars of the Birmingham school, Cohen views that the participants in the collective behavior schemes are seeking "opportunities for excitement, autonomy and sense of action" (Cohen, [1972] 1980, p. 182).

Similarly, Marsh, Rosser, and Harré (1978) write,

> In conspiring to construct a reality which seems to be at variance with their tacit knowledge of orderly and rule-governed action [football] fans are engaged in the active creation (and adoption for the outside) of excitement. For fans, regularity and safety are things to be avoided. They are simply 'a drag.' What the soccer terraces offer is a chance to escape from the dreariness of the weekday world of work or school to something which is adventurous and stimulating (p. 97).

In the United States, Klapp's (1969) and Irwin's (1977) writings on fads, fashion, cultic movements, and urban scenes characterize modern behavioral and stylistic rebellions as a way of creating identity and meaning in life. According to them, people of all classes come to engage in deviant ways of life and in crimes in the course of pursuing leisure activities. Klapp argues that "fun" is becoming a new focal point of mass interest and hedonism is receiving a new validation in the search for and affirmation of identity. He calls this tendency "new romanticism" and sees in it a built-in predilection for deviant behavior. It legitimizes, he argues, offbeat adventures outside one's social position, class, religion—even beyond the pale of morality itself (Klapp, 1969, p. 198).

Anderson (1976) points out that irregular job careers of black youths in Philadelphia often lead to thrill-seeking activities, which are called "good time," "taking a walk," or "beat." Leary's (1977) treatise on the activities of white lower-class youths on the street corner in Bloomington analyzes narratives and street corner myths featuring action-seeking heroes. He argues that the narratives provide a motivating force for the boys' active pursuits. Horowitz's (1983) study of young Chicano men and women along Chicago's "32nd Street" also describes the allure of exciting street life which tempts youths to search for action and occasionally commit illegal behavior.

The results of my own field research on Japanese *bosozoku* (motorcycle gangs) in Kyoto (Sato, 1984, 1985, 1986) also suggest that situational components of play are important parts of deviant behavior. Through the research work,[2] I found that much of the motorcycle gang activity can be characterized as a kind of social play including not only thrills and excitement of high-speed racing but also enjoyments of self-display as a daredevil speedster or ferocious villain. Most of the core members of *bosozoku* are recruited from adolescents called *yankii* (Yankee) who "hang around" street corners of Kyoto. The motorcycle gang activity dramatizes their active lifestyle and provides them with romanticized self-image as action-seeking hero. The gang activities as a whole, indeed, constitute a dramatic world featuring the motorcycle gang as the "picaro."

CONVERGENCES AND DIVERGENCES IN INTERPRETATIONS OF "ACTION"

Convergences

While the ethnographic works already described deal with heterogeneous ethnic groups in various neighborhoods at different historical periods, there is striking similarity where they describe the subjective experience of "action" and its backgrounds. In almost all cases, "action" is said to produce thrills, kicks, and excitement. They also agree that the exhilaration of action contrasts with the boredom of conformity to officially prescribed values. Conventional social institutions, such as schools, the family, neighborhoods, jobs, and the church, cannot restrain these youths' quest for action through coercion or surveillance. They also fail to supply a sense of purpose, self-worth, or meaningful experience. In those studies focusing on action-seeking adolescents, a contrast is drawn between the excitement of action and the boredom of conformity, which parallels the contrast between the social mores of peer groups and those of adult society.

Along with similar interpretations of action and the subjective experience of it, such ethnographic studies have common assumptions concerning the search for action as a collective undertaking. All of them hold that there is some regularity in action-seeking lifestyles and playlike deviance. Moreover, most authors agree that a set of codes accepted by group members regulates the search for action. Sartorial and linguistic standards, as well as behavioral codes, are often designated as "values" and "norms, " although not all of the authors use such terms explicitly. Cressey (1932, pp. 32–33) maintains that the "social world" of a taxi-dance hall is characterized by the completeness of the interests and satisfaction afforded in it and "distinctive patterns of behavior and vocabulary" constitute the keynote of the social world. Willis (1977, p. 17) claims that the lifestyle of British "lads" (corner boys) is closely associated with their distinctive clothes and hairstyles. According to him, the "lad's look" as well as behavioral patterns characteristic of the youngsters manifests their oppositions to the mainstream values exemplified by the lifestyle of school staff and 'ear'oles" (academic achievement-oriented boys).

In my field research with Japanese motorcycle gangs, I found that thematic paraphernalia emphasizing group solidarity and fanaticism plays a crucial role in creating a symbolic universe of discourse characteristic of the gang activity (Sato, 1986, chap. 2). The paraphernalia incudes swastikas, costumes resembling that of a kamikaze party, and nationalistic symbols. The sartorial codes prescribe what are "authentic" modes for gang members and proscribe extreme variations that may jeopardize the group identity.

Thus, there is some regularity in playlike delinquency. In other words, playlike deviance is not the same as what is implied in the word "playground chaos." Playlike deviance does not seem to be equivalent to total "normlessness," but seems to be regulated by some kinds of code or control mechanism.

Divergences

Ethnographers' judgments, however, are divided on two crucial points: (1) the origins and characteristics of codes shared by action-oriented people; and (2) the relative importance of thrills and excitement vis-à-vis psychological strains. A close examination of the theoretical divergences suggests a way in which playlike deviance can be more adequately analyzed and understood.

Social Codes of "Action-seekers"

Two major views can be discerned among the sociological works on delinquency with respect to subcultural codes. On the one hand, some regard codes essentially as the result of collective and primary group processes among adolescents or others engaged in action where ordinary social codes lose firm grip with them (e.g., Thrasher, 1927; Tannenbaum, 1938; Suttles, 1968). In this regard, various works mention the following factors: the attenuation of control resulting from a lack of indigenous community organization; notably in slum areas; ineffective parental control in immigrant families who are incompletely assimilated in the host country; rapid modernization and urbanization, which reduces behavior to an individual level, and leads to "identity deprivation" and the segregation of urban populations; the prevalence of unemployment and poverty, which leads to irregular periods of work and unstable marriages; and "age segregation" (see Coleman, 1974; Scott and Vaz, 1963) in the midst of affluence marked by consumerism and increased media influence. In the absence of social controls and sufficient means to establish self-worth, sociologists argue, certain groups arrive at goals and rules by exploration and improvisation, and thus attempt to achieve meaning and order, as well as experience, thrills, kicks, and excitement.

On the other hand, some ethnographers—and theorists whose work is derivative, rather than based on firsthand observation—contend that codes of behavior and communication are taken from subcultural traditions or denote a self-sustaining subculture within a community (e.g., Cohen, 1955; Miller, 1958; Cloward and Ohlin, 1960; Wolfgang and Ferracuti 1967; Spergel 1964).[3] In many cases, the formulations set forth in these works depict the search for action as undertaken in accordance with subcultural imperatives that are deemed "values" or "norms." This concept, then, makes the pursuit of thrills, kicks, and fun seem obligatory. Miller (1968) takes the most extreme position in this respect, though he opposes the use of the term "value." He argues that subcultural codes supporting or encouraging deviant behavior in the lower class are not specific to adolescents but are shared as well by adults. He also maintains that standards form a distinctive cultural system with its own pattern and integrity, which has its own centuries-old tradition (Miller, 1957, pp. 6, 19). According to him, misbehavior is "explicitly supported by, implicitly demanded by, or not materially inhibited by factors relating to the focal concerns of lowerclass culture" (p. 18). These focal concerns include "trouble," "smartness," "excitement," "fate," and "autonomy."[4]

At first, both theoretical positions—one emphasizing attenuated social control and the other subcultural standards—seem quite plausible. But a close examination of studies dealing specifically with subcultural standards would suggest that the former position actually is the more credible. "Values" and "norms" do not seem to be appropriate terms for rules governing active pursuits; the rules of action are often quite imperative but are highly situation-specific. They do not seem to constitute a self-sustaining and autonomous subsociety, or to ensure full and long term commitments from followers.

In theorists' discussions of subcultural standards, it is often unclear whether the terms used are regarded as determinants of behavior, or used as descriptive terms (Bordua, 1961, p. 131). "Values" and "norms," or more generally "culture" or "subculture," are terms often used as "sponge-like concepts" (Suttles, 1976, p. 12). In this case, they are all inclusive terms embracing all forms of individualism tolerated (if not supported) in a subsociety: moral values, group norms, personal stereotypes, justificatory accounts, and lifestyles. Theorists sometimes treat these miscellaneous "cultural" components as though they were determinants which affect members of a subsociety who in themselves are portrayed as cultural automatons (see Wrong, 1961; Suttles, 1968, p. 169). As in the case of those who use the notion of "culture of poverty," the theorists treat culture "'as a whole way of life,' with no clear distinction between the culture and its environment, between causes and consequence" (Hannerz, 1969, p. 179).

A number of ethnographic studies, however, show that members of these subcultures often have only a partial and ambivalent commitment to group standards (e.g., Finestone, 1957; Rodman, 1963; Liebow, 1967; Hannerz, 1969). Standards emphasizing "toughness," "kicks," and "ultramasculinity" seem to serve only to create social fictions giving members a "rep" and a heightened sense of self. But action-oriented people are generally aware that in many undertakings, fictive accomplishments and great risks lie behind subcultural themes. In many cases, then, they graduate from the action-seeking lifestyle to a conventional way of life (Cressey, 1932, p. 84; Whyte, 1955, pp. 35–51, Gans, 1962, pp. 64–73; Hannerz, 1969, chap. 2).

A number of studies also show that a member's commitment to a subsociety is often partial. Adolescent gangs include many fringe adherents as well as core members, and even the latter do not always "hang around" together (e.g., Thrasher, 1927;

Yablonsky, 1962, Part II; Short and Strodtbeck, 1965, chap. 9; Suttles, 1968, chap. 10). In my own field research with Japanese motorcycle gangs, I found that youths are more or less clearly aware of the fictive nature of their symbolism, and expect to graduate from exciting but quite risky undertakings in the foreseeable future (Sato, 1986, chap. 8). Of course when conflict such as gang fighting is involved, group organization constructed around social fictions may come very close to "reality." At other times membership is in constant flux and participants are only partially committed to gang activities. Similarly, behavior that is supposed to exemplify toughness, masculinity, and "guts" is praised and does enhance one's "rep," but is also regarded as age-specific and, at some points, "kid's stuff."

Fun Versus Strain

Some assumption of psychological strain is often associated with the delinquent's detachment from conventional values and commitment to deviant subcultural values. An examination of such an assumption also supports the argument that the delinquent's commitment to group standards is partial and ambivalent. While students of crime and delinquency often admit that delinquency can be fun, they also discount it by postulating some psychological strain. For example, while Cohen admits that delinquents frequently state that they commit wrongdoings just "for the hell of it," he discounts this type of account by pointing out the "fact" that the majority of those who seek kicks and fun from deviant behavior are lower-class adolescents. He argues that explanation of deviance in terms of fun is not complete as long as one cannot account for the class differential in delinquency (Cohen, 1955, pp. 26–27).[5] He attributes this class differential to a psychological strain induced by unequal distribution of social opportunity, which he calls "status frustration." He argues that group delinquency offers an alternative status system for lower-class boys. In a similar vein, Stinchcombe views the rebellious behavior of high school kids, with respect to such behavior as dating and smoking, as a claim to adult status. This claim is said to compensate for a feeling of degraded personal worth with respect to academic achievement. He argues that a student's resort to ascriptive status symbolism as an adult is an alternative to academic achievement (Stinchcombe, 1964, chap. 5).

The literature on youth and youth subculture abound with similar arguments. Some view prolonged adolescence without means of adequate self-affirmation as an important source of anxiety and frustration leading to various kinds of expressive and rebellious behavior (e.g., Davis, 1940, 1944; Bloch and Niederhoffer, 1958; Vaz, 1967; see Pleck, 1982). Some theorists argue that discontinuity in socialization at different life stages is the cause of masculinity anxiety. Miller and Kvaraceus argue that because a lower-class boy experiences his childhood socialization in matrifocality, or in a household characterized by "serial monogamy," he comes to suffer confusion over his sexual identity in his adolescence. A gang offers an almost ideal solution for this problem (Miller, 1958; Kvaraceus and Miller, 1959, pp. 96–97). Parsons explains how peer groups of white middle-class boys and their "masculine protest" function to fill the gap between the mother's over-involvement in childhood socialization and the emphasis on the masculine role in later life stages (Parsons, 1942; Parson and Bales, 1955).

These explanations assume that the most serious question for adolescents (or ghetto men) is the problem of "How can I be a man?" Most theorists assume that this problem occupies the adolescent's mind for much of his daily life. It follows that the choice between alternative systems is an "either-or" question: The boy has to decide whether he joins a gang and becomes a "man" or stays out of trouble but tolerates being called "sissy"and suffers chronic anxiety. This formulation characterizes the expression of masculinity or action-seeking behavior as obsessive rather than carefree.

This kind of formulation, however, confronts serious difficulties when the actual process of the creation of the "alternative status system" previously depicted by the theorists and other researchers is examined. We frequently find extremely distorted and exaggerated images of masculinity and/or adulthood. These images are far from exact copies; rather, they are caricature or parodies of their model. The boys select external symbols of adult status or masculinity from real world experiences, movie scenes, or other media representations, and discard those elements that threaten their enjoyment (e.g., adulthood responsibility) (Miller, 1958, p. 16; Schwartzman, 1978, p. 105; England, 1967, p. 249; Bloch and Niederhoffer, 1958 p. 13; Matza, 1964, p. 199; Coleman, 1961, p. 128). This exaggeration and distortion of adulthood and masculinity images may be compared to ritualistic performances by primitives, where some of the values, norms, and styles in ordinary life are presented dramatically, comically, and grotesquely. In addition, there is the irony that for adolescents to feel grown up and experience adult enjoyment they must violate adult laws (Henry, 1963, p. 205; Bloch and Niederhoffer, 1958, chap. 1).

Moreover, the causal relationship between status frustration or masculinity anxiety and delinquency in the criminological literature is often merely assumed and not empirically substantiated. Kornhauser (1978, pp. 167–180) points out that there have been few definitive tests concerning the relationship of status frustration to class difference. She also examined a number of empirical studies on the relationship between status frustration and delinquency and found few affirmatory results. Pleck's (1981) review of psychological studies supporting the relationship between "hyper-masculinity" and delinquency also shows that most of the studies have methodological and/or interpretive problems. I have examined a number of psychological studies that attribute the chief motivation for the commitment to motorcycle gang activities to an inferiority complex arising from poor academic achievement (Sato, 1986, chap. 4). I found that these studies have many methodological defects and do not offer any convincing results. My field observations and interviews also suggest that although motorcycle gang members do have inferiority complexes about their own academic achievement, they are not preoccupied with the problem most of the time. They are involved in gang activities chiefly in pursuit of kicks and excitement.

It would be reasonable to assume that displays of masculinity or adult traits can give the feeling of status enhancement mainly on specific occasions such as "sound-ing," "signifying," or verbal duels (see Hannerz, 1969; Matza, 1964; Labov, 1972; Kochman, 1981). They are like role reversals in rituals rather than attempts to establish "alternative status systems," conferring unquestionable prestige and stable self-esteem on adolescents. In other words, such displays are not based on an articulate ideological system, but resemble parodies or make-believe play. Of course, during play, or at moments when delinquents are forced to justify against others' accusations, such parodies or make-believe may appear to arise from a coherent ideological system (cf. Haviland, 1977).

The above argument suggests that action-seeking activities and displays of masculinity are motivated more often by the enjoyment of a thrilling experience or a temporary feeling of status-enhancement than by the compelling need to dissipate anxiety. Even if the display resolves personal conflicts induced by social experiences (Hannerz, 1969, pp. 79–88, chap. 5), it seems to do so more often through cathartic experience in a playlike context that can be controlled and managed by the actor, than through symptomatic, compelling, and automatic "acting-out."

A number of ethnographic studies also suggest that the collective resolution of anxiety and frustration is not the major causal factor in the formation or function of adolescent peer groups. These may be formed for the sake of self-defense (Short and Strodtbeck, [1965] 1974) or as culturally recognized subgroupings in a community (Suttles, 1968; Hannerz, 1969). The question of why action or the display of masculinity becomes one of the dominant patterns of play seems to share the same answer as the question, "What'll we do tonight?" rather than the question, "How can I be a man?" (cf. Berger, 1963; Thrasher, 1927, p. 79).

DUAL PERSPECTIVE MODEL OF PLAYLIKE DEVIANCE

Dual Perspectives of Action-Seekers

It would seem, then, that although action and playlike deviance do not result from the total absence of any norms, and are not mere expressions of hedonistic individual desires, active pursuits are not preprogrammed and induced by values of self-sustaining and autonomous subcultures which compel complete conformity. In other words, such activities are neither "playground chaos" nor automatic responses of "cultural automatons" urged on by subcultural commands. Playlike deviance seems to be ordered by a set of goals and rules that are quite situation-specific. It seems that "action" presupposes two sets of goals and rules—those belonging to the play world and those of the primary reality (see Bateson, 1972; Goffman, 1974; Csikszentmihalyi, 1975; Schwartzman, 1978). The goals and rules in the play world may constitute an alternative definition of the situation by means of which youngsters create a social fiction where they assume the role of daredevil gang member, chic and discerning "dude," or aesthetic drug user. In many cases, various actions of the youngsters evolve around the focal image of such "cultural heroes."

The playlike definition of the situation is not a mere assemblage of fragmentary justificatory accounts such as "value stretch" (Rodman, 1963) and "shadow value" (Liebow, 1967). Nor is it an articulate and consistent system of goals and rules. It includes a great latitude for improvisation and often constitutes a loose dramaturgical system on the basis of which youngsters can generate their own "street corner myth" or other narratives with more or less distinctive plots and themes. The dramaturgical system is flexible enough to allow each of the youngsters a considerable degree of improvisational performances.

In some cases, aspects of the narratives may be adopted by the mass media and become social dramas causing societal moral panic, as in the case of the moral hysteria created over the Hell's Angels (Thompson, 1966) and the Mods and Rockers (Cohen, [1972] 1980). In other cases, youngsters adopt dramaturgical plots and themes from the news industry or the world of mass entertainment. Yet, youngsters are not mere "dupes" or copycats who are influenced by the "pseudo-event" created by the mass media. They often fit the plots and themes of the social drama to their own and their group's needs, situation, and available resources (Gans, 1966, p. 562; Fine, and Kleinman, 1979, p. 12; Marsh, Rosser, and Harré, 1978).

In Japan, a nationwide moral panic was created during the period between the mid-1970s and early 1980s by mass media reportage on motorcycle gangs. The media reports represented the motorcycle gang as an abominable devil responsible for the crime wave beginning in the mid-1970s and as the "first reserve" of *yakuza* (gangster) recruits (Sato, 1986, chap. 3). While sizeable numbers of Japanese youngsters acted out the demonic image by wearing grotesque and flashy costumes and through highspeed driving on city roads, they also distanced themselves from the extremely negative implications of the devilish figure. They defined their performance as make-believe or "mere play" and graduated from gang activity by the age of twenty (Sato, 1986, chap. 8). One of my informants, whose intimidating picture appeared in a picture book about motorcycle gangs, said to me, "That's just a bluff. Just for the picture. You know. Everyone wants to put on airs for the picture."

Youngsters are, then, able to manipulate two perspectives or "frames" of playlike activity to a considerable degree (Bateson, 1972; Goffman, 1974) and choose possible realities.[6] They are not "cultural automatons" who do not have the ability to define the situation by themselves but merely translate subcultural imperatives into action.

Playlike deviance, in its most intense form, emerges when there is a precarious balance between the two standards or perspectives. When conventional institutions do not supply certain groups with a sense of meaning and purpose, they will seek activities in which goals and rules are decidedly unconventional. The inadequacy of surveillance and coercive sanctions will tempt the group further into exploratory undertakings. Such activities also attract those who find it demeaning to seek conventional forms of social prestige, although a sense of inferiority is not the only reason alternative standards are sought. Exploratory behavior is often playful as well when each of the participants find it possible to create his own version of definition of the situation. Urban areas, with their air of mobility and anonymity, are the most likely stages for exploratory and playful undertakings lending themselves to improvisational perform-ances. Situational components of interactional setting become as important or even more important than meaning, purposes, and collective identity supplied by traditional institutions as determinants of social action (see Goffman, 1959; Turner, 1962; Irwin, 1977; Suttles, 1976).

Among the urban population taken as a whole, adolescents who are not fully assimilated into conventional social institutions are most likely to become "action-seekers." They are also most likely to form interactional settings where they "hang around" with no specific purpose and wait for something to happen. The urban milieu includes many places suitable for such social gatherings (see Irwin, 1977; Lofland, 1973): street corners, bar rooms, movie theaters, discotheques.

Youngsters are not fully committed to both the official definition of the situation and alternative, playlike definitions of the situation. They vacillate (or "drift" [Matza 1964]) between the two perspectives, and full but temporary engrossment is obtained more frequently with the alternative definition of the situation than with the official definitions of the situation. While the playlike definition of the situation can provide youngsters with a sense of meaning and purpose, excessive commitment to the definition sometimes leads to fatal and irrevocable consequences, because "action" has an inherent tendency toward "corruption."

Corruption of Play

"Action" does not always end in illegal behavior. Many youthful, active pursuits may be tolerated as "mischief" or lead to relatively harmless adventures. Youngsters themselves avoid extremely risky undertakings likely to lead to fatal consequences. Intense involvement in the kicks, thrills, and excitement of "action," however, often allows one to exceed certain limits and leads to "corruption" of play (Caillois, 1961; chap. 4). At such times, the active pursuit ceases to be playful, and dread and anxiety instead of fun and enjoyment ensue. There are at least three elements in "action" which lead to such consequences: collective encouragement, intense involvement, and a challenge to reach the limit.

Collective Encouragement

An audience and fellow actors are needed if a youth's exploratory behavior is to create an alternative reality, and produce an enhanced sense of self; thus collective action is essential. Language, clothing, and gestures, as well as behavior, are regulated by subcultural codes, which have as an important element a distinctive "style" (cf. Smith, 1974; Hebdige, 1979). In many cases, this style allows considerable latitude for creativity and improvisation. Because an alternative definition of the situation is established—and participants feel that "everyone does it"—each individual is not troubled by fears that he is insane or deviant to an extreme degree (Thomas, 1923, p. 119; Cressey, 1932, p. 85; Granovetter, 1978).[7] Collective participation, then, permits active pursuits on a massive scale, so that one may feel that certainty exists in their alternative reality (Irwin, 1977, p. 27). Collective behavior that leads to action on a grand scale often induces participants to exceed a critical limit and suffer irrevocable consequences. Active pursuits, then, may generate momentum of their own, beyond the control of participants.

A former executive member of a motorcycle gang called the Moko (Fierce Tigers), which in 1978 was the largest motorcycle gang confederation in Kyoto, told me that he abruptly became frightened when the number of participants in a Run (highspeed racing on city roads) exceeded 300. His anxieties were well-founded, when a large Run in Shiga Prefecture (a prefecture adjacent to Kyoto) and a confrontation with the police led to assault on a squad car and a police station. He was arrested on charges arising from this incident, along with twenty other members, and was sent to prison.

Intense Involvement

The alternative reality constructed by playful definitions of the situation may be far more compelling than conventional and official definitions, because it is ordered, like a game, by a set of simplified goals and rules. It may also induce spontaneous involvement free from the overtones of unwilling conformity that youths associate with the monotony, boredom, and seeming endlessness of everyday life. In other words, it provides youths with what Csikszentmihalyi (1975) described as "flow" (see also Csikszentmihalyi and Larson 1978; Mitchell, 1983). Youths can feel that they are the moving agents of their own behavior rather than the objects of others' intentions. To a certain extent, they can devise variations in performance styles where conventional standards allow little scope for individual preferences. Their search for action is, in a sense, an attempt to create meaningful symbols and activities in the midst of a sociocultural void (Moore and Myerhoff, 1977, pp. 16–19; Marsh, Rosser and Harré, 1978, pp. 43, 49, 52). In most cases, action of this sort, undertaken in a spirit of play, is performed in a delimited temporal and spatial context. Thus circumscribed, behavior may be ordered according to goals and rules that are simplified to permit full engrossment. The clear contrast between action and excitement in an alternative reality and the drabness of mundane everyday life also heightens involvement in active pursuits. But at times participants' engrossment precludes other concerns, and past a certain point what began as play becomes an obsession or an addiction. Boys who "play Indian" may eventually burn their companions at the stake (Thrasher, 1927; p. 138).[8] The high-risk Run provides intense involvement and excitement. Many of my informants were involved in severe traffic accidents and suffered severe injuries. Some of their friends died during such activities. Still, the enjoyment of the Run exceeds the consideration of great risks, and some even joined the Run wearing plaster casts on their knees.

Challenge to Reach the Limit

Although action includes legitimate and semi-legitimate pursuits, as well as explicitly illegitimate undertakings, truly exciting and engrossing pursuits often test and challenge conventional standards to their limits. Explicitly deviant styles and outright defiance are among the most effective means of getting thrills and kicks, and of experiencing the joy of showing-off. Systematic deviation from the existing order may, in fact, create another order, though it may be regarded as "noise" or "disorder" by the dominant society (Turner, 1974, p. 55; Hebdige, 1979, p. 113).

Thrasher points to a similar aspect of the image projected by adolescent gangs in Chicago:

The gang . . . however, not having their cultural detachment, usually accepts the code of society but is in rebellion against it. In fact, the diabolical character of disobeying the social codes appeals to gang boys. While they accept the moral authority of the community, still it is external to them and they get a "kick" out of their attitude of disrespect for established rules (Thrasher, 1927, p. 391).

Indeed, evil is often "fun" exactly because it is evil and can provide the excitement of transgression itself. Duncan maintains that,

[O]nce "do" and "do not," "shall" and "shall not," "is" and "is not," becomes "mine and thine," then all the power and radiance of the forbidden arises. The neighbor's wife we must not covet becomes glamorous because she is forbidden, a strange and mysterious creature who haunts us in acts, which to her husband are familiar and even tedious (Duncan, 1968, pp. 220–221; see also Burke, 1962, p. 450).

While doing my field research, I was dismayed but at the same time impressed when an informant commented on the subjective experience of high-risk driving on a city road: "Well, it's rather like raping a girl. It's the terribly thrilling feeling of doing something wrong, with the thought in mind, 'Hell, I'm doing terribly wrong! Can I really do it?' "

Play versus Anarchy

These three aspects of playlike group delinquency—collective encouragement, intense involvement, and challenge to reach the limit—sometimes lead to irrevocable consequences and the "corruption" of play. Chaos ensues when the world of action overflows the limit of the playful definitions of the situation and mob outbreaks take place. Thrilling excursions into the world of action may end with the total loss of freedom to choose possible realities. *"Agon"* (competition) results in accidents, crippling injuries, or death. Belief in *"alea"* (chance) leads to superstition or bankrupt fatalism. What began as playful "mimicry" ends with a fixed deviant role, such as that of the mobster. Excessive pursuits of *"ilinx"* (vertigo) makes one an addict. Many types of playlike deviance presuppose a precarious balance between the tendency toward "corruption" of play (Caillois, 1961, chap. 4), or the contamination of the play frame by the primary reality and the control capacity of playlike definitions of the situation. The tendency toward anarchy, whether it is instinctive, biological, or even culturally conditioned, is liberated when the social controls of conventional institutions are reduced. The playlike definition of the situation provides institutional discipline for the excess of the anarchic tendency: but it cannot entirely restrain playlike deviance, which unlike "domesticated" and "tame" play, such as the vicarious enjoyment of watching a movie, produces deep enjoyment in a manner very close to that of anarchy.

An activity can be playful only when there is an implicit or explicit assumption that a free choice exists between thrilling play and everyday life. Even a thrilling excursion into an extremely dangerous situation presupposes a secure starting point and a safe destination. As Balint (1959) notes, adventurous people such as mountain climbers and skiers often have an almost superstitious confidence in their gear. In a circus, the hero-acrobat begins from a safe area, performs his feats high in the air, and returns to safety where a beautiful girl draws him into security (Balint, 1959, p. 30). Similarly, the "liminal" phase of a rite of passage presupposes preliminal and postliminal periods when the novice is safely ensconced in the sociocultural network (Turner, 1974).

The subculture of action-oriented people, then, tends to include assumptions about the limits of playlike deviance and about eventual graduation into everyday life. Among American delinquents, there may be shared assumptions about an "optimal range of delinquent behavior" within which actions are "deviant enough to establish a negative identity but not so deviant as to repel significant others" (Gold and Peteronio, 1980, p. 525; see also Scott and Vaz, 1963, p. 329; Fine, 1987, p. 120), and most delinquent acts may be considered "kid's stuff" to be abandoned upon reaching adulthood. Street corner gangs may develop a tacit consensus, by which they avoid fights with each other, and maintain prestige by proscribing conflict because of age difference or on other grounds; in many cases there are rumors of gang fights that do not take place (Suttles, 1968, pp. 183, 198–201; Short and Strodtbeck, [1965] 1974).[9]

By common consent young "action-seekers" may, upon maturity, exchange their life style for that of "routine-seekers" (Gans, 1962, pp. 64–73). Many young prostitutes who began their deviant careers from the "impulse to get amusement, adventure, . . . freedom in the larger world which presents so many allurements and comparisons" anticipate settling down as ordinary housewives who achieve their "desire for security" rather than "desire for new experience" (Thomas, 1923, pp. 109, 120). The dancer in a taxi-dance hall also anticipates getting married and settling down, disengaging herself from a romantic and adventurous existence that lies midway between legitimate work and positions at seedier dance halls, until she ends her working life as a prostitute (Cressey, 1932, chap. 5). Many black boys from slum areas hope eventually to retire from their action-oriented careers and establish stable households as they enter adulthood. But it is also likely that economic insecurity and peer pressure will compel them to lead outwardly cheerful but internally anxiety-ridden lives as "street corner men," "hoodlums," or "wineheads" (Liebow, 1967; Hannerz, 1969; Anderson, 1976).

A youngster's commitment to adult life, therefore, constitutes the ultimate limit of playlike deviance. He ceases to vacillate between the primary reality and alternative reality of action-seeking and gains a firm foothold in conventional life. Conventional, adult life may lack opportunities for play and extremely thrilling experiences, but it is also free from the danger of the corruption of play.

CONCLUSION

"Crime as play" is a recurrent theme in the criminological literature, as well as in popular literature. While urban ethnographers present rich descriptive data about the relationship between crime and play, many secondhand observers characterize playlike deviance either as a response to (sub)cultural imperatives or as secondary to turbulent emotions. (Some ethnographers even adopt such interpretations when they try to put their descriptive materials into the straightjacket of existing theories.) Their misconceptions probably are in part due to the transient and ephemeral nature of the playlike definition of the situation. It is far more difficult to discern the dynamics and intricacy of the working of the playlike scheme than to abstract "values" or "norms" from *post hoc* accounts by members of a subsociety. A laborious and patient "time-study" of the leisure life of adolescents on the street is needed in order to analyze the significance of the alternative definition of the situation. During leisure hours, adolescents "do nothing" most of the time except for an episodic search for action.

In this article, I have argued that a dual perspective framework and the consideration of elements of the corruption of play can provide a useful framework by which playlike deviance can be more adequately analyzed and interpreted. Careful analysis of playlike definitions of the situation and elements of "corruption" will provide important clues to the analysis of group delinquency as a type of collective behavior. If integrated with analysis at the societal level and with large scale social surveys, field research carried out on the basis of the framework presented in this article will provide a way to analyze in detail the interrelationship among individual, group, and societal definitions of the situation. Delinquency is just one type of collective behavior that can be understood by a playlike definition of the situation. A more elaborate framework for analyzing the playlike definitions of the situation than the one presented in this article would provide a useful conceptual scheme with which we can understand and analyze other types of playlike activities such as festivals, rituals, and revolutions. Such a scheme would also lead to the formulation of a new theory of social change and modes of individual adaptation and innovation.[10]

ACKNOWLEDGMENT

Research for this article was supported by the Toyota Foundation, the Center for Far Eastern Studies and the Committee on Japanese Studies at the University of Chicago, the Japanese Society for the Promotion of Science, and the Japanese Association of Social Psychology. This is an expanded and refined version of an earlier draft of the concluding chapter of my doctoral dissertation submitted to the University of Chicago. I gratefully acknowledge the helpful comments and encouragement of Professors Gerald Suttles, Mihaly Csikszentmihalyi, Hary Harootunian, Gary Alan Fine, Takekatsu Kikuchi, and the anonymous reviewers. I also would like to thank John Broadus and Elizabeth Horton for their editorial support.

NOTES

1. There are also many observations that suggest pursuit of fun, thrills, kicks, and excitement. This pursuit can sometimes coexist with the consideration of gain and profit and is highly valued among a subsociety of criminals. Biographical or autobiographical accounts of crimes and criminal way of life are full of such observations (e.g., Williamson, 1965; Sutherland 1937; Klockars, 1974; Slim, 1969). Some works on professional criminals also treat this issue (e.g., Schur, 1957; Polsky, 1967).

Moreover, there has been a recurrent argument in folk theories of delinquency that a majority of delinquency is mere "unguided play." This argument has often been directly translated into delinquency prevention programs in which numerous recreational facilities are constructed (see Kett, 1977, pp. 225–227. A criticism of such programs is provided by Tappan (1949, pp. 148–154; set also Sherif and Sherif, 1964, p. 283; Yablonsky, 1970, p. 85; McKay, 1949, p. 38).

2. I conducted field research in Kyoto for one year and three months (from May 1983 to August 1984) and contacted approximately seventy *bosozoku* members belonging to a gang confederation. Research techniques include participant observations (as a "honorary member" of the confederation), interviews, and questionnaires. Various censuses, official documents, mass media reports, and scholarly publications were also examined in order to analyze sociocultural backgrounds of *bosozoku* activity and to explore the process in which official definitions are imposed upon deviant behavior.

The findings of this study show that *bosozoku* activity and symbolism can be comprehended as a form of social play that can be grouped into three genres: (1) speed and thrills (high-speed driving on the city roads), (2) fashion and style (symbolic construction through paraphernalia), and (3) drama and dramatization (creation of a heroic narrative and self-presentation through media). These three genres correspond to three elements of theatrical dramas—performance, props, and script. For details of the research and its findings, see Sato (1984, 1985, 1986).

3. It should be noted that ethnographers sometimes use the term "subcultural" only to summarize their empirical findings and observations about members of a subsociety and their behavior. Their description of a distinctive way of life is not always based on cultural determinism. But when they assume that subcultural codes secure full and longstanding commitment from members, their concept of "subculture" comes close to becoming a sort of determinism (Suttles, 1976, pp. 10, 12; Fine and Kleinman, 1979).

4. Miller's description of focal concerns has much in common with Matza and Sykes's (1961) depiction of "subterranean values." It should be noted, however, that although Matza and Sykes sometimes treat the "values" as (sub)cultural imperatives, they also properly point out that in most cases expressions of the values are acceptable only within bracketed contexts (Matza and Sykes, 1961, pp. 716–717). They, indeed, made a significant contribution to the sociology of deviance by reviving the "attraction" theory of delinquency which, as Bordua has pointed out, had been in abeyance since Thrasher's work (Downes, 1966, p. 81). Matza (1964, 1969) also did much to redress the determinist bias that affected the subcultural theory of delinquency.

In so-called "youth-culture theories of delinquency" there are many references to the subcultural values which resemble the subterranean values. These studies edited by Vaz (1967) include descriptions of playful activities and delinquency of youths from various socioeconomic backgrounds.

5. It is equally plausible that the class differential in search for action is based on the differential in stakes in the conformity, availability of opportunities of legitimate leisure or taste (Downes, 1966; Cohen, [1972] 1980). Cohen's arguments throughout his *The Delinquent Boys* are elusive and he says at one point that the lower-class delinquent can be socialized into a preexisting delinquent subculture even if he does not have status frustration (Kitsuse and Dietrick, 1959). It is also not clear whether Cohen is trying to explain the origin of delinquent subculture or that of the street corner group itself (Suttles, 1968, p. 169).

6. Matza (1964) mentions "pluralistic ignorance" as a crucial feature of subculture of delinquency. His argument seems to have only limited applicability. According to Matza, a subculture of delinquency appears to include articulated norms and values while it actually does not because it is an "oral tradition" among adolescents. In the face-to-face interaction among

street corner boys, "sounding" is one of the most characteristic activities. Through such an activity, Matza argues, each individual thinks that the others support an ideology of delinquency, and so he himself supports it. The essence of the subculture of delinquency lies in this "mutual inference" process. According to Matza, each delinquent is merely under a misapprehension that others around him are committed to delinquency, whereas in reality they are not. In this way, Matza maintains, a "delinquent subculture" is first inferred by the delinquents themselves, and then by sociologists. This "comedy of errors" or "pluralistic ignorance" is supported by a boy's anxiety about his identity as male and acceptance by his peers: he must disguise himself as a hard core delinquent in order to maintain his identity as a "man" and to secure his membership in a peer group. Matza attributes the general background of these membership and masculinity anxieties to a characteristic of adolescence as a developmental stage: suspension between childhood and adulthood. Because adolescence is a stage of "moratorium," an adolescent cannot be confident of his masculinity and depends on his peers for psychological support and acceptance. According to Matza, adolescents mature out of delinquency when they "discover that they had shared misunderstanding with the coming of adulthood" (Matza 1964, p. 55).

His argument may apply to special cases such as gangs in slum areas which are stricken with bitter gang fights involving heavy casualties. But even in such a case, it is unlikely that adolescents cannot have a relatively clear perception of the fictive nature of the social world created by "sounding." For a detailed description and insightful analysis of verbal duels among black youths, see Eabov (1972) and Kochman (1975).

7.   These arguments suggest that Albert Cohen's hypothesis of "exploratory gesture" can be "turned upside down." Cohen assumes that although many lower-class boys have psychological strain (i.e., "status frustration"), they cannot translate it into deviant behavior easily because of the strong pressures toward conformity already internalized through early socialization. "Exploratory gestures" (trial-and-error type expression of deviant motives), then, facilitate mutual inference of others' motives and of their commitment to deviant subcultural values, that are overturned conventional values. According to Cohen (1955, pp. 59–61), these exploratory signs are important factors leading to collective participation in deviance. But it is also possible that mere mimicry of exploratory gestures by others in a minimal way allow youngsters without any significant psychological strain to discover that various kinds of risk taking are fun and intrinsically enjoyable. They may also find that risks accompanying such an undertaking are not as great as they first thought (see Granovetter 1978). Moreover, an exploratory undertaking that began as mimicry of less risky matters (e.g., adopting defiant poses, using gang costumes) may lead to craving for deeper fun and kicks arising from more risky activities (Thrasher, 1927, p. 82). Thus, while Cohen assumes that deviant motives were there beforehand and exploratory gestures facilitate their behavioral translation, it is also possible that motives for risk-taking are "discovered" by such gestures or through reading of official interpretation of motives "behind" the risk-taking in the mass media.

8.   Some theorists, especially those who rely heavily on questionnaire surveys (e.g., Nye, 1958; Richard, Berk, and Forster, 1979) employ a static choice model regarding deviant behavior. They assume that an actor chooses a behavior alternative from several alternatives whose cost/benefit ratios and possible consequences are more or less clearly conceived by the actor beforehand. For example, Nye (1958, pp. 7–8) says, "The objection may be made that many violations are committed for the excitement of the violation itself. However, other possibilities for excitement exist besides violating laws and regulations." These theories fail to take account of the collective behavior process and extremely absorbing nature characteristic of many action-type activities, in which a "rational" choice within the framework of a given reality often becomes irrelevant.

9. But these safety measures do not always work effectively. In particular, the adoption of firearms is a critical factor involving gang violence that cannot be taken back (see Yablonsky, [1962] 1970; Horowitz, 1983).

10. Arguments in this paper are mostly confined to the relationship between "action" and deviant or non-ordinary behavior during adolescence. A truly "general" theory of action will have to include analysis and interpretation of conventional types of search for action by people in general. It seems that action-seeking is a fairly prevalent phenomenon in post-industrial society, where consumption and leisure play crucial roles and escape from boredom tends to become one of the main concerns of people (cf. Klapp, 1969; Cskiszentmihalyi, 1975; Irwin, 1977). For a perceptive, but still somehow normative interpretation of "action," see Goffman (1967).

REFERENCES

Anderson, E. 1976. *A Place on the Corner.* Chicago: University of Chicago Press.
————. 1980. "Some Observation of Black Youth Employment." Pp. 64–87 in B. Anderson and I. Sawhill (eds.) *Youth Employment and Public Policy.* Englewood Cliffs, NJ: Prentice-Hall.
Angell, R. 1945. "A Critical Review of the Development of the Personal Document Method in Sociology 1920–1940." Pp. 177–232 in L. Gottschalk, C. Kluckhohn, and R. Angell (eds.) *The Use of Personal Documents in History, Anthropology and Sociology.* New York: Social Sciences Council.
Balint, M. 1959. *Thrills and Regressions.* London: Hogarth.
Bateson, G. 1972. "A Theory of Play and Fantasy. " Pp. 177–193 in *Steps to an Ecology of Mind.* San Francisco: Chandler.
Berger, B. 1963. "On the Youthfulness of Youth Culture." *Social Research* 30: 319–342.
Bloch, H. and A. Niederhoffer. 1958. *The Gang.* New York: Philosophical Library.
Bordua, D.J. 1961. "Delinquent Subcultures." *The Annals of the American Academy of Political and Social Sciences* 338: 119–136.
Bulmer, M. 1984. *The Chicago School of Sociology: Institutionalization, Diversity and the Rise of Sociological Research.* Chicago: University of Chicago Press.
Burke, K. 1968. "Dramatism," Pp. 445–452 in *International Encyclopedia of the Social Sciences. Vol. 7.* New York: Macmillan and Free Press.
Cressey, P.G. (1932) 1969. *Taxi-Dance Hall.* Montclair, NJ: Patterson Smith.
Csikszentmihalyi, M. 1975. *Beyond Boredom and Anxiety.* San Francisco: Jossey-Bass.
Csikszentmihalyi, M. and R. Larson. 1978. "Intrinsic Rewards in School Crime." *Crime and Delinquency* 24: 322–325.
Davis, K. 1940. "The Sociology of Parent-Youth Conflict." *American Sociological Review* 5: 523–535.
————. 1944. "Adolescence and the Social Structure." *Annals of American Academy of Policy and Social Sciences* 236: 8–16.
Downes, D.M. 1966. *The Delinquent Solution.* New York: Free Press.
Duncan, H.D. 1968. *Symbols in Society.* London: Oxford University Press.
England, R.W. 1967. "A Theory of Middle-Class Juvenile Delinquency." Pp. 242–251 in E. Vaz (ed.) *Middle- Class Juvenile Delinquency.* New York: Harper & Row.
Faris, R.E.L. 1967. *Chicago Sociology* 1920–1932. Chicago: University of Chicago Press.
Fine, G.A. 1987. *With the Boys.* Chicago: University of Chicago Press.

Fine, G.A. and S. Kleinman. 1979. "Rethinking Subculture." *American Journal of Sociology* 85:1–20.

Finestone, H. 1957. "Cats, Kicks, and Color." *Social Problems.* 5: 3–13.

Frith, S. 1981. *Sound Effects: Youth, Leisure, and the Politics of Rock 'n' Roll.* New York: Pantheon.

Gans, H.J. 1962. *The Urban Villagers.* New York: Free Press.

———. 1966. "Popular Culture in America: Social Problem in a Mass Society or Social Asset in a Pluralist Society?" Pp. 549–620 in H.S. Becker (ed.) *Social Problems: A Modern Approach.* New York: Wiley.

Goffman E. 1959. *The Presentation of Self in Everyday Life.* New York: Anchor.

———. 1967. "Where the Action Is." Pp. 149–270 in *Interaction Ritual.* New York: Doubleday.

———. 1974. *Frame Analysis.* New York: Harper & Row.

Gold, M. and R.J. Peteronio. 1980. "Delinquent Behavior in Adolescence." Pp. 495–535 in J. Adelson *Handbook of Adolescent Psychology.* New York: Wiley.

Granovetter, M. 1978. "Threshold Models of Collective Behavior." *American Journal of Sociology* 83: 1420–1443.

Hall, S. and T. Jefferson. 1976. *Resistance through Ritual.* London: Hutchinson.

Hannerz, U. 1969. *Soulside.* New York: Columbia University Press.

Haviland, J.B. 1977. *Gossip, Reputation, and Knowledge in Ziancantan.* Chicago: University of Chicago Press.

Hebdige, D. 1979. *Subculture: The Meaning of Style.* London: Methuem.

Henry, J. 1963. *Culture against Man.* New York: Vintage.

Horowitz, R. 1983. *Honor and American Dream.* New Brunswick, NJ: Rutgers University Press.

Huizinga, J. 1950. *Homo Ludens.* Boston: Beacon.

Irwin, J. 1977. *Scenes.* Beverly Hills: Sage.

Kett, J. 1977. *Rites of Passage: Adolescence in America, 1790 to the Present.* New York: Basic Books.

Kitsuse, J. and D. Dietrick. 1959. "Delinquent Boys: A Critique." *American Sociology Review* 24:208–215.

Klapp, O. 1969. *Collective Search for Identity.* New York: Holt, Rinehart, and Winston.

Klockars, C.B. 1974. *The Professional Fence.* New York: Free Press.

Kochman, T. 1981. *Black and White Styles in Conflict.* Chicago: University of Chicago Press.

Kornhauser, R.R. 1978. *Social Sources of Delinquency.* Chicago: University of Chicago Press.

Kvareceus, W.C. and W.B. Miller. 1959. *Delinquent Behavior: Culture and the Individual.* Washington, DC: National Education Association of the United States.

Labov, W. 1972. *Language in the Inner City.* Philadelphia: University of Pennsylvania Press.

Leary, J.P. 1977. "White Guy's Stories of the Night Street. " *Journal of the Folklore Institute* 14: 59–71.

Liebow, E. 1967. *Tally's Corner.* Boston: Little Brown.

Lofland, L.H. 1973. *A World of Strangers.* New York: Basic Books.

Marsh, P., E. Rosser, and R. Harré. 1978. *The Rules of Disorder.* London: Routledge & Kegan Paul.

Matza, D. 1964. *Delinquency and Drift.* New York: Wiley.

———. 1969. *Becoming Deviant.* New York: Prentice-Hall.

Matza, D. and G. Sykes. 1961. "Juvenile Delinquency and Subterranean Values." *American Sociological Review* 26: 712–719.

McKay, H. 1949. "The Neighborhood and Child Conduct." *Annals of the American Academy of Policy and Social Sciences* 241: 32–41.

Miller, W.B. 1958. "Lower-Class Culture as a Generating Milieu of Gang Delinquency." *Journal of Social Issues* 15: 5–19.

Mitchell, R.G. 1983. *Mountain Experience*. Chicago: University of Chicago Press.

Moore, S.F. and B.G. Myerhoff, 1977. *Secular Ritual.* Assen, Amsterdam: Van Gorcum.

Nye, F.I. 1958. *Family Relationships and Delinquent Behavior.* New York: Greenwood.

Park, Robert E. 1914/15. "The City: Suggestions for the Investigation of Human Behavior in the City." *American Journal of Sociology* 20: 577–612.

Parsons, T. 1942. "Age and Sex in the Social Structure of the United States." *American Sociological Review* 7: 604–616.

Parsons, T. and R.F. Bales. 1955. *Family Socialization and Interaction Process*. Glencoe: Free Press.

Pleck, J.H. 1981. *The Myth of Masculinity.* Cambridge, MA: MIT Press.

Polsky, N. 1967. *Hustlers, Beats, and Others.* Chicago: Aldine.

Richard, P., R.A. Berk, and B. Forster. 1979. *Crime as Play.* Cambridge, MA: Ballinger.

Riesman, D. 1964. *Abundance for What?* New York: Doubleday.

Rodman, H. 1963. "The Lower-Class Value Stretch." *Social Forces* 42: 205–215.

Sato, I. 1984. *Bosozoku no Esunografi* (An Ethnography of Motorcycle Gangs) Tokyo: Shin'yosha.

———. 1985. *Bosozoku, Yankii, Shakaijin* (Motorcycle Gang, Yankee, and Ordinary Citizen). Tokyo: Shm'yosha.

———. 1986. *"Bosozoku* and Yankee: Anomy and Parody in the Affluent Society." Unpublished Ph.D. dissertation, University of Chicago.

———. forthcoming. *"Bosozoku:* Flow in Japanese Motorcycle Gangs." in M. Csikszentmihalyi (ed.) *Flow: Studies in the Psychology of Optimal Experience.* London: Cambridge University Press.

Schur, E.M. 1957. "Sociological Analysis of Confidence Swindling." *Journal of Criminal Law Criminology and Police Sciences* 48: 296–304.

Schwartzman, S.H. 1978. *Transformations.* New York: Plenum.

Scott, J.W. and E.W. Vaz. 1963. "A Perspective on Middle-Class Delinquency." *Canadian Journal of Economics and Political Science* 29: 324–325.

Shaw, C.R. 1930. *The Jack-Roller.* Chicago: University of Chicago Press.

Shaw, C.R. and H.D. McKay. 1931. "Social Factors in Juvenile Delinquency." *Report on the Causes of Crime, vol.* 2. Washington, DC: National Commission on Law Observance and Enforcement.

Shaw, C.R., H.D. McKay, and J. McDonald. 1938. *Brothers in Crime.* Chicago: University of Chicago Press.

Shaw, C.R., F.M. Zorbaugh, H.D. McKay, and L.S. Cottrell. 1929. *Delinquency Areas.* Chicago: University of Chicago Press.

Sherif, M. and C.W. Sherif. 1964. *Reference Groups.* New York: Harper & Row.

Short, J.F. and F. Strodbeck. (1965) 1974. *Group Process and Gang Delinquency.* Chicago: University of Chicago Press.

Slim, I. 1969. *Pimp: The Story of My Life.* Los Angeles: Halloway House.

Smith, T.S. 1974. "Aestheticism and Social Structure: Style and Social Network in the Dandy Life." *American Sociological Review* 39: 725–743.

Spergel, I. 1964. *Racketville, Slumtown, Haulberg.* Chicago: University of Chicago Press.

Stinchcombe, A.L. 1964. *Rebellion in a High School.* Chicago: Quadrangle Books.

Sutherland, E.H. 1937. *The Professional Thief.* Chicago: University of Chicago Press.

Suttles, G. 1968. *The Social Order of the Slum.* Chicago: University of Chicago Press.

————. 1976. "Urban Ethnography: Situational and Normative Accounts." *Annual Review of Sociology* 2: 1–18.

Tannenbaum, F. 1938. *Crime and Community.* New York: McGraw-Hill.

Tappan, P. 1949. *Juvenile Delinquency.* New York: McGraw Hill.

Thomas, W.I. 1923. *The Unadjusted Girl.* New York: Little Brown.

Thomas, W.I. and F. Znaniecki. (1919) 1927. *The Polish Peasant in Europe and America.* New York: Alfred A. Knopf.

Thompson, H.S. 1966. *Hell's Angels.* New York: Ballantine.

Thrasher, F. 1927. *The Gang.* Chicago: University of Chicago Press.

Turner, R.H. 1962. " Role-Taking: Process versus Conformity. " Pp. 20–40 in A. Rose (ed.) *Human Behavior and Social Processes.* Boston: Houghton Mifflin.

Turner, V. 1974. *Dramas, Fields, and Metaphors.* Ithaca, NY: Cornell University Press.

Vaz, E.W. 1967. *Middle-Class Juvenile Delinquency.* New York: Harper & Row.

Whyte, W.F. (1943) 1955. *Street Corner Society.* Chicago: University of Chicago Press.

Williamson, H. 1965. *Hustler!* New York: Avon Books.

Willis, P. 1977. *Learning to Labor.* New York: Columbia University Press.

Wolfgang, M.E. and F. Ferracuti. 1967. *The Subculture of Violence.* London: Tavistock.

Wrong, D.H. 1961. "The Oversocialized Conception of Man in Modern Sociology. " *American Sociological Review* 26: 189–193.

Yablonsky, L. (1962) 1970. *The Violent Gang.* Maryland: Penguin.